THE STRUGGLE FOR IDENTITY
IN THE
CLERICAL ESTATE

STUDIES IN THE HISTORY
OF
CHRISTIAN THOUGHT

EDITED BY

HEIKO A. OBERMAN, Tübingen

IN COOPERATION WITH

HENRY CHADWICK, Cambridge
JAROSLAV PELIKAN, New Haven, Conn.
BRIAN TIERNEY, Ithaca, N.Y.
E. DAVID WILLIS, Princeton, N.J.

VOLUME XXXIII

JOHN STROUP

THE STRUGGLE FOR IDENTITY
IN THE
CLERICAL ESTATE

LEIDEN
E. J. BRILL
1984

THE STRUGGLE FOR IDENTITY
IN THE
CLERICAL ESTATE

*Northwest German Protestant Opposition to Absolutist Policy
in the Eighteenth Century*

BY

JOHN STROUP

LEIDEN
E. J. BRILL
1984

This publication was made possible by grants from the ''Hilles Fund of the Whitney Humanities Center of Yale University'' and the ''Vereinigte Evangelisch-Lutherische Kirche Deutschlands''.

BR
855
.S77
1984

ISBN 90 04 07009 5

Copyright 1984 by E. J. Brill, Leiden, The Netherlands

All rights reserved. No part of this book may be reproduced or translated in any form, by print, photoprint, microfilm, microfiche or any other means without written permission from the publisher

PRINTED IN THE NETHERLANDS BY E. J. BRILL

This book is dedicated to Mrs. Pearl C. Whitener and to Professor Dietrich Gerhard—two teachers who have lived in the Show Me State, even as I have done.

Bis zur modernen Zeit hat unter uns kultivierten Europäern die Religion in der Kultur geherrscht, und nur die moderne Revolution der Kultur gegen die Religion hat diese Herrschaft aufgehoben. Die modernen Theologen machen es aber wie alle erfolgreichen Revolutionäre. Sie verleugnen ihre Vergangenheit oder suchen sich nur auf Schleichwegen zu behaupten, indem sie möglichst unbemerkt zur Ordnung zurück-zukehren suchen. Vor allem wollen sie nicht, daß erkannt werde, wie die alte Ordnung nicht mehr herrsche und die Religion nicht mehr bedeute was sie einmal bedeutet hat.

Franz Overbeck, *Christentum und Kultur*, ed. Carl Albrecht Bernoulli (Basel, 1919; reprint ed., Darmstadt, 1963), p. 14.

CONTENTS

PREFACE

The state of historical scholarship on the Protestant clergy in Germany does not now allow one to state reliably what the lasting results of the Reformation were for the social and political role of the pastorate. While generalities on this score abound, detailed investigation of this theme for the Old Régime has been limited.[1]

The present study has been undertaken in hope of providing a small contribution to the understanding of this matter. Though this investigation deals with the eighteenth century, it is designed to assist in a reassessment of the social, political, and professional status of the Lutheran clergy in Germany before the rise of modern nationalism—not simply to help in evaluating the Enlightenment clergy alone. In this connection I would refer to Prof. Dr. Bernd Moeller, who points out that—contrary to expectation—the urban Reformation of the sixteenth century by no means brought about a complete assimilation of the Protestant clergy to the more secular order represented by the post-Reformation civic community.[2] Similarly, no less an authority on the German Reformation than Hajo Holborn warned against any facile conclusion that the Lutheran tradition prior to the nineteenth century led directly to the consolidation of a temporal government novel in its devotion to power politics.[3]

In a sense, then, in the pages below I am simply following out the suggestions made by these two writers—though sustaining their thesis has required the investigation of a time subsequent to that of Luther himself. How such a study can shed light on the working out of the Reformation will be best appreciated by those who share with me the conviction of Ernst Troeltsch that much is to be gained by considering the Reformation's institutional results as a prolongation of medieval forms of life swept away only by Enlightenment and subsequent revolution. (That I do not share Troeltsch's view of Lutheranism itself should be obvious).[4]

---

[1] Peter Gay, *The Enlightenment: An Interpretation* (New York, 1966), 1:543; Rudolf Vierhaus, "Deutschland im 18. Jahrhundert", in *Aufklärung, Absolutismus und Bürgertum in Deutschland*, ed. Franklin Kopitzsch (Munich, 1976), p. 181.

[2] Bernd Moeller, *Pfarrer als Bürger* (Göttingen, 1972), p. 16.

[3] Hajo Holborn, "Machtpolitik und lutherische Sozialethik", *Archiv für Reformationsgeschichte* 57 (1966): 23-32.

[4] Hermann Fischer, "Luther und seine Reformation in der Sicht Ernst Troeltschs", *Neue Zeitschrift für systematische Theologie und Religionsphilosophie* 5 (1963): 132-72; Dietrich Gerhard, "Periodization in European History", *The American Historical Review* 61 (1955-56): 900-13; Ernst Troeltsch, *The Social Teaching of the Christian Churches*, trans. Olive Wyon (London, 1931, 1949), 2; Troeltsch, *Protestantism and Progress*, trans. W. Montgomery (1912; reprint ed., Boston, Mass., 1958).

A very special expression of gratitude goes to Prof. Dr. Heiko A. Oberman for publishing this book in his series: Studies in the History of Christian Thought. I am also especially pleased to thank the Hilles Fund of the Whitney Humanities Center of Yale University and the Lutherisches Kirchenamt (Hannover) of the Vereinigte Evangelisch-Lutherische Kirche Deutschlands for their very generous support of the publication of this book. Additional gratitude here is due the Herzog August Bibliothek Wolfenbüttel and the Max-Planck-Institut für Geschichte Göttingen. I am also pleased to thank all those who helped in arranging for the publication of this book—especially the Rt. Rev. D. Eduard Lohse, Prof. Dr. Rudolf Vierhaus, Prof. Dr. Hans-Walter Krumwiede, Prof. Hans Frei, Prof. Jaroslav Pelikan, Prof. Thomas Brady, Prof. Robert Berdahl, Prof. Marc Raeff, the Rev. Mr. Gottfried Klapper, D.D., the Rev. Dr. Hans Christian Knuth, the Rt. Rev. Dr. Joachim Massner, Prof. Dr. Paul Raabe, Prof. Dr. Walther Killy, Prof. Dr. Bernd Moeller, Dr. Walter Sundberg, Dr. Sabine Solf, Prof. Dr. Johannes Wallmann, Dr. Walter Sparn, Dr. Horst Günther, Prof. Abraham Malherbe, Mr. David Myers, and Mr. Steven Hosier. Additional words of gratitude are reserved for Mr. Stephen Peterson for his tireless work on the indices and for Dean Leander Keck of the Yale Divinity School, as well as for Dr. John Lewis.

The theme of this study was suggested by Prof. Peter Gay and elaborated with the advice of Prof. Jaroslav Pelikan. Advice came also from Prof. Hans Frei. To them I owe a special debt of gratitude—even as I owe a heavy debt to Prof. Dr. Dietrich Gerhard and Prof. Dr. Rudolf Vierhaus, whom I must acknowledge as the sources for a part of my method. Prof. Dr. Paul Raabe and the staff of the Herzog August Bibliothek graciously put at my disposal the sources and the advice uniquely available at Wolfenbüttel. The staff of the Niedersächsische Staats- und Universitätsbibliothek Göttingen extended to me every courtesy. Likewise, I am indebted to the officials of the Landeskirchenamt Hannover and the Landeskirchenamt Braunschweig; and I have been greatly helped by the staff at the Niedersächsisches Hauptstaatsarchiv Hannover, the Niedersächsisches Staatsarchiv Wolfenbüttel, and the Universitäts-Archiv Göttingen. Assistance also came from the staff of the library and archive at Kloster Loccum (in particular Dr. Ernst Berneburg), and from that of the library of the Predigerseminar Rothenburg/Wümme. Aid came also from many friends of the project, not all of whom can here be mentioned—especially the late Prof. Dr. Hermann Dörries, Prof. Dr. Rudolf von Thadden, Dr. Inge Mager, Prof. Dr. Notker Hammerstein, Dr. Hanno Schmitt, the late Prof. Dr. Ludwig Deike, Prof. Robert Berdahl, the late Dr. Hans Kropatscheck,

Dr. Rand Henson, Herr Ernst-Otto Fehn, and Frau Brigitte Braun. Despite their advice, I fear that I have erred often enough.

Financial support for research was generously provided by many sources: the Danforth Foundation, the Deutscher Akademischer Austauschdienst, the Yale Concilium on International and Area Studies, the Yale Council on West European Studies, the Max-Planck-Institut für Geschichte Göttingen, and the Herzog August Bibliothek. Only their liberality has made an investigation of this kind possible.

In the pages below I rely heavily on the term "utilitarianism" to signify an approach to education and ministry stressing instruction in new techniques for promoting this-worldly welfare (e.g., agronomy, technology). While this approach was developed in close connection with the theories of cameralism and physiocracy advocated by supporters of enlightened centralism, a suitable term for the approach is lacking. I have chosen for it the familiar word "utilitarianism", explicitly disavowing any intent to evoke Bentham. The only alternative would be "eudaemonism", a term so philosophical in its overtones and so unfamiliar to the English reader that I have rejected it. Here it may be recalled that the translator of Schleiermacher's *Reden* did not hesitate to render "das Extrem des nüzlichen" as "the extreme of utilitarianism", thereby setting a precedent for English reference to the temporal version of ministry in an absolutist framework rejected by Schleiermacher and others before him.[5]

Were this study to be expanded, two areas would require treatment. On the one hand, it would be necessary to take account of the relations between church and state throughout Europe so as to set this regional story of differing German Lutheran views on the purpose of the ministry in better perspective. On the other hand, it would also be good to take the account well into the nineteenth century so as to show how the material here analyzed adds a new dimension to how we view the post-Napoleonic period's renewed interest in ministerial authority and confessional identity.

For the present it will suffice to note that what needs to be said will be obvious to any reader who already has some familiarity with these matters in the nineteenth century. For thin air did not by itself produce figures such as Theodor Kliefoth (1810-1895) and August Vilmar (1800-1868), with their views of the ministerial office as a "Gnadenmittelamt" or "ein Institut, an dessen Vorhandensein und Wirksamkeit ...

---

[5] Friedrich Schleiermacher, *Sämmtliche Werke*, 1. Abtheilung (Berlin, 1843), 1:298; Schleiermacher, *On Religion*, trans. John Oman (New York, 1958), p. 131. Cf. p. 82, n. 1 below.

die Seligkeit der Welt gebunden ist."[6] As Karl Barth observes with regard to Vilmar, here one must not overlook the influence of Schleiermacher in inaugurating what was to become a return to a positive evaluation of historic Christianity.[7] As for Schleiermacher himself, the prelude to that revival, in view of what follows he must now appear as in part a continuator of discussions about the proper function of the church which had been in progress for decades before he published the *Reden*.

New Haven, Connecticut
October 31, 1983

---

[6] Emanuel Hirsch, *Geschichte der neuern evangelischen Theologie* (Gütersloh, 1954), 5:194, with reference first to Kliefoth, then to Vilmar.

[7] Karl Barth, *Protestant Theology in the Nineteenth Century* (Valley Forge, 1973), pp. 627, 633.

ABBREVIATIONS

JGNK = *Jahrbuch der Gesellschaft für niedersächsische Kirchengeschichte* (Braunschweig, 1947-)

Jg. = Jahrgang

PRE = *Realencyklopädie für protestantische Theologie und Kirche*, ed. Johann Jakob
Herzog and Albert Hauck, 3rd ed. (Leipzig, 1896-1913)

RGG = *Die Religion in Geschichte und Gegenwart*, 3rd ed. (Tübingen, 1956-1965)

ZGNK = *Zeitschrift der Gesellschaft für niedersächsische Kirchengeschichte* (Braunschweig, 1896-1940)

INTRODUCTION

THE GERMAN PROTESTANT CLERGYMAN IN THE EIGHTEENTH CENTURY

1. *The Standard Picture of the Professional Aims of the Protestant Clergy in the German Enlightenment*

Historians once thought that in eighteenth-century Germany there was only one really significant school of political thought.[1] By whatever name it was called—centralism, mercantilism, *dirigisme*, or absolutism— it served the rationalization of economic and social life for the benefit of the absolutist prince. This political and economic doctrine, without a doubt, was used by princes and their bureaucracies in an attempt to break down and assimilate the structures of the Old Régime—nobles, assemblies of estates, the clergy and the guilds—in order to construct a powerful, new, centralized, allegedly rationalized state.[2]

Since this scholarly consensus was forged by researchers working in libraries and archives founded by the absolutist princes and their bureaucracies, it is not surprising that matters came to look so simple. Fascinated by the growth of the state, and furthermore admiring the way in which absolutist rulers had mastered power politics, the historians of the Prussian school saw the absolutist prince as a virtually irresistible force on the side of the future.[3] After all, he was equipped with a standing army, a court system nearly independent of the imperial courts, and a reliable bureaucracy drawn from the rising bourgeosie.

---

[1] See the historiographical remarks in Rudolf Vierhaus, "Absolutismus", in *Sowjetsystem und Demokratische Gesellschaft*, ed. C. D. Kernig et al. (Freiburg i. B., 1966), 1: cols. 17-37, esp. col. 18 on the tradition since Ranke and Tocqueville; and Kurt von Raumer "Absoluter Staat, korporative Libertät, persönliche Freiheit", *Historische Zeitschrift* 183 (1957): 55-96, esp. pp. 62-64 on the one-sided picture of matters brought about by French and German research on absolutism (e.g., the *Acta Borussica*).

[2] See for example Otto Hintze, "Der preussische Militär- und Beamtenstaat im 18. Jahrhundert", in his *Regierung und Verwaltung*, ed. Gerhard Oestreich (Göttingen, 1967), pp. 419-28; Reinhold August Dorwart, *The Administrative Reforms of Frederick Wilhelm I of Prussia* (Cambridge, Mass., 1953); and Klaus Deppermann, *Der hallesche Pietismus und der preußische Staat unter Friedrich III. (I.)* (Göttingen, 1961). The studies on absolutism are numerous. See *Der Aufgeklärte Absolutismus*, ed. Karl Otmar von Aretin (Cologne, 1975); *Absolutismus*, ed. Walther Hubatsch (Darmstadt, 1973); *Aufklärung, Absolutismus und Bürgertum in Deutschland*, ed. Franklin Kopitzsch (Munich, 1976); and Volker Sellin, "Friedrich der Große und der aufgeklärte Absolutismus", in *Soziale Bewegung und politische Verfassung*, ed. Ulrich Engelhardt et al. (Stuttgart, 1976), pp. 83-112.

[3] See the remarks by Vierhaus and von Raumer cited in n. 1 above.

Church historians, too, have tended to present the history of the German religious Enlightenment as a simple process of steadily accelerating capitulations before the secularizing pressures of the modern state and its theoreticians.[4] This impression seemed to be supported adequately by the evolution of Enlightenment theology. For its development had of course consisted of the progressive surrender of traditional metaphysical and historical content. The more advanced of the Enlightenment theologians in every generation of the eighteenth century had taken the reduction of doctrine a step further. The disciples of Christian Wolff denied that revelation could contradict human reason; yet they remained relatively conservative by leaving reason and revelation in a relationship of peaceful coexistence: they claimed that some truths of divine revelation were simply above the capacity of human reason to comprehend them.[5] The next generation, the "Neologians" of Berlin, redefined revelation to eliminate any historical content that seemed contradictory to reason, and developed a moralistic version of Christianity supported by the reasonable doctrines of God, virtue, and immortality.[6] The final generation, the Rationalists, dropped the concept of revelation altogether, or consistently reinterpreted its contents into truths of reason and nothing else.[7] Modern church historians have assumed that most Enlightenment churchmen marked off the stages of this evolution, and in consequence have characterized the theological Enlightenment as unresisted secularization.[8]

---

[4] For this viewpoint in the older literature see Gustav Ecke, *Die theologische Schule Albrecht Ritschls und die evangelische Kirche der Gegenwart* (Berlin, 1904); Christian Tischhauser, *Geschichte der evangelischen Kirchen Deutschlands in der ersten Hälfte des 19. Jahrhunderts* (Basel, 1900); Horst Stephan and Hans Leube, *Handbuch der Kirchengeschichte, 4. Teil. Die Neuzeit*, 2nd ed. (Tübingen, 1931), pp. 90-92. In newer literature: Klaus Scholder, "Grundzüge der theologischen Aufklärung in Deutschland", in Kopitzsch, *Aufklärung*, pp. 310-13; and Johannes Wallmann, "Zwischen Reformation und Humanismus", *Zeitschrift für Theologie und Kirche* 74 (1977): 368-70. Use of the term "secularization" in this study implies my belief that a change has taken place in the Western world since the Gregorian reform, with the result that certain ecclesiastical institutions and theological structures of thought have lost influence. On the problems connected with this concept, see Bryan Wilson, "The Debate over 'Secularization,'" *Encounter* 45 (October, 1975): 77-83; and Hermann Lübbe, *Säkularisierung: Geschichte eines ideenpolitischen Begriffs* (Munich, 1965). Also worth noting are Trutz Rendtorff, "Christentum", in *Geschichtliche Grundbegriffe*, ed. Otto Brunner, Werner Conze, and Reinhart Koselleck (Stuttgart, 1972-), 1:772-814; cf. however n. 19 below and Manfred Baumotte, *Theologie als politische Aufklärung* (Gütersloh, 1973).

[5] Karl Aner, *Die Theologie der Lessingzeit* (Halle/Saale, 1929), pp. 144-201.

[6] Aner, pp. 144-342.

[7] Aner, pp. 3, 343-361; Wolfgang Philipp, "Rationalismus", *Evangelisches Kirchenlexikon*, ed. Heinz Brunotte and Otto Weber (Göttingen, 1959), 3: cols. 439-45.

[8] Cf. n. 4 above (though Scholder would scargely share this opinion); also for example Paul Graff, *Geschichte der Auflösung der alten gottesdienstlichen Formen in der evangelischen Kirchen Deutschlands*, 2nd ed., 2 vols. (Göttingen, 1937); Reinhard Krause, *Die Predigt der späten*

The metaphysical or Orthodox theology abandoned during the Enlightenment had clearly served during the sixteenth and seventeenth centuries to establish a relative autonomy of the church in religious affairs: the divinely-ordained character of the church had obviously helped to restrain the efforts of the state to manipulate the church for crassly political purposes.[9] Therefore it seemed clear to modern scholars that the abandonment of that traditional metaphysical dogmatics necessarily brought about a loss of ecclesiastical autonomy. For with the virtual abandonment of pre-Enlightenment theology during the eighteenth century, the very purpose of the church was indeed called into question. Scholars naturally concluded that what had remained of the church lost its distinctive character and so was easily put to work by temporal governments during the eighteenth century.[10]

Such a view harmonized nicely with the opinion of general historians that in eighteenth-century Germany there existed only the absolutist school of political thought. Thus church historians set to work depicting, not simply the theological features, but also the institutional aspects of the ecclesiastical Enlightenment as unresisted secularization. In particular, scholars contended that the majority of Enlightenment theologians and churchmen, because of their sympathy with absolutism, had co-operated with or acquiesced in the suppression of the independence which the old Orthodox Lutheran clerical establishment had maintained in the face of the temporal government.[11] Hence it followed that the majority of Enlightenment churchmen must have sought and found their *raison d'être* in serving as an arm of the bureaucracy that made absolutist régimes possible. The enlightened clergy did this, it is held, by

---

deutschen Aufklärung (1770-1805) (Stuttgart, 1965). Cf. the judgment in Dagobert de Levie, *Die Menschenliebe im Zeitalter der Aufklärung: Säkularisation und Moral im 18. Jahrhundert* (Bern, 1975), p. 12.

[9] Friedrich August Gottreu Tholuck, *Geschichte des Rationalismus.* 1. (einzige) Abteilung (1865; reprint ed., Aalen, 1970), pp. 119, 167; Hans Liermann, "Laizismus und Klerikalismus in der Geschichte des evangelischen Kirchenrechts", *Zeitschrift [der Savigny-Stiftung] für Rechtsgeschichte, Kanonistische Abteilung*, 39 (1953): 1-27; Martin Honecker, *Cura religionis Magistratus Christiani*, (Munich, 1968).

[10] The most influential studies are those on Prussia: Georges Pariset, *L'État et les Églises en Prusse Sous Frédéric Guillaume Iᵉʳ (1713-1740)* (Thèse, Paris, 1896); Erich Foerster, *Die Entstehung der Preußischen Landeskirche unter der Regierung König Friedrich Wilhelms des Dritten*, 2 vols. (Tübingen, 1905-1907); and Robert M. Bigler, *The Politics of German Protestantism. The Rise of the Protestant Church Elite in Prussia, 1815-1848* (Berkeley, Calif., 1972). Attempting a more general treatment of this problem, but still assuming that the process is a simple one of the transformation of the pastor into a governmental bureaucrat, is the obsolete yet provocative work by Manfred Köhler, "Über die soziale Bedeutung des Protestantischen Pfarrhauses in Deutschland" (Diss., Heidelberg University, 1952).

[11] This viewpoint is represented in the works cited above in nn. 4 (especially Tischhauser and Ecke, which have not been superseded), pp. 8 and 10. Other statements of this view could be adduced.

functioning as census takers, adjuncts to the recruiting officer, public health officers, and county agents giving cameralistic instruction on how the populace could augment their wellbeing and the prince's wealth.[12]

Important in the establishment of this interpretation as standard was the Neo-Pietist Friedrich August Tholuck. Over a century ago he recognized that the absolutist state in Germany had been founded on natural law, and furthermore focused on Christian Thomasius (1655-1728) as the figure decisive for later developments. At the earliest stage of the Enlightenment Thomasius had called on princes to withdraw all financial and legal support of autonomy from the Lutheran pastorate so that princes could control it. This challenge to clerical independence, according to Tholuck, set in the tone for the next century:

> The changed view concerning the relation of church and state resulted in an alteration in the position of the clergy. The more there spread Thomasius' view of the clergyman as servant of the state, the more there vanished the religious nimbus with which the clerical estate had previously been adorned: the clergyman entered the ranks of the servants of the state.[13]

Tholuck's opinion remains standard among scholars to the present day. It has often been restated in sweeping and unreserved terms—e.g., by Gustav Ecke and Christian Tischhauser, who around the turn of the century sought a scapegoat to explain the institutional church's loss of influence and found it in the Enlightenment.[14] Recent church historians have kept Tholuck's thesis alive. Reinhard Krause suggested on the basis of sermonic evidence that the Protestant clergy in the later German Enlightenment were chiefly occupied with this-worldly matters of economics and politics, and had thus surrendered their identity to the state-backed process of secularization.[15] Klaus Scholder took the argu-

---

[12] The classic formulation of this view is Tischhauser, pp. 131-32.

[13] Tholuck, *Rationalismus*, p. 167. See also the remarks on the spread of Thomasius' "Caesaropapism" in Tholuck, *Vorgeschichte des Rationalismus. 2. Das kirchliche Leben des siebzehnten Jahrhunderts, 2. Abtheilung* (Berlin, 1862): 95. This and all other translations are my own unless otherwise noted.

[14] Ecke, pp. 65-108; Tischhauser, pp. 131, 136, 138-39, 145, 151. The importance of and the weaknesses in the presentations by Ecke and Tischhauser were pointed out long ago by Stephan and Leube, pp. 91-92, who therefore called for new research (p. 86). That call has yet to be answered. Of the original contributions evoked by Tischhauser and Ecke, the rebuttal of their entire view of secularization suggested by Paul Drews remains important. See Drews, "Der Rückgang der Kommunikanten in Sachsen," *Zeitschrift für Theologie und Kirche*, 10 (1900): 148-66.

[15] Krause, "Der Übergang zu reinen Natur- und Zeitpredigten, zu politischen und ökonomischen Kanzelreden als konsequente Fortentwicklung der praktischen und sozialen Leitgedanken," in his *Predigt* (n. 8 above), pp. 116-42. Krause's study makes no effort to evaluate such preaching in the territorial setting in which it evolved, and makes no systematic effort to put it within the framework of the eighteenth-century argument about the purpose of the clerical estate.

ment a step further by claiming that the only abiding result of the German ecclesiastical Enlightenment was a clerical sanction of absolutism.[16] Edward Dixon Junkin, in a discussion of the attitude of German Enlightenment churchmen to the French Revolution, concluded that they failed to protect either their professional integrity or the distinctively biblical content of their message. Both, he alleged, were delivered up to reactionary governmental manipulation because already during earlier phases of the Enlightenment the clergy had surrendered the basis for defending them. Having bowed to governmental pressure, the enlightened pastor supposedly agreed with secular governments that he was "a public official" whose "calling" required him "to teach good morality and to encourage decency and order in public affairs."[17] Without any attempt at systematically investigating what theological faculties and consistories actually held on the point, Junkin claims that for these churchmen "the primary task" of the clergyman was that of a "moral pedagog" striving to "protect society from violent upheaval."[18] Similar sweeping judgments have come from Friedrich Wilhelm Kantzenbach, who holds with regard to Protestant Germany around 1800 that

> ... the state insisted that it must administer the church by means of its functionaries. The clergy were regarded as bureaucratic functionaries entrusted with popular education and even (with a few exceptions) regarded themselves as such.[19]

Secular historians as well have not hesitated to approve Tholuck's thesis. They, too, have regarded the churchmen of the German Enlightenment as docile tools of secular government, so eager to curry favor with absolutist rulers and to make themselves useful that they could not resist a decisive secularization of their profession. Instead, shaken by scepticism, these churchmen are said to have sought professional contentment in fostering civil obedience and economic productivity. This willingness to serve as agents of government allegedly manifested itself in a universal enthusiasm for remodeling their preaching and ministry to fulfill administrative, economic, and ideological tasks for the state.

For example, Dagobert de Levie writes that the religion and pastors of the German Protestant Enlightenment, by their "tendency to secularize

---

[16] Scholder, p. 313, contending that, out of the Enlightenment impulse to ethical activity in this world there survived "ultimately merely the sanction of absolutism."

[17] Edward Dixon Junkin, *Religion versus Revolution* (Theol. Diss., Basel University, 1968; Austin, Texas, 1974), 2:708-10; cf. 852-54.

[18] Junkin, 2:481.

[19] Friedrich Wilhelm Kantzenbach, "Das Phänomen der Entkirchlichung als Problem kirchengeschichtlicher Forschung und theologischer Interpretation," *Neue Zeitschrift für Systematische Theologie und Religionsphilosophie*, 13 (1973): 82.

all aspects of life, undermined the very position of religion and ultimately led to the enthronement of nationalism as a secularized religion.''[20] Again, Karl Otmar von Aretin contends that

> Neither in Prussia nor in Denmark or Sweden did ... Protestantism retard enlightened absolutism. Of all Christian confessions the Protestant churches have been the most permeated with Enlightenment thought. ... There was no other independent force which could have protected itself against enlightened absolutism in these lands or have fought the measures taken by absolutism.[21]

Finally, Thomas P. Saine has recently held that most Protestant churches during the German Enlightenment, and by implication their clergy as well, were defenseless against the temporal government's desire to manipulate spiritual institutions in the service of this-worldly goals. He writes:

> The fact, that the church was always simultaneously a national [sic] church, and could in potential and in fact be directed by governmental ministers according to raison d'état, furnished the state with an irresistible power over public intellectual life.[22]

Theologicans and churchmen who did not share this general enthusiasm for the absolutist variety of Enlightenment have been regarded as exceptions: as anachronistic survivals from the age of witch hunts (e.g., Lessing's opponent Johann Melchior Goeze);[23] as isolated fanatical mystics (Johann Kaspar Lavater);[24] or as forerunners of the nineteenth century's Idealistic, romantic, and nationalistic overcoming of the Enlightenment (Herder).[25]

2. Revising the Standard Picture: The Occasion and the Way of Proceeding

One of the premises on which this standard view of Enlightenment churchmen is based is no longer tenable. This is the case because recently our entire picture of eighteenth-century Germany has been revised by general historians. Meinecke's classic work on the origin of Historismus,

---

[20] Dagobert de Levie, "The Patriotic Sermons of Christian Ludewig Hahnzog, Germany, 1785," The Journal of Modern History, 26 (1954): 36.

[21] Aretin, "Einleitung," in his Absolutismus, pp. 35-36.

[22] Thomas P. Saine, "Was ist Aufklärung?" in Aufklärung, ed. Kopitzsch, p. 333.

[23] Cf. the judgment in Stephan and Leube, p. 107, according to which Goeze has been regarded as the embodiment of "barbaric Orthodoxy."

[24] (1741-1801). Cf. Emanuel Hirsch, Geschichte der neuern evangelischen Theologie, 1 (Gütersloh, 1949-1954), 4: 185-92.

[25] Gustav Frank, Geschichte der Protestantischen Theologie, 3. Theil = Geschichte des Rationalismus und seiner Gegensätze (Leipzig, 1875), pp. 190-263; Tischhauser, pp. 131-38, 161-62; Rudolf Haym, Herder nach seinem Leben und seinem Werken, 2 (Berlin, 1877), 1:571-594; Hirsch, 4:18-22, 527; 5:145-231; Krause, pp. 21-27, 34, 116-42.

published before the Second World War, began the revision. It helped direct attention to the way in which a number of eighteenth-century German thinkers (e.g., Justus Möser) had stressed the theme of local particularism as an alternative to the theory and practice of centralized regimentation (absolutism).[26] The ramifications of this point were subjected to systematic investigation by Dietrich·Gerhard and others during the 1960's.[27]

As a result, historians have concluded that German proponents of particularism exercised a real influence during the era of Enlightenment. They managed to propagate a widely-discussed critique of the theory of absolutist centralism. As Geraint Parry and Helen P. Liebel have demonstrated, a number of writers in Germany sharply attacked the use of natural law ideas by the theorists of enlightened centralism.[28] Invoking Montesquieu's claim that the rise of despotism can be prevented only if the central government is restrained by *pouvoirs intermédiaires* (i.e., the corporate bodies in the Old Régime),[29] these thinkers constituted an important party of opposition throughout the German Enlightenment. That they cannot be dismissed as mere cranks or obscurantists has been shown

---

[26] Friedrich Meinecke, *Die Entstehung des Historismus*, ed. Carl Hinrichs = Meinecke, *Werke*, ed. Hans Herzfeld, Carl Hinrichs, Walther Hofer, no. 3 (Munich, 1959), 303-54.

[27] See for example Dietrich Gerhard, "Regionalismus und standisches Wesen als ein Grundthema europäischer Geschichte," *Historische Zeitschrift*, 174 (1952): 307-37; Werner Conze, "Staat und Gesellschaft in der frührevolutionären Epoche Deutschlands," *Historische Zeitschrift*, 180 (1961): 1-34; Geraint Parry, "Enlightened Government and its Critics in Eighteenth-Century Germany," *The Historical Journal*, 6 (1963): 178-92; Rudolf Vierhaus, "Deutschland im 18. Jahrhundert: soziales Gefüge, politische Verfassung, geistige Bewegung," in Kopitzsch, ed., pp. 173-91; Vierhaus, "Die Landstande in Nordwestdeutschland im späteren 18. Jahrhundert," in *Ständische Vertretungen in Europa im 17. und 18. Jahrhundert*, ed. Dietrich Gerhard (Göttingen, 1969), pp. 73-93; Vierhaus, "Land, Staat und Reich in der politischen Vorstellungswelt deutscher Landstande im 18. Jahrhundert," *Historische Zeitschrift*, 223 (1976): 40-46; Vierhaus, "Politisches Bewusstsein in Deutschland vor 1789," *Der Staat*, 6 (1967): 175-96; Helen P. Liebel, *Enlightened Bureaucracy vs. Enlightened Despotism in Baden, 1750-1792* (1965); William Frederick Sheldon, *The Intellectual Development of Justus Möser* (Osnabrück, 1970); Mack Walker, *German Home Towns: Community, State, and General Estate 1648-1871* (Ithaca, New York, 1971). These themes were touched on by pre-war research. See Arnold Berney, "Reichstradition und Nationalstaatsgedanke (1789-1815)," *Historische Zeitschrift*, 140 (1929): 57-86; cf. Notker Hammerstein, "Das politische Denken Friedrich Carl von Mosers," *Historische Zeitschrift*, 222 (1971): 316-38.

[28] See Parry and Liebel as cited in n. 27; cf. also Liebel, "Der aufgeklärte Absolutismus und die Gesellschaftskrise in Deutschland im 18. Jahrhundert," in *Absolutismus*, ed. Hubatsch, pp. 488-544.

[29] See for example Charles de Montesquieu, *De l'esprit des lois*, 2-4 = *Oeuvres completes*, ed. Roger Caillois, 2 (Paris, 1958): 248. Cf. Vierhaus, "Montesquieu in Deutschland. Zur Geschichte seiner Wirkung als politischer Schriftsteller im 18. Jahrhundert," in *Collegium Philosophicum. Studien Joachim Ritter zum 60. Geburtstag* (Basel, 1965), pp. 403-37, esp. pp. 427-28. On "despotism" as a term for unlimited absolutism, cf. Vierhaus, "Absolutismus," col. 17.

by Parry, who notes that they were influenced by Vico and Hume as well
as by Montesquieu and Herder.[30] Paradoxically their defense of traditionalist particularism was rooted in some of the ideas of the Enlightenment itself.

The significance of this revision in our picture of the complexity of
political *theory* in Enlightenment Germany can be grasped only if we consider it in connection with current scholarship on the reality of administrative and political *practice*. Especially important is the research of
Rudolf Vierhaus, which emphasizes the tenacious power of anticentralist
or particularist institutions such as assemblies of estates and the imperial
courts.[31] In addition, it has become increasingly clear that, with the
passage of time, absolutist governments tended to become the captives of
their own bureaucracies.[32] Thus in practice a variety of elements imposed
severe limitations on the power and influence of absolutist governments.
It can no longer be contended that the German eighteenth century was
the age of uncontested absolutism, either in theory, or in practice.

The most recent, and the most comprehensive, statement of this new
view is that of Peter Hanns Reill, who maintains that eighteenth-century
Germany was completely polarized between the proponents and the
critics of absolutist centralism:

> On the political level, a conflict existed between those social groups that
> desired a destruction of traditional political ties in favor of a strong cen-
> tralized absolute monarchy, and those that favored a reformation of the
> German body politic without destroying the traditions of the *Ständestaat* [i.e.,
> the central government sharply limited by the power of assemblies of estates
> and the jurisdiction of the imperial courts].[33]

These two parties tended to localize in different kinds of areas:

> The former [i.e., members of the radically innovative centralist group
> described immediately above] were centered in the court and looked to
> French intellectual traditions favorable to the establishment of "Enlighten-
> ed Absolutism." The latter [i.e., members of the conservative and par-
> ticularist reform group described above] were found in provincial towns,
> especially university towns, in mercantile centers, and in bureaucracies that
> had won or retained a certain degree of independence from monarchial
> supervision.[34]

Furthermore (and of capital importance for our study), the entire
eighteenth-century Enlightenment, considered as a nonnoble or

---

[30] Parry, p. 185 and n. 35.

[31] See n. 27 above.

[32] Hans Rosenberg, *Bureaucracy, Aristocracy and Autocracy: The Prussian Experience
1660-1815*, Harvard Historical Monographs, no. 34 (Cambridge, Mass., 1958).

[33] Peter Hanns Reill, *The German Enlightenment and the Rise of Historicism* (Berkeley,
Calif., 1975), p. 4.

[34] Reill, p. 4.

"bürgerlich" movement, is closely associated with the antiabsolutist party:

> The leaders of the Aufklärung [i.e., German Enlightenment] belonged to the latter [i.e., particularist] group. They turned toward intellectual traditions emphasizing the necessity of … historical continuity, traditions more favorable to checking the power of the monarchy through the revitalization of "constituted bodies."[35]

Reill, then, defines the German Enlightenment as a non-courtly, non-noble movement, and hence a movement opposed to absolutist centralism and the "Enlightened Bureaucracy" favored by Prussia and its imitators. While Reill's statement of the matter may be somewhat overdrawn, it sums up a body of current research that cannot be ignored.

Yet when considering the ecclesiastical Enlightenment, historians still operate on the assumption that absolutism was the only significant variety of political thought at the time. Even so knowledgeable a scholar as Scholder asserts that, because the ecclesiastical Enlightenment lacked "critical reflection" on society, its one lasting result was the ideological underpinning of absolutism.[36] Though Scholder rightly points out that most churchmen in the German Enlightenment were not—as has too often been assumed—radical Rationalists; and though he correctly insists that most Enlightenment churchmen did not aim to destroy the church, but instead wished by means of moderate reform to preserve as much of institutional Christianity as possible; nonetheless Scholder feels comfortable with the standard picture of the political stance of these churchmen.[37] It does not occur to him that an orientation of conservative reform such as he rightly ascribes to these churchmen does not fit with his characterization of them as unthinking champions of absolutism; nor does he consider the possibility that the enlightened churchmen may have recoiled from the secularism and religious indifferentism implicit in the absolutist doctrine.

General historians have concluded that Enlightenment Germany produced, not one, but two schools of thought and practice with regard to the direction of government. This realization raises the possibility that the Enlightenment churchmen, like their lay contemporaries, divided into two major parties on the issue of governmental centralism and its consequences. If such proves to be the case, it would then be necessary to con-

---

[35] Reill, p. 4. The similarity to the "court-country" polarization discussed by some historians dealing with the "general crisis of the seventeenth century" is obvious. See *Crisis in Europe 1560-1660*, ed. Trevor Aston (New York, 1965).

[36] For Scholder on the "Mangel an kritischer Reflexion," see Scholder, p. 314. Note his lament, p. 311, that the Neologians desired reform rather than revolution.

[37] Cf. Scholder, pp. 310-14.

sider the related possibility that one party among these churchmen cannot be considered as promoters of the secularization of institutional Christianity, but rather as opponents of it. The present study will investigate these two closely related possibilities.

Scholars have neglected to consider these two possibilities because the assumptions on which they have proceeded excluded them from the outset. This has been the case, not simply because political life in the German eighteenth century was wrongly taken to be monolithically absolutist in character, but also because of another unquestioned assumption. That was the belief that only a dogmatic or doctrinal structure ideologically employed can provide the motivation and the means for the clergy to resist assimilation by the state and by secular culture. This assumption has long governed the way in which the history of the ecclesiastical Enlightenment has been written: it has been taken as established that the loss of traditional dogmatic substance necessarily induced among Enlightenment churchmen a paralysis when confronted with absolutism and its advocates.

This belief is clearly formulated in two works from the turn of the century which still provide the basis for how Enlightenment churchmen are regarded—even though, as was pointed out forty-five years ago, these studies are based on inadequate research.[38] The first of these unsuperseded works, Gustav Ecke's attempt to explain the institutional church's loss of influence in Wilhelmine Germany, discerned a double process of decay dating from the eighteenth century:

> [since the Protestant Church was] weakened in its essence—inwardly by Rationalism, outwardly by the destruction of its organization—it was unable to resist the attack of the spirit of the modern world.[39]

The argument here is plain: because of inner erosion of theological substance, the Enlightenment clergy were rendered incapable of resisting the attempts of absolutism and its propagandists to transform the church into the adjunct of secular culture. Ecke's contemporary Christian Tischhauser made the same argument: because the identity of the churchmen was weakened by scepticism and rationalistic philosophy, they naturally fell into the habit of servility and therefore were unable to resist the state's secularization of church property, the government's reduction of ecclesiastical rights and privileges, and the absolutist demand that the parish clergy become instructors in agronomy and first aid.[40]

---

[38] Cf. n. 14 above.
[39] Ecke, p. 103.
[40] The classic statement: Tischhauser, pp. 131, 136, 138-39, 145, 151.

This line of argumentation has continued to dominate postwar scholarship on the subject. It can be summarized in two theses which recur in most postwar treatments of the ecclesiastical Enlightenment:

1. Because of an inner collapse, that is, because of the loss of doctrinal substance giving rise to a sort of professional vacuum that needed filling, the Enlightenment churchmen completely lacked any will to resist governmental and propagandistic pressures toward the remodelling of their role in a this-worldly direction;

2. on this account there occurred a steady and almost unopposed secularization of the clerical role throughout the eighteenth century, culminating in the preponderance of economic and political preaching in the Rationalist era after 1785.

These ideas can be readily documented in postwar scholarship. For example, Dagobert de Levie argues

> that the weakening of dogmatic orthodoxy extended the scope of the sermon to include a wide range of social and political topics[41]

with the result that the enlightened clergy

> preached on kindness, envy, jealousy, and hate; the significance of glory; marriage, education, and agriculture; politeness, games, and fashions; and what not. On this intellectual soil, finally, grew a new kind of sermon, a characteristic outgrowth of the Enlightenment, the patriotic sermon.[42]

De Levie does not pause to consider whether this pattern is valid for only one group of enlightened churchmen, and thus does not inquire whether another group, despite their abandonment of Orthodoxy, may nonetheless have put up some resistance to such secularization. Again—to take an example of a conclusion that will be challenged in a subsequent chapter of the present study—Alexandra Schlingensiepen-Pogge holds that the Göttingen theology professor Johann Peter Miller (1725-1789), because his anthropology or doctrine of human nature had been affected by Enlightenment currents, relocated the main task of the clergy in the education of people for their this-worldly tasks.[43] The same line of argumentation underlies Reinhard Krause's research on the preponderance of this-worldly themes in Rationalist preaching.[44] It also provides the basis for Scholder's claim that the one lasting effect of ecclesiastical Enlightenment in Germany was the legitimation of absolutism. For the necessary precondition of this development was

---

[41] Levie, "Hahnzog," p. 36.
[42] Levie, "Hahnzog," p. 37.
[43] Alexandra Schlingensiepen-Pogge, *Das Sozialethos der lutherischen Aufklärungstheologie am Vorabend der Industriellen Revolution* (Göttingen, 1967), p. 14; cf. pp. 87f. below.
[44] Cf. n. 15 above.

allegedly the devaluation of dogma in favor of practical activity, and the concomitant failure to develop a theoretical or ideological orientation. Scholder does not ask whether this explanatory model can rightly be applied to all Enlightenment churchmen.[45] The same model has been employed by Johannes Wallmann, who recently has contrasted Lutheran Orthodoxy's impassioned criticism of temporal government with the absence of this criticism among the undogmatic theologians who led up to the Enlightenment.[46]

The present study assumes neither that all Enlightenment churchmen in Protestant Germany were proponents of absolutism and secularization, nor that their undeniable surrender of Orthodoxy necessarily led them to give up all independence of spirit. It will instead argue that a significant number of Enlightenment churchmen opposed the secularizing consequences of absolutism, and did so with some ingenuity. It will make this case, not by examining the entirety of the Lutheran clergy, but rather by looking at the articulators and shapers of clerical opinion and ecclesiastical policy in influential places—members of consistories, superintendents with a rank comparable to that of a bishop, and professors of theology in the universities and in other institutions for training clergy. That is to say, the evidence to be cited here will in the main be drawn from the examples of those clergymen who had access to the means of disseminating their ideas in print. While this delimitation will exclude a certain amount of evidence, it is certainly a defensible approach: for this substantial body of printed material has never been surveyed with a view to determining how the eighteenth-century clergy conceived their role.

The principal theme to be investigated here is the debate about the aims and function of the clerical estate during the later eighteenth century: were the clergy to find their *raison d'être* in service to other-worldly goals, or in service to the this-worldly needs of the state—were they to serve the traditional religious needs of mankind, or the needs of absolutist governments? This theme cannot be pursued in the abstract. By way of introduction we must first examine the structure, circumstances, and orientation of the clerical leadership in the eighteenth century. Then we shall turn to the phases in which the secularist challenge to traditional

---

[45] Scholder, p. 311, traces the failure of the Neologians to develop a revolutionary stance to their prior lack of a "radikale, theoretische Position." The presupposition here is that a stance critical of the temporal government must be occasioned and supported by some kind of ideological structure—either the rhetoric of Rousseau, Tom Paine, and Robespierre, or the dogmatic assertions of Lutheran Orthodoxy. For the significance of the Enlightenment devaluation of dogma and the ultimately conservative implications of the concentration on practical reform in Scholder's account, cf. pp. 294-303, 310-14.

[46] See n. 4 above.

clerical identity was made and to the clerical responses to the theological, legal, and professional varieties of challenge posed by secularism; we shall concentrate on the last challenge in particular. In so doing it will become possible to understand the full dimensions of the Enlightenment argument about the purpose for which the clergy should be trained. An investigation of this theme offers the chance to see how conservatively the leading churchmen in much of the ecclesiastical Enlightenment in fact reacted to the radically secular reform demands made on them by the supporters of absolutism.

In the course of this investigation it will become clear that the negative response of many of these churchmen to pro-absolutist concepts of the ministerial office can be adequately understood only if the traditional identity of the clergy is taken as a variant on the particularistic self-understanding characteristic of the members of the various constituted bodies making up the Old Régime—an orientation which was, by its very nature, opposed to the unchecked growth of centralistic absolutism. Hence it will also become evident that anticentralist plans for the strengthening of traditional clerical identity were not simply ad hoc expedients invented in order to provide an answer to pro-absolutist projects for reform of the clergy; these anticentralist plans were furthermore a sort of clerical variant on traditional political particularism: a variation on the claim made by advocates of political particularism that the solution to Germany's problems lay in what Reill terms "the revitalization of 'constituted bodies'" as a means of restraining monarchies.[47] All this will in turn suggest that much evidence of clerical opposition to radical secularism during the eighteenth century has been ignored by scholars: because they have failed to question the basic assumptions on which the standard view of the ecclesiastical Enlightenment rests, scholars have mistakenly detected surrender to absolutistic secularization where in truth there was only apologetic maneuvering with a decidedly traditionalist intent.

Thus this study will be delimited in two ways: by its concentration on leading churchmen with access to the press, and by its preoccupation with the debate about the clerical *raison d'être*. A third delimitation will be geographical. This study will be confined to two small territories so as to investigate the kind of territory which, according to Reill, provided the natural homeland for that anticentralist party which put forward its deliberate alternative to Prussian centralism.[48] Any ecclesiastical representatives of a noncentralist or nonabsolutist viewpoint will be most

---

[47] Reill, p. 4.
[48] Reill, p. 4.

likely to have flourished in such smaller territories. Yet we do not wish simply to examine the ecclesiastical counterpart to the anticentralist movement, but wish also to see how churchmen influenced by pro-absolutist ideas behaved. Therefore we must also see to it that the area to be studied was one affected as well by radically secular notions on the ministry.

Both these needs can be met if we concentrate here on the leading churchmen in two small, adjacent, closely linked, yet altogether distinct territories: Braunschweig-Wolfenbüttel and Electoral Hannover (Kurhannover). These two territories will for the sake of convenience be referred to jointly as "Northwest Germany."[49]

These two territories present a useful opportunity for comparison and contrast. Both were ruled by different branches of the same family, the Welfs or Guelphs. Yet the members of this family had come to adopt different orientations in the rule of the two territories. The dukes of Braunschweig pursued a centralized and absolutistic policy. The other branch of the family, the kings of England as Electors of Hannover, were forced by their absence to tolerate particularism in Electoral Hannover.

Braunschweig (as we may term the territory for short) had become an absolutist territory at least as early as the reign of Duke Anton Ulrich (1685-1714), whose imitation of Louis XIV was kept in bounds only by limited resources.[50] The assemblies of estates had ceased meeting in 1682 and did not meet again until 1768, when a financial crisis brought on by courtly expenditures and military involvement forced Duke Karl I (1735-1780) to seek help.[51] His reign had been characterized by lavish spending on the army and the court theatre, and by elaborate and unsuccesful economic experiments based on mercantilist theory.[52] His successor, Karl Wilhelm Ferdinand (1780-1806) attempted to cope with the financial problems inherited from his predecessor; like him, he was an imitator of Friderician Prussia. The history of Braunschweig can be seen to exemplify the stages in the development of absolutism—from the

---

[49] Adapting the usage of the Lessing-Akademie (Wolfenbüttel) in its symposium of October 26-30, 1976 on "Das Zeitalter der Aufklärung in Nordwestdeutschland." However, "Northwest Germany" will here indicate only the territories ruled by the Welfs—Hamburg, Oldenburg, and Schleswig-Holstein are here excluded from consideration. For the main features of the political, economic, and social conditions in the two territories the reader is referred to Appendix A.

[50] For an overview of Braunschweig-Wolfenbüttel in this period, see Joseph König, "Landesgeschichte," in Richard Moderhack, ed., *Braunschweigische Landesgeschichte im Überblick* (Braunschweig, 1977), pp. 61-110, esp. pp. 80-87; and Albert Rhamm, *Die Verfassungsgesetze des Herzogthums Braunschweig* (Brauschweig, 1907), pp. 1-23.

[51] Wilhelm Schmidt, *Der braunschweigische Landtag von 1768-1770* (Phil. Diss., Göttingen University, 1912).

[52] König, p. 82.

architectural and administrative emulation of the French court under Anton Ulrich to Karl Wilhelm Ferdinand's try at an administrative, financial, and pedagogical reorganization under the leadership of the young K. A. von Hardenberg of later Prussian fame.[53]

Hannover, on the other hand, presents a different picture. The departure of George I for England in 1714 had meant that here—in contrast to Braunschweig—the assemblies of estates retained their traditional powers and the nobility and Protestant prelates their traditional governmental functions. The power of the assemblies of estates in Electoral Hannover actually *grew* in the course of the eighteenth century.[54] Thus the climate in Hannover encouraged a number of writers who favored particularism and administrative practice based on experience gained at the local level; among them may be named August Ludwig Schlözer (1735-1809), August Wilhelm Rehberg (1757-1836), and Ernst Brandes (1785-1810).[55] In consequence the center of the nonnoble and antiabsolutist movement in the German Enlightenment was Electoral Hannover's new university in Göttingen.[56]

---

[53] On the young Hardenberg's activity, cf. Franz-Ludwig Knemeyer, *Regierungs- und Verwaltungsreformen in Deutschland zu Beginn des 19. Jahrhunderts* (Köln and Berlin, 1970), p. 183. In general: Selma Stern, *Karl Wilhelm Ferdinand. Herzog zu Braunschweig und Lüneburg* (Hildesheim, 1921). On pedagogical reform attempts in Braunschweig, see Ulrich Herrmann, ''Modell der Schulreform: Das Braunschweigische Schuldirektorium 1786-1790,'' *Braunschweigisches Jahrbuch* 52 (1971): 163-81.

[54] See Otto von Heinemann, *Geschichte von Braunschweig und Hannover* (Gotha, 1892), 3:379-81; Ernst von Maier, *Hannoversche Verfassungs- und Verwaltungsgeschichte* (Leipzig, 1898-99); Stephen Skalweit, ''Edmund Burke, Ernst Brandes und Hannover, '' *Niedersächsisches Jahrbuch für Landesgeschichte* 28 (1956): 28-29; and Joachim Lampe, *Aristokratie, Hofadel und Staatspatriziat in Kurhannover* (Göttingen, 1963).

[55] Reill, p. 8; Parry, p. 181; Klaus Epstein, *The Genesis of German Conservatism* (Princeton, N.J., 1966), pp. 547-94.

[56] Reill, p. 8; Parry, p. 181.

CHAPTER ONE

THE CLERICAL ESTABLISHMENT
IN NORTHWEST GERMANY

1. *The Institutional Church and its Clergy*

The character of the institutional church and its clergy in Electoral
Hannover and Braunschweig-Wolfenbüttel was in large measure shaped
by the character of the general population which the church served and
from which many of the clergy were recruited. The character of that
population, and thus implicitly the nature of the church, was summed up
eloquently by the late-eighteenth-century Hannoverian official Ernst
Brandes.[1] In a largely unpublished[2] memorandum concerning Electoral
Hannover sent in 1796 to Edmund Burke, Brandes ventured these
judgments:

> In Germany the national Character of its northern inhabitants differs very
> much from that of the people in the western and eastern part of it. We can
> not well be look'd upon as one nation, except in point of language and lit-
> terature and even in these points the difference is very considerable. Good
> sense is certainly a quality with which we in this country seem to be more
> largely endow'd than the Germans of the West, but we have perhaps less wit
> and by far a less livelier imagination than these.[3]

Going further, Brandes then made an observation which the student
of ecclesiastical affairs in Northwest Germany can readily apply to the
indigenous clergy:

> Our people is much attach'd to ancient practices, follows regularly the mode
> of proceeding of its forefathers and is not prone to innovation of any kind.
> We learn not easily, but we retain well what we have learn'd. ... The spirit
> of invention is not great in the nation, but the progresses which we have
> made, not in a long period, in adopting the useful inventions of other Coun-
> tries, notwithstanding the bias of the national Character, which is averse to
> innovations, have on the whole been very great.[4]

---

[1] Cf. Carl Haase, *Ernst Brandes 1758-1810* (Hildesheim, 1973-74).

[2] Part of this memorandum has been published in Stephen Skalweit, "Edmund Burke,
Ernst Brandes und Hannover," *Niedersächsisches Jahrbuch für Landesgeschichte* 28 (1956):
15-72.

[3] Cited according to Stephen Skalweit's transcript of the MS in the Central Library in
Sheffield, Acc. 4 157 in the Niedersachsisches Hauptstaatsarchiv Hannover, MS Q, Nr.
010: "Denkschrift von Ernst Brandes an Edmund Burke über Verfassung Verwaltung
und Landesnatur des Kurfürstentums Hannover (October 29, 1796)," p. 56-57.

[4] Brandes, "Denkschrift," p. 57.

Brandes concludes with more general observations equally applicable to the temperament of the ecclesiastical establishment:

> The Nation is rather of a cold phlegmatic disposition. Its good nature does not shine in effusions of a warm heart. But tho' its good nature is not easily to be perceiv'd in conversing with the people, much more certainly is done here by all ranks to relieve the distresses of the indigent and miserable, than in most of the other parts of Germany. We are not lively but inclined to sullenness and difficult to be pleased. We are more apt to feel disagreeable sensations than to be elated by pleasure and enjoyments. We are constant, firm and faithful, ...[5]

This population, numbering in Electoral Hannover just under a million[6] and in Braunschweig-Wolfenbüttel just over 200,000[7] supported at the end of the Old Régime a very considerable Lutheran ecclesiastical establishment. Though Lutherans today have the reputation of putting great weight on the invisible church (to the alleged disadvantage of their sense for practical arrangements insuring the integrity of the visible church), in eighteenth-century Germany the visible church was much in evidence. Black-clad clergy,[8] feudal payments due the church, the regulation of engagements and marriages, frequent worship services, clerical supervision of schools, and programs of poor relief all gave

---

[5] Brandes, "Denkschrift," p. 57.

[6] Friedrich Thimme, *Die inneren Zustände des Kurfürstentums Hannovers unter der Französisch-Westfälischen Herrschaft 1806-1813*, 2 vols. (Hannover and Leipzig, 1893), 1:1.

[7] Carl Venturini, *Das Herzogthum Braunschweig in seiner gegenwärtigen Beschaffenheit* (Helmstedt, 1826), p. 19.

[8] In accord with the custom of the English-speaking world the term "clergy" will be used for the Protestant pastorate in Germany, a custom fully in accord with the legal realities and practice of the Old Régime in Germany. While it is the case that *Clerisey* had a pejorative connotation for the Enlightenment, it could be and was applied to the Protestant pastors. It is of course perfectly appropriate in English to speak then of a kind of anticlericalism in the eighteenth century directed against the established church's Protestant servants. I recognize of course that present-day German usage regards the *Klerus* as being simply Roman Catholic.—It has proven impracticable to try to render the nuances of eighteenth-century terminology for the clergy in English. For the period of Pietism and Enlightenment the standard term was *Lehrer* or *Religionslehrer* (teacher or teacher of religion), just as the apologetic substitute for *Predigt* (sermon) was *Religionsvortrag*. To avoid confusion with schoolteachers and university lectures I have decided to ignore these nuances and to call the clergy clergy and sermons sermons: a study of this kind has no investment in perpetuating the camouflage developed by the clergy in an age hostile to the traditional forms of religion. The custom of terming the clergy and laity *doctores et auditores, Lehrer und Zuhörer* is a Pietist and natural-law reaction against the Orthodox doctrine of three estates within the church and the exaggerated importance for the clergy thereby claimed. The use of the term "teacher" for the clergyman is associated with Pietism and the territorialist and collegialist schools of Protestant church law. See Martin Honecker, *Cura religionis Magistratus Christiani: Studien zum Kirchenrecht im Luthertum des 17. Jahrhunderts* (Munich, 1968), p. 81.

testimony to the significance of the visible church and to the importance of the distinction between clergy and laity.[9]

As a result of the sixteenth-century Reformation the clergy in the territorial churches of both Braunschweig-Wolfenbüttel and Electoral Hannover were bound to the Lutheran confessional writings, though certain regional variations did obtain. The most significant variation was the fact that in Braunschweig-Wolfenbüttel, despite the early part played by a duke of Braunschweig in the origin of the Formula of Concord, that document was nonetheless not formally recognized there as binding.[10] Still the common basis in the ecumenical creeds, the Augsburg Confession, Luther's catechisms, and other shared confessional writings provided a unity of doctrine in the area that ultimately proved more important than the differences registered in the regional church orders.

From its inception in Northwest Germany the local version of the faith of the Church of the Augsburg Confession had been marked by cautious avoidance of extremes. This tendency can be seen already in such early documents as the *Formulae caute loquendi* of 1535.[11] It became the dominant trait in the theology of ecumenical and irenical compromise elaborated at Helmstedt University in Braunschweig-Wolfenbüttel (a university until 1737 serving as well the rest of the Welf territories) by the most influential theologian in Northwest Germany, Georg Calixt (1586-1656).[12] The Melanchthonian humanism implicit in the tradition of Calixt made for a relatively flexible, traditionalistic theology, receptive to the proto-Pietistic emphases of such writers as Johann Arndt (1555-1621); but at the same time, the discouragement of extreme scholastic Orthodoxy and the readiness of local churchmen to find a place for the practice of piety which resulted from this kind of theology meant that, in the whole, extra-ecclesiastical Pietism as a protest movement was of little significance in

---

[9] On the legal authority of the church and its clergy over the laity see Philipp Meyer, "Der obrigkeitliche Zwang in den deutschen evangelischen Landeskirchen des 16. bis 18. Jahrhunderts, *ZGNK* 34/35 (1929/30): 278-314.

[10] Johannes Meyer, *Kirchengeschichte Niedersachsens* (Göttingen, 1939), p. 105; cf. H.-W. Gensichen, "Die Lehrverpflichtung in der Hannoverschen Landeskirche," *JGNK* 48 (1950): 98-108; K. Knoke, "Der lutherische Bekenntnisstand der Prediger an der Universitätskirche zu Göttingen," *ZGNK* 23 (1918): 95-112.

[11] J. Meyer, *Kirchengeschichte*, p. 80; cf. Paul Fleisch, "Hannoversche 'Vorsicht' in kirchenregimentlichen Äußerungen [1576-1866]," *Evangelische Wahrheit* 31 (1940): 74-76.

[12] On Calixt and his influence see for example Horst Reller, "Die Auswirkungen der Universität Helmstedt auf Pfarrer und Gemeinden in Niedersachsen," *JGNK* 74 (1976): 35-52; Inge Mager, "Bibliographie zur Geschichte der Universität Helmstedt (mit besonderer Berücksichtigung der theologischen Fakultät," *JGNK* 74 (1976): 237-42; Johannes Meyer, "Literatur zur Einführung in die Kirchengeschichte Niedersachsens," *ZGNK* 41 (1936): 262-78; and Friedrich Uhlhorn, "Die Bedeutung Georg Calixts für die lutherische Kirche der welfischen Lande," *ZGNK* 32/33 (1927-28): 201-17.

most parts of the Welf territories.[13] What we find here is rather a gradual modification of the basic theological position of the territorial churches to include elements of Pietism and moderate Enlightenment as the decades passed. Only in the later eighteenth century, with the advent of radical Rationalism, were sharp lines drawn.[14]

Despite the doctrine of the universal priesthood, the Lutheran Reformation had retained and adapted the division between clergy and laity, and with it the traditional notion of three orders or estates within society.[15] For the mentality of the Old Régime in Protestant Europe this fact was of immense significance: it meant that, even after the Reformation, one of the fundamental categories of medieval European society would be perpetuated: some would be clergy; all the rest would be laity. The ramifications of this fact must not be minimized: in truth, a great variety of marks set off the clergy from the laity, and a number of factors created a clerical *esprit de corps*—and subjected the clergy to lay criticism. To ignore the extent of these ramifications would be easy for a modern observer living in a society largely divested of the sacral trappings of the Old Régime; but such ignoring would constitute a failure of historical imagination.[16]

So prominent appeared the Protestant clergy that to the laity it often seemed that the pastors *were* the church. In the words of Bernd Moeller concerning the Lutheran territorial churches after the Reformation: ''The 'church' as an institution was composed in practice of only a single estate, that of the pastors.''[17] Such was the case theologically because in

---

[13] Rudolf Ruprecht, *Der Pietismus des 18. Jahrhunderts in den Hannoverschen Stammländern*, Studien zur Kirchengeschichte Niedersachsens, no. 1 (Göttingen, 1919); Martin Schmidt, ''Der Pietismus in Nordwestdeutschland,'' *JGNK* 70 (1972): 147-77.

[14] Cf. Hans Beyer, ''Niederdeutsche Kirchenkämpfe im ausgehenden 18. Jahrhundert,'' *JGNK* 53 (1955): 108-16; 121-26.

[15] Wilhelm Maurer, *Luthers Lehre von der drei Hierarchien und ihr mittelalterlicher Hintergrund* (Munich, 1970); cf. Jean Batany, ''Des 'Trois Fonctions' aux 'Trois États'?'' *Annales: Économies, Sociétés, Civilisations* 18 (1963): 933-38; on the distinct notion of three estates *within* the church in Orthodox Lutheran theology, see Johann Gerhard, *Loci Theologici*, ed. Johann Friedrich Cotta, 20 vols. (Tübingen, 1762-81), 12b:2; Honecker, pp. 51-136; Martin Heckel, ''Staat und Kirche nach den Lehren der evangelischen Juristen Deutschlands in der ersten Hälfte des 17. Jahrhunderts,'' *Zeitschrift der Savigny-Stiftung für Rechtsgeschichte, Kanonistische Abteilung* 42 (1956): 117-247 and 43 (1957): 202-308; 43:239-68; Werner Elert, *Morphologie des Luthertums*, 2 vols. (1931; reprint ed., Munich, 1965), 2:49-64.

[16] On the need to derive the categories for the analysis of the Old Régime from the Old Régime itself rather than from subsequent notions, see Roland Mousnier, ''Problèmes de Méthode dans l'étude des structures sociales des seizième, dix-septième, dix-huitième siècles,'' in *Spiegel der Geschichte: Festgabe für Max Braubach*, ed. Konrad Repgen and Stephen Skalweit (Münster/Westfalen, 1964), pp. 550-57; p. 556.

[17] Bernd Moeller in *Ökumenische Kirchengeschichte*, 3 vols.: *2. Mittelalter und Reformation*, ed. R. Kottje and B. Moeller (Mainz and Munich, 1973): 430.

late Orthodoxy and down into the period of Enlightenment the Protestant pastor represented more or less what the Roman Catholic parish priest of the day did: namely, as Timothy Tackett has put it, "the essential link within the rural world between man and the supernatural, man and his salvation."[18] Such was the case also because in practice in the clergy were the sole group educated in matters of religion and theology (at least until the onset of Enlightenment), had the authority to teach and administer the sacraments, and possessed the legal authority to manage the incomes and property of the church.

The Lutheran clergy throughout Germany were derived neither from the nobility nor, to any considerable degree, from the peasantry or the poorer artisans. Many were the sons of pastors, for pastors and learned theologians ran in dynasties.[19] Figures on the social origin of the clergy in Northwest Germany are rare. For Lüneburg, and indeed for all of Electoral Hannover, it would appear that, during the period 1800-1930, about 40% of the clergy were sons of pastors; 16% sons of teachers; 10% sons of artisans; 8% sons of high functionaries; 7% sons of functionaries of the middle rank; 7% sons of farmers, 6% sons of merchants; and 6% sons of professionals. During the period before 1800 it would appear that sons of peasant origin entered the clergy only rarely.[20] These figures can be taken as representative for most of Protestant Germany, for they fall well within the range of those for Brandenburg-Prussia around 1700 as ascertained by another study putting the percentage of pastors' sons among the clergy there between 32 and 50.[21]

In Braunschweig-Wolfenbüttel before the Napoleonic invasion there were a total of 236 full-time pastors, not counting assistants; they served a total of 398 churches and chapels. Of these, 116 parishes were under ducal patronage; 44 were filled by manorial lords, 40 by prelates, 10 by

---

[18] Timothy Tackett, *Priest and Parish in Eighteenth-Century France: A Social and Political Study of the Curés in a Diocese of Dauphiné 1750-1791* (Princeton, N.J., 1977), p. 152.

[19] Cf. W. H. Bruford, *Germany in the Eighteenth Century: The Social Background of the Literary Revival*, 2nd ed. (Cambridge, 1971), p. 247; Gerd Heinrich, "Amtsträgerschaft und Geistlichkeit: Zur Problematik der sekundären Führungsschichten in Brandenburg-Preußen 1450-1786," in *Beamtentum und Pfarrerstand 1400-1800*, ed. Günther Franz (Limburg/Lahn, 1972), pp. 179-238; p. 194; Gebhard von Lenthe, "Zur Geschichte des Beamtentums in Niedersachsen," in *Beamtentum und Pfarrerstand*, pp. 239-47; Karl E. Demandt, "Amt und Familie: Eine soziologisch-genealogische Studie zur hessischen Verwaltungsgeschichte des 16. Jahrhunderts," *Hessisches Jahrbuch für Landesgeschichte* 2 (1952): 79-133; Friedrich Wilhelm Euler, "Entstehung und Entwicklung deutscher Gelehrtengeschlechter," in *Universität und Gelehrtenstand 1400-1800*, ed. Hellmuth Rössler and Günther Franz (Limburg/Lahn, 1970), pp. 183-232; and Georges Pariset, *L'État et les Églises en Prusse Sous Frédéric Guillaume Ier (1713-1740)* (Thèse, Paris, 1896), pp. 253-62.

[20] Eduard Salfeld, "Der Landpfarrer und seine Gemeinde im Fürstentum Lüneburg zur Zeit der Orthodozie," *ZGNK* 45 (1940): 203-24; p. 204.

[21] Pariset, pp. 253-62, esp. p. 255.

city governments, 7 by congregations, and 19 by cloisters outside the territory.[22]

In Electoral Hannover in 1787 there seem to have been about 893 parishes.[23] Another reckoning from 1789 lists a total of 818 pastors, of whose posts 513 were under royal patronage and 305 were conferred by other agencies. Of these, 597 positions were supervised by the consistory in Hannover; the remainder were supervised by smaller consistories.[24]

These clergymen, and with them as well schoolteachers and sextons, formed a distinct body governed by laws of its own and judicable in the consistory acting as an ecclesiastical court—not in temporal courts.[25] Furthermore they enjoyed certain privileges. For example, they were granted immunities: besides the traditional freedom from military service, they had also freedom from imperial taxes and from imposts on wine and beer as well as freedom from charges levied by the temporal arm for recovery of unpaid incomes.[26]

Clerical incomes were of several types, as might be expected in the Old Régime. Pastors received payments in cash, either as salaries and interest from capital, or from collections and occasional fees (accidental payments of *jura stolae*) for the performance of offical acts such as marriage, burial, or hearing private confession without enumeration of individual sins (the fee for which was the infamous *Beichtpfennig*). In some places the clergy also received from peasants a tithe in kind. The clergy in many places had parish lands which they either put under cultivation themselves or leased out.[27]

Aside from the elite of the clerical leadership in urban areas, the parish clergy were not well off despite the fact that they enjoyed free lodging and certain payments in retirement due them or their widows. Their situation worsened appreciably in the inflationary period of the later eighteenth century. To give estimates in absolute figures means little but can be at-

---

[22] Carl Venturini, *Das Herzogthum Braunschweig in seiner gegenwärtigen Beschaffenheit* (Helmstedt, 1826), pp. 65-66.

[23] See "Anzahl der Pfarren in den Churhannoverschen Landen," *Magazin für die Geschichte und Statistik und das Territorialstaatsrecht von Niedersachsen*, 1:1 (Lemgo, 1787): 59-63; p. 63.

[24] See "Anzahl der sämmtlichen evang. Prediger in Sr. Königl. Majestät von Groß-Brittanien und Kurfürstl. Durchl, von Braunschweig-Lünenburg Deutschen Landen, nebst einer Anzeige, wie viel davon auf Königlichen, und wie viel auf Patronat-Pfarren, stehen," *Journal von und für Deutschland*, 6ter Jg., 1.-6. Stück (1789), p. 131.

[25] Johann Karl Fürchtegott Schlegel, *Churhannöversches Kirchenrecht*, 5 vols. (Hannover, 1801-6), 1:119-230.

[26] See for example Johann Christoph Stübner, *Historische Beschreibung der Kirchenverfassung in den Herzogl. Braunschweig-Lüneburgischen Landen seit der Reformation* (Goslar, 1800), pp. 215-19.

[27] Stübner, pp. 198-202.

tempted: in Electoral Hannover under the Old Régime more than half the parish clergy made do with an average income of at *most* 300 *Reichsthaler* a year; only a few churchmen (e.g., consistorial councillors or pastors of large urban congregations) could look forward to 800 to 900 *Thaler* a year.[28]

Regulation prescribed a course of education and examination for students planning to enter the ministry. Students in Braunschweig-Wolfenbüttel were required to spend a minimum of two years at Helmstedt University after Latin school and to undergo examination by the consistory.[29] Regulations in Electoral Hannover were equally strict: students as of 1727 were required to place themselves under the direction of the consistory once they began to seek a parish.[30] They were ordinarily required, at least by the turn of the eighteenth to the nineteenth century, to spend a minimum of three years at Göttingen University; furthermore, it was normally expected that "foreigners" from territories other than Electoral Hannover would not obtain parishes unless they had been certified by the consistory in Hannover. An exception was made for the sons of pastors from the Electorate who had taken calls elsewhere.[31]

An additional educational possibility available in both territories was post-university study[32] in one of the small seminaries attached to former Roman Catholic cloisters such as Loccum in the electorate and Riddagshausen near Braunschweig; these institutions trained perhaps three to six students at a time and provided future leadership for the clerical estate in the two territories.[33]

---

[28] Christian Tischhauser, *Geschichte der evangelischen Kirchen Deutschlands in der ersten Hälfte des 19. Jahrhunderts* (Basel, 1900), p. 132.—It should be noted that the upper reaches of the clergy were assigned a place in the tables of ranks issued for use at court; see C. E. von Malortie, *Der Hannoversche Hof unter dem Kurfürsten Ernst August und der Kurfürstin Sophie* (Hannover, 1847), pp. 230-33; Johann Christian Lünig, *Theatrum ceremoniale historico-politicum*, 2 vols. (Leipzig, 1719-20), 2:1504, 1508-9; "Controversie wegen des Rangs der Geistlichen," *Unschuldigen Nachrichten Von alten und Neuen theologischen Sachen*, ed. Valentin Ernst Löscher, Jg. 1709 (Leipzig, 1707 [*sic*]), pp. 860-62; Johann Georg Walch, *Historische und Theologische Einleitung in die Religions-Streitigkeiten Der Evangelisch-Lutherischen Kirchen*, 5 vols. (Jena, 1730-34), 3:15-57.

[29] Stübner, p. 268.

[30] Schlegel, 2:295.

[31] Schlegel, 2:299-301.

[32] Most candidates did not enter cloistered seminaries, nor did they find a call immediately after completing studies and examinations. Rather did they serve as tutors in some well-to-do family; cf. Georg Schnath, *Geschichte Hannover im Zeitalter der neunten Kur und der englischen Sukzession 1674-1714*, 2 vols. (Hildesheim, 1976), 2:413.

[33] Cf. Christoph Erich Weidemann, *Geschichte des Klosters Loccum*, ed. Friedrich Burchard Köster (Göttingen, 1822); Friedrich Düsterdieck, *Das Hospiz im Kloster Loccum* (Göttingen, 1863); Johannes Beste, "Das Predigerseminar zu Riddagshausen," *ZGNK* 10 (1905): 197-230; Zacharias Conrad von Uffenbach, *Merkwürdige Reisen durch Niedersachsen Holland und Engelland*, 3 vols. (Ulm and Memmingen, 1753-54), 1:301-4.

The churchmen-abbots at the head of these and other Lutheran cloisters in the two territories were, like consistorial councillors, endowed with sufficient income to make them in some measure independent of governmental pressure and hence capable of serving as voices for particularist self-interest on the part of the clerical estate. The importance of this group of churchmen was signified by the fact that the heads of the surviving cloisters and pious foundations formed a special group in the assemblies of estates—the so-called curia of prelates. In the estates of Calenberg-Göttingen in the Electorate, for example, the abbot of the Lutheran cloister at Loccum and the two other Lutheran prelates, together with the Catholic abbot of Cloister Marienrode, took precedence over the assembled nobility; indeed, the abbot of Loccum, a Lutheran churchman, was director of the assembly, a post with considerable financial responsibility.[34] In Braunschweig-Wolfenbüttel the standing "large committee" of the estates numbered among its members four Lutheran prelates endowed with the incomes of Lutheran cloisters.[35] Thus the churchmen, not in their capacity as clerics, but rather as landholding feudal lords, were possessed of sufficient means to assume an independent stance despite the claims to sovereignty made by the temporal government; moreover, these churchmen were by reason of self-interest so caught up in the fabric of particularism that at times they had reason to see as did the nobles the merit of limiting the prince's claims.

The bulk of the clergy were not, of course, prelates or prominent churchmen; they were rather parish pastors. For these parish clergy many features of life were regulated by law—not only were the immunities, incomes, and education of the parish clergy prescribed by law; their duties were also listed. For example, besides maintaining already as students the proper *decorum clericale*, or grave and upright conduct becoming a clergyman, the clergy in Braunschweig-Wolfenbüttel were obligated to give public instruction in the Christian religion to their congregations, administer according to the valid church order the sacraments and rites of their office, wear clerical garb, read aloud spiritual and temporal orders before the congregation, exhibit respect toward their superiors, observe the precepts of Christian doctrine, inspect schools, supervise poor-houses, keep church records and parish statistics,

---

[34] See Ebhard Sperling, "Evangelische Klöster und Stifte in Niedersachsen," *JGNK* 72 (1974): 137-49; Walther Lampe, "Grundsätzliches zur Frage der Prälatur in besonderer Verbindung zu den alten Provinziallandschaften," *JGNK* 63 (1965): 264-71; Schnath, 2:412-13; Heinz Weidemann, *Gerard Wolter Molanus, Abt zu Loccum* (Göttingen, 1925, 1929).

[35] Joseph König, "Landesgeschichte," in *Braunschweigische Landesgeschichte im Überblick*, ed. Richard Moderhack (Braunschweig, 1977), pp. 61-110; pp. 86-7.

and send in regular reports to their ecclesiastical superiors on any number of matters.[36]

Supervision of the parish clergy was carried out by a network of superintendents and general superintendents, clergymen who in part took the place of the Roman Catholic hierarchy—though the powers of these married churchmen were relatively limited. Lutheran doctrine ascribed after all a purely functional significance to degrees within the one ordained ministry.

In the latter half of the eighteenth century Braunschweig-Wolfenbüttel was divided into the general superintendencies of Wolfenbüttel (seat of the consistory, even after the court removed to the city of Braunschweig in the middle of the century), Braunschweig, Helmstedt, Schöningen, Greene, and Holzminden; an additional general superintendency had jurisdiction over the separate territory of Blankenburg.[37] These were then subdivided into superintendencies. Electoral Hannover in this period was divided into general superintendencies with seats at Calenberg, Göttingen, Grubenhagen, Celle, Harburg, and Hohnstein; these were likewise further subdivided.[38]

Decisions in policy matters and in court cases concerning the church and clergy were made by the consistory, or board for church, school, and marital affairs. The most important consistories were located in the cities of Hannover and Wolfenbüttel. Originally formed to take the place of episcopal courts in ecclesiastical and marital cases, consistories continued to have jurisdiction in litigation involving clergy and marital matters. Consistorial councillors or *Räthe* were appointed by the duke or Elector from both the laity and the clergy. The fact that appointment to the consistory was made by the territorial lord did not signify that the consistory was simply a tool of the temporal government; it, like most institutions in the Old Régime, had a life of its own. Therefore, even with the progress of ecclesiastical centralization in the eighteenth century and with the gradual tightening of consistorial supervision over pastors and students of theology, the total result was not simply greater *government* (i.e., temporal) control over church and clergy: for the clerical members of the consistory and the churchmen on whom they were dependent for the execution of their orders could reinterpret or ignore orders perceived as inimical to the self-interest of the clergy as a particularist corporation. As anyone who has leafed through handbooks of church law from the period knows, consistorial and governmental orders in ecclesiastical affairs were

---

[36] Stübner, pp. 191-95.

[37] Stübner, pp. 183-85.

[38] Schlegel, *Kirchenrecht*, 2:239-45; cf. Christian Barthold Scharf, *Der Kirchen-Staat des Churfürstentums Branunschweig-Lünenburg* (Hannover, 1776).

reissued with astonishing frequency in that age of "absolutism," a circumstance necessitated by the ease with which orders from on high could be obstructed.[39]

In the later eighteenth century the consistory in Hannover was composed of four salaried spiritual councillors and three salaried temporal councillors; in addition there were unpaid councillors and so-called assessors and other assistants; the presidency was normally held by a layman.[40] The consistory in Wolfenbüttel was in a less happy state in this period, reflecting the efforts of the absolutist government to reduce the independency of the institutional church and its clergy. Whereas the ancestor of the consistory in Wolfenbüttel had originally been made up of two lay and three or four clerical members, during a good part of the eighteenth century the consistory had only one or two clerical members and—in the great days of absolutism from 1758 to 1765—for a time had no clerical members at all. The damage to ecclesiastical interests caused by this arrangement was only in part offset by the duke's reliance on his court pastor for advice and by his eventual naming of two clerical councillors to the consistory by the 1770's—for in the 1770's there were in any case six lay councillors.[41]

---

[39] See the collections by Schlegel and Stübner cited above; also Karl Friedrich Bege, *Uebersicht der Verordnungen, welche im Herzogthume Braunschweig in Ansehung der weltlichen Geschäfte der Prediger ergangen sind* (Helmstedt, 1828). It would be intriguing to develop at length a comparison of the "ständisches Beamtentum" poised in the secular world between crown and estates as discussed (see below) by Dietrich Gerhard, and the clerical consistorial councillors and their clerical subordinates, pulled between responsibilites to the prince and to their own estate as a particularistic corporation. See Dietrich Gerhard, "Amtsträger zwischen Krongewalt und Ständen—ein europäisches Problem," in *Europa und die moderne Gesellschaft: Festschrift für Otto Brunner*, ed. Alexander Bergengruen and Ludwig Deike (Göttingen, 1963), pp. 230-47. While the struggle against venality of clerical office (simony) is ancient (Acts 8:20), it cannot be said that the battle against this form of resistance to rationalization of the clerical bureaucracy had been totally won by the eighteenth century; see the oath required in Stübner, p. 269; cf. K. W. Swart, *The Sale of Offices in the Seventeenth Century* (The Hague, 1948).—It must be emphasized that in the Old Régime the Lutheran parish clergy, even in the later eighteenth century, were to a surprising degree free from total integration into the network of ecclesiastical supervision, Thus, even when one allows that the consistory was to an extent subject to pressure from the temporal government, the consequences for the parish clergy, geographically at a remove from the consistory, must not be overestimated. Cf. the arguments developed at length in Manfred Köhler, "Über die soziale Bedeutung des protestantischen Pfarrhauses in Deutschland" (Phil. Diss., Heidelberg University, 1952).

[40] Johann Christoph Salfeld, ed., *Sammlung zur Geschichte des Königl. Churfürstlichen Consistorii zu Hannover, und zur Biographie des zeitigen ersten Raths in demselben, Hrn. Geh. Just. Rth. Dr. E. A. Heiliger* (Hannover, 1803), pp. 124, 129; cf. Walther Lampe, "Beitrag zur Personalgeschichte des hannoverschen Konsistoriums 1744-1844," *JGNK* 59 (1961): 105-9.

[41] Vitus Dettmer, *Das Konsistorium zu Wolfenbüttel* (Braunschweig, 1922), pp. 12, 80, 84-95. However, it should not be imagined that the lay members of consistories *always* voted against the self-interest of the clergy as a particularist body simply because they were laymen. Counter examples can readily be cited.

2. *The Professional Identity of the Clergy: Models for Ministry*

If we are to chronicle the changes in the self-understanding of the Lutheran clerical estate in Northwest Germany during the eighteenth century we must take as our point of departure the common understanding at the start of that period concerning the main purpose and nature of Christian ministry as it was to be carried out by the ordained clergy. That understanding was derived from the Reformation.

Both the "Reformation" notion of the priesthood of all believers and the idea of a clergy set apart go back to the early church. As Jaroslav Pelikan has pointed out, Clement of Rome and the *Didache* apply the traits of the Levitical priesthood to the servants of the church; on the other hand, Irenaeus maintains that "all the righteous have a priestly order."[42] This ancient complexity of views regarding order and office in the church is made even greater by the existence of at least three distinct views in the ancient church concerning ecclesiastical office itself—views that were to live on for centuries. Hans von Campenhausen writes:

> The documents of the sub-apostolic age which we have discussed thus fall naturally into three definite groups, from three different provinces of the Empire; and each of the three groups displays a different concept of ec-clesiastical office and of the powers pertaining to it. The three might almost be classified as embryonic forms of the Roman Catholic, the Greek Orthodox, and the Lutheran thinking on this subject.[43]

The differences are not inconsiderable:

> In Rome the bishop is primarily the supreme cultic official of his congregation, [punctuation *sic*] in Syria he is its spiritual example and sacral focus, [punctuation *sic*] in Asia Minor he is above all the ordained preacher of the apostolic teaching. These are the three main possible evaluations of church office; and in later Church history we hardly ever again find them in isolation and in such a pure form as we do here in Clement, in Ignatius, and in the Pastoral Epistles...[44]

In the church of the Augsburg Confession, then, the prime task of the clergy was classically to be that of preaching the apostolic teaching—a teaching held to consist in the communication of the word of God con-

---

[42] Jaroslav Pelikan, *The Christian Tradition: A History of the Development of Doctrine. 1. The Emergence of the Catholic Tradition (100-600)* (Chicago and London, 1971): 160, citing 1 Clement 32.2; 40.5; 52; *Didache* 13.3; Irenaeus, *Haereses*, 4.8.3; cf. 4.34.3.

[43] Hans von Campenhausen, *Ecclesiastical Authority and Spiritual Power in the Church of the First Three Centuries*, trans. J. A. Baker (Stanford, Calif., 1969), p. 120.

[44] Campenhausen, p. 120; cf. Martin Schmidt, "Das pietistische Pfarrerideal und seine altkirchlichen Wurzeln," in *Bleibendes im Wandel der Kirchengeschichte*, ed. Bernd Moeller and Gerhard Ruhbach (Tübingen, 1973), p. 248.

tained in scripture, and hence a teaching supernatural[45] in its effectiveness for conversion and salvation. Yet it would be misleading to single out the office of the word alone as the only feature in the Lutheran doctrine or practice of ministry; the significance of the sacraments (visible word) and of other non-salvific responsibilities must also be kept in mind while giving priority to care for word and sacrament.

The major features of the Lutheran doctrine of the ministry have been summarized by Arthur Carl Piepkorn as they are to be found in the sixteenth-century confessional writings of the German Lutherans; that summary can serve as a conspectus of the chief points.[46]

For the Lutheran Confessions the church is more than the ministers alone; it consists of preachers and people. However, the ministry is important, for, in Piepkorn's summary,

> God instituted the sacred ministry ... of teaching the Gospel and of administering the sacraments. His purpose in so doing is that men might obtain the faith that God forgives them by grace for Christ's sake through faith. The divine Word and the sacraments are ... means by which God gives the Holy Spirit that works faith when and where God wills in those who hear the Word and receive the sacraments.[47]

---

[45] Hermann Schultz, "Der *Ordo salutis* in der Dogmatik," *Theologischen Studien und Kritiken* 72 (1889): 350-445; Martin Greschat, *Zwischen Tradition und neuem Anfang: Valentin Ernst Löscher und der Ausgang der Lutherischen Orthodoxie*, Untersuchungen zur Kirchengeschichte, no. 5 (Witten, 1971), pp. 262-81. The belief in the supernatural efficacy of sacred texts was commonplace in the ancient world; cf. Johannes Leipoldt and Siegfried Morenz, *Heilige Schriften: Betrachtungen zur Religionsgeschichte der antiken Mittelmeerwelt* (Leipzig, 1953), esp. p. 178: "Der Unterschied zwischen Büchern, die in Gottesdiensten benutzt werden, und Zaubertexten ist nicht immer zu erfassen." Not surprisingly, this belief survived into the early modern period. That the Orthodox Lutheran dogmaticians of the seventeenth and other centuries have gone rather far in the same direction of claiming an extraordinary character and supernatural efficacy for scripture is generally recognized; see in this connection Robert D. Preus, *The Theology of Post-Reformation Lutheranism: A Study of Theological Prolegomena* (St. Louis, Mo., 1970), pp. 254-403. Cf. Georg Graf, "Der vom Himmel gefallene Brief Christi. (Nach Cod. Monac. arab. 1067)," *Zeitschrift für Semitistik und verwandte Gebiete* 6 (1928): 10-23; Franz Overbeck, *Christentum und Kultur*, ed. Carl Albrecht Bernoulli (Basel, 1919; reprint, Darmstadt, 1963), pp. 16-17; Adolf Harnack, *History of Dogma*, trans. Neil Buchanan, 7 vols. in 4 (1900; reprint ed., New York, 1961), "Prolegomena," 1:9; Theodor Reik, "Dogma and Obsessional Idea," in his *Dogma and Compulsion*, trans. Bernard Miall (1951; reprint ed. New York, 1973), pp. 13-164.

[46] Arthur Carl Piepkorn, "The Sacred Ministry and Holy Ordination in the Symbolical Books of the Lutheran Church," *Concordia Theological Monthly* 40 (1969): 552-73. As Piepkorn observes, p. 552, the Lutheran Symbols or Confessions have been interpreted as setting forth many different doctrines of the ministry ranging from the Congregationalist to something near to the Roman Catholic position. Cf. M. le Maitre de Claville, ancien Doyen du Bureau des Finances à Rouen, *Traité du vrai mérite de l'homme* (Frankfurt [a.O.?], 1755), front matter: "On ne trouvera point dans six Consistoires de Luthériens le même dogme rendu ou entendu de même façon."

[47] Piepkorn, p. 553.

The necessity of the ministry is upheld:

> The Lutherans reject the position that the Holy Spirit is received by purely interior preparation ... without the external Word of God personally communicated through the sacred ministry. ... The antithesis here is the asserted position of the Enthusiasts, who depreciated the sacred ministry.[48]

The Confessions are explicit concerning the content of the ministry:

> The content of the sacred ministry is the responsible public proclamation of the Gospel and the administration of the Sacraments. ... It is not the offering up of an expiatory sacrifice which earns forgiveness of sins for the living and the dead.[49]

Implied at the same time is the proclamation of divine law:

> The obligation of the incumbents of the sacred ministry to proclaim and apply the Gospel of divine grace in Christ does not exclude the proclamation of the Word of God as judgment. On the contrary, it implies the latter as a necessary corollary of the sacred minister's primary task.[50]

As one might expect from the divine authority of the ministry, the ministry is asserted to have an existence over and above its purely functional character; recognized is the ministry as an abstraction, so that an authority by divine right is asserted to inhere in all who rule over churches regardless of their title.[51] So important is the ministry that the church is divinely obliged to call and ordain pastors and teachers, *pastores et doctores*[52] for the teaching of the Gospel, the pastor's primary function.

Though the Lutheran tradition recognizes that the ministry exists for the purpose of service,[53] and though the doctrine of the universal priesthood as a property of the church is affirmed,[54] the sixteenth-century confessional writings nonetheless abound in passages which underscore the divine authority of the ministry and what ministers do. The confessions speak of the ministry as an order in the church with an existence separate from its exercise, terming the ministry an office (*ministerium* or *Amt*) and an estate or order (*Stand* or *ordo*) within the church.[55] Furthermore, in Piepkorn's summary:

> In his proclamation and application of the Gospel and his administration of the sacraments, the officiant or celebrant acts in the place of God and in the stead of Christ ..., not in his own person. ...[56]

---

[48] Piepkorn, p. 553.
[49] Piepkorn, p. 553.
[50] Piepkorn, p. 553.
[51] Piepkorn, p. 554.
[52] Piepkorn, p. 554.
[53] Piepkorn, p. 555.
[54] Piepkorn, p. 557.
[55] Piepkorn, p. 555, with documentation.
[56] Piepkorn, p. 555.

Thus Piepkorn can equally well summarize the Confessions as saying that "God preaches through the chosen clergy of the churches" and that "it is God Himself who baptizes."[57] Likewise, according to Piepkorn's summary:

> The absolution is to believed as nothing less than a voice sounding from heaven ..., that is, from God Himself.[58]

Unless special circumstances intervene it is expected that absolution and administration of the sacraments will be carried out only by an ordained clergyman.[59] To such a clergyman is committed both the *potestas ordinis*, the power to proclaim the gospel and to administer the sacraments, and the *potestas jurisdictionis*, or the power of excommunication.[60] The clergy are in effect regarded as spiritual fathers of the laity;[61] they are set apart by a second sanctification at vocation following upon the first sanctification that was accomplished by word and baptism.[62] Ordination is viewed as being of divine right and altogether essential for public ministry.[63] However, in opposition to the Roman Catholic view, the ministry is seen as having what Piepkorn terms a "unitary character" in that the "postapostolic differentiation of grades" within the ministry is held to exist only by human right.[64]

In the course of the seventeenth century, Lutheran Orthodoxy was to make only minor modifications in this doctrine of a clergy operating with a supernaturally effective power in word and sacraments. The doctrine of three estates (with the clergy as the leaders) *within* the church was elaborated so as to strengthen the theoretical claim of the clergy to direct a church protected by the temporal government.[65] In response to radical spiritualism's devaluation of the ministry the claim was developed that the clergy possessed a sacral status as persons deriving from their ordination and from their occupation with the exegesis of the divine word, in which a transferable sacral quality was held by some late Orthodox

---

[57] Piepkorn, p. 555.
[58] Piepkorn, p. 555.
[59] Piepkorn, p. 555.
[60] Piepkorn, p. 556.
[61] Piepkorn, p. 557.
[62] Piepkorn, p. 557 and n. 9; on vocation, cf. Hermann Dörries, "Geschichte der vocatio zum kirchlichen Amt," in his *Wort und Stunde* (Göttingen, 1970), 3:347-86.
[63] Piepkorn, pp. 560-61.
[64] Piepkorn, p. 558.
[65] See the works on this point cited in n. 15 above; also Emanuel Hirsch, *Hilfsbuch zum Studium der Dogmatik: Die Dogmatik der Reformatoren und der altevangelischen Lehrer quellenmäßig belegt und verdeutscht*, 4th ed. (Berlin, 1964), p. 368, citing Johann Andreas Quenstedt, *Theologia didactico-polemica* (1691), 4:393.

theologians to inhere.[66] This claim would not long survive the Enlightenment.

A final late change in the doctrine of the ministry was made in response to the radical spiritualist and Pietist tendency to question the older doctrine of an objective efficacy inhering in the supernaturally effective word of God, and to counter the consequent Pietist emphasis on the unbound and inward power of the Holy Spirit transmitted only through a converted ministry. This area of change was the doctrine of confession and absolution.

In late-seventeenth-century Lutheranism the custom of mandatory private confession and absolution of sins before communion still existed. It involved a somewhat mechanical going through of a set of memorized responses to pastoral questions. Joined to it was a perfunctory bit of instruction in Christian doctrine followed by an absolution. Though the process was carried out quickly in urban congregations,[67] it did give the pastor a potentially effective hold on the lives and emotions of his parishioners, one that could not be eliminated if the parishioner wished to receive the sacrament of the altar.

Against this version of penance the Pietists at Halle and elsewhere protested. They found this practice so rapid that it could not contribute to nor sustain an inner conversion of the heart. Nor did they believe that pastoral absolution conferred grace. The Pietist protest, and the Pietist plan to introduce a substitute (ultimately, a general confession as a part of the church service accompanied by a less "priestly" formula of absolution for the entire congregation) was aided by Enlightenment protests against the superstition and priestcraft alleged to be inherent in the traditional penitential practice of Lutheranism. In consequence the entire eighteenth century saw continuing campaigns against Orthodox formulae of absolution; the result was a trend toward abandonment of private confession.[68] Such abandonment brought with it a diminution in the kinds of pressure available to the local pastor for the purpose of main-

---

[66] See for example Johann Gerhard, *Loci communes theologici*, ed. Johann Friedrich Cotta, 20 vols. (Tübingen, 1762-81), 12b: 168; Hans-Martin Rotermund, *Orthodoxie und Pietismus: Valentin Ernst Löschers "Timotheus verinus"* (Berlin, 1954), p. 39, n. 28; also p. 40; Johann Georg Walch, *Historische und theologische Einleitung in die Religionsstreitigkeiten der evangelischen lutherischen Kirchen*, 3 vols. (Jena, 1730-39), 2:465; and Greschat, *Zwischen Tradition*, p. 269.

[67] Walter Wendland, "Die praktische Wirksamkeit Berliner Geistlicher im Zeitalter der Aufklärung (1740-1806)," *Jahrbuch für Brandenburgische Kirchengeschichte* 11/12 (1914): 295-96.

[68] Kurt Aland, "Die Privatbeichte im Luthertum von ihren Anfängen bis zu ihrer Auflösung," in his *Kirchengeschichtliche Entwürfe* (Gütersloh, 1960), pp. 452-522; and Helmut Obst, *Der Berliner Beichtstuhlstreit: Die Kritik des Pietismus an der Beichtpraxis der lutherischen Orthodoxie* (Witten, 1972).

taining social control over the congregation. This newly-lost control was all the more significant in view of the fact that the consistories had arrogated the power to excommunicate for public offenses. Already deprived in the seventeenth century of local authority to excommunicate because of the growth of consistorial power, the pastor in the eighteenth century, faced with the additional threat of loss of psychological and social pressure hitherto available by means of his role as confessor and dispenser of absolution, was forced to ask what powers remained for him to use in his effort to keep a congregation faithful to the apostolic teaching.[69]

At issue was the pastor's function as a quasi-priestly intermediary between God and the congregation—admittedly a subordinate element in the Lutheran doctrine of the ministry, but hitherto a real one nonetheless. The Lutheran formulae for absolution in the sixteenth and seventeenth centuries varied considerably, often containing a paradoxical combination of elements. A typical early formula might mention the fact of the sinner's repentance; then make an announcement of God's general forgiveness of the sinner; and then continue with a formula signifying that the pastor himself by divine authority absolved the penitent. With the spread of Pietism and Enlightenment *two* changes occurred. *First*, the beleaguered Orthodox clergy moved into increasingly "priestly" statements concerning their powers in absolution. For example, the late-seventeenth-century dogmatician Johann Andreas Quenstedt categorically affirmed:

> The servants of the church have the power of forgiving sins in such a way that they forgive sins, not merely historically by way of declaration [declarative] and announcement [annuntiative], but also effectively [effective], yet instrumentally [sc. as an instrument used by God].[70]

The *second* development, the one to which the future belonged,[71] was that the spiritualist and Pietist position—the one rejected by Quenstedt according to which the pastor merely declares logically prior divine forgiveness but does *not* pronounce an absolution effected by the supernaturally active divine word operating on the penitent elect—triumphed in most of Germany in the course of the eighteenth and nineteenth cen-

---

[69] Cf. Pariset, pp. 491-94; Wendland, p. 295, citing Johann Friedrich Ulrich, *Ueber den Religionszustand in den preußischen Staaten* (Leipzig, 1778-80), 2:146; Paul Graff, *Geschichte der Auflösung der alten gottesdienstlichen Formen in der evangelischen Kirche Deutschlands* (Göttingen, 1937), 1:375-76; 2:285-87.

[70] Hirsch, *Hilfsbuch*, p. 369, citing Quenstedt.

[71] In line with this general evolution is the English-language *Lutheran Book of Worship*, ed. Inter-Lutheran Commission on Worship (Minneapolis, Minn. and Philadelphia, Penn., 1978), p. 98.

turies.[72] Thus a heightening of the Orthodox claims with regard to clerical powers was in fact the immediate preparation for an Orthodox defeat.

The local concretion of this general pattern can be made evident by examining the church orders in force in the Welf territories at the outset of the Enlightenment. The influential "Calenberg" *Church Order* of 1569, valid in a good part of Electoral Hannover, represents an early form of the classic Lutheran view of the ministry.[73] Beginning with stress on the importance of preaching a doctrine founded on divine scripture and the Lutheran distinction between law and gospel,[74] it proceeds to a treatment of repentance, confession, and absolution, incorporating as well a number of other classic Lutheran elements. Auricular confession in the Roman sense is repudiated, but confession before a clergyman without enumeration of sins is retained for the sake of ecclesiastical discipline, pastoral care, proper preparation for communion, and giving of private absolution.[75] Absolution is understood in the sense of an application to the individual of the promise of forgiveness of sin on account of faith in divine grace through Christ; thus it is the private counterpart to an objective word of promise applied to the whole congregation (that is, a private counterpart to the sermon).[76] This dynamic understanding of absolution does not by itself exhaust the interpretation of such ministerial action; in the formula of absolution there occurs language approaching the "quasipriestly" objectivity elaborated more explicitly by some of the Saxon theologians of Late Orthodoxy.[77]

Concern for the objective element in ministry and for the privileges of the clerical estate emerges from other passages in the *Calenberger Church Order* as well. To the sacraments is ascribed a more than natural efficacy,

---

[72] Cf. nn. 68-69 above.

[73] See Schlegel, *Kirchenrecht*, 1:35-42; J. Meyer, *Kirchengeschichte*, p. 94. For the text see "Kirchenordnung unser, von Gottes genaden Julii, herzogen zu Braunschweig und Lüneburg etc. ... Gedruckt zu Wolffenbüttel durch Cunradt Horn 1569," in *Die evangelischen Kirchenordnungen des XVI. Jahrhunderts*, ed. Emil Sehling (Tübingen, 1955-), 6:1:1: 83-280. (Here cited as *Calenberger KO.*).

[74] *Calenberger KO*, pp. 89-91, 98-99.

[75] *Calenberger KO*, pp. 119-22.

[76] *Calenberger KO*, pp. 120-21. On the significance of the doctrine of justification by faith for the doctrine of the ministry see Wilhelm Preger, *Die Geschichte der Lehre vom geistlichen Amte auf Grund der Geschichte der Rechtfertigungslehre* (Nördlingen, 1857).

[77] *Calenberger KO*, p. 167, emending "im rahmen des Vaters ..." to correct the obvious typographical error: "... [since] I, a servant of God, am established [verordnet] to comfort poor sinners, since Christ has spoken to me [cf. Joh. 20:23; Matt. 18:18]; Whose sin you forgive, it is forgiven him, and again, what you loose on earth, is loosed in heaven, upon such promise of God and according to his command I absolve you [spreche ich euch loss von] from all your sins here in the stead of God in the name of the Father and of the Son and of the Holy Spirit. Amen. Go in peace and sin no more."

with a clear definition of the real presence of the body and blood of Jesus Christ.[78] The section concerning ordination[79] and installation emphasizes not only the importance of preaching, but as well the divine commission of the ministerial office so that proper pastoral care for the flock with the word of God can be accomplished. Furthermore, the congregation is admonished to hold the ministry in respect.[80] The incomes and immunities of the clergy are dealt with in detail.[81] In accord with the high position accorded the clergy, their duties in connection with care of schools, the poor, and the sick are set forth.[82]

The newer church order in force for Braunschweig-Wolfenbüttel during the eighteenth century shows only minor departures from this pattern.[83] It stresses the importance of teaching the pure doctrine that leads to blessedness, and develops an Orthodox view of the ministry on this basis.[84] Though by this time the exercise of church discipline required the prior consent of the consistory,[85] and though the absolution formulae are cast in a somewhat less objective or "quasi-priestly" mold in response to the currents of the day,[86] nonetheless the formula for ordination makes extensive use of the classic passages (e.g., Matt. 16 and 18; Joh. 20) identifying the ministerial power of the keys in disciplinary matters and the pastoral authority to teach with the very divine power of Jesus Christ.[87] Nor can any noticeable effort be detected to widen the scope of the minister's temporal duties so as to benefit the state at the expense of the cure of souls. The Orthodox Lutheran concept of the ministry was then, at least on paper, largely intact in Braunschweig-Wolfenbüttel at the start of the Enlightenment despite the issue of a new church order under the authority of a duke desirous of emulating Louis XIV.

Nonetheless the church order of 1709 in Braunschweig betrayed at one point an influence of Pietism and incipient Enlightenment that would eventually work great changes: it separated private instruction from the confessional—and thereby pointed the way toward eventual abolition of

---

[78] *Calenberger KO*, pp. 122-34.

[79] On ordination in this area see Edgar Hennecke, "Zur Gestaltung der Ordination mit besonderer Rücksicht auf die Entwickelung innerhalb der lutherischen Kirche Hannovers," *Forschungen zur Geschichte Niedersachsens* (Hannover and Leipzig, 1906-07) 1, no. 1: 1-58.

[80] *Calenberger KO*, p. 189.

[81] *Calenberger KO*, pp. 192-94.

[82] *Calenberger KO*, e.g., pp. 196-97; 225-26; 262-69.

[83] See *Erneuerte Kirchen-Ordnung Unser Von Gottes Gnaden Anthon Ulrichs Hertzogen zu Braunschweig und Lüneburg*, 2 vols. (Braunschweig, 1709); reprint, Braunschweig, 1862). (Here cited as Anton Ulrich, *KO*).

[84] Anton Ulrich, *KO*, 1:7.

[85] Anton Ulrich, *KO*, 1:24, 39.

[86] Anton Ulrich, *KO*, 1:40; 2:7.

[87] Anton Ulrich, *KO*, 2:93-94.

private confession and absolution.[88] After a lengthy public campaign against it, obligatory private confession was abolished in Braunschweig-Wolfenbüttel in 1775.[89] Though no such general measures seem to have been taken in Electoral Hannover, similar criticism was voiced and in some places the obligation was abolished.[90] It must however be pointed out that a number of Enlightenment churchmen in Northwest Germany continued to defend private confession purged of "superstition" as an instrument of pastoral care useful for the purpose of the clergy.[91]

Although the traditional Lutheran concept of the ministry as proclamation of the apostolic preaching by an ordained man, including as well a bit of "quasi-priestly" overlay and an additional component of responsibility for education and poor relief, remained largely intact at the start of the eighteenth century, far-reaching changes were soon to come. This can be surmised in view of the Pietist and Enlightenment campaign against the notion of the ministry as bearer of a supernaturally effective divine word just alluded to. The alternative model for ministry to be proposed by the end of the eighteenth century was already foreshadowed in some German writers at the turn of the seventeenth to the eighteenth century.

For the classic Lutheran view the teaching aspect of ministry is central; but that teaching is a teaching of a supernaturally effective word in principle identical with its embodiment in the visible form of the sacraments.[92] This classic view became increasingly problematical, as we have seen, as a result of changes in the common understanding of the doctrine of the word of God in Pietism and elsewhere. What occurred was the diffusion within Lutheran circles of the views originally associated with such figures as Caspar Schwenckfeld (1489-1561) and the Lutheran

---

[88] Cf. Johannes Beste, *Geschichte der Braunschweigischen Landeskirche von der Reformation bis auf unsere Tage* (Wolfenbüttel, 1889), p. 450.

[89] Beste, *Geschichte*, p. 457.

[90] Cf. for example, "Ueber Einführung der öffentlichen Beichte in einzelnen Orten," *Annalen der Braunschweig-Lüneburgischen Churlande* 2 (1788); no. 2: 171; no. 3: 181; 3 (1789); no. 3: 710; 6 (1792); no. 2:364; also Stadtsyndicus Lüders, "Ueber die Abschaffung des Beicht—und Leichengeldes in Hameln," *Neues Hannöversches Magazin*, Jg. 1804, cols. 193-208.

[91] Cf. Beste, *Geschichte*, pp. 450-56; Gottfried Less, *Ueber Christliches Lehr-Amt Dessen würdige Fürung, Und die Schikliche Vorbereitung dazu. Nebst einem Anhange von der Privat-Beichte* (Göttingen, 1790), p. 166: "Nach diesen Betrachtungen kann es nicht mehr zweifelhaft seyn, was erleuchtete Freunde des Christenthums, in Absicht der Privat-Beichte zu thun haben. Sie ganz abschaffen und mit der Allgemeinen verwechseln: heißt, das Christliche Lehr-Amt grossentheils und in seinen günstigsten Zeit-Punkten, unwirksam und unnüz machen." Hence he will recommend some reforms. Cf. J. O. Thiess, *Ist die Einführung der Allgemeinen Beichte oder die Beibehaltung des Beicht-Stuhls rathsamer?* (Hamburg, 1788).

[92] See "Confessio fidei exhibita invictissimo imperatori ... in comitiis Augustae Anno MDXXX," in *Die Bekenntnisschriften der evangelisch-lutherischen Kirche*, ed. Hans Lietzmann et al., 2nd ed. (Göttingen, 1952), pp. 31-137, esp. p. 58 and p. 69.

pastor Hermann Rathmann (1585-1628). Rathmann had aroused controversy with his view that scripture was but the mediate product of the Holy Spirit, who had operated immediately upon the human authors. Therefore scripture could be termed the external word of God. It was not in itself effective upon the hearts of men; this immediate effect came only from the operation of the Holy Spirit accomplished independent of the "external instrument" of scripture. Without this immediate and separate operation of the Holy Spirit, scripture remained but an inefficacious source of historical information.[93]

Ideas of this kind became common in the course of the seventeenth and eighteenth centuries among spiritualist and Pietist writers; they were then taken up in transformed shape by Enlightenment writers affected by theories of natural religion. These notions, joined with the criticism of Christian Orthodoxy carried out by anticlerical writers representing the schools of revived Stoic natural law and philosophical empiricism, led to the most considerable revision in opinion concerning the teaching of the church and the necessity of the clergy. The effect upon the doctrine of the Christian ministry has in part been touched upon already; as we are about to chronicle the long-term effects below in detail, what is necessary here is an overview of the development.

The first result in the course of the eighteenth century was that the classic Lutheran notion of the clergyman was simplified in that the element of teacher was ever more completely stripped of supernaturalist or "quasi-priestly" trappings. This process can be seen in the conflicts over the grace conferred at ordination and over the significance of absolution precipitated by the Pietists; it is also evident in the Pietist furore over the danger of an unconverted ministry—over, that is, the danger of coming into contact with a pastor who had not felt the immediate operation of the Spirit upon his inner self: for in the Pietist view such a pastor would scarcely be able to transmit the true divine spark despite his ordination.[94] As a result, with the simultaneous growth of Enlightenment and the increasing tendency of the Pietists to resort to moralism, the pastor became regarded increasingly as a teacher pure and simple—first as a teacher of divine wisdom, then more and more as a teacher of virtue.[95] With the

---

[93] Greschat, pp. 267-75; Martin Schian, *Orthodoxie und Pietismus im Kampf um die Predigt*, Studien zur Geschichte des neueren Protestantismus, no. 7 (Gießen, 1912); Otto Ritschl, *Dogmengeschichte des Protestantismus*, 4 vols. (Göttingen, 1912-27), 4:158-65; Emanuel Hirsch, "Zum Verständnis Schwenckfelds," in *Festgabe für Karl Müller* (Tübingen, 1922), pp. 145-70.

[94] Cf. Schian, *Orthodoxie*.

[95] Cf. Schmidt, "Pfarrerideal," p. 247; Johann Joachim Spalding, *Ueber die Nutzbarkeit des Predigtamtes und deren Beförderung* (Berlin, 1772).

further advance of Enlightenment, with the complete identification of the truths of revelation with those of reason, and with the growing influence of cameralistic propaganda upon the clergy, the content which the clergy were urged to teach would depart ever more from the apostolic preaching as understood hitherto. Instead that content to be taught would come to depend ever more upon revived Stoic natural law, common sense philosophy, and the latest trends in agronomy and industrial technology favored by theoreticians of absolutism.[96]

When the disadvantages of such a reduction of the ministerial task to that of teaching chiefly the wisdom of this temporal world eventually became evident to those churchmen who had the self-interest of the clerical estate at heart; when, that is, in the course of the Enlightenment the fact became clear that such an exaggeratedly pedagogical and utilitarian concept of the clerical role might be ultimately more of a threat than a benefit to the well-being of the clergy as a group with a distinctive function that alone could legitimate its continued existence at public expense; then gradually some theologians and churchmen began to cast about for a more satisfying and plausible version of the clerical role.

Here the names of Herder and Schleiermacher come instantly to mind: names long associated in scholarship with the revival of ''mystical' or ''priestly'' or ''irrationalist'' components in the concept of ministry. Yet this move was, as is commonly admitted, not a revival of Roman Catholic sacerdotalism with its idea of sacrifice.[97] The ideas of Herder and Schleiermacher, upon which we shall touch briefly below, represent rather an attempt to restore some distinctive and inherent worth to the clerical estate despite the Enlightenment abandonment of the view of word, sacraments, and revelation formerly entertained in Christian Orthodoxy. Under such conditions, in a climate conditioned by panentheism and German Idealism, in a milieu permeated with the rhetoric of personal development through educational *Bildung* or cultivation to achieve an harmonious personality, there could be no question of a true revival of the notion of priestly intermediation in the classic Roman sense of an offering of a representation of Christ's sacrifice for the sins of the laity. (Indeed, the changed notion of sin current in the later eighteenth century eliminated the need for such a sacrifice in any case.) Instead

---

[96] See for example Dagobert de Levie, *Die Menschenliebe im Zeitalter der Aufklärung: Säkularisation und Moral im 18. Jahrhundert* (Bern and Frankfurt, 1975). The documentation for these assertions will be supplied below.

[97] Cf. in general Emanuel Hirsch, *Geschichte der neuern evangelischen Theologie* (Gütersloh, 1954), 5: 144-231; Holsten Fagerberg, *Bekenntnis, Kirche und Amt in der deutschen Konfessionellen Theologie des 19. Jahrhunderts* Uppsala, 1952); Henry C. Sheldon, *Sacerdotalism in the Nineteenth Century* (New York, 1900).

figures such as Herder and Schleiermacher, and to a lesser but not insignificant degree also several Northwest German theologians, began to try to restore dignity to the clergy by combining with the remnants of the classic Lutheran doctrine of the ministry other traits drawn from a tradition utterly distinct from that of Lutheranism in its Orthodox form.

The proximate source for this newer version of the ministerial role was *radical* Pietism.[98] Now here the complexity of German Pietism must be kept in mind. On the one hand, despite all its seeming radicalism in criticism of the clergy,[99] institutional Pietism remained in the long run supportive of the fundament to the classic Lutheran ideal of ministry, the notion of the pastor as teacher. For Halle Pietism, and with it a good number of Enlightenment theologians, notwithstanding the fundamental Pietistic premise of the necessity of conversion for effective ministry, remained true to the older Lutheran faith in the value of strong academic and philological training as a perequisite for scriptural exegesis. Thus the Halle tradition of August Hermann Francke and a good number of the Enlightenment churchmen influenced by Pietism contributed not a small amount to keeping alive the old Lutheran ideal of a learned ministry devoted to teaching the theoretical knowledge of God as well as carrying out the cure of souls.[100]

On the other hand, the more radical, more anti- or extra-institutional tradition of mystical spiritualism did not die out with the advent of Pietism. Furthermore, one of its most influential German spokesmen made current within ecclesiastical and Enlightenment circles throughout Germany a model for ministry fundamentally different from any previously received into Lutheranism. It was this alien model, released into the milieu of Enlightenment Germany and subsequently transformed in the periods of *Sturm und Drang* and Romanticism, which constituted the necessary precondition for the elaboration by Herder, Schleiermacher, and others in Northwest Germany of a revision of the doctrine of ministry that would to some degree incorporate the notion of

---

[98] Rudolf Vierhaus, "Bildung," *Geschichtliche Grundbegriffe*, ed. Otto Brunner, Werner Conze, and Reinhart Koselleck, 1 (Stuttgart, 1972-): 508-51; Schmidt, "Pfarrerideal"; cf. Wilhelm Dilthey, "Die herrnhuterische Erziehung," in his *Leben Schleiermachers: Erster Band*, ed. Martin Redeker, 1 (Göttingen, 1970), pp. 13-27. It would be pointless to cite here the secondary sources remarking upon the way in which Pietism influenced the religious structure behind Schleiermacher's *Reden*.

[99] Cf. Schmidt, "Pfarrerideal," p. 213, citing for radical criticism of the clergy by mystical spiritualists Elias Praetorius, i.e., Christian Hoburg, *Ministerii Lutherani Purgatio: Das ist Lutherischer Pfaffenputzer* (1648); cf. Schian, *Orthodoxie*.

[100] See August Hermann Francke, "Idea Studiosi Theologiae oder Abbildung eines der Theologie Beflissenen, wie derselbe sich zum Gebrauch und Dienst des Herrn und zu allem guten Werk gehörigermaßen bereitet," in his *Pädagogische Schriften*, ed. G. Kramer (Langensalza, 1885), pp. 369-445; cf. Schmidt, "Pfarrerideal," p. 219.

the clergyman as mystically gifted mediator of a higher wisdom—one derived from both classical texts and from his own superior personality, a wisdom that could be effective in giving the souls of his circle of followers a more harmonious equilibrium. That this notion of the pastor as agent of mystical *Bildung* has its roots in radical Pietism has long been ignored; but the existence of these roots, and their ultimate derivation from the ancient church, has been demonstrated by a leading authority in this field, Martin Schmidt.[101]

The Pietist writer in question was the influential church historian and theologian Gottfried Arnold (1666-1714).[102] As Schmidt has established, though in his opinions on the significance of the laity as bearers of the Holy Spirit Arnold relies heavily on Origen, in his development of the concept of ministry Arnold is heavily dependent on the thought of Ignatius of Antioch (fl. ca. 107-110 A.D.).[103] The thought of Ignatius, developed by Arnold on the basis of the Pietistic and Lutheran theme of partaking of the divine nature[104] and stripped of its "hierarchical" elements, was in Arnold to serve as the way in which there was to be introduced into Lutheranism a doctrine of the ministry differing in its fundamental emphases from those of the classic Lutheran tradition: namely, what von Campenhausen dubs the "Syrian-Greek Orthodox" ideal of the clergyman as "spiritual example and sacral focus."[105] Since—at a later point in the present study—we shall encounter a number of Northwest German theologians and churchmen who,[106] like Herder and

---

[101] Cf. Schmidt, "Pfarrerideal," pp. 221-550; Vierhaus, "Bildung"; also n. 153 below.

[102] See Erich Seeberg, "Christian Thomasius und Gottfried Arnold," *Neue kirchliche Zeitschrift* 31 (1920): 337-58; E. Seeberg, *Gottfried Arnold: Die Wissenschaft und die Mystik seiner Zeit* (Meerane i. Sa., 1923); Hermann Dörries, *Geist und Geschichte bei Gottfried Arnold* (Göttingen, 1963); Jürgen Büchsel, *Gottfried Arnold: Sein Verständnis von Kirche und Wiedergeburt* (Witten, 1970). On Arnold's influence, cf. Johann Wolfgang von Goethe, *Dichtung und Wahrheit*, Zweiter Teil, Achtes Buch.

[103] Schmidt, "Pfarrerideal," p. 249; Philipp Vielhauer, *Geschichte der urchristlichen Literatur* (Berlin, 1975), p. 545.

[104] 2 Pet. 1:4; cf. Schmidt, "Pfarrerideal," p. 248; M. Schmidt, "Teilnahme an der göttlichen Natur. 2. Petrus 1,4 in der theologischen Exegese des Pietismus und der lutherischen Orthodoxie," in *Dank an Paul Althaus: Eine Festgabe zum 70. Geburtstag* (Gütersloh, 1958), pp. 171-201; Hugo Rahner, "Die Vorstellung von der Gottesgeburt in der Seele bei den griechischen Kirchenvätern," *Zeitschrift für katholische Theologie* 59 (1935): 333-418; M. Schmidt, *Wiedergeburt und neuer Mensch* (Witten, 1969); Steven Ozment, "Eckhart and Luther: German Mysticism and Protestantism," *The Thomist* 42 (1978): 259-80; Otto Ritschl, "Das Theologumenon von der *unio mystica* in der späteren orthodox-Lutherischen Theologie," in *Harnack-Ehrung* (Leipzig, 1921), pp. 335-52.

[105] Cf. nn. 76-77 above.

[106] For a striking example of the supplement to the classic Lutheran pastoral role accomplished by suggesting that the pastor operate as an agent of *Bildung*, see Johann Friedrich Christoph Gräffe, "Zweiter Haupttheil. Vierter Abschnitt. Von den

Schleiermacher, assume that a part of the clergyman's task consists in the formation (*Bildung*) of beautiful and balanced souls by the communication of a higher wisdom gleaned from carefully-studied classic religious and cultural texts; and since this concept of ministry fosters the notion of the clergyman as a "virtuoso" who serves as sacral focus in part because he can mediate access to some higher wisdom with which he has gained especially close acquaintance; and since the single most important source for this ideal of ministry in eighteenth-century Protestant Germany was Gottfried Arnold; therefore it is necessary to examine Arnold's notion of the ministerial role in our overview of these matters.[107]

As Martin Schmidt observes, the ideal of ministry in Arnold is so rigorous that it requires its representatives to be "model Christians": Arnold moves within the same circle of ideas as Ignatius of Antioch, who in the salutations to his epistles is styled "Theophorus" ("the God-bearer").[108] Such a view of authority is one founded on the conviction that, because of possession of the Spirit, one is in special touch with the heavenly order; therefore the possessor of the spirit forms the sacral focal point for all in the congregation.[109] All these elements of thought about the ministry will be met with again in Gottfried Arnold; but Ignatius' other theme, that of a graded hierarchy of ministerial offices, will be in Arnold studiously eliminated.[110]

Arnold put his ideas on the ministry into a book entitled *Die geistliche Gestalt eines Evangelischen Lehrers* (Halle, 1704).[111] Deeply marked by Arnold's central idea of the fall of the church, this theology of the ministry concentrates on the theme of how, in Schmidt's words,

---

ästhetischen Gefühlen," in his *Die Pastoraltheologie nach ihrem ganzen Umfange*, 2 vols. (Göttingen, 1803), 1: 190-92.

[107] Cf. for example Schmidt, "Pfarrerideal," pp. 248-50.

[108] Vielhauer, pp. 543-44; Schmidt, "Pfarrerideal," p. 249; Ignatius of Antioch, "To the Ephesians," salutation.

[109] Cf. von Campenhausen, pp. 97-106; Vielhauer, pp. 543-44: "Aber er nennt sich in jedem Präskript 'Theophorus' = 'Gottesträger' und bringt damit seinen eigentlichen Anspruch zur Geltung: Er ist Pneumatiker in einem Sinn, den es nur in der Gnosis gibt, ..." On Ignatius' comparison of episcopal authority with that of God and the "ikon-theology" behind it, cf. Alfred Adam, *Lehrbuch der Dogmengeschichte* (Gütersloh, 1965), 1: 135; Ignatius, "To the Ephesians," 6:1; Martin Werner, *Die Entstehung des christlichen Dogmas problemgeschichtlich dargestellt*, 2nd. ed. (Bern and Tübingen, 1941), pp. 652-55.

[110] Cf. Vielhauer, p. 544; von Campenhausen, p. 97. It should be noted that such an elimination of the hierarchical component can be carried out all the more readily since Ignatius' concept of authority is not founded on legal argumentation as in the Latin West, but rather on the notion of a mysterious union between God, Christ, the bishop, and the congregation which "accords with the inner logic of a concept of the Church in terms of musical or cosmic harmony" (von Campenhausen, p. 102).

[111] Cf. Schmidt, p, 222, n. 58, citing Gottfried Arnold, *Die geistliche Gestalt eines Evangelischen Lehrers Nach dem Sinn und Exempel der Alten Auff vielfältiges Begehren Ans Licht gestellet* (Halle, 1704).

the essence of a genuine teacher, who can be regarded as fully-empowered
messenger of God, lies in his inner form, in his "inner man," as Arnold
says with the language of the mystics.[112]

Such a notion of communication of the inward form to one's circle of
followers, though stripped of much of its biblical wrapping, was to
become a key precept in the later quasi-religion of *Bildung* in Germany,
and it would make in its own way demands for literary, aesthetic, and
personal "cultivation" on the would-be sacral leader quite as rigorous as
the demands for piety and holiness placed upon the pastor by radical
Pietism. Stressing the importance of rebirth and predestination,[113] Arnold in his treatise went on to maintain that the true grace of the
ministerial office consisted in the experience of the Holy Spirit. In so doing he reiterated for a wider audience the old mystic spiritualist distrust of
learned education of the ministry,[114] an emphasis that would in the
course of the eighteenth century find little favor with the figures who were
to take up the Ignatian ideal of ministry. (They would rather try to infuse
deep personal relevance into the sacred texts and add to the collection
works from the Greek and Roman classics that would attain to near-
canonical status with the advance of Neohumanism.) According to Arnold, a true teacher must receive the secret instruction of heaven that
leads to union with God and partaking in the divine nature.[115] Such
rebirth was for Arnold—as for later Neohumanists among the clergy—far
more important than the rite of ordination, which Arnold in any case
regarded as superfluous on the basis of his interpretation of the Lutheran
Confessions.[116] Since everything depended on the experience of the Holy
Spirit and the birth of God in the soul and the resulting holiness of a life
humbly put in the service of others, there could be no place at all in
theological activity for the kind of scholastic theological polemic
characteristic of the debates of the Counter-Reformation and
seventeenth-century Protestant Orthodoxy.[117] Here, again, Arnold
sounded a note that was to echo for a century.

In Arnold we see a concept of ministry that is highly personal: it
depends for its authority upon the individual's displayed ability—the
ability to convince others that one possesses a higher and secret wisdom
and power, a power in principle different from the objectively efficacious
power of the preached word of apostolic teaching that had been the

---

[112] Schmidt, "Pfarrerideal," p. 223.
[113] Schmidt, "Pfarrerideal," pp. 224-25.
[114] Schmidt, "Pfarrerideal," p. 226.
[115] Schmidt, "Pfarrerideal," pp. 226-27.
[116] Schmidt, "Pfarrerideal," p. 229.
[117] Cf. Schmidt, "Pfarrerideal," pp. 229-46.

source of legitimating authority for the classic Lutheran doctrine of the ministry. Such a personal concept of authority is to be met with first of all in the leaders of countless spiritualistic and extra-ecclesiastical Pietistic conventicles.[118] But it is, in transformed shape of course, to be met with within the mainstream—in Herder, with his "divine orator," or in Schleiermacher, with his "religious virtuoso" able to carry out the religious cultivation of the admiring souls gathered around him to receive his mediation of mysterious intuitions of the infinite universe.[119]

These late-eighteenth-century variants on the pastoral ideal of the agent of *Bildung*[120] differ from Arnold's ideal of ministry, to be sure, for the pastoral ideal of the religion of *Bildung* as it was fully elaborated in Herder and the Neohumanists[121] de-emphasized holiness of life and put in place of contact with the Holy Spirit instead closeness of contact with a view of the cosmos to be gained by total immersion in the ancient authors as the one thing needful in order to establish the sacral leader in his function of shaping the inner selves of his devotees. Nonetheless the core of the concept of the ministerial role in Herder, Schleiermacher, and in various late-Enlightenment Northwest German counterparts (at least when the last-named begin to discuss the pastor as agent of *Bildung* for humanity, even though at other times they remain more classically Lutheran) is the same as that adapted by Arnold from Ignatius of Antioch.

Since the ideal of ministry in Herder, Schleiermacher, and others of like disposition was in the course of the nineteenth century to be hailed by many as a key to the "overcoming" of the eighteenth-century Enlightenment, below we may properly pay some attention to the way in which—already in the eighteenth century—the ecclesiastical leadership began to prepare itself to embrace such "Arnoldian" or "Herderian"

---

[118] For a look at the kind of figures to be found in such conventicles, see Walter Grossmann, *Johann Christian Edelmann* (The Hague, 1976); Karl Philipp Moritz, *Anton Reiser: Ein Psychologischer Roman*, ed. Wolfgang Martens (Berlin, 1785; reprinted, Stuttgart, 1972).

[119] Schmidt, "Pfarrerideal," p. 249.

[120] Cf. n. 106 above; and Fritz K. Ringer, *The Decline of the German Mandarins: The German Academic Community 1890-1933* (Cambridge, Mass., 1969), pp. 86-90; A. Flitner, "Bildung," *RGG*, 1 (Tübingen, 1957): cols. 1278-1281. Flitner, col. 1279, points out that the two of the most important figures in the history of the concept of *Bildung* are Gottfried Arnold, who speaks of "forming" the soul as well as the body ("Ach bild mich ganz nach Dir") and the German translation of Shaftesbury in 1738, which began to give to *Bildung* an aesthetic overtone of harmony of the person with the cosmos in such phrases as "God is the moral architect which forms the inward form." Such concepts are the prerequisite for the rise of Neohumanism. Its effects on the concept of ministry will be dealt with below.

[121] M. Fuhrmann and A. Reble, "Neuhumanismus," *RGG*, 4 (Tübingen, 1967): cols. 1416-1419; Friedrich Paulsen, *Geschichte des gelehrten Unterrichts auf den deutschen Schulen und Universitäten*, 3rd ed., 2 vols. (Berlin and Leipzig, 1919-21).

ideas as a supplementary means of strengthening the position of the church and its clergy: in this way the subterranean connection between Lutheran Orthodoxy and the "conservative" Lutheranism of the nineteenth century can be traced. Yet our chief job in the pages below is not to chronicle in detail the way in which the pastoral ideal of the religion of *Bildung* (the pastor as *Kulturträger*) and of German Idealism began to emerge in Northwest Germany in the later eighteenth century—though that topic will be treated in sufficient detail to suggest that Herder and Schleiermacher ought not to be regarded as the *only* early elaborators of such an ideal of ministry. Our main attention below will instead go to the *prior* issue of how it was that the classic Lutheran ideal of the minister as teacher came to be so problematical that toward the end of the eighteenth century a good many churchmen began to move toward supplementing it with the additional ideal of the pastor as agent of a mystically efficacious *Bildung*, an education of the human race in a non-Orthodox-Lutheran sense. As we shall see, this prior issue cannot be resolved unless we return to the theme sounded in our introduction above: namely, the struggle of the churchmen with the doctrines of enlightened absolutism. Since an important part of those doctrines consisted in a variety of Protestant anticlericalism as a political program rooted in the absolutist version of natural law theory, we must next turn to the absolutist campaign against the Protestant clerical estate.

CHAPTER TWO

SECULARIST ATTACK AND PROTESTANT CLERICAL RESPONSE IN NORTHWEST GERMANY BEFORE 1760

1. *The Secularist Attack on the German Protestant Clergy*

Recent scholarship on the Enlightenment has emphasized not only pure history of ideas, but as well the human and social aspect in which these ideas became significant. Turning from the nineteenth century's investigation of deism and epicureanism, scholars have acknowledged that the animus in the Enlightenment was to a significant degree a desire to have done with the pretensions, authority, and financial burden of an Orthodox Christian clergy supported at public expense. Furthermore, the notion that Enlightenment opposition to the clergy was confined to Roman Catholic countries must now be abandoned; for, as Peter Gay has pointed out with regard to Protestant Germany, "anticlericalism was rife among religious men."[1] Throughout the Enlightenment a growing number of people agreed with Hume that "priests of all religions are the same," and therefore that

> all wise governments will be on their guard against the attempts of a society [sc. the Christian clergy], who will for ever combine into one faction; and while its acts as a society, will for ever be actuated by ambition, pride, revenge, and a persecuting spirit.[2]

---

[1] Peter Gay, *The Rise of Modern Paganism* = vol. 1 of his *The Enlightenment: An Interpretation* (New York, 1966): 350. Cf. Martin C. Battestin, *The Moral Basis of Fielding's Art* (Middletown, Conn., 1959), pp. 130-49; Eric J. Evans, "Some Reasons for the Growth of English Rural Anti-Clericalism *c.* 1750-*c.* 1830," *Past & Present*, no. 66 (February, 1975): 84-109; John Toland, *Letters to Serena*, ed. Günter Gawlick (London, 1704; reprint ed., Stuttgart-Bad Cannstatt, 1964); Norman Sykes, "Benjamin Hoadly, Bishop of Bangor," in *The Social & Political Ideas of Some English Thinkers of the Augustan Age*, ed. F. J. C. Hearnshaw (London, 1928), pp. 112-55; Sander L. Gilman, "The Anti-clerical Novel and its Offshoots," in his *The Parodic Sermon in European Perspective* (Wiesbaden, 1974), pp. 60-65; and John Redwood, *Reason, Ridicule and Religion* (Cambridge, Mass., 1976).

[2] David Hume, "Of National Characters," in his *Essays Moral, Political and Literary* (Oxford, 1963), pp. 202-20; pp. 204 and 206n.; also pp. 204-5, to the effect that it is only an exception when a few clergymen promote by rational means the interests of society as a whole to the detriment of their particular estate's self-interest, since "the greater number" of clergy behave differently: they must eventually discover that their ambitions can be satisfied "only by promoting ignorance and superstition, and implicit faith, and pious frauds." Cf. Immanuel Kant, *Religion within the Limits of Reason Alone*, trans. Theodore M. Greene and Hoyte H. Hudson (reprint ed., New York, 1960, p. 168:

The spread of such opinions and the elaboration of a program of action in conformity with them caused a considerable change in how the clergy regarded themselves during the eighteenth century. In this chapter we shall consider the onset of this process during the early Enlightenment, at a time when the mentality and ecclesiastical structures of Orthodoxy were still strong enough to exert some influence.

Anticlerical writers of the later seventeenth and the eighteenth centuries such as Hobbes, Bayle, Mandeville, Voltaire, Hume, Helvétius, Holbach, and a host of the now-forgotten, agreed that priests and clergymen throughout history had conspired. This conspiracy over time had been aimed at defrauding and oppressing the general population: by dint of imposture and superstition the priests had kept the population in such ignorance and fear that it willingly paid good money for the illusory services rendered by the priestly class. The priests when threatened by occasional waves of enlightenment inimical to the self-interest of their faction had not hesitated to promote bloody persecution to maintain their privileged position.[3]

This Enlightenment view of the clergy rested on two premises.[4] The first premise concerned the nature of true and false religion. True religion was inward, "spiritual," "moral," and consisted in the ethical service of a highest Good rendered according to rational principles ultimately discoverable by human reason. Underlying this was the more basic assumption that supernatural revelation of the traditional variety

---

"Wherever credal statutes find a place among the laws of the constitution [of a church], a *clergy* rules which believes that it can actually dispense with reason ... because it has authority ... [to] command."

[3] See for example Bernard Mandeville, *Free Thoughts on Religion, the Church, and National Happiness* (London, 1720); Mandeville, *An Enquiry into the Origin of Honour and the Usefulness of Christianity in War* (London, 1732); Irwin Primer, ed., *Mandeville Studies* (The Hague, 1975); Claude Arien Helvétius, *De L'Homme, de ses facultés et de son éducation* (n.p., 1772); [Paul Henri Thiry, Baron d'Holbach?], *Éthocratie ou le gouvernement fondé sur la morale* (Amsterdam, 1776). The anticlerical material and its ramifications in the sources is too numerous to cite here; nor can we deal with the immense literature on Bayle, Hobbes, Hume, and Rousseau. See for example Frank E. Manuel, *The Eighteenth Century Confronts the Gods* (Cambridge, Mass., 1959). For earlier periods see for example Hans-Martin Barth, *Atheismus und Orthodoxie: Analysen und Modelle christlicher Apologetik im 17. Jahrhundert* (Göttingen, 1971); and on Hobbes, J. G. A. Pocock, "Time, History and Eschatology in the Thought of Thomas Hobbes," in his *Politics, Language and time* (New York, 1973), pp. 187, 195.

[4] In addition to the literature cited immediately above, see Hans-Walter Krumwiede, "Zur Entstehung des neuzeitlichen Staates und seiner Stellung zur Religion," *Evangelische Theologie* 36 (1976): 527-49; Helvétius, *De L'Esprit* (Paris, 1759); Walter Glawe, *Die Hellenisierung des Christentums in der Geschichte der Theologie von Luther bis auf die Gegenwart* (Berlin, 1912); and Reinhart Koselleck, *Kritik und Krise* (Freiburg and Munich, 1959).

was irrelevant, impossible, or a distortion of natural theology. As a corollary it was assumed that the outward signs, sacraments, and cultic paraphernalia of the historic positive religions were all ultimately dispensable and that images and representations of the deity were dangerous: for they had ever been subject to abuse by the priestly class, who deluded the populace into mistaking such earthly service for service of the invisible and intangible highest Good, and hence into confounding service directed toward the well-being of the priestly class with service of God Himself.

A second premise was that the clergy as a traditional constituted body were in need of reform. The causes adduced were two: first, the condition of the clergy themselves (ignorant, superstitious, immoral, prejudiced, removed from practical life, greedy, opposed to the well-being of the commonwealth); and second, the need for the central government to enforce its claim to undivided sovereignty by removing the basis in financial and legal privilege for potential resistance by the clergy to the demands of the temporal magistrate.[5]

These two premises amounted to a call for reform of theology, of professional training of the clergy, and of the legal relationship of the church and its clergy to the state. Since programs for such radical reform of theology are a major part of the more general problem of Enlightenment religious criticism and have only a partial connection with the question of clerical identity, they will largely be ignored here.[6] As for calls for a radical reform of professional training, it can be said that only in the later Enlightenment, after 1760 or so, did such calls for *radical* professional reform (amounting to either disestablishment or a total secularist reshaping of the professional aims of the clergy) become a significant theme in the German Enlightenment; hence they will not concern us at this point overmuch. It will suffice to recall that from the sixteenth century on numerous radical spiritualist groups had called into question the very existence of the clergy as a distinct group, and that in response already during the period of Orthodoxy and Pietism traditionalist churchmen

---

[5] Cf. for general background Mario A. Cattaneo, "Hobbes Théoricien de l'Absolutisme Eclairé," in *Hobbes-Forschungen,* ed. Reinhart Koselleck and Roman Schnur (Berlin, 1969), pp. 199-210; Klaus Schlaich, "Der rationale Territorialismus. Die Kirche unter dem staatsrechtlichen Absolutismus um die Wende vom 17. zum 18. Jh.," *Zeitschrift der Savigny-Stiftung für Rechtsgeschichte, Kanonistische Abteilung* 54 (1968): 269-340.

[6] Important here as well was the view that Christianity was harmful to the well-being of the state and to the maintenance of a martial spirit. A long chain of opinions on this point ranging from Bayle to the Abbé Galiani and later Enlightenment writers is summarized in the judgments on the military weakness of a Christian republic in the last chapter of Rousseau's *Social Contract.*

had called for conservative reform.[7] The significance of those calls for conservative reform will concern us below.

The third radical demand, that for a far-reaching revision in church-state relations which would subject the clergy more thoroughly to state control, is of great importance here. This demand was issued at the outset of the German Enlightenment by the initiator of that movement, Christian Thomasius (1655-1728). Thomasius is remembered for his stress on practical Enlightenment and his introduction of secularized natural law as a means of promoting the growth of the central government at the expense of the traditional estates so as to benefit the nonnoble entrepreneurial class. Thomasius found the perfect opportunity to elaborate and disseminate his view in the anti-Orthodox Pietist circles of the University of Halle, of which he was a co-founder.[8]

Thomasius' views on these matters were a reaction to the foregoing school of church law among Lutheran Orthodox churchmen, the school called "episcopalism," characterized by its doctrine that the prince exercised a right of custody over religion in virtue of the episcopal rights which had by default devolved upon him at the Reformation; the episcopalists held that there existed within the church three estates, of which the pre-eminent was neither that of the political nor the familial order, but rather that of the ecclesiastical or clerical order, to which pertained the government of religious affairs in the church.[9]

Against such ideas was articulated the so-called territorialist position, which emphasized the undivided sovereignty of the territorial lord over the church and its clergy. Leaving out of consideration the earlier Dutch background[10] of this set of ideas, we can for the sake of brevity consider Thomasius as the principal spokesman for this radically secularist position.

The most recent scholarship on territorialism as propounded by Thomasius sees it as an attempt to employ secular law so as to reshape the church and its law according to the yardstick of the state so that ecclesiastical institutions would serve secular purposes. This attempt was *total* in that secular law was used, not simply to regulate the relationship

---

[7] See Hans Leube, *Die Reformideen in der deutschen lutherischen Kirche zur Zeit der Orthodoxie* (Leipzig, 1924); Arnold Schleiff, *Selbstkritik der lutherischen Kirchen im 17. Jahrhundert* (Berlin, 1937).

[8] H. Hohlwein, "Thomasius," *RGG*, 3rd ed. (Tübingen, 1962), 6: cols. 866-67.

[9] Schlaich, "Territorialismus"; Martin Heckel, *Staat und Kirche nach den Lehren der evangelischen Juristen Deutschlands in der ersten Hälfte des 17. Jahrhunderts* (Munich, 1968); cf. Klaus Schlaich, *Kollegialtheorie: Kirch, Recht und Staat in der Aufklärung* (Munich, 1969).

[10] Josef Bohatec, "Das Territorial- und Kollegialsystem in der holländischen Publizistik des XVII. Jahrhunderts," *Zeitschrift der Savigny-Stiftung für Rechtsgeschichte, Kanonistische Abteilung* 35 (1948): 1-149.

between church and state, but also in order to regulate the constitution of the institutional church even in its inward aspect, leaving out of consideration only the private conscience of the individual.[11] Starting with the idea that the sovereign power to command could not logically be divided lest the welfare of the commonwealth be endangered by competing allegiances, the territorialists ended by redefining the *jus sacrum* (church law) as a mere subdivision of the *jus publicum* (law of the commonwealth).[12] The consequences for the independence of the institutional church were far-reaching, for this position represented a return to the formal identification of the Christian religion (reinterpreted according to Stoic natural law) with the civic ideology of the ancient Mediterranean city states and the ancient Roman empire. Thus with regard to church law, as in so many other areas, the initial impact of the courtly Enlightenment consisted in a conscious revival of classical antiquity.[13]

The territorialism of Thomasius was not based on the episcopalist notion that the territorial lord exercises government over the church in virtue of episcopal rights that have devolved upon him as first member and custodian of the church; nor does this doctrine recognize a delegation by the church of its rights properly speaking to the territorial lord (the view of later collegialism). Rather does the view of Thomasius derive the entirety of the territorial lord's right over the church from his mere sovereignty (*jura territorialia* or *maiestatica*).

For Thomasius the state was not founded for religious purposes, and indeed the territorial lord has a certain duty to protect his subjects from

---

[11] See Schlaich, "Territorialismus," p. 277. We dispense here with citations of the endless works of Thomasius and his circle, since Schlaich gives an adequate guide. See Rolf Lieberwirth, *Christian Thomasius: Sein wissenschaftliches Lebenswerk. Eine Bibliographie* (Weimar, 1955); Hildegard Doerr, *Thomasius Stellung zum Landesherrlichen Kirchenregiment* (Phil. Diss., Bonn University, 1917).

[12] Schlaich, "Territorialismus," p. 294; cf. Horst Stephan and Hans Leube, *Die Neuzeit* = vol. 4 of *Handbuch der Kirchengeschichte*, 2nd ed. (Tübingen, 1931): 31-32.

[13] Besides Gay's study of the revival of paganism in his work on the Enlightenment, see Johann David Heilmann, *Traits de parallèle entre l'esprit d'irreligion d'aujourdhui et les anciens adversaires de la religion chrétienne dédiés à ... Monsieur Baumgarten ...* (n.p., 1750); Günter Gawlick, "Cicero and the Enlightenment," *Studies on Voltaire and the Eighteenth Century* 24-27 (1963): 657-82; Gerhard Oestreich, "Politischer Neustoizismus und Niederländische Bewegung in Europa und besonders in Brandenburg-Preußen," in his *Geist und Gestalt des frühmodernen Staates* (Berlin, 1969), pp. 101-56; Ernst Troeltsch, "Das stoischchristliche Naturrecht und das moderne profane Naturrecht," in his *Aufsätze zur Geistgeschichte und Religionssoziologie* = vol. 4 of his *Gesammelte Schriften*, ed. Hans Baron (1925; reprint ed., Aalen, 1925): 166-90; and on the penetration of natural law into theology, Martin Greschat, "Der Bundesgedanke in der Theologie des späten Mittelalters," *Zeitschrift für Kirchengeschichte* 81 (1970): 44-63; Gottlob Schrenk, *Gottesreich und Bund im älteren Protestantismus vornehmlich bei Johannes Coccejus* (Gütersloh, 1923); Leonard J. Trinterud, ed. *Elizabethan Puritanism* (New York, 1971), pp. 302-13; and A. F. Stolzenburg, *Die Theologie des Jo. Franc. Buddeus und des Chr. Matth. Pfaff* (Berlin, 1926).

over-agressive clergy so as to preserve toleration and freedom of conscience.[14] The church is not a part of the state, but rather an equal society
made up of teachers and taught. It is based on social contract and
represents merely a human association; the visible church is not of divine
foundation. In agreement with the principles of secularized natural law,
Thomasius accords to the church only powers of persuasion and denies
the right of compulsion or coercion to the church.[15]

According to Thomasius, since the church is but a society, it lacks a
structural principle. Therefore the church is completely subject to the territorial sovereign. In order to insure the completeness of this subjection
Thomasius teaches that the Orthodox doctrine of three estates within the
church (the foundation of the primacy of the Orthodox clergy in ecclesiastical affairs) is without foundation.[16] As a further means of depriving the visible church of any structure, Thomasius rejects the traditional
distinction between the *potestas ecclesiastica interna* (preaching, administration of sacraments, and the power of discipline, all of which traditionally
pertained to the Protestant clergy) and the *potestas ecclesiastica externa* (subdivided into *propagatio religionis, jurisdictio ecclesiastica,* and *cura et defensio
religionis,* all of which traditionally pertained to the prince as chief
member and custodian of the church). This traditional distinction, the
customary legal form of the doctrine of the division of powers in the Germany of the Old Régime, is rejected because Thomasius repudiates as
well the idea that the prince as a member of the church has special rights
and duties. Rather does Thomasius insist that the prince has rights over
the church simply on account of his sovereignty. The prince makes decisions in church affairs on the mere basis of secular *raison d'état,* the sole
consideration that is now to determine the extent of the "rights" of the
visible church—a radical departure from the Lutheran Orthodox notion
of a prince whose actions are informed by his care for the church.[17]

Consequently Thomasius redefines the purpose of public support of
religion. The state's support of the religion of its subjects is indeed continued, but it now becomes simply the state's service to itself, or, in the
words of Klaus Schlaich, "the care for a state religion" which, though it
has the guise of Christianity, is nonetheless at every visible point subject
to reinterpretation at the pleasure of the prince.[18] Religion as an eternal
matter becomes then an individual affair: the relationship of the soul to
God is a matter ultimately unconnected with the operation of the visible

---

14 Schlaich, "Territorialismus," pp. 283-84.
15 Schlaich, "Territorialismus," pp. 277-81.
16 Schlaich, "Territorialismus," pp. 287-89.
17 Schlaich, "Territorialismus," p. 291.
18 Schlaich, "Territorialismus," p. 301.

church. In consequence for Thomasius the church is to be understood as "spiritual"; its essence is untouched by the mutable arrangements of the visible, institutional church.[19] Thomasius goes so far as to deny that the visible, external church and its external worship were instituted by Christ—and thus implicitly places the church, the clergy, and public worship wholly in the hands of the prince acting according to *raison d'état*.[20]

Fully in accord with this approach is Thomasius' claim that the church has no power to legislate for itself, since Christ did not make provision for this. The visible church is then composed of the totality of persons absolutely subject to the temporal government—a principle which Thomasius invokes to banish the danger that the church might constitute a corporate entity claiming its own sovereignty, that is, a *status in statu*.[21]

The administrative results are startling. Beginning with the principle that all government of the church is merely a part of the sovereign rights of the territorial lord ("jus sacrorum pars summae in republica potestatis"),[22] Thomasius goes on to assert the prince's complete control over ecclesiastical adiaphora, or matters which, since they do not pertain to the holding of articles of faith, are indifferent in themselves. The prince may issue commands concerning worship and liturgy.[23] Thomasius defines this area of princely intervention broadly and admits a divine right in ecclesiastical affairs *only* in the realm of private conscience; thus there are in effect no limits to the territorial lord's power over the institutional church.[24] According to Thomasius the prince can in theory do away with preaching, excommunication, and church holidays, for all of them exist by merely human, not divine, right. Indeed, Thomasius denies that the sacrament of the altar was instituted by Christ as a mark of the church; therefore it, too, can in theory be abolished by the prince.[25] Furthermore, Thomasius makes the prince the final judge of dogmatic controversies and will admit a juridical authority of the consistory over the clergy only if it be understood that that authority is delegated from the prince.[26] It will be seen, then, that Thomasius'

---

[19] Schlaich, "Territorialismus," pp. 307-9; cf. Walther Bienert, *Die Glaubenslehre des Christian Thomasius* (Diss., Halle, 1934).

[20] Schlaich, "Territorialismus," p. 310.

[21] Schlaich, "Territorialismus," pp. 313-14. On the phrase "status in statu," used to denote concepts of church polity that refused to extend temporal sovereignty over the church and its clergy, cf. Bohatec, p. 26, n. 80, deriving this set of concepts from Optatus of Milevis, *De schismate Donatistarum adversus Parmenianum*, 3.3.

[22] Schlaich, "Territorialismus," p. 317, with documentation in n. 195.

[23] Schlaich, "Territorialismus," pp. 319-20.

[24] Schlaich, "Territorialismus," p. 323.

[25] Schlaich, "Territorialismus," p. 325.

[26] Doerr, pp. 47-48.

modern-sounding stress on the freedom of private conscience has as its goal the total subjection of the institutional church and its clergy to the central government.[27]

Though Thomasius taught at Prussian Halle, he did not remain a distant figure for the churchmen in Northwest Germany. In 1705 his opinion was sought by the duke of Braunschweig-Wolfenbüttel in order to justify his over-riding of the objections raised by Lutheran Orthodox clergy to the pressure the duke was applying to his grand-daughter to convert to Roman Catholicism in order to bring about a marriage with the house of Habsburg. Thomasius issued a formal opinion on the matter, justifying the duke's conduct and arguing that the clergy had not the right to exclude the prince from receiving the sacrament of the altar. This document, one of Thomasius' most important statements of temporal supremacy in ecclesiastical affairs, was issued and then reprinted at Wolfenbüttel.[28]

Additional pressure along Thomasian lines came from Johann Georg Pertsch, junior (1694-1754), a student of Thomasius who occupied important posts in the courts in Hannover and Wolfenbüttel. In 1749 Pertsch joined the legal faculty in Helmstedt. By means of historical and legal treatises Pertsch carried out a vitriolic attack on clerical rights and privileges, demanding that clerical influence over the consciences of the laity be radically diminished and that princes abolish the payment of fees to the clergy for ceremonial acts.[29] Other pressure toward the reduction of clerical privilege was not lacking: the consistory in Hannover had been forced to struggle fiercely in order to assert its autonomy at the end of the seventeenth century, and the duke of Braunschweig during the 1750's encouraged by neglect the decline of clerical influence in the Wolfenbüttel consistory. Thereby was promoted a laxity in the enforcement of clerical rights when contested at law.[30]

2. *Johann Lorenz von Mosheim, Organizer of the First Clericalist Defense*

The first phase of the Enlightenment in Northwest Germany was marked by a negative clericalist reaction to the secularist and pro-

---

[27] Schlaich, "Territorialismus," p. 339.

[28] Thomasius, *Bedencken über die Frage: Wieweit ein Prediger gegen seinen Landes-Herrn Welcher zugleich Summus Episcopus mit ist sich des Bindeschlüssels bedienen könne?* (Wolfenbüttel, 1706; 2nd ed., 1707); cf. Johannes Beste, *Geschichte der Braunschweigischen Landeskirche von der Reformation bis auf unsere Tage* (Wolfenbüttel, 1899), pp. 333-46.

[29] Johann Georg Pertsch, *Recht der Beicht-Stuhle*, 2nd ed. (Wolfenbüttel, 1738); Pertsch, *Recht des Kirchen-Bannes*, 2nd ed. (Wolfenbüttel, 1738).

[30] Vitus Dettmer, *Das Konsistorium zu Wolfenbüttel* (Braunschweig, 1922), p. 80-82 (on Braunschweig); and on Hannover, Heinz Weidemann, *Gerard Wolter Molanus, Abt zu Loccum*, 2 vols. (Göttingen, 1925, 1929), 1:48-96.

absolutist attack. The defense consisted largely of outright rejection; however, since strict Orthodoxy was to a growing degree recognized as an untenable position, at the same time there was necessitated a comprehensive remodeling of the traditional clericalist position so as to disguise or supplement its foundation in supernaturalist divine right. The attempt to do this by the adaptation of natural law principles mixed with the appeal to supernatural revelation and historic custom was undertaken by the great church historian, theologian, and churchman Johann Lorenz von Mosheim (1693-1755), whom Adolf Harnack termed "the Erasmus of the eighteenth century."[31] A professor at Helmstedt, co-founder and only chancellor of the new Hannoverian university at Göttingen, and founder of modern scientific church history, Mosheim was in a position to exercise a unique influence on ecclesiastical life: even after his death his transcribed lecture notes served as standard textbooks in more than one field of theology.

Although Mosheim's role as an opponent of secularizing absolutist theory has largely been ignored,[32] in his own time he was the most significant spokesman for upholding the independency of the church and its clergy among the North German Protestant theologians. A considerable part of Mosheim's writing and teaching was undertaken as either a direct or an indirect defense against the territorialism of Thomasius. Mosheim's words on Thomasius are not gentle; he criticizes Thomasius frequently, attributing to him the remark that the prince had the right to depose the clergy at will and to prescribe the content of sermons, since the clergy were of no greater dignity than the princely masters of the hunt. Behind Thomasius' denial of the divine right of the clergy Mosheim saw

---

[31] Adolf Harnack, *Lehrbuch der Dogmengeschichte*, 5th ed., 3 vols. (Tübingen, 1931), 1:29.—On Mosheim: Karl Heussi, *Die Kirchengeschichtsschreibung Johann Lorenz von Mosheims* (Gotha, 1904); Heussi, *Johann Lorenz von Mosheim: Ein Beitrag zur Kirchengeschichte des 18. Jahrhunderts* (Tübingen, 1906); bibliography of Mosheim's works in Johann Georg Meusel, *Lexikon der vom Jahr 1750 bis 1800 verstorbenen teutschen Schriftsteller* (Leipzig, 1809), 9:347-64; Martin Schian, *Die Sokratik im Zeitalter der Aufklärung* (Breslau, 1900); Nathanael Bonwetsch, "Johann Lorenz von Mosheim als Kirchenhistoriker," in *Festschrift zur Feier des hundertfünfzigjahrigen Bestehens der Königlichen Gesellschaft der Wissenschaften zu Göttingen* (Berlin, 1901), pp. 235-61; Johannes Reinhard, *Die Prinzipienlehre der lutherischen Dogmatik von 1700 bis 1750* (Leipzig, 1906); Martin Peters, *Der Bahnbrecher der modernen Predigt Johann Lorenz Mosheim* (Leipzig, 1910); Glawe, pp. 150-76; Emanuel Hirsch, *Geschichte der neuern evangelischen Theologie im Zusammenhang mit den allgemeinen Bewegungen des europäischen Denkens*, 5 vols. (Gütersloh, 1949-54), 2:354-70; Hirsch, *Die Umformung des christlichen Denkens in der Neuzeit: Ein Lesebuch* (Tübingen, 1938), pp. 8-13; and E. P. Meijering, "Mosheim on the Philosophy of the Church Fathers," *Nederlands Archief voor Kerkgeschiedenis* 56 (1975): 367-83.

[32] Schlaich's *Kollegialtheorie* is a recent exception, though its highly technical character as a specialized monograph on Protestant canon law has lessened its impact on the general reader.

lurking the figure of Hobbes.[33] According to Mosheim, Thomasius intended to abolish every right of the clergy and the church and to transform the servants of the gospel into servants of the temporal government. The instrument for doing this was, according to Mosheim, the doctrines of natural law, which Thomasius utilized to derive the unlimited power of the prince from his territorial sovereignty at the expense of the divine right of the church and clergy: since in principle the clergy were rendered unnecessary by the royal priesthood of the laity, the existence and function of the clergy were for Thomasius determined by the convenience of the state.[34] In order to oppose persuasively this secularizing tendency, Mosheim came to propose traditionalist reform in three areas: theology, church law, and the training and supervision of the clergy. Since Mosheim's proposals were in the long run to have great influence, we must gain a thorough understanding of them. That can be done only if we know something about Mosheim's life and approach to questions of politics and church-state relations, and only if we investigate the background to his traditionalist reform proposals.

Mosheim in his early years enjoyed the patronage of the ducal house of Braunschweig-Wolfenbüttel.[35] Having studied at Kiel, where he was educated in the tradition of the mild-tempered Helmstedt Calixtine theology, Mosheim in 1723 received a call to Helmstedt, which at that time served both Braunschweig-Wolfenbüttel and Electoral Hannover. There he remained until 1747; there he achieved his international reputation as a church historian, as an apologist for Christianity, and as a powerful preacher. His skill and fame brought with it rewards: membership in the consistory in Wolfenbüttel and the prestige and incomes from two Lutheran abbacies. With these abbacies went an honored seat in the assemblies of estates. In addition, Mosheim in 1739 became head of the theological faculty at Helmstedt. This position and Mosheim's seat on the consistory gave him a good acquaintance with the character of theological students.

Mosheim's opinion was sought after during the founding of the new university for Electoral Hannover at Göttingen, and numerous efforts were made in the period 1734-35 to attract him to the new institution. But Mosheim declined, protesting his contentment and his debt of gratitude to the ducal house.[36]

---

[33] Mosheim, *Allgemeines Kirchenrecht der Protestanten, Nach dessen Tode herausgegeben und mit Anmerkungen versehen von Christian Ernst von Windheim* (Helmstedt, 1760), pp. 533-34, 594-95. (Hereafter cited as Mosheim, *KR*.)

[34] Cf. Mosheim, *KR*, pp. 190, 591; also p. 195.

[35] For details of Mosheim's career see Heussi's 1906 biography.

[36] Heussi (1906 biography), pp. 157-65, 191-97; Emil F. Rössler, *Die Gründung der Universität Göttingen* (Göttingen, 1855), pp. 173-219.

Yet twelve years later, in 1747, Mosheim decided to make the move to Göttingen. Behind the decision was a disagreement with the young duke Karl I, a difference of opinion that had begun shortly after the duke's accession in 1735. Mosheim's correspondence with Gottsched reveals that the underlying cause was Mosheim's disapproval of the militarism which the new ruler pursued in his effort to imitate Louis XIV and the Hohenzollerns. Mosheim regarded the new régime's militaristic orientation as being at variance with what a theologian should stand for. He criticized the new government's devaluation of eloquence and learning.[37] Mosheim's disaffection with the ducal régime was increased by the duke's heavy expenditure on opera, theatre, and court pageantry. Though Mosheim himself gladly participated in such worldly diversions, he was sufficiently in touch with financial reality to see that a régime spending 70,000 *Thaler* a year on opera and theatre alone could scarcely hope to improve the lot of the impoverished clergy, many of whom had to make do with less than 200 *Thaler* a year. Had Mosheim lived into the 1760's, he would not have been surprised by the total financial collapse that overtook the régime of Karl I: Mosheim's published comments show he was disturbed by the financial consequences of ducal absolutism.[38]

Mosheim's work throughout his career, especially after his removal to Göttingen, was motivated by his particularistic understanding of the academic theologian's task. Adopting from the theological tradition of Calixt the distinction between the parish clergy as servants of the congregation's religious needs and the academic theologians as guardians of the true faith serving the church at large, Mosheim however modified it to fit the conditions of his time.[39] He stressed that the main task of the academic theologian must now consist, not simply in refuting theological error, but as well in refuting atheism, scepticism, and secularism of the sort associated with Hobbes. In his lectures on theology during his Göt-

---

[37] Heussi in his biography provides a transcription of the correspondence on p. 165, n. 2, apparently based on archival materials in Universitätsbibliothek Leipzig, Cod. MS 1274u (Gottscheds Briefwechsel), March 9 and August 24, 1735.

[38] Wilhelm Havemann, *Geschichte der Land Braunschweig und Lüneburg*, 3 vols. (Göttingen, 1857), 3:620; Yorck Alexander Haase, "Theater," in *Braunschweigische Landesgeschichte im Überblick*, ed. Richard Moderhack (Braunschweig, 1977), pp. 301-12; pp. 304-6; Beste, *Geschichte*, p. 381; on Mosheim as a gambler, see Heussi's 1906 biography, p. 126; Mosheim, *Sitten-Lehre Der Heiligen Schrift*, 3rd ed. (Helmstedt, 1742), 1:533 (hereafter: Mosheim *SL*); Wilhelm Schmidt, *Der braunschweigische Landtag von 1768-1770* (Phil. Diss., Göttingen University, 1912).

[39] Johannes Wallmann, *Der Theologiebegriff bei Johann Gerhard und Georg Calixt* (Tübingen, 1961), pp. 148-61; Georg Calixt, *Gründliche Widerlegung eines unwarhafften Gedichts unterm Titul: Crypto-papismus Novae Theologiae Helmstadiensis*, 2 vols. (Lüneburg, 1641), 2:337-40; Mosheim, *Kurze Anweisung, die Gottesgelahrtheit vernünftig zu erlernen, in academischen Vorlesungen vorgetragen*, ed. Christian Ernst von Windheim (Helmstedt, 1756), pp. 170-75 (hereafter cited as Mosheim, *AG*); Mosheim, *SL*, 1:521-24.

tingen period, Mosheim explained that the academic theologian's service to the church, since it did not consist merely in the training of future pastors, but as well in defense, was in his day an arduous task. Because of the increasing intensity of attacks on Christianity from the learned in every discipline, this task demanded that a theologian become "well-nigh a universal scholar."[40]

Such an understanding of the theological task lay behind Mosheim's work in special apologetics and in scholarly church history: Mosheim tried to rescue the historic uniqueness of Christian doctrine without sacrificing its intellectual credibility or its claim to participation in the mainstream of the Western philosophical tradition. A look at Mosheim's neglected work in dogmatics, practical theology, and church law demonstrates a similar concern to defend Christianity, and indeed shows that he consciously took on the role of the opponent of the secularism advocated by the pro-absolutist natural law school. If this activity is taken into account, Mosheim's career can be seen as an effort to refute three secularist claims:

— the claim that Christian doctrine ought to be radically revised to bring it into conformity with purely natural religion;

— the claim that the organization of the church ought to be radically restructured on the secularist principles of natural law advocated by Thomasius;

— the claim that the identity and functioning of the clergy ought to be reshaped so as to meet the demands of natural law put in the service of the prince.

In order properly to evaluate Mosheim's responses to these claims, we must first sketch Mosheim's general position on questions of politics in connection with church-state relations; in this way we can locate the foundation of Mosheim's commitment to clerical particularism.

The political and ecclesiastical standpoint of most leading churchmen in the Northwest German Enlightenment can be seen as a clerical counterpart to what Klaus Epstein has termed "reform conservatism."[41] Unlike the Rationalistic theologians who flourished in the absolutist environment of the Berlin Enlightenment, most of these churchmen undertook only so much theological, legal, and professional revision as the currents of opinion made necessary. The emphasis was on "practical"

---

[40] Mosheim, *AG*, p. 171.

[41] Cf. Klaus Epstein, *The Genesis of German Conservatism* (Princeton, N.J., 1966), pp. 3-25. I am aware that Epstein's application of the "conservative" label to the so-called Hannoverian school of political thought is open to objection. However, since these thinkers have been made familiar to English readers by Epstein's treatment, I here adopt the label as a label, reserving for another place argument about its ultimate fitness.

reform, that is, on showing that, if updated by cautious modification, the traditional faith and institutions of Christianity could still meet the needs of mankind. Such an approach was intended to refute both sceptics and proponents of Thomasian natural law territorialism. Thus the Prussian variety of ecclesiastical Enlightenment could find in Northwest Germany only limited acceptance: the dominant point of view represented a clerical counterpart to the attitude of the Northwest German particularist or anticentralist political writers. Among the churchmen, as among the writers of the political school of Justus Möser, August Ludwig Schlözer, August Wilhelm Rehberg, and Ernst Brandes, hopes were put in a gradual and local reform of the traditional estates in society rather than in a program of centrally-executed rapid reforms. Furthermore the churchmen, like their lay colleagues, opposed reforms of institutions and ideologies based solely on secularized natural law and human reason, instead stressing the advantages of continuity and accumulated tradition refined over centuries.[42]

Although Mosheim wrote no treatise on government, his writings consistently adopt a viewpoint akin to that of the anticentralist writers when he touches on church-state relations. For Mosheim was at one with the particularist writers in his rejection of "despotism" (absolute, unrestrained monarchy).[43]

Mosheim's negative view of "despotism" can be amply documented. He criticized theoretical attempts to support it, whether they took the form of divine right theories invoking the kings of ancient Israel, or the shape of secularized natural law doctrines advocated by Hobbes and Thomasius.[44] Going on beyond the contention that kings were *not* to be regarded as divine representatives, Mosheim leveled specific charges against the absolutist courts of his day. His criticism of heavy taxation, military expenditures, and courtly extravagance are already familiar. In return for their tax money, Mosheim suggested, the population received an immoral, irreligious, and unreliable clique of courtiers whose worst flaw was their failure to withhold obedience when their superiors issued unjust commands. As Mosheim put it, despotism was growing steadily and gave the whole world cause for complaint.[45]

Mosheim's positive views on politics stressed the so-called mixed con-

[42] Cf. Epstein, pp. 547-94; Johannes Meyer, *Kirchengeschichte Niedersachsens* (Göttingen, 1939), pp. 134-88.

[43] On "despotism" as a term for unlimited absolutism, see Rudolf Vierhaus, "Absolutismus," in *Sowjetsystem und Demokratische Gesellschaft*, ed. C. D. Kernig et al. (Freiburg i.B., 1966-), 1: col. 17.

[44] Mosheim, *KR*, pp. 585, 605, 570, 193; in general, pp. 591-607.

[45] Mosheim, *SL*, 1:138, 529-34; *KR*, pp. 591-606.

stitution,[46] or, more precisely, government by separate powers restraining each other. Mosheim, like the political writers in the anticentralist party, held ideas reseembling those of Montesquieu. Like the antiabsolutist writers he found what he wanted in an idealized concept of the English constitution.[47] Mosheim the churchman, like the antiabsolutist political thinkers, prescribed rejuvenation of the historic corporate bodies in the Empire as the cure for German ills. In so doing Mosheim hoped to arrest the growing tendency in Germany for the will of princes to become the sole force in government. In a passage strongly reminiscent of Montesquieu, Mosheim urged that Germans take a cue from the French example. In France, he pointed out, despotism was still held in check by three forces: the nobility, the law courts or *parlements*, and the clergy. Immediately thereafter he invoked that other favorite example of the particularists—the idealized English constitution. According to Mosheim, the English also furnished an example worthy of emulation, for they would say that

> our bishops must enjoy esteem; our religion and church must resist [widerstehen] the king, in order that he not acquire all the power. In order to do this, the clergy need prestige and incomes. They must sit in Parliament; ...[48]

And wise are the English, contends Mosheim; for without such arrangements, despotism necessarily gains the upper hand.

The congruence of Mosheim's ideas with those of the advocates of political particularism is enhanced then, not merely by the high regard for historical study and for the exemplary worth of tradition which were shared by both Mosheim and these writers, but as well by the shared opinion that the *clergy* as a constituted body could be especially useful as a restraint on monarchs. Particularist writers in Germany favoring the separation of powers and the maintenance of political equilibrium by *pouvoirs intermédiaires* customarily invoked Montesquieu in support of their political ideas. In *De l'esprit des lois* Montesquieu wrote concerning the clergy:

---

[46] Cf. n. 27 to the Introduction above; also G. J. D. Aalders, *Die Theorie der gemischten Verfassung im Altertum* (Amsterdam, 1968); Arnaldo Momigliano, "Polybius' Reappearance in Western Europe," in *Polybe* (Vandoeuvres and Geneva, 1973), pp. 345-72; J. G. A. Pocock, "Civic Humanism and its Role in Anglo-American Thought," in his *Politics, Language and Time* (New York, 1973), pp. 80-103.

[47] Cf. Hermann Christern, *Deutscher Ständestaat und englischer Parlamentarismus am Ende des 18. Jahrhunderts* (Munich, 1939); Rudolf Vierhaus, "Montesquieu in Deutschland," in *Collegium Philosophicum: Studien Joachim Ritter zum 60. Geburtstag*, ed. Ernst-Wolfgang Böckenförde (Basel and Stuttgart, 1965), pp. 403-37. The ideas of Mosheim are discussed below.

[48] Mosheim, *KR*, pp. 605-6.

To the degree that the power of the clergy is dangerous in a republic it is appropriate in a monarchy, especially in those approaching despotism. Where would Spain and Portugal be after the loss of their laws without this power that is the sole hindrance to arbitrary power? Always a salutary barrier when there is no other: for, since despotism visits the most hideous evils upon human nature, the very evil that checks it is a good.[49]

Mosheim's contention was the same as Montesquieu's concerning the political function of the clergy—even though, as an apologist for the clerical estate, he was not about to admit that its necessary power was a necessary *evil*. Not only did Mosheim hold that the clergy were of surpassing importance in a monarchy precisely because they could restrict princely power; Mosheim even contended that a good case could be made for augmenting the power of the clergy on purely political grounds without taking theological arguments into account. For Christianity and the traditional power of the clergy were indispensable to the political wellbeing of the state and the entire commonwealth.[50] Therefore the secularist territorialism of Thomasius threatened more than the clergy and religion: it endangered the traditional structure of political community. The application of natural law and natural religion as the sole standards in politics and religion, according to Mosheim, led to a common destination, irreligious despotism, a threat to the traditional order of society.[51]

Clearly Mosheim's particularism, despite his Enlightenment tendencies, has close affinities with the Lutheran Orthodox critique of absolutism and Thomasian territorialism.[52] This point must be emphasized: for those few scholars who do recognize that Lutheran Orthodoxy attempted to restrain the growth of absolutism have ordinarily seen such restraint as ending with the spread of Enlightenment.[53] It did not. However, as we shall see below, Mosheim is no longer in the position of the Lutheran Orthodox: he cannot make a convincing case by the sole method of piling up scriptural proof passages that establish the theology,

---

[49] Charles de Montesquieu, *De l'esprit des lois*, 2.4. = his *Œuvres complètes*, ed. Roger Caillois (Paris, 1958), 2:248. The translation is my own.

[50] See for example, Mosheim, *KR*, pp. 604-6; and *SL*, 1:533.

[51] Mosheim, *KR*, pp. 184-85; also pp. 193 and 591-607.

[52] Theodor Wotschke, "Löschers Bemühungen um einen Theologenbund," *Zeitschrift für Kirchengeschichte*, 47 (1928): 145-61; Wotschke, "Niedersächsiche Mitarbeiter an den Unschuldigen Nachrichten," *ZGNK* 31 (1926): 73-112; Martin Greschat, *Zwischen Tradition und neuem Anfang: Valentin Ernst Löscher und der Ausgang der lutherischen Orthodoxie* (Witten, 1971); Hajo Holborn, "Machtpolitik und lutherische Sozialethik," *Archiv für Reformationsgeschichte* 57 (1966): 23-32; Wilhelm Bofinger, "Zur Rolle des Luthertums in der Geschichte des deutschen Ständeparlamentarismus," in *Geist und Geschichte der Reformation: Festgabe Hanns Rückert* (Berlin, 1966), pp. 397-417.

[53] For example, Johannes Wallmann, "Zwischen Reformation und Humanismus," *Zeitschrift für Theologie und Kirche* 74 (1977): 344-70.

the law, and the professional status of Lutheran clericalism by divine right. He must also argue that the pre-Enlightenment *status quo* in theology, ecclesiology and clerical privilege (if purged of certain unimportant features) is exactly what enlightened right reason judging in accord with natural law ought to approve. Yet all the while, in order to obtain an adequate safeguard against secularist demands, Mosheim must contend as well that the pre-Enlightenment *status quo* possesses an unshakable foundation in divine right. Mosheim is in a far more delicate position than the churchmen of seventeenth-century Orthodoxy, and must therefore resort to such double argumentation to defend the clericalist cause.

Mosheim's interest in the cause of clerical particularism was heightened by his position as an abbot and by his seat in the assembly of estates at Helmstedt; there he could see the divergence in princely and particularist (i.e., clerical) self-interest. His sense for the decline in the prestige of the clergy was sharpened by his work as a theological educator. The particularist in Mosheim was brought to the fore by his observation of the militarism and extravagance of the young duke Karl. Mosheim in fact evolved toward an ever-firmer advocacy of particularism. His public utterances against "despotism" increase in intensity and frequency late in his career, in the period during which he contemplated and carried out the move to Göttingen. For after all Göttingen, Mosheim's final location, was the center of that anticentralist Enlightenment with which Reill's study has made us familiar. So careful a writer and planner as Mosheim cannot have moved to such a site without considering its advantage as a location for executing a defense of religion, church, and clergy against the linked threats of secularism and despotism.

Mosheim's opposition to radical deism and naturalism took the form of a careful reworking of traditional Christian theology. His effort here was aided by the nature of the theological tradition indigenous to the Welf territories. This tradition, originating in Helmstedt and continued in Helmstedt's daughter university at Göttingen, was characterized by its avoidance of doctrinal polemic, its aversion to extreme formulations, and by its liking for "practical" good works. In such a way the possibility of development in a truly radical or naturalist direction was reduced by means of prudent concessions to the temper of the day.

The starting-point here was Melanchthon, who revised Luther's doctrine of justification by faith alone, defining the Holy Spirit as the gift of the power needed to meet the demands of the law. Melanchthon's theology, with its slogan that to know Christ is to know his benefits, and its heavy use of the humanist tradition, anticipates the apologetic stress on "practical" virtue and good works characteristic of the Enlightenment. Such an emphasis was the main feature in the irenical theology of Georg Calixt (1586-1656), the founder of the Helmstedt tradition, who aimed at unifying Christendom on the basis of a consensus on basic doctrines.[54]

In his vain effort to achieve this, Calixt separated religious faith from learned theology and distinguished between theological ethics and doctrinal theology. He aimed to insure that, in the face of the challenge of revived pagan humanism, morality and ethics would remain the province of theologians and churchmen; but in so doing he inadvertently set in motion a process that would increasingly make dogmatic theology the concern of academic specialists.[55]

The first effect of Calixt's theology, however, was to reinforce the importance of clerical authority by encouraging the clergy to maintain a high regard for the function of their estate. It is therefore not surprising that the Helmstedt tradition repeatedly produced churchmen who clashed with the dukes of Braunschweig over the autonomy of church and clergy.[56]

Calixt's theology in the Welf territories was easily reworked on Wolffian principles during the early Enlightenment. The age of Mosheim in the Welf territories was not a period of radical Enlightenment, nor was radical Enlightenment to be prominent among most churchmen there even in the 1770's. The Calixtine tradition did not on the whole develop into radical Neology of the Berlin variety with its potential for a consistent Rationalism attacking the very concept of immediate revelation; for decades most churchmen remained content with a mild variety of Wolffianism that eventually shaded off into a moderate Neology conceived as an apologetic means of refuting the naturalistic denial of revelation. The revision of the Calixtine tradition for these purposes was accomplished all the more readily since Calixt himself had already held a relatively optimistic view of the capabilities of human reason in religion.[57]

Even in the generation or so after Mosheim, even in absolutist Braunschweig-Wolfenbüttel, radical Rationalists could not count on going unchallenged. The most outspoken champion of natural religion, Wilhelm Abraham Teller (1734-1804), found it necessary to leave for the

---

[54] Inge Mager, *Georg Calixts theologische Ethik und ihre Nachwirkungen* (Göttingen, 1969); Hermann Schlüssler, *Georg Calixt: Theologie und Kirchenpolitik* (Wiesbaden, 1961).

[55] Wallmann, *Theologiebegriff*, pp. 107-9; Ernst Luthardt, *Die Ethik Luthers in ihren Grundzügen* (Leipzig, 1867), p. 15, as cited in Mager, p. 134.

[56] Beste, *Geschichte*, pp. 330-58; Dettmer, *Konsistorium*, pp. 58-68; Georg Seebaß and Friedrich-Wilhelm Freist, *Die Pastoren der Braunschweigischen Evangelisch-Lutherischen Landeskirche* (Wolfenbüttel, 1974), 2:161.

[57] Mager, pp. 29, 173.

freer air of Friderician Prussia. For to the end of the century, despite the presence of such Neologians and Rationalists as Johann Friedrich Wilhelm Jerusalem (1709-1789) and Heinrich Philipp Conrad Henke (1752-1809), there flourished in Braunschweig a traditionalist theological party opposed to truly radical Rationalism.[58] There, as in Electoral Hannover, the university theologians, most of the consistory, and most of the parish clergy opposed any wholesale abandonment of the supernatural core of the historic Christian proclamation. The contrast here between indigenous caution and the more radical variety of theology prevalent in absolutist Prussia was commented upon at the time. The issue was the preservation or abandonment of the concept of an immediate divine revelation; and it is clear that, whereas champions of the Berlin Enlightenment held that natural religion alone was desirable since it would alone suffice to maintain political health, the thinkers in Northwest Germany were of a different opinion. In Northwest Germany opinion favored rather the retention of revealed religion on the grounds that it was necessary for the health of the state.[59]

Evidently a correlation existed between theological traditionalism and political particularism on the one hand, and theological Rationalism and openness to centralist absolutistic doctrines on the other. The leading churchmen in Northwest Germany shared the political and intellectual orientation of their lay colleagues who criticized unrestrained absolutism in language akin to that of Montesquieu. As we saw above, the churchmen, like the conservative political writers, feared a central government based on secularized natural law as discerned by the prince; they suspected that it would soon become dangerously independent of the checks imposed by historical tradition, positive religion, and existing forms of governmental and administrative practice (e.g., assemblies of estates). The churchmen, like traditionalist political writers such as Schlözer, rejected the radical Enlightenment attempt to reshape religion and government according to purely "rational" principles defined solely by human reason. Both the Northwest German political writers and most of the theologians in that area shared the conviction that historical tradition (the mores and privilege of the entrenched particularist powers, and

---

[58] Beste, Geschichte, pp. 441-43; Johannes Meyer, Kirchengeschichte Niedersachsens (Göttingen, 1939), pp. 153-78; Karl Aner, "Die Historia dogmatum des Abtes Jerusalem," Zeitschrift für Kirchengeschichte, 47 (1928): 76-103; Hirsch, Geschichte, 5:11-14; Heinrich Philipp Conrad Henke, Lineamenta institutionum fidei christianae (Helmstedt, 1795).

[59] See for example Johann Friedrich Jacobi, "Nähere Entdeckung eines neuen Lehrgebäudes der Religion," in his Sämtliches Schriften, 3. Theil (Hannover, 1784), pp. 125-92; Hirsch, Geschichte, 5:57-59; Karl Aner, Die Theologie der Lessingzeit (Halle/Saale, 1929), n. 3, pp. 121-22; Arnold Berney, "August Ludwig Schlözers Staatsauffassung," Historische Zeitschrift 132 (1925): 46-57.

the traditional religious ideology reinforcing them) ought to be of continuing and vital significance. This general conviction was to have lasting consequences for the shape of Enlightenment theology in Northwest Germany.

The apologetic reworking of traditional religious ideology was successfully undertaken at the start of the Enlightenment by Mosheim; the skill with which he accomplished it was to a considerable degree responsible for the persisting conviction among later churchmen of the Northwest German Enlightenment that some variety of revealed religion was intellectually defensible—even in the age of Kant and Fichte. We are well advised, then, to glance at Mosheim's antisecularist reform of the religious and theological tradition.

Mosheim's theology can be seen as an effort to uphold two claims traditionally made by the church: that Christian doctrine did not contradict human reason, but rather supplemented it; and that the Christian message was of unique significance both because of its supernatural validation and its positive content. The kind of Enlightenment theological apologetic inaugurated by Mosheim constitutes a last heroic effort to defend both of these claims so as to avoid making a choice between obscurantist irrationalism and universalist relativism deprived of the validation of timeless truth. The denial of these two traditional claims by spiritualist and secularist writers had suggested that, since the church and its clergy could be justified by neither an appeal to reason nor an appeal to other sources of legitimation, therefore the temporal government might be well advised to curtail the privileges and authority of the church and its clergy in public life. Mosheim's theology is designed to refute the secularist position by defending the two traditional claims of the church in the belief that the fallen prestige of the Christian religion must be raised so as to promote the eternal salvation and the temporal morality of mankind. In raising this prestige Mosheim discerned one of his primary tasks as a theologian.[60]

Though Mosheim repeatedly stressed his caution and hesitancy in revising the dogmatic tradition, nonetheless he was prepared to propose a traditionalist reform as a necessary alternative to radical change. His revision of dogmatics was carried out by the introduction of two principles: he reshaped Lutheran dogmatics according to the requirements of Wolffian philosophy[61] and in agreement with the plan of the federal or

---

[60] Mosheim, *SL*, 1:517.

[61] Mosheim, "Vorrede," in his *Heilige Reden*, Erster Theil (Hamburg, 1732), p. 22; Mosheim, *Elementa theologica dogmatica*, ed. Christian Ernst von Windheim (Nürnberg, 1758), p. 410 (hereafter: Mosheim, *ED*); Hirsch, *Geschichte*, 2:365. On Wolffianism and Mosheim, cf. Carlo Antoni, *Der Kampf wider die Vernunft*, trans. Walter Goetz (Stuttgart, 1951), p. 162.

covenant theology previously developed in Reformed circles. By proceeding according to these principles he accomplished what apologetic necessity demanded: he reaffirmed for his contemporaries both the rational and the uniquely valid content of Christian revelation in a way that seemed persuasive to his readers.

In accord with these principles Mosheim's theology abandoned the verbal inspiration of scripture as a doctrine, stressing instead the ethical results brought about by the study of scripture. Sin he redefined as "spiritual imperfections" instead of total corruption, so that grace was held to effect gradual improvement rather than bringing about a transformation of the natural state. Christology was revised to de-emphasize the communication of properties and to move toward an abandonment of the doctrine of the anhypostasia (impersonality) of the human nature in Christ. Simultaneously Lutheranism was made into a religion based on moral performance, for with Mosheim the receipt of the divine promises depended on human acceptance of the "conditions of the covenant of grace"; conversion was moreover presented as a free decision under the influence of supernatural grace; and faith was characterized as justifying only if it carried with it the effective intent of doing good.[62]

Yet Mosheim managed to uphold the unique character of the supernatural revelation in historic Christianity. Wolffianism allowed the historicity of miracles and the affirmation of the Christian revelation, and the covenant theology as adapted by Mosheim reinforced the importance of a supernaturally-validated relationship between God and man. Mosheim's covenant theology, unlike that of some of his contemporaries, had at its center the notion of the kingdom of God, a doctrine which was alone capable of preventing the supernatural character of the covenant, once stated in juristic terms, from gradually disappearing so as to leave behind only the Stoic pantheism which formed the core of covenant theology. So as to avoid this attrition of the supernatural, Mosheim recurred to the originator of the covenant theology (Coccejus) rather than following the example of the later federal theologians: for example, Mosheim insisted on the transcendent and supernatural character of the kingdom, which he based in an eternal covenant between the first and second persons of the trinity (Luke 22:29); and he made the notion of the

---

[62] Reinhard, pp. 80, 91-92; Peters, p. 22; Mosheim, *KR*, p. 546; Hirsch, *Geschichte*, 2:366-68; Mosheim, *SL*, 1:233, 321; Mosheim, *AG*, p. 128; Mosheim, *ED*, pp. 572-602; 509, 681, 730, 828-29; but *ED*, pp. 738, 751, 714-15 and 577; cf. *ED*, pp. xix-xx; also Ernst Bizer, "Coccejus," *RGG*, 3rd ed. (Tübingen, 1957), 1:cols. 1841-42. Cf. for background Robert C. Schultz, *Gesetz und Evangelium* (Berlin, 1958); and for an example of the pressure moving theologians in a Pelagian direction, see Christian Ludwig Liscow, *Über die Unnöthigkeit der guten Werke zur Seeligkeit*; cf. Berthold Litzmann, *Christian Ludwig Liscow* (Hamburg and Leipzig, 1883), pp. 8, 21-23.

kingdom the key to his doctrine of the church as an expression of the supernatural character of the covenant initiated by God in Christ for the salvation of mankind. Similarly conservative is the christocentricity of Mosheim's entire theology, in clear contrast to the religion of Thomasius. Furthermore, in the classic tradition of Latin Christendom, religion's real purpose according to Mosheim remained getting eternal souls into heaven; its orientation remained other-worldly.[63]

Likewise, though Mosheim, in the words of Emanuel Hirsch, knew

> no other connection between God and man than that of didactic revelation, with an appeal to the [human] will on God's part, and with an acceptance of this instruction and this appeal on man's part; ....[64]

and though Mosheim at times seemed to see natural reason as capable by study of scripture of obtaining an accurate knowledge of the truths of salvation; still Mosheim expressly denied that the church and its revelation were potentially superfluous. On the contrary, in true conservative fashion Mosheim defended the necessity of ecclesiastical instruction in the truths of revelation for the vast majority of mankind.[65]

Thus, though as Hirsch puts it, Mosheim suppressed as many of the "metaphysical and mystical intrusions of Orthodoxy" as possible so as to replace them with a sober concern "for the experientially perceptible moral reality" typical of the German Enlightenment,[66] still, all things considered, Mosheim must be reckoned as a traditionalist. Despite his didactic moralism, his regard for rationality, his clear universalist tendencies and his taint of Semipelagianism, Mosheim nonetheless concluded that divine revelation is of paramount importance for religion and theology: the connection between God and man was asserted to occur by means of supernatural revelation. Thus Mosheim defended the doctrinal basis for the traditional supernatural or other-worldly *raison d'être* of the church and its clergy. That purpose remained for Mosheim the promotion of the health of the eternal soul by means of preaching the word of God and administering sacraments in which an incomprehensible quality was still held to inhere.[67] In the eighteenth century such a position was tradition-oriented.

---

[63] Hirsch, *Geschichte*, 2:57-58; 73-74; Stolzenburg, pp. 346-48, 356-57; Peters, p. 74; Mosheim, *ED*, pp. 579-80 and p. 577, 879; *SL*, 1: fol. C 3 recto; *AG*, p. 143; Mosheim, *Pastoral-Theologie von denen Pflichten und Lehramt eines Dieners des Evangelii* (Leipzig and Ansbach, 1763), p. 13 (hereafter: Mosheim, *PT*); Mosheim, *Institutes of Ecclesiastical History*, trans. James Murdock (New York, 1861), 1:41; cf. Bienert, p. 57.

[64] Hirsch, *Geschichte*, 2:369.

[65] Mosheim, *SL*, (Helmstedt, 1752), 5:433; Reinhard, pp. 81, 98; Peters, pp. 125-27; Mosheim, *SL*, 3:81, 90-91; Hirsch, *Geschichte*, 2:368-70. Cf. Augustine, *Retractiones* 1.13.

[66] Hirsch, *Geschichte*, 2:369.

[67] Hirsch, *Geschichte*, 2:368; Mosheim, *PT*, pp. 13, 70; Peters, p. 74; and Mosheim, *Auserlesene akademische Abhandlungen*, ed. Johann Peter Miller (Leipzig, 1766), pp. 63, 27 (hereafter: Mosheim, *AA*).

Mosheim's opposition to the Thomasian call for a radical reorganization of the church under the authority of the state was carried out in his Göttingen lectures on Protestant church law, which provided Mosheim with an opportunity to elaborate a rival system of church law as an alternative to territorialism. This system, called collegialism because it proceeded on the premise that the church was a *collegium* or society to which definite rights pertained, allowed Mosheim to argue that the church enjoyed certain rights other than those flowing from the sovereignty of the prince; at the same time, this system gave far greater scope to ecclesiastical privileges based on divine right than did territorialism.

Though collegialism originated among the Dutch opponents of Grotius' system of secularized natural law,[68] and though Mosheim was not the only theologian to introduce collegialism to Germany, here we shall limit ourselves to a consideration of the system as presented by Mosheim. There can be no doubt that Mosheim and the other proponents of collegialism were cognizant of the significance of the territorialist challenge. For in truth, as Gerhard Masur puts it, writers in the natural law camp such as Thomasius, on account of their indebtedness to the heritage of Stoic thought, were demanding

> as complete an identification of state and church as the states of antiquity had known: not only the subordination of the church, but rather its total subjection, indeed dissolving into the state.[69]

Mosheim was fully aware of the background and aims of this movement. His 600-page Göttingen lectures on Protestant church law cite every significant commentator on church-state relations from Eusebius to Barbeyrac, and conclude that Thomasius and his followers intended to furnish the prince with "a *jus absolutum* and *illimitatum* even with regard to religion and the conscience" and thereby to transform the clergy from "servants of the gospel" into "temporal servants."[70] Mosheim abhorred this tendency: however much he might approve promoting liberty of conscience and curtailing the pernicious effects of theological disputes,[71] he was still convinced that the real goals of the natural law party, if realized, would result in despotism and irreligion. Not surprisingly, Mosheim

---

[68] See the study by Bohatec. Recent scholarship on the marked differences between territorialism and collegialism is summed up in the important studies by Schlaich.

[69] Gerhard Masur, "Naturrecht und Kirche," *Historische Zeitschrift* 148 (1933): 39.

[70] Mosheim, *KR*, pp. 591-92.

[71] Liberty of conscience: Mosheim, *KR*, p. 261 and pp. 474-75 and PT, pp. 13-14; as background, Pierre Bayle, *Commentaire philosophique sur ces paroles de Jésus-Christ: "Contrains les d'entrer"* (Amsterdam, 1686). Controversy: Mosheim, *KR*, p. 529; Mosheim, *De Odio theologico commentatio* (Göttingen, ca. 1747), commenting on the celebrated "Tantum religion potuit suadere malorum" (p. 3; cf. p. 22n.). Clearly Mosheim espouses a "tolerant" standpoint.

turned to Dutch collegialism for a solution—to a school of church law explicitly designed to protect the clergy from becoming creatures of the civil magistrate and to prevent what one Dutch collegialist had characterized as the degeneration of ecclesiastical office into secular rule with consequent loss of the characteristic spiritual or religious nature of that office.[72]

Offering a course of lectures on this topic within the theological rather than the legal faculty was something of an innovation at the time, an innovation born of necessity. In these lectures Mosheim sought not only to provide the learned world with a persuasive defense of the relative autonomy in religious matters enjoyed by the pre-absolutist church and clergy, but as well to suggest to his students that acquaintance with ecclesiastical and clerical rights under existing law was the necessary precondition to an effective defense of those rights.

Collegialism in its German context reasserted the ecclesiastical rights formerly upheld by the episcopalist system with its doctrine of devolution of churchly rights upon the prince. In place of this with its corollary assertion of the ecclesiastical primacy of the clerical estate on the basis of divine right came now Mosheim's newer collegialist system, carefully interweaving divine right, federal theology, and "unsecularized" natural law with an appeal to right reason. The collegialist system ought to be seen as a thorough but traditionalist and ultimately clericalist reform of, or substitute for, its episcopalist predecessor.[73] The collegialist system is then Mosheim's response based upon his understanding that what Thomasius had put forward was indeed a "reformation" in church law, and that Thomasius understood himself as a "reformer" of law. In order to avoid the Erastian, even despotic, consequences of territorialism, Mosheim at Göttingen argued that secularist reform was unnecessary, since an alternative reform would satisfy the demands of reason without disturbing the religious and ecclesiastico-political equilibrium of Protestant Germany.[74]

The full force of Mosheim's defense of ecclesiastical rights becomes clear when his legal system is seen in its connection with his theological system—a point generally overlooked. For the link between these two systems is furnished by the covenant theology borrowed from the Dutch Reformed. The Janus-like double orientation was vital here—looking simultaneously toward the domain of the supernaturally-established

---

[72] Bohatec, p. 31, citing Jacques Trigland, *Dissertatio de potestate civili et ecclesiastica* (Amsterdam, 1642), pp. 283, 311; cf. Gisbert Voetius, *Politica Ecclesiastica*, 4 vols. (Amsterdam, 1663-76), 1: no. 1:136.

[73] Following here largely the judgments of Schlaich, who however does not undertake a full theological analysis.

[74] Cf. Mosheim, *KR*, pp. 519-606.

kingdom of Christ and the domain of legally-delimited rights and obligations. In the supernaturally-grounded natural law thinking of the covenant theology Mosheim found the ideal means for re-emphasizing the
uniquely transcendent character of the church as well as the proper way
of giving sharp definition to those rights of the church against which
earthly sovereigns were not to transgress on pain of violating both divine
and natural law.

In his dogmatics Mosheim moves from a definition of the church as the
"particular kingdom of Christ" (i.e., the salvific dominion of Christ over
believers rather than his dominion over all of mankind)[75] to a more
precise definition of the church as

> that society which is gathered under Christ its king for the purpose of
> obtaining eternal salvation.[76]

Thus Mosheim's theology of the church as a society is so formulated as to
supply a ready bridge to the "unsecularized" natural law terminology
employed in the collegialist attack on territorialism. After we have taken
a look at what Mosheim's theology of the church implies, we shall be
ready to cross that bridge and to appreciate how law can be used for the
purposes of theology.

Mosheim's view of the purpose and nature of the church is derived
from one of the central themes in the covenant theology, the theme of the
kingdom of God in Christ. For this theology the covenant of grace,
replacing the covenant of works broken in the Fall, is seen to be based in
an eternal covenant in which God the Father promises God the Son a
kingdom the content of which is eternal life. Christ as king must have
objects over which he rules: they are those believers who make up his
church, thereby sharing in eternal life by accepting the conditions of
Christ's covenant. Thus the church, membership in which confers the
content of the eternal covenant (eternal life) on believers, can be defined
as a society whose head is Christ and whose purpose is obtaining eternal
salvation. For the church is the result of Christ's covenant with mankind,
according to which those who accept the promise of divine grace offered
by Christ to mankind receive in exchange that eternal life which at the
same time is the purpose for which the church is formed. Although
Mosheim does not hold that the church as an earthly institution is in itself
of a transcendent character, it nonetheless is seen as of a more than earthly nature insofar as it, as an object of Christs's rule, shares passively in
that dominion exercised by Christ its head, thereby participating in the
transcendent glory of eternal life. For Mosheim, then, the nature of the

---

[75] Mosheim, *ED*, p. 879.
[76] Mosheim, *ED*, p. 879.

church remains in traditional fashion transcendent, eternal, and supernatural: the church itself is an object of Christ's dominion; and the visible
church and its clergy are still held to have been instituted by Jesus Christ
himself—in direct contradiction to the denial of this claim by Hobbes and
Thomasius.[77]

In addition, Mosheim's theology of the church is in continuity with
Lutheran Orthodoxy in that it firmly upholds the necessity of the church
and its clergy. According to Mosheim, the word and sacraments are ordinarily necessary for salvation, and inner experiences such as those
favored by the Quakers are too uncertain to replace the external word.
Mosheim insists that the church, the clergy, public worship, and instruction are all indispensable as means for the perpetuation of the Christian
faith. Furthermore, despite the inner nature of faith, for Mosheim the ex-
ternals of institutional religion remain too important to be neglected or
left to the care of the prince. Explicitly refuted is the claim that public instruction in religion is unnecessary; explicitly affirmed is the necessity
and the divine origin of the teaching office and public worship—which,
according to Mosheim, ought not to be despised by the educated who feel
themselves no longer in need of them.[78]

On the basis of this doctrinal position Mosheim can in his lectures on
church law contend that the church, by virtue of its divine institution and
transcendent purpose, possesses rights of a status not approached by the
rights pertaining to the temporal government. For Mosheim recognizes
two sources of right—divine, contained in revelation, and human,
discovered by reason. Against the Thomasian school Mosheim upholds
the traditional Christian claim that the commands of Christ constitute
binding laws. The church's inalienable rights are seen to possess, not
simply a foundation in mutable human right, but moreover a foundation
in immutable divine right not subject to alteration by the civil
magistrate.[79]

However, since Mosheim is seeking to persuade an enlightened audience, he must first demonstrate his good faith: before pressing his

---

[77] Mosheim, *ED*, pp. 575-602, 880-81; Peters, pp. 20, 125-27.—Mosheim avoids both
the Roman Catholic claim that the eternal right to rule in the church belongs to the hierarchy and the sectarian and natural law view of the church as a purely human arrangement
deprived of direct connection with what occurs between God and the human soul.
[78] It should be noted that Hobbes and Thomasius denied that the Christian ministry
was instituted by Jesus Christ, whereas Mosheim upholds this claim. See Peters, p. 20;
Mosheim, *KR*, p. 273; pp. 274, 277. On the necessity of external means of salvation, see
Mosheim, *SL*, 3:39-99; Peters, pp. 125-27; Mosheim, *Institutes*, trans. Murdock, 1:84;
Mosheim, *Anweisung erbaulich zu predigen*, ed. Windheim (Erlangen, 1763), pp. 29-30
(hereafter: Mosheim, *AP*).
[79] Mosheim, *KR*, pp. 9, 15-16, 220, 227, 563.

clericalist juridical claims, he must first show that he is truly enlightened—that he does not represent unreconstructed Lutheran Orthodoxy with a simple assertion of clerical primacy on the bare basis of divine right. Mosheim must make some concessions.

Mosheim's first juridical concession to the natural law party is to allow that, since the church as a society has a peculiar (i.e. an inner) nature, therefore the power of the church should rightly be restricted to inward persuasion: external compulsion of the sort exercised by Lutheran Orthodoxy in co-operation with the secular arm has rightly been abandoned by the natural law party. Mosheim then concedes the ultimate unimportance of external, ''Neoplatonic'' ceremonies, agreeing with critics of Orthodoxy that the important thing is inward worship consisting of fear, love, and reverence toward God so as to minimize the chance for the clergy's obtaining by its manipulation of ceremonies an irrational hold over the laity. Likewise Mosheim concedes that too often in the past the clergy have misused their authority by furthering controversies over metaphysics, dogmatics, and ceremonies, at times even leading to civil strife. Mosheim condemns this, and with it the notion that clerical exemption from secular jurisdiction and from regular taxation can exist by divine right; they are to be defended only on the basis of human right. In addition, Mosheim agrees with the territorialists that the only valid distinction between clergy and laity is one between teachers and learners: no divinely-constituted priestly caste of intermediaries between God and man (or a Protestant counterpart to it) is to be allowed. Finally, in a *captatio benevolentiae* Mosheim concedes that a certain demoting of the status of the clerical estate is advisable, in that it is proper to accord to the temporal power far-reaching rights of supervision over church and clergy by way of preventing religious civil war.[80]

This final concession satisfies the demand of the secularist party for specific guarantees against ecclesiastical incitement to a renewal of the Thirty Years' War. However Mosheim's way of doing this provides at the same time the opening for the juridical reassertion of the rights pertaining to the institutional church. For Mosheim the collegialist satisfies the secularist demands by conferring on the temporal government *two* entirely distinct sets of juridical rights. Here he follows the earlier example

---

[80] For all this see Mosheim, *ED*, p. 879; Mosheim, *PT*, pp. 13-14; Mosheim, *SL*, 5:73, 395-442; Peters, p. 24; Mosheim, *SL*, 1:460 and Glawe, p. 162; Mosheim, *KR*, pp. 253, 258, 270, 308; Mosheim, *Heilige Reden*, 3. Theil, pp. 1299-1300; Mosheim, *KR*, pp. 106, 324, 486 and on tax-exemption pp. 323-25 and n. 57, pp. 325-27 and also n. 58, p. 327; also *KR*, pp. 528-29; Werner Elert, *Morphologie des Luthertums* (Munich, 1931; reprint ed., Munich, 1965), 1:297-335; 2:49-64; Mosheim, *KR*, pp. 273-74; also *KR*, pp. 514-17; cf. F. Edward Cranz, *An Essay on the Development of Luther's Thought* (Cambridge, Mass., 1959), p. 156, n. 135.

of the Dutch collegialists, who had distinguished between the inner rights pertaining to the church as a society (e.g., the rights of preaching the word, administering the sacraments, and selecting the clergy) and the sovereign's ecclesiastical rights or *jus majestatis sacrum circa sacra, non in sacris* (the civil magistrate's right to administer the external affairs of the church in their connection with civil matters).[81] This distinction as employed by the Dutch had been used to preserve the autonomy of the church as a religious institution. In this connection the collegialists first argued on the basis of natural law, holding that the nature of the state's power (commanding) prevented it from reaching into the religious sphere (persuasion). Then they contended that the episcopal powers that had devolved upon the sovereign after the wars of religion could not extend to the internal affairs of the church because such an extension was contradictory to revealed divine law; consequently, the magistrate exercised authority over "internal" ecclesiastical matters only on the basis of human (i.e., ecclesiastically delegated and thus potentially revocable), not divine, right. Thus the collegialist defense from the start preserved ecclesiastical rights by an appeal to divine right (positive doctrine and law derived from scriptural revelation as it had been historically interpreted) in order to counteract the conclusions reached by such proponents of secularized natural law as Grotius. This collegialist point of view was to become dominant in Germany due to the efforts of Mosheim and Georg Ludwig Böhmer (1715-1797) at Göttingen and Christoph Matthaeus Pfaff (1686-1760) at Tübingen.[82]

Mosheim employs the distinction between the sovereign's own *jus circa sacra* and the delegation of collegial rights to the sovereign so as to protect the rights of the church. To begin with, whereas Hobbes had held that the *jura circa sacra* pertain to the prince by divine right, Mosheim argues the collegialist view that they do so only because reason and good order demand it—that is, the prince possesses them simply by human right. Only on this potentially mutable basis can the prince claim to decide whether a particular church will be tolerated, require churches to submit their confessions of faith for inspection so as to determine whether their doctrine might lead to rebellion, and inspect and perhaps regulate church discipline and worship to protect the public welfare.[83]

In dealing with the internal, collegial rights of the church Mosheim shows, not only that one can theoretically restrict the nature and extent of

---

[81] Bohatec, pp. 39-40, 34, 103-4.

[82] Stephan and Leube, p. 31.

[83] Mosheim, *KR*, pp. 514-17; cf. 533-34 with 594-95; Martin Heckel, "Ius circa Sacra," *RGG*, 3rd ed. (Tübingen, 1959), 3: cols. 1073-74. Also Mosheim, *KR*, pp. 567, 573, 563, 580-86; and Thomas Hobbes, *Leviathan*, 3.42; 2.18; 3.35; 3.41; and Mosheim, *KR*, p. 214.

the prince's claim to rights in ecclesiastical affairs, but also that one can defend the church's claim to its own domain of rights founded on an authority higher than the prince's claim on the church. Mosheim manages to do this although he must admit that the content of the collegial rights cannot be readily listed since it varies according to territory. Mosheim nonetheless argues that only *certain* of the church's collegial or internal religious rights are among those collegial rights that may by custom be delegated to the prince for his administration. Thus Mosheim begins with the assertion that certain other of the collegial rights, including the right of the congregation to call its own pastor, should be numbered among the inalienable rights *not* susceptible of delegation to the prince.[84]

There follows Mosheim's detailed argument elevating the authority of the church in ecclesiastical affairs over that of the prince. Hobbes and the natural law school had contended that, while "the pastoral authority of sovereigns only is *jure divino*," on the other hand "that of other [*sic*] pastors is *jure civili*."[85] As mentioned above, Mosheim denies this. According to Mosheim, the prince's right to administer some of the delegated (alienable) collegial rights (as well as his *jura circa sacra*) is founded only on a claim *de jure humano*. Specifically, the prince's authority over delegated collegial rights is held to be merely a concession by the church. Thus Mosheim's system is a direct assault on that of Hobbes and Thomasius; he rejects as pernicious the Thomasian derivation of princely ecclesiastical rights from the mere fact of sovereignty. Far from allowing this, Mosheim insists that the church has a right, through the clerical members of the consistory, to participate in the administration of even the sovereign's *jura circa sacra*. Moreover, Mosheim points out, according to the Peace of Westphalia and the opinions of the Lutheran theologians, the church has the right (*jus retrahendi*) of reclaiming all of even the *jura circa sacra* in the event the prince should administer them to the disadvantage of the church.[86]

Mosheim's presentation of the church's collegial rights makes a powerful assault on territorialism. Against the Hobbesian claim that the rights of the clergy can be established only *jure civili*, and not by divine right,

---

[84] Cf. Mosheim, *KR*, p. 563 on inalienable rights.

[85] See esp. Hobbes, *Leviathan*, 3.42.

[86] Mosheim, *KR*, pp. 214, 579-80, 586, 576, 565, 564, 566-79; *KR*, p. 211, 585-606. Note *KR*, pp. 585-86 and also n. 30 there: "Sollte es aber geschehen daß ein Landesherr sein Jus circa Sacra zum Nachtheil der Kirche gebrauchte: so wird niemand läugnen daß die Gemeinde das Jus retrahendi habe"; and with reference to the same right: "Diese ist selbst dem Westphälischen Frieden gemäß, denn das Instrum. pacis Osnabr. Art. V. n. 16 §. 48 schränkt die geistliche Gerichtbarkeit nach den Bekenntnissen der Unterthanen an, und verstattet denselben eine völlige Gewissensfreyheit."

Mosheim sets a counterclaim: the church possesses certain *divinely-instituted* rights. These include the rights of congregations to call a pastor, to provide for public worship, to set up confessions of faith, and to exercise discipline. Since the rights are of divine institution, they are held to be immutable and are accorded a foundation exceeding in status the purely human foundation given to the prince's potentially mutable administration of the *jura circa sacra*.[87]

At the same time, since Mosheim is trying to persuade an enlightened public, he must provide a defense of the church's rights on the basis of reason alone. He furnishes an additional list of the church's collegial rights on the basis of reason, roughly coinciding with the list of divinely instituted rights. Enumerated here are the church's right to make laws for itself through synods, to call pastors and teachers, to establish doctrinal standards, to administer its affairs, to collect money, and to assemble regularly.[88]

Noteworthy here is the way in which the first of the rights asserted on the basis of reason constitutes a denial of the Thomasian claim that the church as an entity distinct from the state has no authority to give itself laws. Since Mosheim accords to the prince as governor of the church's external affairs no more than a foundation in human right, and since the same foundation in human right is ascribed to the church's authority to give itself laws for the regulation of its internal affairs, and as Mosheim elsewhere provides a defense in the divine right of revelation for the church's rights: it is clear that Mosheim refuses to allow the church as an institution serving a religious purpose to be subjected to the temporal power. This refusal is grounded in Mosheim's argument that both sources of law, reason and revelation, agree in refuting the radical territorialism of Thomasius.

Mosheim states that he undertook this refutation of Hobbes and Thomasius as a result of a growing conviction among the clergy that the study of church law could not safely be left to the jurists. He declares that, if the rights of the church are to be preserved and defended, they must first be studied and given a systematic basis. No one, he adds, will contest the practical utility of such a study under existing circumstances.[89]

Plainly Mosheim intended to encourage his students to undertake the defense at law of the church's traditional rights should they be attacked. Below we shall see that the churchmen of the later Enlightenment did not

---

[87] Mosheim, *KR*, p. 426 and pp. 345, 362, 368, 369, 395; cf. pp. 215-16.

[88] Mosheim, *KR*, pp. 10, 213-14, 195, 441-55, 37, 68, 331, 338, 397, and 514; cf. Bienert, e.g., pp. 21-23.

[89] Mosheim, *KR*, "Einleitung," pp. 1-2.

hesitate to threaten litigation when faced with governmental attempts to realize the Thomasian program for the subjection of the clergy to secular authority. Mosheim's readiness to recommend such a tactic, and the readiness of later churchmen to follow this suggestion, shows how many Enlightenment churchmen continued to behave as members of a constituted body within the Old Régime even during the "Age of Absolutism." For, as recent research emphasizes, the defense of corporate self-interest by means of the threat of litigation was one of the main characteristics of the struggle between particularism and centralism in the eighteenth century.[90] In such tugs of war, and not in dramatic confrontations, is to be found the characteristic method of "resistance to authority" in the German version of the Old Régime.

Mosheim's refutation of the secularist claim that the identity and functioning of the clergy ought to be revised so as to transform the clergy into servants of the temporal power necessitated Mosheim's moving from the domain of theory into that of practice. For here he had to make suggestions regarding the curriculum of theological study and the condition of the parish clergy. The first kind of practical suggestion (curricular) was required because Pietist, sectarian, and Enlightenment writers now denied the once-axiomatic necessity of equipping clergy with the traditional metaphysical and theological tools. It and the second kind of practical proposal for reform of financial conditions among parish clergy were both necessary so as to improve a clerical image harmed by generations of decrying of the clergy as deceivers of the people, purveyors of superstition, exploiters moved by greed and immorality, betrayers of the state, and ignorant retarders of progress. For the currency of these criticisms had long since made the clergy objects of secularizing proposals aimed at depriving them of financial and legal autonomy who were so disheartened that they could scarcely function effectively.

Mosheim's two linked varieties of practical reform are a direct outgrowth of his theology of the Christian ministry. Though in classic Enlightenment fashion the didactic element is important in Mosheim's view of the ministry, and though the pastoral, proclamatory, and priestly components of ministry are perhaps less important than had traditionally been the case, nonetheless it would be mistaken to suggest that in Mosheim's *theology* of the Christian ministry the didactic is the central concept.[91] In fact Mosheim employs a wide variety of terms other than those of a didactic nature for the clergy, and in his dogmatic system he uses only *one* central term for the clergyman:

---

[90] Rudolf Vierhaus, "Land, Staat und Reich in der politischen Vorstellungswelt deutscher Landstände im 18. Jahrhundert," *Historische Zeitschrift* 223 (1976): 48.

[91] Cf. Mosheim, *AA*, pp. 7-13; *SL*, 1:529-33; *KR*, pp. 312-14.

> The *minister* [emphasis supplied] is a man, called mediately by God, for the purpose of publicly expounding and interpreting the laws of Christ, and for exhorting and encouraging the citizens in Christ's Kingdom to obedience in faith and morals, so that in their assemblies all things are done as the laws of the church intend.[92]

The importance of this term "minister" is confirmed by the frequency with which Mosheim employs elsewhere the German equivalent to the Latin, namely *Diener* ("servant" or "helper"). Mosheim speaks of the servants of God, of the Gospel, of the Kingdom of Christ, of the Lord, and of Jesus.[93] Indeed, it would appear that the fact that "minister" requires qualification (service of or to someone) is what makes the term so attractive to Mosheim: in using the term one must state unequivocally whose servants the clergy are—and by implication, whose they are *not*. Getting this point straight was the goal in Mosheim's lectures on church law, which attack the Thomasian plan to transform "the servants of the gospel into temporal servants."[94]

In order to insure that the clergy be conceived as servants of the gospel Mosheim defines the purpose of the Christian ministry precisely. For him the main purpose of the parish ministry is the traditional cure of souls, that is, their conversion and preparation for eternal bliss by use of the supernaturally efficacious word of God so as to instruct the understanding and move the will. Since Mosheim moves within the traditional framework of a theology based on the idea of an eternal and personal God external to the created universe, Mosheim can elsewhere state Christian ministers can "have no other purpose" than laboring toward the reconciliation of sinful mankind with a perfect God; for this purpose Jesus Christ instituted the ministry.[95]

In order plausibly to defend the transcendent character and purpose of the ministry in an age of Enlightenment, Mosheim must however make certain concessions. Having upheld the divine institution by Jesus Christ and the consequent dignity of the clerical office,[96] Mosheim finds it wise to repudiate the Orthodox claim that the clergy participate in a divine or quasi-priestly character derived from intermediation between God and humanity.[97] As the pastor is no longer to be regarded as a direct instru-

---

[92] Mosheim, *ED*, p. 889.

[93] Mosheim, *AA*, p. 246; *KR*, pp. 589-90; *SL*, 1:530-32; *PT*, pp. 12-13.

[94] Mosheim, *KR*, p. 591.

[95] Mosheim, *AA*, pp. 21, 63, 27; *PT*, pp. 12-14, 44, 70; Peters, p. 74; *AG*, p. 26; *AP*, p. 14.

[96] Mosheim, *KR*, pp. 274, 220, 227; *AP*, pp. 29-30.

[97] Cf. Mosheim, *KR*, pp. 589-91: "Wir glaubten noch [that is, Lutherans during the seventeenth century believed], die Kirche wäre hauptsächlich die Geistlichkeit, und die Diener des Evangelii wären Repräsentantes der Gemeinde. Wir hielten dafür, unsere

ment of the divinity immune from the changes and chances of temporality (unlike the angels, prophets, and apostles), the Orthodox doctrine of three divinely-instituted estates within the church, the late Orthodox doctrine of a special and perduring ministerial grace, and the exaggerated Orthodox claims regarding ordination are all abandoned. Out of apologetic necessity Mosheim holds that, although ordination is to be retained, nonetheless it has "no divine power connected with it" but is rather a "ceremonial action" that is time-conditioned and potentially dispensable.[98]

Similarly cautious is Mosheim's basically traditionalist treatment of the powers of the ministry. The minister is empowered to interpret scripture, admonish the laity concerning their duties, and administer public worship. This sober list, though less grandiose than the treatments of Orthodoxy, does contain the essentials. Elsewhere Mosheim allows a pastoral right to require the confession of sins before communion, a custom defended as useful but only of human right—for, says Mosheim, it enhances the prestige and effectiveness of the pastor. In addition, the pastoral role in enforcing church discipline (exclusion from communion) is upheld.[99]

Mosheim's defense of the divine institution and transcendent dignity of the pastoral office is closely connected with his realization that the predicament of the Christian religion in his day resulted to a considerable degree from the low esteem in which the ministry was held. Operative here was the church's difficulty in recruiting competent, well-trained, socially acceptable candidates for the ministry.[100] Both at Helmstedt and

---

Prediger wären Nachfolger der Propheten und Apostel. ..." He then continues "Daher sind verschiedene Streitigkeiten entstanden. Es sind aber diese Sätze seit funfzig Jahren also bestritten worden, daß sie itzo fast alle vertilget sind. Wir glaubten im vorigen Jahrhunderte noch daß jedweder Prediger *ein unmittelbarer Diener des Höchsten*, ein sogenanntes *Subjectum inviolabile* wäre, und daß der, welcher einen Pfarrer angriffe, sich Gotte selbst widersetzte und ihm Unrecht zufügte. Jetzt unterscheiden wir das Amt selbst, und die Person, die dieses Amt führet. Das erste oder das Amt ist *Juris divini* und ein göttliches Amt. Die Personen oder *individua* aber sind nicht unmittelbarere Diener Gottes."

[98] Mosheim, *KR*, pp. 295-98; cf. Hellmut Lieberg, *Amt und Ordination bei Luther und Melancthon* (Göttingen, 1962), p. 124.

[99] Mosheim, *ED*, pp. 886-87; *KR*, pp. 335-36, 395-97.—Mosheim concedes explicitly or implicitly that external compulsion in religious matters, the abuse of private confession, and the extreme late Orthodox position affirming objectively effective absolution are beyond defense. For Mosheim, the pastor can confer forgiveness of sins merely "conditionally," in view of true repentance. Underlying these concessions is a more general admission that in the past metaphysical dogmatics in its abstraction has been too much stressed, with the result that the clergy have overawed the laity with mystery and led polemical campaigns. See Mosheim, *PT*, pp. 13-14; *KR*, pp. 330-36. *PT*, p. 56. Cf. Christian Specht et al., *Augustana Confessio brevibus Aphorismis illustrata* (Braunschweig, 1965), p. 64.

[100] Cf. for example Mosheim, *SL*, 1:517-18.

Göttingen Mosheim issued plans for dealing with the institutional causes of this. His reform plans for theological education, for the placement of candidates, and for the financing of parish ministry are highly significant, both because they were to serve as an example to later churchmen in the Enlightenment, and because they constituted a reworking of long-standing plans for a traditionalist or particularist reform of the clergy that could serve as an attractive alternative to the territorialist plan to transform the clergy into servants of the temporal government.

Mosheim's reform plans built upon a deeply-rooted tradition of thinking about how the reform of the clergy should be carried out. This tradition may be called particularist, for its presupposed that the functioning of the clergy ought to serve ends peculiar to the church as a distinct institution and the clergy as a corporate body—and not chiefly the ends defined by spokesmen for the central state. Particularist reform planning had from the days of Calixt rested on the assumption that functional qualification for membership in the clerical estate required a certain kind of education—the study of metaphysically-based doctrinal theology, biblical exegesis of the original text, and training in the practice of the pastoral calling itself (preaching, teaching, cure of souls, church administration). The central place of this kind of study, and the "intellectualism" inherent in the academic training in such an approach would eventually be called into question by spokesmen for the cameralistic ideology of utilitarian absolutism in the eighteenth century.

The Protestant theological faculties had in the sixteenth and seventeenth centuries assumed from the medieval bishops the role of guarantors of theological orthodoxy. Consequently the Protestant *clerical* estate of the Old Régime regarded itself as part of the larger *learned* estate.[101] This attitude was the most basic ingredient in Protestant clerical identity: the clergy constituted a corporation or guild composed of university-trained, Latin-reading professionals, chiefly occupied with the study of religious doctrine, and further set off by the right of trial in special courts and by the enjoyment of privileges. It was above all the possession of a

---

[101] See for example in Johann Heinrich Zedler, "Stand, Zustand, Stand der Menschen, oder Personen," *Universal-Lexicon* (Leipzig and Halle, 1741-44), 39: col. 1097: "Indessen werden gemeiniglich alle Stände bekanntermassen in drey Haupt-Stände getheilet, in den Lehr- oder Geistlichen, Wehr- oder Obrigkeitlichen, und Nehr- oder Bürgerlichen und Bauer-Stand; ... Abermahl theilet man ... die Gelehrte in Geistliche, Juristen, und Medicos." Here a division of the learned estate according to the body of knowledge peculiar to each subdivision is clearly implied. On the learning peculiar to the clerical estate, that is, on the rigorous philological and metaphysico-doctrinal training traditionally presupposed as the condition for membership in the Protestant clerical estate before the onset of cameralistic Enlightenment, see "Prediger" and "Predigtamt," in Zedler, 24: cols. 241-46; 269-79.

special kind of learning (in religious doctrine and biblical exegesis) that constituted the clerical identity.

This traditional identity, stressing learning and the divine institution of the clerical estate,[102] was deeply rooted in the Welf territories. Its intellectualism had been enhanced by the development of the Helmstedt theological tradition, which had been elaborated by Calixt with the intention of providing an elitist ideology for the training and legitimation of a clerical leadership that could be assured of preponderance over the temporal government in all matters of ecclesiastical life and order.[103]

In order to back up this approach, which assigned external church government to the clergy instead of to the prince, Calixt had innovated by distinguishing ecclesiastical from academic theology. Ecclesiastical theology, for students aiming at the parish, would consist of a two-year survey of the faith and the scriptural basis for it, giving only slight attention to the church fathers and the intricacies of polemical theology. Academic theology, on the other hand, was intended for professors of theology and church administrators, who together were to provide church leadership and the defense of the true faith in public controversy. This program of study would last up to twelve years, allowing exhaustive study of dogma, patristics, and polemics. Calixt further elaborated this scheme so as to distinguish three categories (*Gattungen*) of theologically-trained persons, two at the extremes of academic and parish-oriented theology, the third occupying a middle position designed for urban congregations.[104]

The conception of the clerical estate in these plans is thoroughly elitist. This elitism extends to Calixt's conception of all grades of the clergy: the Lutheran pastorate, itself an elite within society, is to be arrayed into a hierarchy. Rank within it is to depend, not on sacramental consecration, but on intellectual qualifications and academic training so that the church will receive leadership capable of defending its interests. With the spread of territorialist ideas this clerical elitism was not abandoned; rather did the continuators of the Calixtine tradition offset the loss of clerical influence over public affairs by grafting Calixt's ideas about professional training onto another set of traditional ideas. The stem onto

---

[102] Emil Sehling, ed., *Die evangelischen Kirchenordnungen des XVI. Jahrhunderts*, 6.1. no. 1, *Niedersachsen. Die Welfischen Lände* (Tübingen, 1955), p. 43 and p. 299, showing that the divine institution of the three estates in society (''oberkeit ... predigampt ... und ... ehestand'') was accepted from the sixteenth century in Northwest Germany; cf. Beste, *Geschichte*, pp. 83-90.

[103] Cf. Wallmann, *Theologiebegriff*; background in Ernst Ludwig Theodor Henke, *Georg Calixtus und seine Zeit*, 2 vols. (Halle, 1853-60).

[104] Wallmann, *Theologiebegriff*, pp. 148-61; E. L. Henke, 1:331; Calixt, *Gründliche Widerlegung*, 2:337-40.

which the Calixtine ideas were grafted was the notion that the surviving medieval cloisters could serve a justified and important function within Lutheranism. This point was argued by the influential Hannoverian churchman Justus Gesenius (d. 1673), a student of Calixt. He held that because of poor preparation and incompetence the clergy were held in ever-lower esteem, and that the answer lay in a reform of theological education to be effected by the establishment of seminaries apart from the universities—located, that is, in cloisters, where learning, piety, and practical training could be furthered among candidates who had finished their university study.[105]

These suggestions were then put into practice in Northwest Germany. The prime mover in Electoral Hannover in its short-lived absolutist phase was the Calixtine theologian and particularist churchman Gerard Wolter Molanus (d. 1722), who consistently upheld a rigorously episcopalist standpoint against all the encroachments of territorialism, and who allied with the assemblies of estates to defend church rights against the new claims made by the Electors of Hannover. Under the leadership of Molanus as abbot of Cloister Loccum the beginning was made in turning Loccum into a center for constantly training two to four future leaders of the church along elitist lines. Other plans from this period in the Electorate called for the establishment of regional seminaries to give theological candidates post-university practical training. In imitation of the plans at Loccum there was issued in 1690 a document setting up Cloister Riddagshausen (outside the city of Braunschweig) as the first true seminary for pastors in the history of the Protestant church. This institution, which was designed to train up to twelve candidates at a time for leadership positions in the church of Braunschweig-Wolfenbüttel, had as its further goal the raising of the prestige of the clerical estate and the creation of churchmen able to defend ecclesiastical self-interest. Rigorous academic requirements and high standards of discipline at Riddagshausen combined to create a strong clericalist *esprit de corps* among future churchmen well educated in dogmatic, confessional, and exegetical theology of the traditional variety.[106]

---

[105] Wallmann, *Theologiebegriff*, p. 161; Carl Bertheau, "Gesenius, Justus," *PRE*, 3rd ed. (Leipzig, 1899), 6:622-24; Justus Gesenius, "Vorrede," in his *Fest-Predigten: Erster Theil* (Helmstedt, 1664), fols.):(iii verso -):():(ii recto.

[106] Heinz Weideman, *Gerard Wolter Molanus* (Göttingen, 1925, 1929), 1:47-96; 2:1-29; Christoph Erich Weidemann and Friedrich Burchard Köster, *Geschichte des Klosters Loccum* (Göttingen, 1822); Friedrich Schultzen, *Zum Jubiläum des Klosters Loccum* (Hannover, 1913); J. Feltrup, "Zur Geschichte des Predigerseminars Hannover-Erichsburg," *ZGNK*, 29/39 (1924-25): 1-2; Christian Specht, *Christliche Leich-Predigt ... Bey Christlicher Bestattung Des ... Herrn Johannis Lucae Pestorfen* (Braunschweig, 1695); Johann Georg Justus

The creation of seminaries at Loccum and Riddagshausen should be seen as part of a particularist reform movement closely akin to the more general belief in much of Germany that the welfare of the Holy Roman Empire depended on the reform and rejuvenation of the corporations, assemblies of estates, law courts, and other components of pre-absolutist society. It should furthermore be remembered that clerical particularism of this kind, often taking the form of anticentralist alliances between the late Orthodox clergy and assemblies of estates, was a feature in many territories of Germany during the seventeenth and eighteenth centuries.[107]

Mosheim's plans for Enlightenment reform bear a similar elitist stamp in their stress on separation from the world and on rigorous examination before placement. His general hope was to bring about an augmentation of the prestige, independence, and well-being of the clergy that would in turn facilitate a renewal of religion; this augmentation was to be effected by persuading the prince to reorganize the resources of the realm to effect the reforms necessary to protect the particularist self-interest of the clergy.

Mosheim's program takes the form of an "imaginary picture" of what might be done by a mythical prince. Its main features may be summarized:[108]

(a) In future parents alone will not determine whether their sons study theology; instead a committee of six experienced and pious men will screen all applicants, investigating mind and heart. Those who qualify will undergo a rigorous preparation, set apart from others so as to acquire retiring and quiet habits.

(b) No one is to be admitted to the theological curriculum who has not attained the eighteenth year and acquired the rudiments of learning.

(c) Four years of study in theology and other fields is expected during the university stay.

(d) At the university future clergymen are to be divided into three categories (*Gattungen*) according to the intensity of their academic preparation. Though Mosheim follows Calixt's lead in proposing that those destined for rural parishes undergo a less intense academic train-

---

Ballenstedt, *Beiträge zur Geschichte unsers Landes. Zweites Stück. Geschichte des Klosters Riddagshausen* (Schöningen, 1809), pp. 125-37; Johannes Beste, "Das Predigerseminar zu Riddagshausen," *ZGNK* 10 (1905): 203-17; Johann Georg Hagemann, *Oratio secularis de beneficiis coenobio Riddagshusano* (Braunschweig, ca. 1717); Philip Julius Rehtmeyer, *Historiae ecclesiastica inclytae urbis Brunsvigae, Pars. V. Supplementa* (Braunschweig, 1720); "Fürstliche Verordnung, Die Beförderung der Closter-Collegiaten zum Predig-Ambt betreffend [February 28, 1704]," in *Erneuerte Kirchen-Ordnung ... Anton Ulrichs, Erster Teil* (Braunschweig, 1709); reprint edition, Braunschweig, 1862), pp. 147-49; Specht, *Augustana*.

[107] The studies by Reill and by Greschat on Löscher should be kept in mind here.

[108] Summarizing Mosheim, *SL*, 1:520-25; cf. Mosheim, *AG*, pp. 30-32; 170-84.

ing, he has in fact made the demands for *all* more rigorous; for, unlike Calixt, who required only two years, Mosheim requires four years at the university. Furthermore, Mosheim, unlike Calixt, expects the entirety of the parish clergy to acquire a working knowledge of the ancient languages and of the basis of doctrinal theology in metaphysics and scholasticism which, in Mosheim's opinion, was necessary if the parish clergy were to conduct effective apologetic.[109] Furthermore, Mosheim requires practical training in preaching, catechetical instruction, and pastoral care of the sick. The result is that all branches of the theological calling as reformed by Mosheim would constitute an elite within society led by an inner elite of academic theologians.

(e) By means of supervision of clothing, morals, and conduct, the clergy will from their earliest years acquire a strong *esprit de corps*.

(f) In order to round off the training of all branches of the clergy, all who expect a post under princely patronage are to spend time in post-university seminaries on the lines of Loccum and Riddagshausen.

(g) Placement to posts under princely patronage is to take into account the kind and intensity of academic training received by the candidate.

These proposals represent an effort to put the resources of the central government behind clericalist self-interest. Not only do they call for support of seminaries with public tax monies, but they also provide life-long tenure for clergymen—a guarantee against that precarious tenure advocated by Thomasius.

Closely related are Mosheim's plans for insuring that the clergy once in the field will be well-provided for, insuring that the prestige of the clergy will thereby be gradually raised. In putting forward plans of this kind Mosheim hopes to recruit in future persons of a higher social standing (and thus of a more independent disposition) to the clergy.[110] In fact, these must be read as a slap at absolutism, for Mosheim states that the existing serious financial problems of the Protestant clergy result from the secularization of ecclesiastical property and the temporal government's curtailment of historic clerical rights and privileges. As a result of this loss of financial independence in the face of the growing power of the central state, the clergy are threatened with a total loss of moral authority.[111]

---

[109] On radical Pietist opposition to Latin in the theological curriculum, and Mosheim's opinion that its study was necessary if the parish clergy were in future to be reckoned among the learned ("den Gelehrten"), see Mosheim, *AG*, pp. 31-32.

[110] Cf. Mosheim, *SL*, 1:525-26; *KR*, p. 604.

[111] See Mosheim, *SL*, 1:529; on Mosheim's criticism of pressures on the parish clergy to engage in agriculture for their support rather than caring for their congregations, and for Mosheim's argument that clerical poverty results in lay contempt for the clergy, see *SL*, 1:528-31. Closely connected is Mosheim's campaign against patronage of pulpits by the territorial lord and in favor of augmenting the congregation's say in the choice of the

The only cure, in Mosheim's view, lies in a reduction of courtly and secular bureaucratic expenses so as to free more resources for the pay of an independent-minded clergy. Such a redistribution of resources is, according to Mosheim, the only answer: for the existing burden of taxation is as heavy as the subjects can bear.[112]

Clearly for Mosheim the plans for the education of future clergy constitute the most important element in professional reform. The full significance of those plans was to be discovered only in the later Enlightenment, after Mosheim's death. Only then would their value as examples of defensive particularist reform become clear. For in the course of the centralist Enlightenment the theoreticians of the absolutist state put forward a two-part program for dealing with pre-absolutist society. In the first or negative phase,[113] the traditional corporate bodies were to be stripped of the financial and juridical basis of their existence independent of the central state: guilds, nobles, and clergy were to be rendered dependent on the good will of the prince and hence subservient to him. Then, in the second or positive phase,[114] these groups were to be assimilated to the structure of the absolute state itself—that is, made a part of its "machinery" so that they might perform the tasks assigned by the state. In this connection it was contended that the traditional estates in society could justify their existence only by serving a common good

---

new pastor. Cf. *KR*, p. 603: "... it is indisputable that the congregation possesses a right in the choice of the clergyman. ... Preachers who are nonetheless installed contrary to the wishes of the congregation receive little love and respect. They are regarded as creatures of the princes. ... This right to the choice of the clergyman ought according to all fairness to be extended in our churches and ought to be better arranged: for these are matters of conscience, in which no king, no monarch, no territorial lord, has a right to exercise dominion, but alone the almighty God."

[112] Mosheim, *SL*, 1:533-34.

[113] See for example Hans von Voltelini, "Die naturrechtlichen Lehren und die Reformen des 18. Jahrhunderts," *Historische Zeitschrift* 105 (1910): 65-104; F. L. Carsten, "The Defeat of the Estates of Prussia," in his *The Origins of Prussia* (Oxford, 1954), pp. 202-28; Deppermann; Carl Hinrichs, "Der Hallische Pietismus als politisch-soziale Reformbewegung des 18. Jahrhunderts," in his *Preussen als historisches Problem*, ed. Gerhard Oestreich (Berlin, 1964), pp. 171-84.

[114] Hans Rosenberg, *Bureaucracy, Aristocracy and Autocracy* (Cambridge, Mass., 1958); Hermann Weill, *Frederick the Great and Samuel von Cocceiji* (Madison, Wisc., 1961); Otto Hintze, *Die Behördenorganisation und die allgemeine Staatsverwaltung Preussens im 18. Jahrhundert* = *Acta Borussica*, 6: no. 1 (Berlin, 1901); Walter L. Dorn, "The Prussian Bureaucracy in the Eighteenth Century," *Political Science Quarterly* 46 (1931) 402-23 and 47 (1932): 75-94, 259-73; Hintze, "Die Hohenzollern und der Adel," in his *Regierung und Verwaltung*, ed. Oestreich (Göttingen, 1967), pp. 30-55; Günter Birtsch, "Zur sozialen und politischen Rolle des deutschen, vornehmlich preussischen Adels am Ende des 18. Jahrhunderts," in *Der Adel vor der Revolution*, ed. Rudolf Vierhaus (Göttingen, 1971), pp. 77-95; and Henning von Bonin, "Adel und Bürgertum in der höheren Beamtenschaft der preussischen Monarchie 1794-1806," *Jahrbuch für die Geschichte Mittel- und Ostdeutschlands* 15 (1966): 139-74; cf. Hubert C. Johnson, *Frederick the Great and his Officials* (New Haven, Conn., 1975).

defined by the spokesmen for the absolutist state. This second phase would find its most characteristic and far-reaching expression in the plans for reform of education and professional training elaborated in the latter phases of the absolutist Enlightenment. In the words of Rudolf Vierhaus:

> The concept of an education fitted to each estate was retained by enlightened absolutism in its Friderician or later phase, but it was reinterpreted for the pedagogical purposes of the state. Each citizen in the state was to receive the training which would enable him to make the greatest possible contribution to the functioning of the welfare state's economic system.[115]

This second or positive phase is especially characteristic of the mid- and late eighteenth century. It is the pedagogical counterpart to the celebrated reintegration of the Junkers into the Hohenzollern bureaucracy after they had been rendered more or less harmless. This absolutist pedagogics occasioned lengthy debates over school policy throughout the Germany of the later Enlightenment: at issue was the main purpose of education—was it to create citizens serving the state, or persons serving their own autonomous ends as members of humanity?[116] Inevitably the question was raised whether the clergyman as teacher of a moral religion was chiefly to prepare citizens for the state or men for humanity. At this point in the late-eighteenth-century debate the proponents of clerical particularism would make common cause with the defenders of the priority of the education of the man over that of the citizen, and would thus be in a position fully to appreciate the particularist or traditionalist view on reform of clerical education as it had been stated by Mosheim.

---

[115] Rudolf Vierhaus, "Bildung," in *Geschichtliche Grundbegriffe*, ed. Otto Brunner, Werner Conze, and Reinhart Koselleck (Stuttgart, 1972), 1:513.
[116] Cf. Vierhaus, "Bildung"; and Karl-Ernst Jeismann, *Das preußische Gymnasium in Staat und Gesellschaft* (Stuttgart, 1974).

CHAPTER THREE

SECULARIST PRESSURES AND PROTESTANT CLERICAL RESPONSE IN NORTHWEST GERMANY 1760-1786

1. Cameralism and Clerical Utilitarianism

In the generation after Mosheim the pressure for secularization concentrated, not on theology or legal theories of church-state relations, but on the proposals for a change in the duties of the clerical role and the training for them. To these proposals the clerical response was up to a point favorable. This response, which contrasted with the negative response to the ideas of Thomasius, earned for the ecclesiastical Enlightenment its reputation for surrendering to secularism. Though the model for ministry remained that of the teacher, what was to be taught took on an increasingly this-wordly character. Yet the total significance of this change can, as we shall see, be properly determined only once we have assessed developments continuing down to the turn of the century.

Pressing clergy toward a greater concern with this-wordly matters was pedagogical utilitarianism—the movement to reduce poverty and advance prosperity by inculcating in the idle a skill and the discipline for its use. The clergy readily became involved in this movement: they had long been active in education and poor relief; here they saw a new way to disprove the Enlightenment charge of clerical parasitism.

Proposals for utilitarian pedagogical projects were spread by spokesmen for the economic doctrines of cameralism or mercantilism associated with absolutism. They held that one must strive for economic self-sufficiency by restricting imports and by exporting manufactured goods.[1]

---

[1] The term "utilitarianism" seems the readiest designation for this movement; no connection with Bentham is implied.—On cameralism and mercantilism see for example Louise Sommer, "Cameralism," *Encyclopaedia of the Social Sciences* (New York, 1938), 3:158-61; Herman Kellenbenz, "Probleme der Merkantilismusforschung," *Comité International des Sciences Historiques*, XIIᵉ Congrès. *Rapports*, 4 (1965): 171-90; Mack Walker, *German Home Towns* (Ithaca, N.Y., 1971), pp. 145-84; Heinz Holldack, "Der Physiokratismus und die Absolute Monarchie," *Historische Zeitschrift* 145 (1931-32): 517-49; Helen P. Liebel, "Der aufgeklärte Absolutismus und die Gesellschaftskrise im Deutschland im 18. Jahrhundert," in *Absolutismus*, ed. Walther Hubatsch (Darmstadt, 1973), pp. 488-544; "Mercantilism," *Encyclopaedia Britannica*, 15th ed., 6:798. On clerical involvement: Harold J. Grimm, "Luther's Contributions to Sixteenth-Century Organization of Poor Relief," *Archive for Reformation History* 61 (1970): 222-33; Hermann Brödel, "Die Arbeits- und Industrieschulen vor Ferdinand Kindermann," *Zeitschrift für Geschichte der Erziehung und des Unterrichts* 21 (1931): 308-19; 22 (1932): 35-49; Brödel, "Braunschweigische Industrieschulpläne um 1750," *Zeitschrift für Handelsschulpädagogik* 3

Programs based on this premise were elaborated within a framework of state interventionism sanctioned by appeal to natural law thinkers such as Pufendorf, Thomasius, and Wolff. In such a way the corporate components of pre-absolutist society, formerly shielded from princely intervention, could be either eliminated or transformed into agents of the prince. Pedagogical utilitarianism implied the overriding of custom legitimated by an appeal to natural law: so arose educational programs in line with the absolutist program of depriving traditional components in society of their independence so as to transform them into parts in a political machine serving aims defined by the central government.

Particularly important were training programs to create a disciplined labor force for incipient industry.[2] In these programs the state was to serve as the ultimate co-ordinator and arbiter, even as the instigator: for cameralism depended on government leadership to bring about "proto-industrialization" in the absence of wealthy entrepreneurs. Central governments created bureaucrats, professionals, and mobile entrepreneurs symbiotic with the state in order to introduce economic and political integration. Pressures for the educated to participate in this movement came from both direct programs fostered by the state and from the cameralist ideology propagated throughout the literate classes. In view of the aim of pedagogical utilitarianism, clerical participation in it was inevitably perceived as an act of siding with political centralization in opposition to traditionalist particularism.[3]

(1931): 245-315.—The significance of such utilitarianism can best be appreciated against the background provided by Marc Raeff, "The Well-ordered Police State and the Development of Modernity in Seventeenth- and Eighteenth-Century Europe," *American Historical Review* 80 (1975): 1221-43. Raeff argues that the absolute state contributed decisively to forming the continental style of maximizing the "resources" for improvement of society's "way of life" (p. 1222). Thus the transition from "absolutism" to "Enlightenment" signifies "the transformation of felicity from a mere instrument of a transcendental political goal" into an "end" for the individual "to be achieved for its own sake" (p. 1239). See the allied work of Gerhard Oestreich on the diffusion of a new ethos of social discipline in the period of "absolutist" policy; thus Oestreich, "Eurooppalaisen Absolutismin Rakenneongelmia," *Historiallinen Aikakauskirja* 66 (1968): 234-49; also Oestreich, *Geist und Gestalt des frühmodernen Staates* (Berlin, 1969). Cf. Otto Hintze, "Calvinism and Raison d'Etat in Early Seventeenth-Century Brandenburg," *The Historical Essays of Otto Hintze*, ed. Felix Gilbert and Robert Berdahl (New York, 1975), pp. 88-154.

[2] Cf. Sommer, pp. 159-60; John C. Gagliardo, *From Pariah to Patriot* (Lexington, Ky., 1969), pp. 84-87; Reinhardt Koselleck, "Begriffsgeschichte und Sozialgeschichte," in *Historische Semantik und Begriffsgeschichte*, ed. Koselleck (Stuttgart, 1979), p. 22.

[3] Peter Kriedte et al., *Industrialisierung vor der Industrialisierung* (Göttingen, 1977); Ludwig Renatus Caradeuc de la Chalotais, *Versuch über den Kinder-Unterricht* (Göttingen and Gotha, 1771); Hans Seel, *Beiträge zur Geschichte des Begriffs einer deutschen Nationalerziehung am Ausgang des 18. Jahrhunderts* (Phil. Diss., Münster University, 1925); Enno Fooken, *Die geistliche Schulaufsicht und ihre Kritiker im 18. Jahrhundert* (Wiesbaden-Dotzheim, 1967); Hans Hubrig, *Die patriotischen Gesellschaften des 18. Jahrhunderts* (Weinheim/Bergstrasse, 1957).

Absolutist Brandenburg-Prussia pointed the way with clerical experiments in clerical utilitarianism. Important were the schools, orphanage, publishing house, and the textile and pharmaceutical factories at Pietist Halle. The Calvinist kings encouraged these ventures as a way of breaking down resistance to Hohenzollern sovereignty on the part of Orthodox Lutheran Junkers, clergy, and guilds.[4]

Significant intensification of pressure came toward the end of the Seven Years' War from the pro-Prussian writer Thomas Abbt (1738-1766). Abbt, a deist, propagandized for putting religion and the clergy in the service of the state. In his widely-read works he argued that the "general good" of society implied but a single political virtue, that defined by the prince; the self-interest of various estates must be subordinated to the general good. As a result, since every person is simply a citizen, the distinction between the traditional estates disappears. Therefore it becomes the duty of the clergy to whip up patriotic devotion in wartime so as to aid the recruiting officer. The mere preaching of repentance in the conventional style will no longer suffice.[5]

Abbt urged the clergy to fit their peacetime activities to Friderician absolutism. To aid in this Abbt put forward the concept of "merit" to categorize the contributions of various social groups to the advancement of that general good defined by the prince. This quasi-Wolffian classification of merit, inspired by the Prussian military decoration *Pour le mérite*, used its analysis to arrive at ways of moving citizens to meritorious actions. Of great, though now forgotten, influence was Abbt's four-part division of cameralistic merits into "high," "great," "beautiful" and "simple" merits.[6]

---

[4] Carl Hinrichs, *Preussentum und Pietismus* (Göttingen, 1971); Klaus Deppermann, *Der hallesche Pietismus und der preussische Staat unter Friedrich III. (I.)* (Göttingen, 1961).

[5] Dagobert de Levie, "Patriotism and Clerical Office," *Journal of the History of Ideas* 14 (1953): 622-27; F. Pressel, "Abbt," *Allgemeine Deutsche Biographie*, 1: 2-4; Oskar Claus, *Die historischpolitischen Anschauungen Thomas Abbts* (Phil. Diss., Leipzig University, 1905); Annie Bender, *Thomas Abbt* (Bonn, 1922); "Abbt," in J. S. Ersch und J. G. Gruber, eds. *Allgemeine Encyclopädie* (Leipzig, 1818), 1: 52-3; Friedrich Nicolai, *Ehrengedächtniß Herrn Thomas Abbt* (Berlin and Stettin, 1767); Otto Gruber, *Herder und Abbt* (Phil. Diss., Marburg University, 1934); Gertrud Brück, *Die Bedeutung Justus Mösers für das Leben und Denken Thomas Abbts* (Phil. Diss., Munich University, 1937); cf. Gagliardo with reference to Abbt, pp. 85-6: "One of the tactics involved in the struggle of princes to become truly sovereign ... was that of appealing to the country at large against the 'selfish' ... machinations of whatever group happened to be in the absolutist shooting-gallery at the moment. From this was developed the picture of the prince as ... an objective arbiter of interests whose goal was the welfare of all persons within his sovereign jurisdiction" measuring "institutions and ideas ... in terms of" their contribution to the general welfare "as defined by the prince." Cf. Abbt, *Vom Tode fürs Vaterland* reprinted in Fritz Brüggemann, ed., *Der Siebenjährige Krieg im Spiegel der zeitgenössischen Literatur* (Leipzig, 1935), pp. 47-94.

[6] Abbt, *Vermischte Werke, 1. Theil welcher die Abhandlung vom Verdienste enthält* (Berlin, 1768) (hereafter: Abbt, *Verdienste*), p. 190; Bender, pp. 171-75; Edmund Pentzhorn, *Thomas Abbt* (Phil. Diss., Giessen University, 1884), pp. 64-77.

According to Abbt the clergy must serve the state, not their own estate. Leaving eternal matters out of consideration, rejecting Orthodoxy and Pietism, suggesting that Christianity could if necessary be replaced by other systems of belief better able to promote war-time self-sacrifice, Abbt nonetheless hesitated to replace the clergy with lay overseers of morals. Instead he suggested that the proper response to anticlericalism was simple transformation of the clergy into guardians of morale and morality: after all, the peasants still trusted the clergy, who on that account could aid the recruiting officer more effectively than a secular functionary.[7]

The pastor thus becomes a temporal ideological officer on the assumption that the well-managed central state provides the only framework within which parishioners can unfold and develop their economic and personal potential in the face of the constraints of traditional society. For Abbt the freedom of the man (*Mensch*) is inseparably connected with the freedom of the citizen (*Bürger*); and the freedom of the man as individual can be secured only by protecting the freedom of the citizen. Abbt cannot imagine that the claims of the man may war against those of the citizen, or that under some circumstances the clergyman may do well to put service to the man above service to the citizen in order to subordinate the demands of the state.[8]

2. *Pressure and Response in Braunschweig-Wolfenbüttel*

In Braunschweig-Wolfenbüttel the government had followed policies akin to cameralism at least as early as the sixteenth century. From the Reformation on the Protestant clergy in the Welf territories had been required to read from the pulpit government orders on temporal matters ranging from begging to care of ducal mulberry trees to protect the health of silkworms. In 1748 the militaristic Karl I, sensing the economic potential of the clergy, strongly urged all preachers to take up bee-keeping. Clerical reaction was unfavorable.[9]

New pressure came from the ducal councillor Bernhard Schrader von Schliestadt (1706-73). Impressed by English and Dutch hospitals and workhouses, he proposed alternating book-learning with instruction in

---

[7] Abbt, *Verdienste*, pp. 199-201, 276-80.

[8] Abbt, *Verdienste*, p. 311.

[9] Friedrich-Karl Burmeister, *Der Merkantilismus im Lande Braunschweig-Wolfenbüttel* Wirtschafts- und Sozialwissenschaftliche Diss., Frankfurt a.M. University, 1928); Philipp Meyer, "Zur Verlesung landesherrlicher Verordnungen von den Kanzeln Niedersachsens im 16. bis 19. Jahrhundert," *JNGK* 48 (1950): 109-19; Landeskirchliches Archiv in Braunschweig, Signatur V 1177; Karl Friedrich Bege, *Uebersicht der Verordnungen* Helmstedt, 1828); on bee-keeping, see Frieda Biehringer, *Herzog Karl I von Braunschweig* (Wolfenbüttel, 1920).

useful skills (e.g., knitting)—thus anticipating the industry school pioneered in Göttingen in the 1780's. Between 1748 and 1756 Schrader applied his influence on the government in Braunschweig to urge that the ecclesiastical superintendents see to it that schools teach such skills. He arranged for the government to print a translation of an English pamphlet of 1725 arguing that the idle and orphaned be put to work in closely-regulated Christian workhouses or factories to benefit the commonwealth.[10]

The clerical reaction was mixed. For example, the translator of the pamphlet, the theologian Johann Friedrich Wilhelm Jerusalem (1709-89) himself regarded it as insignificant and translated it only at government request. Furthermore, Jerusalem himself in his capacity as a leading churchman personally promoted a far more traditionalistic, otherworldly view of clerical activity.[11]

Yet with time there occurred a *limited* reception of the calls for utilitarian reform of the clerical task among the Northwest German churchmen. Illustrative is a journal published from 1779 to 1783 by a pastor in Wolfenbüttel.[12] It presented the initial reworking of Abbt's ideas by the clergy; at this point Abbt's rhetoric of merit had not yet been used in definitions of the theological task in textbooks, nor made the organizing principle in treating the whole ministerial office.

---

[10] Brödel, "Industriepläne," pp. 246-54, 311, and p. 246 on Hannoverian parallels; Johann Friedrich Wilhelm Jerusalem, trans. *Nachricht von denen Armen- und Arbeits- oder Werck-Häusern in Engelland* (Braunschweig? 1745); Jerusalem, *Nachgelassene Schriften, Zweiter und letzter Theil* (Braunschweig, 1793). Jerusalem's introduction under Schrader's influence, fols.)( )(2 verso,)( )(3 recto and)( )(5 recto, uses the distinction between man and citizen, *Mensch* and *Bürger*, familiar since Hobbes: children cared for in workhouses grow up to be both "useful citizens" and "happy people," thus avoiding their burdening the commonwealth and their ending in hell. Yet Jerusalem avoids making the temporal component primary in ministry.—On the natural law distinction between the man as a member of human society and the citizen as a member of that civil society constituted by the state (or between the individual and the citizen as part of civil society) see Manfred Riedel, "Bürger, Staatsbürger, Bürgertum," in *Geschichtliche Grundbegriffe*, ed. Otto Brunner et al. (Stuttgart, 1972), 1:706; Jürgen Schlumbohm, *Freiheit* (Düsseldorf, 1975), pp. 119-21; Josef Bohatec, "Die Vorgeschichte der Menschen- und Bürgerrechte," in *Zur Geschichte der Erklärung der Menschenrechte*, ed. Roman Schnur (Darmstadt, 1964), pp. 268, 373-74; and Reinhart Koselleck, *Kritik und Krise* (Frankfurt a.M., 1973).

[11] Jerusalem, *Nachgelassene Schriften, 2. Theil*, pp. 157-292; cf. Fritz Meyen, "Johann Friedrich Wilhelm Jerusalem, Abt von Riddagshausen," *Braunschweigisches Jahrbuch* 53 (1972): 159-81.

[12] *Der patriotische Landprediger. Erstes Stück. Mit einer Vorrede herausgegeben vom Herrn Doktor Miller*, ed. Johann Heinrich Ress (Leipzig, 1779); *Zweites-Viertes Stück* (1780-83). See Wagenmann, "Miller," *Allgemeine Deutsche Biographie*, 21: 749-50; Franz Milske, "Joh. Peter Miller als Pädagog," (Phil. Diss., Würzburg University, 1921); Paul Zimmermann, "Ress," *Allgemeine Deutsche Biographie*, 28: 249-51. The term "patriotic" at this time implied no endorsement of chauvinism; it underscored the need for co-operation for the common good.

The journal in question was the product of collaboration between a pastor and a professor of theology. The latter, from Göttingen in Electoral Hannover, provided the theological legitimation for a limited expansion of the temporal and utilitarian component in parish ministry; the former provided details on how utilitarian principles could be put into practice. Though the pastor was from Wolfenbüttel, and though the bulk of the journal came from his pen, the clearest statement of the purpose of the journal was made by Johann Peter Miller (1725-89), professor of theology at Göttingen.[13]

Miller was an older cousin of Abbt, stamped by Swabian Pietism. From a standpoint of "moderate, tolerant Orthodoxy" that inclined toward "Latitudinarianism and Rationalism" he completed Mosheim's unfinished moral theology.[14] In 1779 he joined forces with the Wolfenbüttel churchman Johann Heinrich Ress (1732-1803) to produce a journal showing how the numerous rural clergy could introduce utilitarian activities. It was entitled *Der patriotische Landprediger*. In the introduction to its first number Miller furnished the theological justification for the enterprise.[15]

Miller's entire theology reveals how deeply affected he was by the Enlightenment charge that the clergy were harmful to human society. Yet he did not move hastily toward acceptance of Abbt's views. Even though Miller's nephew, a theology student at Göttingen in the early 1770's, reported that five out of six theology students abandoned the discipline in disgust at the bad reputation of the clergy, still Miller in his textbook on the pastoral ministry published for use at Göttingen in 1774 does not place major emphasis on temporal utility. Instead he retains the traditional emphasis on preaching, teaching, sacramental ministry, and pastoral care aimed at showing "the way through Christ's mediation" toward a blessed immortality.[16]

Important concessions to Abbt, though by no means unqualified surrender to Abbt's views, show up in Miller's introductory statement in the journal co-edited with Ress in 1779. Miller urges that the pastor cooperate with the governmental bureaucracy in imparting to the peasantry the latest methods of improving crop yield and the well-being of livestock, of modernizing care of the sick and education, and of rationalizing poor

---

[13] See n. 12 above.

[14] Cf. Wagenmann; also Mosheim, *Sitten-Lehre der Heiligen Schrift, 8. und 9. Theil, Verfasset von D. Johann Peter Miller* (Göttingen and Leipzig, 1767, 1770).

[15] Miller, "Vorrede," *Landprediger, 1. Stück*, pp. iii-xlviii.

[16] Johann Martin Miller, *Briefwechsel drey Akademischer Freunde* (Ulm, 1778-79), 1:113; Johann Peter Miller, *Ausführliche Anleitung zur ... Verwaltung des evangelischen Lehramts* (Leipzig, 1774), p. 8.

relief. The pastor should also encourage laity to undertake cameralistic and physiocratic projects for economic self-improvement. In this way the pastor can "acquire merit"—an Abbtian theme developed in Ress's section in exhaustive detail.[17]

Yet Miller's acceptance of Abbt is not unqualified and is motivated by the aim of defending traditional Christianity. Miller's view of Christianity, though affected by Reformed and Enlightenment theology, is conservative in its defining of the main goal of the church as fostering perfect blessedness in eternity. Furthermore—despite the impression given by Alexandra Schlingensiepen-Pogge that Miller's theology represents a break with the Lutheran tradition—Miller retains the Orthodox view that, since scriptural doctrines operate upon the soul with divine power, there exists a unique clerical task in ministering to the human condition by means of these doctrines.[18]

In keeping with this traditionalism, Miller develops a model of ministry preserving intact the supernatural core of traditional ministry while still allowing the pastor to undertake on a peripheral basis some of the this-worldly tasks advocated by spokesmen for absolutism. Miller carefully retains a conventional emphasis on preparing the souls of the parishioners for eternity by means of instruction in revealed divine truth.[19]

At the juncture of the this- and the other-worldly, Miller reinterprets Abbt's temporal emphases. According to Miller, pastoral involvement in agronomy can be justified as necessary on pedagogico-theological grounds. Such had been the method of Jesus Christ: showing the lowly who were oppressed by rulers how one can become "virtuous ... in this world" and "eternally blessed" in the other.[20] In order to fix the thoughts of simple people on things eternal, argues Miller, Jesus Christ first spoke with the people about things of daily life that they could readily grasp—crop yield, sheep, fishing—and only gradually led them on to

---

[17] Miller, "Vorrede," pp. xxi-xlv; for Miller's awareness of secularist criticism of the clergy (e.g., Mandeville), see Mosheim [Miller], *Sitten-Lehre, 8. Theil*, pp. 8-9, 19-29; 9. Theil, pp. 4, 13, 535; for Miller's particularist and anticentralist, anticourt interpretation of patriotism, see *Anleitung*, p. 20. On Ress see n. 23 below.

[18] Mosheim [Miller], *Sitten-Lehre, 9. Theil*, pp. 17-18; Miller, *Anleitung*, pp. 10, 23-24. The assessment by Wagenmann of Miller as traditionalist in his theology provides a valuable corrective to the misleading judgments in Alexandra Schlingensiepen-Pogge, *Das Sozialethos der Lutherischen Aufklärungstheologie* (Göttingen, 1967), p. 14, according to which Miller adopted a this-wordly view of the pastoral role. On the contrary: Miller placed a heavy stress on preparing the soul for eternity, however "optimistic" his emphasis on shaping people for temporal activity; cf. Miller, *Anleitung*, pp. 8-9. Schlingensiepen-Pogge does not perceive the apologetic purpose in expansion of temporal duties.

[19] Miller, "Vorrede," p. xxxvii; *Anleitung*, p. 10.

[20] Miller, "Vorrede," p. xxvi.

matters intangible. This was the effective way to teach that the main issue was preparing the immortal soul for eternity, and even today it must be followed by pastors: they must gain the interest and respect of the peasantry by conversing first about earthly matters so as to lead to higher things.[21]

Miller intended then to defend the other-wordly, biblically-oriented content of Christianity, and with it the core of the traditional role of the clergyman. He did not wish to transform the Christian religion into a subdivision of cameralistics or the pastor into a state-paid jack-of-all-trades. The notion long current in scholarship that such was the real aim of the ecclesiastical Enlightenment cannot be supported by invoking the example of Miller, who rather envisioned such a possibility only to inveigh against it.[22]

For the churchman Miller, tied to the historic identity and self-interest of his estate, the claim that the clergy must improve their image by greater utilitarian involvement could be made with sincerity. His more secular relative Abbt, however, used this claim as a pretext for proposing that the clergy become instruments of the state. Thus mere use of the rhetoric of utilitarianism in itself provides no sure index of how "secularized" the writer in question has become.

Similarly traditionalistic in total emphasis was the body of the journal written by Miller's co-worker Ress in Wolfenbüttel. Though Ress makes heavy use of the Abbtian concept of merit, he evidently does so only to show the clergy how by greater involvement in agricultural education they can make an apology for their estate in an age of anticlericalism. He at no point, however, rejects the traditional concept of the clergy as a group chiefly devoted to furthering eternal salvation.[23]

3. Pressure and Response in Electoral Hannover

The economic difficulties after the Seven Years' War led to many cameralistic and physiocratic attempts at amelioration. At Celle in the

---

[21] Miller, "Vorrede," pp. xxvi-xxxvi; for Miller's apologetic aim in urging pastors to counter by deeds the Enlightenment charge that the pursuit of clerical self-interest necessarily undermines state and society, see Mosheim [Miller], Sitten-Lehre, 8. Theil, p. 9; 9. Theil, pp. 7-21 [first sequence of pp.].

[22] For Miller's supernaturalistic view of Christianity see for example Anleitung, pp. 23-24. For the call made in 1773 to abolish the paid clergy in hope of replacing them with utilitarian-oriented lay preachers, see Karl Christoph Reiche, Ueber das Schädliche des Predigerordens und dessen Abänderung (Brandenburg, 1773). For Miller's rejection of this "new religion" in favor of the authoritative biblical word of God, see Miller, "Vorrede," pp. xxxvi-xl.

[23] See esp. Ress in Landprediger, 1. Stück; cf. on Ress's conservative theology Wolfgang Kröger, "Das Publikum als Richter" (Phil. Diss., Tübingen University, 1977), pp. 79-107.

electorate the churchman Johann Friedrich Jacobi (1712-91) set an example of clerical participation in agricultural education and experimentation. This, coupled with his measured scepticism concerning the value of intensive philological study in the theological curriculum, marks him as a forerunner of later radical trands—though his own view of the clerical office was other-wordly in emphasis.[24]

More important for the future were developments in the university town of Göttingen. Despite its importance as a center of political particularism, it was still suited for experimentation with clerical utilitarianism. The decay of traditional religiosity was observed by a theology professor there, who in 1763 noted that the mere mention of Pietist rhetoric about washing souls in the Blood of the Lamb brought about in polite society a "general hush and a rolling of the eyes"; faces reddened when religion had to be mentioned.[25] As attendance at the university church declined during the later Enlightenment, the building itself was secularized into a wing of the library.[26]

Readiness for utilitarian experimentation was heightened by the declining appeal of theology as an academic career. As for the Göttingen theology, it will suffice to remark that, despite its seeming conservatism, it provided ample scope for experimentation with utilitarianism. Though Göttingen theologians were noted for their interest in supernaturalistic apologetics linked to biblical revelation, still the so-called "biblical" theology at Göttingen in the later eighteenth century moved progressively closer to abandoning the normative character of scripture altogether. In the 1790's some of the Göttingen theologians painlessly moved into a vaguely supernaturalistic Rationalism or a mitigated Kantianism.[27]

Furthermore, governmental efforts in the 1730's to attract more well-to-do students to theology had failed, and with them the hope of raising the intellectual level of the clerical estate: the impoverished and poorly educated were those attracted by the low cost of theological study. Those who could do otherwise escaped, leaving behind a general student body that poked fun at both traditional and Enlightenment sermons and theology students who were troubled because of the prevalent belief that the clerical estate was a "plot" against humanity.[28]

---

[24] On Jacobi see Appendix B.

[25] Johann David Heilmann, *Der Prediger und Seine Zuhörer* (Göttingen, 1763), pp. 45-46.

[26] Philipp Meyer, ed., *Die Pastoren der Landeskirchen Hannovers* (Göttingen, 1941), 1:161.

[27] Gotthilf Traugott Zachariä, *Biblische Theologie* (1771-75), 1:175 as cited in Hans W. Frei, *The Eclipse of Biblical Narrative* (New Haven, Conn., 1974), p. 170; Johannes Meyer, *Kirchengeschichte Niedersachsens* (Göttingen, 1939), pp. 173-74; Johannes Meyer, "Geschichte der Göttinger theologischen Fakultät," *ZGNK* 42 (1937): 9, 29-30, 38-40.

[28] On governmental hopes for Göttingen see Reinhardt Wittram, *Die Universität und ihre Fakultäten* (Göttingen, 1962), pp. 7-8; cf. E. F. Rössler, *Die Gründung der Universität Göt-*

The low quality of the theology students aroused alarm. In 1750 and 1788 we find official complaints of a decline in philological and theological skills.[29] The Göttingen theologian Gottfried Less in 1790 saw his students as poorly educated, recruited only from the lowest social orders, untalented: whereas formerly the sons of country preachers had been numerous, now they do not follow their fathers' profession. They are scared away by theological chaos and the general contempt for theology. Those who do matriculate in theology neglect thorough study. Modern criticism destroys the old faith. The ranks of the clergy can be filled only with the ignorant, arrogant, and base, resulting in universal bitterness toward religion and hatred of the clergy.[30]

Two roads toward reform presented themselves: one stressing "practical" or utilitarian skills, another emphasizing refurbished traditionalist academic preparation. The former was first taken; by further lowering the academic level it prepared the way for extreme outcries such as that of Less in 1790. Once the theologians and churchmen had satisfied themselves that utilitarian reform was of only limited use for their purposes, they turned in the second direction—one looking back to Mosheim. Here we shall concentrate on the "practical" reform proposals at Göttingen, postponing our look at the subsequent traditionalist reaction in clerical reform.

The Göttingen theologians after the Seven Years' War responded favorably to calls for a moderate increase in pastoral concern with this-worldly matters.[31] Practical experimentation had been under way since

---

tingen (Göttingen, 1855). On escape, cf. J. M. Miller, *Briefwechsel*, 1:113, 96, 311; 2:94; 1:214; 2:610.—The church in Electoral Hannover late in the eighteenth century did not want for ministerial candidates; see Ernst Brandes, "Ueber den gegenwärtigen Zustand der Universität Göttingen," *Neues Hannöversches Magazin*, Jg. 1802 (February 5, 1802), col. 235, reporting that many reached the age of 36 without a call; cf. Gottfried Less, *Ueber Christliches Lehr-Amt* (Göttingen, 1790), p. v. The percentage of the Göttingen student body enrolled in the theological faculty remained relatively constant, fluctuating from 26% in the 1760's to 28% in the 1770's to 31% in the 1780's to 21% in the 1790's, where it remained in following decades. Total average enrollment for the whole university grew from 649 in the 1760's to an average of 714 at the turn of the century; see F. Eulenburg, *Die Frequenz der deutschen Universitäten* (Leipzig, 1904), pp. 162-65, 294-301, 313. By this time Helmstedt had entered such a decline that figures for it are of little statistical significance.

[29] J. Meyer, "Facultät," p. 26; Philipp Meyer, "Die theologischen Prüfungen in den lutherischen Kirchen Calenberg-Göttingens und Lüneburgs," *JGNK* 53 (1955): 85, n. 331; Johann Christoph Salfeld, "Beförderung der humanistischen Studien," *Neue Beyträge zur Kenntniß und Verbesserung des Kirchen- und Schulwesens*, ed. J. C. Salfeld and J. P. Trefurt, 2 (Hannover, 1810): 1-55.

[30] Less, *Lehr-Amt*, pp. v-xii.

[31] Mosheim [Miller], *Sitten-Lehre, 9. Theil*, pp. 12-45; J. P. Miller, *Grundsätze eines Blühenden christlichen Staates* (Leipzig, 1773); Christian Ludwig Gerling, *Nachricht von seinen Vorlesungen über die Practische Theologie* (Göttingen, 1771), pp. 4-10; cf. also Christoph Christian Sturm and Jacob Friedrich Feddersen, *Gesellschaftliche Bemühungen, der Welt die*

Pietist students in Göttingen had begun in 1736 to imitate the Halle example. At the Göttingen orphanage, under Electoral charter since 1747, theology students taught catechism while future school teachers taught reading, figuring, and wool-spinning.[32]

This experimentation joined to the influence of local theorists of cameralism led to the so-called industry school movement. Important here was the cameralist Johann Heinrich Gottlob Justi (ca. 1720-71), who had formerly served Maria Theresia. Justi's Göttingen cameralism followed the same approach in its theory that the Hohenzollerns had followed in practice with the Junkers: not to eliminate the particularist elements in pre-absolutist society, but to transform them into cogs in the centralized state. Justi taught that economic advance was possible in traditional society only if central government intervened "to regulate each occupation ... in such a fashion as it would govern itself ... if it had sufficient insight and understanding."[33] Justi's school of thought would press the clergy to become what Mack Walker terms "intermediate mechanisms" transmitting order between individuals and a common good defined on centralist principles so that the clergy and other particularist elements could aid the state in carrying out the "total administration of civic life."[34]

Justi, who in 1755, became city administrator and university lecturer at Göttingen, urged setting up orphanages and trade schools to inculcate the children of the poor with a "drive toward commerce."[35] Shiftless adults must be put into "manufacture houses" or workhouses to learn a trade. The common weal for Justi demanded instruction of children in their "future duties to the common good" so that there could be implanted in them a "genius for commerce and trade."[36]

The next stage in this development would be to arrive at a pedagogical concept of industry or the spirit of diligence, to put it into the curriculum

---

christliche Religion anzupreisen, 2 parts (Göttingen and Gotha, 1772-73). For future developments the concept of "Glückseligkeit," would be crucial as an ambiguous expression of a religion of virtue preparing the soul for immortal happiness even as it leads to temporal prosperity. See Johann Benjamin Koppe, *Genauere Bestimmung des Erbaulichen im Predigen* (Göttingen, 1778), p. 10; and G. W. Leibniz, *Philosophische Schriften*, trans. Hans Heinz Holz, 1:391, as cited by Karl Heinz Broecken, "Mensch und Bürger bei Rousseau und den Philanthropisten," *Pädagogische Rundschau* 32 (1978): 762.

[32] Rudolf Ruprecht, *Der Pietismus des 18. Jahrhunderts in den Hannoverschen Stammländern* (Göttingen, 1919), pp. 116-67 and 69; E. Beyreuther, "Halle und die Herrnhuter," *JGNK* 73 (1975); 115; Horst Grüneberg, "Die Anfänge des Göttinger beruflichen Schulwesens," *Göttinger Jahrbuch*, Jg. 1966 (Göttingen, 1966), pp. 167-71.

[33] Justi cited in Walker, p. 169; cf. Inama, "Justi," *Allgemeine Deutsche Biographie*, 14: 747-53.

[34] Thus Walker, p. 169.

[35] Grüneberg, p. 175.

[36] Grüneberg, p. 175.

of schools, to co-ordinate such pedagogy with the city poor relief, and to integrate the furthering of such utilitarian activity into the formal definition of the clerical task so that such a role model could be propagated. The clergy and the schoolteachers they supervised would thus be treated precisely as Justi had treated the particularist structures of towns and guilds—transforming the clergy into "intermediate mechanisms to transmit harmony and order between individuals and the common weal."[37] All these moves were made by the Göttingen theologian Heinrich Philipp Sextroh (1746-1838).[38]

Sextroh had been educated at Göttingen. After declining a call as second preacher to George III, he instead in 1779 became pastor of St. Alban's in Göttingen. Active in poor relief and as a teacher of pastoral theology at the university, he published in 1782 a textbook on pastoral care of the sick in conjunction with the formation of new training facility in practical theology: it was to combine lectures on pastoral theology with practical training exercises in the public hospital.[39] The new venture was succesful, and in 1784 Sextroh was named extraordinary professor. By 1786 he had in print a syllabus of his lectures on pastoral theology and the conduct of the ministry.[40] Sextroh received the theological doctorate from Helmstedt in 1788 and became an Ordinarius there in 1789. He was named as well General Superintendent, pastor of St. Stephen's in Helmstedt, and abbot of the Lutheran cloister at Marienthal. The decline of Helmstedt caused him to return to the Electorate: in 1798 he was named first court preacher at Hannover, consistorial councillor, and General Superintendent of Hoya.

Sextroh's theological position in the 1780's was a variant on the Göttingen biblical theology moving rapidly in the direction of the Kantian Rationalism that he was to espouse in the 1790's. Yet, for all Sextroh's utilitarian interests in the early part of his career, he never surrendered the respect for ancient philology as a part of the pastor's equipment that was traditionally a part of the Lutheran ideal of ministry. His inclinations here are signaled by his close connections with the classicist Heyne. Nor

[37] Walker, pp. 168-69.
[38] Paul Zimmermann, "Sextro," *Allgemeine Deutsche Biographie*, 34:77-79; Friedrich Rupstein, *Dr. Heinrich Philipp Sextro* (Hannover, 1839). Sextroh had studied history under Gatterer and Pütter and read the classics in Heyne's seminar; he studied theology with Walch, Less, and Michaelis.
[39] Sextroh, *Ueber Materialien zum Religionsvortrage an Kranke* (Göttingen, 1782); Johann Stephan Pütter, *Versuch einer academischen Gelehrten-Geschichte*, 2 (Göttingen, 1788), p. 243-47.
[40] Sextroh, *Ueber Pflicht, Beruf und Verdienst des Predigers* (Göttingen, 1786); cf. Sextroh, *Ueber praktische Vorbereitungsanstalten zum Predigtamt* (Göttingen, 1783); Sextroh, *Abriß der Geschichte Jesu aus den Evangelien* (Göttingen, 1785); and Sextroh, *Ueber die Beförderung des Praktischen Studiums der Geschichte Jesu* (Göttingen, 1785).

did Sextroh ever formally abandon the traditional proposition that the clerical role is distinguished by its unique occupation with transcendental concerns.[41]

Yet in the 1780's Sextroh took the pastoral role in theory and to a degree in practice as far in the direction of teaching in service to this-worldly ends as one possibly can without formally surrendering the historic priority of the other-worldly element. In so doing, Sextroh helped bring on a crisis in the clerical profession, a crisis in which the churchmen were forced to decide what their chief function was to be in coming decades.

Sextroh's contribution to utilitarianism began with his work in the in-dustry school movement. Sextroh both in his publications and in his work at Göttingen propagandized for combining instruction in reading and religion with training for the lower orders in the disciplined practice of textile manufacture; thereby he set in motion a movement that was soon to encompass much of central Europe.[42] In so doing he also hoped to counteract the effects of what he regarded as a generalized *Verfall der Menschheit* (Fall of mankind), a failure to develop human potential for work which not only corrupted human life on earth, but also adversely affected the fate of the immortal soul.[43]

Given this highly ambiguous use of the remnants of traditional theological concepts such as "Fall," it is evident that with Sextroh in his early or Göttingen period one can scarcely be certain whether the this-worldly or the other-worldly element predominates: temporal life is a preparation for immortal existence in the sense that here on earth are formed by work the capacities that must be utilized in the Beyond.[44] In view of this crass work-righteousness and this stress on the temporal, it is not surprising that a similar ambiguity characterized Sextroh's formal presentation of the pastoral task. In it *all* the pastor's activities, whether "other-worldly" or "utilitarian," are evaluated by the yardstick of usefulness to state and society.

Sextroh's formal conception of the clerical task is unfolded in his long-neglected syllabus of lectures in pastoral theology published at Göttingen in 1786 under the title *Ueber Pflicht, Beruf und Verdienst des Predigers.*[45] It is

---

[41] Zimmermann, p. 78; Rupstein, pp. 29-31; cf. Carl H. G. Venturini, *Ideen zur Philosophie uber die Religion und den Geist des reinen Christenthums* (Altona, 1794).

[42] Cf. Fritz Trost, *Die Göttingische Industrieschule* (Berlin, 1930), pp. 15-18; Heinz-Joachim Heydorn and Gernot Koneffke, eds., *Studien zur Sozialgeschichte und Philosophie der Bildung: 1. Zur Pädagogik der Aufklärung* (Munich, 1973).

[43] Cf. Heydorn-Koneffke, pp. 51-82, esp. p. 70, 75; Sextroh, *Über die Bildung der Jugend zur Indüstrie* (Göttingen, 1785), esp. pp. 18-20.

[44] Sextroh, *Bildung*, pp. 3, 16.

[45] Cf. n. 40 above.

heavily dependent on Abbt's treatise on merit (*Verdienst*), a fact that has gone unnoticed in modern scholarship. Abbt had, it will be recalled, redefined the cure of souls to stress the temporal utility of moral supervision; and he had elaborated and popularized a scheme of merit in which the estates in society could be measured according to their contribution to the "general good" of a society run on principles congenial to absolutist governments.

Sextroh's syllabus on pastoral theology of 1786 incorporates much of Abbt's thought and language; in so doing it states a utilitarian doctrine of the ministry that could exercise considerable influence among conservative churchmen because it came from a respected theologian, not from a pamphleteer.

Sextroh distinguishes between the traditional religious and moral duties of the pastor proper (the *Wirkungskreise seines Amts*) and pastoral activities not pertaining to the ministry in the strict sense (*ausser dem eigentlichen Wirkungskreise seines Amts*).[46] At first glance, Sextroh's treatment of the duties pertaining to the pastoral task in the strict sense appears rather traditional. These duties include public preaching and teaching and private instruction (all based on biblical doctrine), the conduct of public worship, the administration of the sacraments, and moral supervision of the congregation. But the conventional look is deceptive. For Sextroh undertakes to show that moral supervision, *moralische Aufsicht* (what Abbt had called the task of the *Sittenaufseher*), constitutes the chief business (*Hauptgeschäft*, printed in blackletter for emphasis) of the preaching office. Moreover, arguing in Abbtian fashion that *Seelsorge* or cure of souls has been open to misunderstanding, Sextroh then implies that moral supervision is the true sense of *Seelsorge*; in so doing, moreover, Sextroh necessarily evokes a recollection of Abbt's redefinition of the cure of souls, which had concentrated on this-worldly supervision of morals, largely leaving out of account other-worldly matters.[47]

What does Sextroh understand by "moral supervision"? It consists in an application of the means available to the pastor (i.e., admonition, persuasion, and example) for correcting moral flaws and for promoting improvements or progress in virtuous conduct—that is, socially useful and socially acceptable behavior. This moral supervision requires careful observation of the "moral pathology" common to each estate of mankind, and then private work with members of each estate so as to further the smooth functioning of "virtue" (i.e., socially useful patterns of behavior). The preacher is a "moral physician" dealing, not with

---

[46] Sextroh, *Pflicht*, p. 30.
[47] Sextroh, *Pflicht*, pp. 4-26; cf. Abbt, *Verdienste*, p. 277.

original sin, but with corrigible flaws of adults, the physically ill, youth, criminal evil-doers, ecclesiastical separatists, the superstitious, doubters, tempted persons, and those suffering from an excess of either religious awakening or depression. Though Sextroh clearly intends that the pastor's religious function of preaching, teaching, conducting worship, and counseling be carried out on the basis of biblical doctrine, nevertheless, by reinterpreting the cure of souls in an Abbtian sense to mean moral supervision, he transforms the pastor's distinctive religious function into that of an ideological officer responsible for the upholding of group morale. Concern with supernatural and other-worldly matters, aside from the attainment of immortal bliss through earthly utilitarian conduct, is almost totally absent from Sextroh's scheme.[48]

Sextroh's assimilation of Abbt is not limited to the *core* of the ministerial role; it goes beyond this to encompass the way in which the *total* role is to be evaluated. The final section of Sextroh's syllabus is entitled "Vom Verdienst des Predigers." In this section Sextroh provides an explicit rationale for the pastor's efforts to further the this-worldly welfare of his parishioners. To be sure, certain points of connection for joining on utilitarian activity had been provided already in Sextroh's treatment of moral supervision as the most important part of the pastor's duties. There, for example, Sextroh had urged future pastors to undertake the "advancement of a wise Christian and lasting charitable program in the congregation for the benefit of the poor." He had encouraged a study of the "character" of people condemned to correctional in-

---

[48] Sextroh, *Pflicht*, pp. 15, 17, 22, 8-9; cf. Abbt, *Verdienste*, p. 277.—Sextroh was aware of the necessity and the difficulty of equipping the parish clergy conceived as teachers of virtue with a function that would be both uniquely their own and highly prized by contemporary society. Sextroh also knew that his version of relevant ministry ran the risk of depriving the clergy of any distinctive task peculiar to their estate. He attempts (*Pflicht*, p. 15) to meet this problem by stressing the "religious" and "moral" content of clerical instruction as something peculiarly the property of the clergy, and by protesting that "moral supervision" is different from "political, economic, etc." supervision. That this uniqueness (given the widespread trend toward abandoning belief in a positive supernatural revelation of unique salvific significance) was of an illusory character emerged only in the subsequent debates. Schleiermacher faced—*mutatis mutandis*—a similar problem in his *Reden*: addressing an audience which makes the aesthetic all-important, he had to defend the purpose of religion and the clergy by invoking aesthetic categories (cf. the third of the *Reden*). Yet simultaneously Schleiermacher had to suggest that religion is somehow distinct from aesthetic experience and superior to it. The similarity of situation is not accidental: as the third of the *Reden* shows, Schleiermacher's concept of the ministerial function resulted directly from his rejecting the radical utilitarian version of the minister as teacher of temporal virtue. Schleiermacher tried to solve the same problem facing Sextroh; yet, unwilling to accept either utilitarianism or supernaturalism, Schleiermacher could only de-emphasize the teaching role and look elsewhere—to a remodeling of Gottfried Arnold's Ignatian version of ministry: the pastor was transformed into a sacral focus and an agent of *Bildung*.

stitutions in order to see how to work in them a "thorough and enduring moral improvement" coupled with "a love for industriousness in the correctional institution itself."[49] However, in the final section of the syllabus Sextroh provides a rationale for systematically expanding the boundaries of the clerical role in a utilitarian direction; it is derived from Abbt's notion of merit as service to the common good as defined by the modern state.

According to Sextroh, every "striving" beyond the bounds of the "customary" determination of clerical duties constitutes "the beginning of merit." That is, the pastor can make a real claim on public esteem only if he pushes on into a variety of activities not traditionally expected of the clergyman; Sextroh's own work in poor relief and in campaigning for industry schools gives a good idea of what sorts of new activities he had in mind here. Sextroh makes it plain that merit can be acquired both within and outside the clergyman's distinctive sphere of activity. The former variety of merit comes from preaching, teaching, the conduct of worship, providing a good "moral example" and "the business of moral supervision," whereas merit from extra-official activities must be derived from activities dependent on one's particular circumstances.[50]

Sextroh then turns to the problem of measuring merit, and in so doing gives certain proof that, though Abbt's name appears nowhere in the syllabus, still Sextroh's evaluation of merit is derived from Abbt's absolutist thought. Sextroh's syllabus presents a classification of the "determination of worth of clerical merit" that constitutes only a superficial revision of Abbt's categories: there are recognized sublime, great, and noble merits in addition to simple merits. By his heavy dependence on Abbt Sextroh signaled instantly his agreement with Abbt on the need for a redefining of the pastoral role to meet the needs of the modern sovereign state. This impression was further strengthened by Sextroh's adjacent discussion of acquiring merit as an army chaplain or a country preacher, roles in which the pastor could readily be seen to have a function of immediate utility to the state as a fortifier of morale.[51]

With all this redefining Sextroh intended to present a defense of the utility of the ministry. In the introduction to his syllabus, Sextroh speaks of the "usefulness" of the preaching office, a theme beloved of Enlighten-

---

[49] Sextroh, *Pflicht*, pp. 23, 21.

[50] Sextroh, *Pflicht*, pp. 30-31, Grüneberg, pp. 179-86.

[51] Sextroh, *Pflicht*, pp. 31-32. Since a Pietist vocabulary had been transformed by patriotic writers such as Abbt, the re-appropriation for "religious" purposes of Abbt's rhetoric was not difficult. For background see August Langen, *Der Wortschatz des deutschen Pietismus* (Tübingen, 1954); and Gerhard Kaiser, *Pietismus und Patriotismus im literarischen Deutschland* (Wiesbaden, 1961).

ment theologians.[52] Elsewhere he explains the "rights of preachers" and "the obligation to protect the esteem in which the office is held."[53] Furthermore, the function of the entire final section on clerical merit in the syllabus is that of convincing the clergy and the laity of the utility (merit) with respect to the common good that pertains to the clerical estate. Just to be on the safe side, though, Sextroh concludes his syllabus with yet an additional word of comfort—"Grounds for consolation, if contemporaries do not recognize the value of merit and of striving after merit."[54]

With Sextroh the accommodation of the ministerial role to the demand for relevance had proceeded as far as it possibly could without explicitly asking the clergy to concentrate their energies chiefly on this-worldly matters at the expense of attending to the other-worldly needs traditionally met by instruction on the basis of scriptural and metaphysical theology. The demand for precisely such a drastic revision in priorities was not long in coming, and it came in Braunschweig-Wolfenbüttel in the guise of a further development of Sextroh's ideas.

---

[52] Cf. Sextroh, *Pflicht*, p. 4; and Johann Joachim Spalding, *Ueber die Nutzbarkeit des Predigtamtes und deren Beförderung* (Berlin eds. of 1772, 1773, 1791). On the Spalding controversy: Joseph Schollmeier, *Johann Joachim Spalding* (Gütersloh, 1967), p. 243.

[53] Sextroh, *Pflicht*, p. 26.

[54] Sextroh, *Pflicht*, p. 26.—Sextroh was also a pioneer in the development of clinical pastoral education. Not only did he in his lectures show students how to widen clerical activities to achieve a claim on public recognition, but also did he give his students a savor of a psychologically satisfying reward. That was the chief latent function of his Pastoral Institute with its supervised preaching and private religious sessions at the Göttingen hospital: students who gained skill in hospital counselling could render patients a "veritable good deed." As a result students would have "the refreshing feeling of having performed ... an action really of general utility and benevolence" (Sextroh, *Vorbereitungsanstalten*, p. 33). The unspoken premise was that the pre-Enlightenment ministry was *not* of general utility and benevolence. The establishment of the Göttingen Pastoral Institute with its hospital exercises represented an effort by Sextroh to provide something besides a feeling of frustration for theology students; it was a try at strengthening the professional commitment of students affected by the general low opinion of the clergy.

CHAPTER FOUR

RADICAL SECULARIST PRESSURES AND PROTESTANT CLERICAL RESISTANCE IN NORTHWEST GERMANY AFTER 1785

1. *The Radical Secularist Attack on Clerical Identity*

a. The General Intensification of Secularist Demands: The Example of Carl Friedrich Bahrdt

In Northwest Germany at the close of the eighteenth century pressure for secularization of the institutional church was chiefly directed toward the activities of the clergy and the programs for training future clergymen. In the two other areas in which secularist natural law thinkers had proposed radically secular reform, attempts at secularization had been to a surprising degree thwarted. The triumph of collegialism had provided a universally accepted alternative to Thomasian territorialism. Furthermore, at least in Northwest Germany, the blend of reason and revelation advocated in theology by Mosheim and his followers held the field until such time as the advent of Kantianism and Romanticism could stimulate renewed interest in positive theology: radical Rationalism found few supporters, and those who advocated it did so in a cautious manner. However, in the third area in which secularizing reform had been urged, namely, that of the functioning of the clergy, new proposals were made in the 1780's that seemed to have a real chance of being realized, thereby turning the clergy into mere servants of the prince.

In the previous chapter the steps leading up to such a proposed secularizing transformation of both the training and the functioning of the clergy were traced. In order to see how pressure for such a metamorphosis was intensified, we must glance at a figure who lived outside the Welf territories; this propagandist. made proposals emblematic of demands made by any number of other writers at the time in official Prussian circles. As these demands were immediately taken up (though not by churchmen) in Braunschweig-Wolfenbüttel itself, their prehistory deserves our attention.

The propagandist in question was the controversial Carl Friedrich Bahrdt (1741-1792) in Halle.[1] Bahrdt was influenced by two related

---

[1] Martin Schmidt, "Bahrdt," *RGG*, 3rd ed. (Tübingen, 1957), 1: col. 845; Paul Tschackert, "Bahrdt," *PRE*, 3rd ed. (Leipzig, 1897), 2: 357-59; Gustav Frank, "Bahrdt," *Allgemeine Deutsche Biographie* (Leipzig, 1875), 1: 772-74; Gustav Frank, *Dr.*

pedagogical movements that relied very greatly on the central state: the movement for national education and the Philanthropist movement. Proponents of the former movement propagandized for secularized education which—freed from clerical control—would educate all citizens to labor toward the welfare of the state; in so doing, the education of the individual man (*Mensch*) was to be subordinated to the common interest of the entire citizenry, whose wills were to be united by education to produce the *Nationalgeist* or spirit of the nation: national education was to lead to a complete devotion of the individual to the state.[2]

A similar trust in the absolutist state characterized the Philanthropists. Their movement, founded by Johann Bernhard Basedow (1724-1790), was in its initial phase based on an unquestioning approval of the absolutist state, on an expanded study of the vernacular languages and literatures, and on pleasurable education leading to utilitarian training. The Philanthropists stressed hygiene, physical education, manual training, physical labor, and sex education; they favored complete reorganization of all existing schools to increase state control and to insure both religious instruction based on natural religion and the elimination of ecclesiastical school supervision. Only in this way could state-oriented utilitarian curricular programs be effectively introduced.[3]

In the North Germany of the 1780's occurred a confluence of secularizing streams—utilitarian pedagogical theory influenced by cameralism and the industry school movement; Abbtian rhetoric; radical deism; pressure for "national" education with elimination of clerical control over schools and de-emphasis on classical languages; and Philanthropism. What this meant for the clergy was explained by Bahrdt.

The son of an Orthodox Lutheran theologian at Leipzig, Bahrdt began teaching sacred philology in 1766 at the same university in the odor of or-

---

Karl Friedrich Bahrdt = *Historisches Taschenbuch*, ed. von Raumer, 3. Folge, 7. Jg. (Leipzig, 1866), pp. 207-370; Günter Mühlpfordt, "Karl Friedrich Bahrdt und die radikale Aufklärung," *Jahrbuch des Instituts für Deutsche Geschichte, Tel Aviv*, ed. Walter Grab, 5 (1976): 49-99; Sten Gunnar Flygt, *The Notorious Dr. Bahrdt* (Nashville, Tenn., 1963).

[2] See Hans Seel, *Beiträge zur Geschichte des Begriffs einer deutschen Nationalerziehung* (Phil. Diss., Münster University, 1925); Helmut König, *Zur Geschichte der Nationalerziehung* (East Berlin, 1960); Karl Ernst Jeismann, *Das preußische Gymnasium in Staat und Gesellschaft* (Stuttgart, 1974).

[3] Albert Pinloche, *Geschichte des Philanthropismus* (Leipzig, 1914); Reinhold Schumann, *Die Auffassung des Philanthropismus von Gesellschaft und Staat* (Phil. Diss., Leipzig, 1905); A. Reble, "Philanthropinisten," *RGG*, 3rd ed. (Tübingen, 1961), 5: cols. 329-30; Reble, "Basedow," *RGG*, 3rd ed. (Tübingen, 1957), 1: col. 904; Max Müller, "Basedow," *Allgemeine Deutsche Biographie* (Leipzig, 1875), 2: 116; Enno Fooken, *Die geistliche Schulaufsicht und ihre Kritiker im 18. Jahrhundert* (Wiesbaden, 1967); Hanno Schmitt, "Leistungen, Widersprüche und Grenzen pädagogischer Reformarbeit am Ausgang des 18. Jahrhunderts ... im Herzogtum Braunschweig-Wolfenbüttel," 2 vols. (Diss. Erziehungswissenschaften, Marburg University, 1977).

thodoxy. But in 1768 owing to a misadventure involving a young woman he was obliged to resign. From this point, as Gustav Frank notes, his theological development consisted of steady abandonment of the positive doctrines in Christianity.[4]

After being decried as heretical by the celebrated Ernesti and after issuing sensational publications for the laity, Bahrdt was in 1775 removed from his teaching post at Erlangen by governmental action. Attracted to Philanthropist ventures, he took a post as General Superintendent and educator at Dürckheim, from which he was deposed on account of heresy in 1778. In Prussian Halle he enjoyed the favor of Karl Abraham Freiherr von Zedlitz (1731-93), head of the "Spiritual Department of the Lutheran Church and School Affairs." Zedlitz obtained for Bahrdt the *venia legendi* at Halle in 1779 over the opposition of the theological faculty and the academic senate. As an unsalaried philosophical *Docent* Bahrdt lectured on classical literature, rhetoric, and dietetics to as many as 900 students at once.

Here Bahrdt continued his publishing career, espousing natural religion in place of traditional theology. Under the influence of the Northwest German Philanthropist Ernst Christian Trapp, Bahrdt held that the state should limit religion to the general concepts of reason so that all might participate equally in the public religion. Bahrdt's Jesus was a devotee of natural religion who had aimed by a campaign of Enlightenment to eliminate all positive religions and pretended revelations, which were the products of priestly deception. Both Moses and Jesus had led graded organizations akin to Enlightenment Freemasonry; after the "Ascension" Jesus had lived on secretly in the Mother Lodge up to the time of Paul's becoming a member.

In the theologico-political reaction after the death of Friedrich II, Bahrdt was forced to give up his lecturing. He retired to his restaurant and tavern outside Halle. On account of his satire on the reactionary Religion Edict of Wöllner, Bahrdt was imprisoned for a year in 1789. He died in 1792 poisoned by mercury taken for medicinal purposes.

Bahrdt's position is of interest because it combined radical deism with social criticism, while maintaining a faith in the absolutist state as the best agent for beneficial change. Bahrdt's underlying indebtedness to "nationalist," utilitarian, and Philanthropist currents can be seen in the demands for reform of clerical education made in his book, *Ueber das theologische Studium auf Universitäten*. It was published at Berlin in 1785 and

---

[4] Frank (1866), p. 224, 302; Frank (1875), p. 773; cf. n. 1 above for background and the works from which these biographical remarks are drawn. The two works by Frank are still the best introduction to Bahrdt's theology. Cf. Ulrich Herrmann, "Ernst Christian Trapp (1745-1818)," *Braunschweigisches Jahrbuch* 53 (1972): 183-95.

dedicated to Zedlitz; it attributes the low esteem in which the clergy are held, and the apparent fact that the clergy have become superfluous to the state, to the failure of the clergy to keep pace with the progress of Enlightenment.[5] Since the "decisive cause" for this lies in the way pastors and schoolteachers are educated at the university, the problem can be remedied by reform. For, as Bahrdt argues, whereas formerly in an age of ignorance and barbarism, the mere superstitious veneration attached to the pastoral office had sufficed to establish the good reputation of the clerical estate, now, in an age of Enlightenment, when the mass of the people no longer regard the clergy as divine emissaries capable of sending the parishioner to eternal perdition or bliss, it has become necessary to found the prestige of the clerical estate upon the actual capacities and performance of its individual members.[6]

In order to achieve this reshaping of the clerical estate, Bahrdt proposes that the training of the future clergy be reorganized so as to produce *Volkslehrer* useful to the common good. As Enno Fooken has recently pointed out, "in the age of the Enlightenment the term '*Volkslehrer*' was standard, and signified an educator in the service of the state" whose job it was to give advice in the practical affairs of daily life.[7] Precisely such was Bahrdt's understanding of the term—implying one who

> in an official capacity dedicates himself either to the instruction and the education of the young, or to lectures from the pulpit and to care for souls—one who makes himself useful in his place of operating as a schoolteacher or as a preacher or as both at once.[8]

What Bahrdt meant by teaching, preaching, and the cure of souls may be surmised readily enough from our previous acquaintance with his general evolution: one should here recall that seven years later, in 1792, he was to call for setting up a deistic state religion complete with a uniform public worship service based on natural religion.[9] A further look at Bahrdt's earlier proposals to Zedlitz in 1785 will prove worthwhile, for they show how Bahrdt intended to train future pastors as state-supervised *Volkslehrer* responsible for the people's this-worldly welfare.

Bahrdt begins with the premise that the study of the oriental languages (Hebrew and Aramaic), dogmatical and polemical theology, patristics, the whole of church history, exegesis of the Old Testament, and perhaps

---

[5] Carl Friedrich Bahrdt, *Ueber das theologische Studium auf Universitäten* (Berlin, 1785), pp. 7-15; cf. Mühlpfordt, pp. 84-93.

[6] Bahrdt, *Studium*, pp. 10, 16-17.

[7] Bahrdt, *Studium*, pp. 28-29; Fooken, p. 111.

[8] Bahrdt, *Studium*, pp. 28-29.

[9] Bahrdt, *Rechte und Obliegenheiten der Regenten und Untertanen in Beziehung auf Staat und Religion* (Riga, 1792), pp. 251-300.

even exegesis of the New Testament contribute absolutely nothing to turning a student into a *Volkslehrer*. For a *Volkslehrer* must be competent as advisor and counselor in matters of childrearing and practical economics, as well as able to serve as the model of a diligent and useful person. According to Bahrdt, it is not simply that the theological curriculum is irrelevant; beyond this, it is positively harmful, for the stiffness of theological method coupled with the ponderous character of theological language insures that the student will become incapable of communicating with ordinary people. By promoting a love for abstractions traditional theology damages the capacity for human feeling, so that finally religion comes to seem no more than "learned nonsense" [*gelehrter Kram*].[10]

In all this Bahrdt operates with an exaggerated variety of Johann Salomo Semler's distinction between religion and theology, arguing that the clergyman in the field has no need to be acquainted with such mysteries of theology as the divinity of Christ, the personality of the Holy Spirit, and the real presence in order to proclaim by word and example the true moral religion.[11]

What does Bahrdt's proposed three-year university curriculum for the future parish clergy look like? To begin with, Bahrdt still supposes that the student entering the university will have a knowledge of the Greek and Latin authors in the original, so that further use of these languages is possible; in this regard, Bahrdt (an ex-professor himself) retains some continuity between the future clergy and the traditional Latin-reading learned estate of the Old Régime.[12] Given this, then, the student is to pursue the following course:[13]

(1) Philosophy, consisting of logic and elementary metaphysics, without "useless subtleties or scholastic nonsense."[14]

(2) Religion, that is, the knowledge necessary for moral perfection—namely, a doctrine of happiness, motivated by self-love, and including a classification of the motives for and types of enjoyment, as well as the development of the understanding leading to attention to such matters as superstition, existence of and prayer to God, formation of taste, respect for oaths and contracts, and promotion of the health of the body (with units on the importance of health, the evil of suicide, the

---

[10] Bahrdt, *Studium*, pp. 34, 31-32.

[11] Cf. Emanuel Hirsch, *Geschichte der neuern evangelischen Theologie* (Gütersloh, 1952), 4: 53; Bahrdt, *Studium*, pp. 43-55.

[12] Bahrdt, *Studium*, pp. 62-63.

[13] For these points in sequence, see Bahrdt, *Studium*, pp. 64-113.

[14] Bahrdt, *Studium*, pp. 64-65.

preservation of health, and general dietetics); there is to follow an appendix on the history of Christianity.

(3) The reading of the New Testament in the original in order to supply scriptural examples so that the future pastor can, when reasoned argument fails, invoke the words and example of Jesus and the apostles. In all this the student must grasp the true goal of Jesus: the enlightenment of the human race.

(4) Natural history, physics, and anatomy, useful because of their importance for giving a vivid presentation of the goodness and wisdom of nature's God, because of their utility in combating superstition, and because of their utility in making the pastor knowledgeable in matters of agronomy, first aid, and public health so as to increase general respect for the *Volkslehrer* as a well-rounded person.

(5) Arithmetic and geometry, so that the *Volkslehrer*, by his knowledge of surveying, can settle disputes over boundaries, thereby promoting congregational harmony while demonstrating his general usefulness.

(6) Agronomy (which Bahrdt in the usage of the day terms *Oekonomie*), for, as Bahrdt holds:

> Would it not aid astonishingly much in securing love and respect for the preacher, thereby augmenting his utility for the congregation, if he could also be the wisest man in the village in the area of husbandry, the advisor and example for his flock?
> Would not the preacher then be able to support the governmental orders ... concerning improvement of agriculture and be able to put them into practice, if he—as an expert and a man of authority—were in a position to speak with his congregation about the reasons for them?[15]

(7) Roman and Greek mythology and literature, for they are obviously indispensable to the schoolteacher, and it is advantageous to the state that both varieties of *Volkslehrer* (preacher and school teacher) be so trained that, in case of need, either can serve in the capacity of the other.

(8) History and modern literature, for the study of them makes the preacher a far better conversationalist and educates the taste much more satisfactorily than do the study of dogmatics, polemical theology, and oriental philology, and thus are of greater use in helping the preacher to "acquire esteem" and to make his company more desired.[16]

(9) A survey of the history of past doctrinal controversies, the symbolical books, the history of New Testament exegesis, and a brief guide to some of the best modern theological books.

(10) An introduction to clinical medicine (in case one must serve as a country preacher in areas remote from a physician). Studying medicine

---

[15] Bahrdt, *Studium*, p. 85.
[16] Bahrdt, *Studium*, pp. 89-91.

would transform the clerical estate from dreaded announcers of death into the most honorable of estates, simultaneously refuting once and for all the common charge that rural ministry is the refuge of the slothful. In order to acquire the proper acquaintance with the physiology, dietetics, *materia medica*, pathological states, diagnosis, and therapy, the theological student must be required to spend five hours a week for three semesters on these topics.[17]

(11) Theory and practice of pedagogy, including methodology; practice in "socratic teaching," useful in conducting catechetical instruction along Philanthropic lines; rhetoric; formation of a good German prose style; and public speaking.[18]

These proposed curricular reforms are accompanied by the further recommendation that the existing estate of schoolteachers be abolished. In its place, and utilizing the funds thereby liberated, is to be set up a system of interns: every theological graduate is to spend three to six years as resident assistant to a pastor, teaching in the school, preaching on occasion, and functioning as an auxiliary physician. If this plan be followed, Bahrdt assures the reader, the clergy, as teachers and physicians, will become one of the most important and respected groups in the state; otherwise, if the clergy are not given a "nobler" sphere of activities, warns Bahrdt, the estate will become more despised and useless with each decade, until at last they constitute "a nil" in the state.[19]

While Bahrdt himself was by 1785 regarded as something of an extremist, his plans were not so far-fetched as to seem impossible of realization. Suggestions for a radical reform of the clergy in a similar fashion were everywhere to be found. Many Protestant writers in Germany toward the close of the eighteenth century argued—in the manner of Thomas Abbt—that the joining together of the clerical office with all matter of temporal tasks (e.g., pedagogy, medicine, legal counsel, agronomy, and aid to the recruiting officer) would be a positive advantage to the clergyman, for it would increase his utility, his prestige, and his influence.[20]

Bahrdt's proposals can be taken as emblematic of a major challenge to the traditional *raison d'être* and the traditional institutional loyalty of the clergyman. It is of central importance for our study that Bahrdt's challenge was reissued by one of his admirers in the Northwest German territories during these years.

---

[17] Bahrdt, *Studium*, pp. 94-101.
[18] Bahrdt, *Studium*, pp. 107-113.
[19] Bahrdt, *Studium*, pp. 134-37.
[20] Fooken, pp. 98-103; see Appendix C.

b. Joachim Heinrich Campe: Radical Reform at the Braunschweig Court

Bahrdt's secularist challenge was restated in very radical terms by Joachim Heinrich Campe (1746-1818).[21] Since he was entrusted by the Duke of Braunschweig-Wolfenbüttel with responsibility for a complex program of educational reform, he had to be taken seriously when he suggested that future parish clergy ought to devote the bulk of their time to caring for parishioners' temporal welfare.

Campe had studied at Enlightenment Helmstedt, a university in decline and deeply divided on account of the presence of conservative and enlightened theological factions. Because of his support of the radical exegete Wilhelm Abraham Teller (1734-1804), Campe's scholarship from the assembly of estates was withdrawn, forcing him to move to Halle.[22] After work as a military chaplain in Potsdam, Campe was offered a preaching post in Braunschweig, which he refused because he found clerical decorum intolerable. Deeply affected by Rationalism and deism, Campe had come to find the traditional clerical role oppressive. As he wrote to his brother-in-law in 1777 from Potsdam:

> How can an honorable man feel happy when every day he must play the role of a hypocrite? And such a role is what every clergyman must play, regardless of who he may be—except of course for the nitwit.[23]

Campe sought a new career in the pedagogy advanced by Rousseau and Basedow. In 1776 Prince Franz von Dessau made him co-curator of the Philanthropin in Dessau, over which school he assumed the directorship when Basedow resigned. Under Campe's direction it prospered, preparing children for a happy and utilitarian life in line with Campe's

---

[21] G. Bauer, "Campe," *Allgemeine Deutsche Biographie* (Leipzig, 1876), 3: 733-37; Jakob Anton Leyser, *Joachim Heinrich Campe*, 2nd ed. (Braunschweig, 1896); Friedrich Koldewey, "Campe's Vorschläge zur Verbesserung des braunschweigischen Schulwesens," *Braunschweigisches Magazin* 2 (1896): 97-103; F. Behrens, ed., *Das Fürstliche Schuldirektorium im Herzogthum Braunschweig vom Jahre 1786* (Braunschweig, 1888); Eugen Stech, *Das braunschweigische Schuldirektorium* (Langensalza, 1909); Ulrich Herrmann, "Modell der Schulreform: Das Braunschweigisches Schuldirektorium 1786-1790," *Braunschweigisches Jahrbuch* 55 (1971): 163-81; Heinz-Joachim Heydorn and Gernet Koneffke, *Studien zur Sozialgeschichte und Philosophie der Bildung. 1. Zur Pädagogik der Aufklärung* (Munich, 1973); and Schmitt.

[22] On theology at Helmstedt and Teller's conservative enemies, and on the ties of the conservatism at Helmstedt to the conservative Orthodoxy of the Carpzov dynasty in Saxony, see Appendix C. On Campe's involvement see Leyser, 1:12, n. 2; and Johannes Beste, *Geschichte der Braunschweigischen Landeskirche* (Wolfenbüttel, 1889), pp. 11-12.

[23] Leyser, 1:25-26, n. 5; cf. David Hume, "Of National Characters," in his *Essays, Moral, Political and Literary* (Oxford, 1963), pp. 205-5, n. 2; cf. Gottfried Less, *Ueber Christliches Lehr-Amt* (Göttingen, 1790), pp. 104-5n.

dictum that more merit was due the introducer of potato planting than was to be accorded the poet of the *Iliad* and the *Odyssey*.[24]

In the spring of 1786 Campe was asked to assist Karl Wilhelm Ferdinand, the Duke of Braunschweig-Wolfenbüttel, in planning a far-reaching series of school reforms. He was to receive the title of *Hochfürstlich Braunschweig-Lüneburgischer Schulrath* and was to work with others in bringing about the reforms.[25]

Campe, like all the Philanthropists, conceived of true religion only in rational terms. The Christian religion was to be interpreted in accord with sound reason and human needs. Indicative of the Philanthropist viewpoint here was the argument of one of Campe's associates that the chief goal of Enlightenment instruction must be to remove the outmoded prejudice that divine forces can operate immediately on physical bodies, which was a perennial source of superstition and barbarism.[26]

Such was Campe's general view of religion when he responded affirmatively to the duke's request in 1785-86 for help with the educational reform of Braunschweig-Wolfenbüttel. In the course of reflection on the shape of reform Campe was led to support a radicalized version of Bahrdt's ideas on the revision of the *raison d'être* of parish ministry.

The dukedom of Braunschweig-Wolfenbüttel was the home of Jerusalem and Lessing. Under the late Duke Karl I (1735-1780) connections with Berlin had been good: the duke and Friedrich II of Prussia had married each other's sisters. The late duke, it will be recalled, had emulated Prussia in carrying out various cameralistic experiments and in fielding a large army (in the year 1760 there had been 16,000 men under arms out of total population of 159,000). Enlightenment on the French and Prussian models had been and continued to be encouraged. However, the worsening economic situation of the 1760's, the costs of war, and the duke's undiminished love for courtly pageantry had led to a burden of debt exceeding twelve million imperial dollars.[27]

In view of the fact that foreign sources had refused additional loans, Duke Karl I had been forced in 1768 to convoke an assembly of estates, the first since 1682. This event is of interest in more than one connection. The negotiations between duke and estates, lasting until 1770, resulted in a solution of the immediate financial problems. The estates agreed to a twenty-five-year plan according to which new taxes were to reduce the

---

[24] Baur, pp. 733-34.
[25] Baur, p. 735.
[26] Schmitt, 1:85.
[27] Joseph König, "Landesgeschichte," in Richard Moderhack, ed., *Braunschweigische Landesgeschichte*, 2nd ed. (Braunschweig, 1977), pp. 82-83; Wilhelm Havemann, *Geschichte der Lande Braunschweig und Lüneburg* (Göttingen, 1857), 3:620; Eduard Vehse, *Geschichte der Höfe des Hauses Braunschweig* (Hamburg, 1853), p. 230.

debt. In return the duke agreed to abolish the court opera, to reduce the army, and to carry out other austerity measures. As the deliberations demonstrate, the estates—including to a degree the clergy—had become suspicious of the absolutist policies of the central government. Demands were voiced for a full reconfirmation of the historic privileges of the nobles, clergy, and corporations; in addition, the anticourt party sought guaranteed periodicity of assemblies of estates and consent of the estates to taxation, legislation, and declaration of war. Though not all these demands were to be obtained, the fact that they were made illustrates the intention of the estates to reassert their self-interest in the face of centralizing tendencies on the part of the ducal régime.[28]

The evidence of desire to defend clerical particularist self-interest is of special concern here. Though the clerical segment of the estates began as allies of the duke in his request for new taxes, the Lutheran prelates present at the assembly from 1768-1770 exhibited a growing reluctance to grant automatic approval to government proposals.[29] Especially significant of the reawakening of clerical self-interest vis-à-vis the ducal régime is the intransigent refusal of the clergy to surrender their traditional exemption to the tax on beer and wine, a refusal in which they were joined by the nobility. Likewise, in negotiations the Lutheran prelates forced the duke to return to the clergy the right of presentation to offices in Lutheran cloisters, a right lost in 1741.[30]

The reservations of the clergy concerning the ducal régime resulted ultimately from a long-standing ducal neglect of clerical and ecclesiastical interests. In the period immediately preceding the convocation of the assembly of estates, that is, from 1758 to 1764, the consistory had been seriously understaffed, and had been manned only with lay members. Indeed, for a time it appeared that—as a consequence of administrative reorganization resulting from the removal of the court from Wolfenbüttel to Braunschweig in 1753—the consistory might be abolished altogether. In the period 1758-1764 the duke depended for ecclesiastical advice solely

---

[28] Vehse, p. 233; Wilhelm Schmidt, *Der braunschweigische Landtag von 1768-1770* (Phil. Diss., Göttingen, 1912), pp. 3, 33-38.

[29] Johann Friedrich Wilhelm Jerusalem, *Zwey Predigten* (Braunschweig, 1770); Schmidt, *Landtag*, pp. 14-15, 25-27.

[30] Schmidt, *Landtag*, pp. 26, 31; König, p. 85. The consistory and its noble allies also protested the constitutional innovation implied by the ducal establishment of a medical board in 1747, a protest taken into account in the organization of the *Ober-Sanitäts-Collegium* in 1772. Similar displeasure with ducal policy is evidenced in the demand of the prelates and their allies that the professorial chairs at Helmstedt be once agin filled in their entirety instead of siphoning off money from theology, law, medicine, and philosophy to finance the ducal military academy in Braunschweig (the Collegium Carolinum). Cf. Fritz Meyen, "Johann Friedrich Wilhelm Jerusalem," *Braunschweigisches Jahrbuch* 53 (1972): 165-67.

on his favorite, the *Abt* Jerusalem, who at that point did not sit or vote in the consistory. Thus it seemed plausible that eventually the consistory might be done away with, the privy council then being expanded to allow it to handle ecclesiastical affairs. The lack of clerical representation on the consistory in Wolfenbüttel at this point meant that many affairs of the church were decided to the disadvantage of ecclesiastical and clerical independence.[31]

All this ought not to be taken to mean that the clergy and estates were opposed to reform in any shape. In 1768 the Lutheran prelates took the negotiations with the duke as opportunity for requesting that the schools, especially the Latin schools, be improved. This petition was repeated in other negotiations between the estates and the duke at a later point in 1775. This request was to provide the duke's son and successor, Karl Wilhelm Ferdinand, with the pretext for putting forward a program of far-reaching school reforms in which Campe was to play a major part.[32]

The Braunschweig-Wolfenbüttel into which Campe came was a center of intellectual life still unsettled by the controversy about Lessing's publication of the Wolfenbüttel *Fragments*.[33] Duke Karl Wilhelm Ferdinand, who reigned from 1780 until he was mortally wounded by a French bullet through his eye at Auerstedt in 1806, was a devotee of the French Enlightenment; he had been tutored as well in the principles of the Berlin Enlightenment by the *Abt* Jerusalem. The new duke continued his father's pro-Prussian policies, joining in 1785 the anti-Habsburg *Fürstenbund* and fostering Enlightenment at home.

He differed from his father, however, in the seriousness with which he pursued financial and administrative reform. The new duke was determined to run his territory on the soundest and most advanced cameralistic principles. Already before his accession at the age of forty-five, Karl Wilhelm Ferdinand had persuaded his father to introduce a number of reform measures—the foundation of a central financial board, a more adroit juggling of debts, a decrease in public expenditures, and trade in mercenaries. On his accession he reduced court expenditures. By 1785 financial conditions had improved sufficiently to allow the contemplation of more grandiose reforms beginning with the schools.

---

[31] Vitus Dettmer, *Das Konsistorium zu Wolfenbüttel* (Braunschweig, 1922), pp. 80-85. Only in 1765, feeling the need for allies because of financial crisis, did Duke Karl mitigate his policy of governmental management of ecclesiastical affairs by making clear that the consistory would not be abolished—though clerical appointees remained in the minority for a time.

[32] Behrens, p. 10.

[33] For conditions see Karl Steinacker, *Abklang der Aufklärung und Widerhall der Romantik* (Braunschweig, 1939); Selma Stern, *Karl Wilhelm Ferdinand* (Hildesheim, 1921); König, p. 83; Schmitt, 1:28-29.

The new ruler's determination to proceed apace was signaled by his turning for help to Karl August von Hardenberg (1750-1822), who was given the title of *Wirklicher Geheimrath*. Hardenberg—the later *Staatskanzler* of Prussia and the architect of Prussian reform—had before coming to Braunschweig worked as an administrator in the government of Electoral Hannover. Hardenberg's entire career shows considerable continuity; his policies in Braunschweig-Wolfenbüttel can be viewed as an outgrowth of his policies in Kurhannover.[34]

In Hardenberg's period of activity as privy councillor in Hannover from 1771-1781, he took as his point of departure the rationalistic and cameralistic principles of the Enlightenment. His reform efforts, in part thwarted by the conservative local aristocracy managing affairs in Kurhannover, had been aimed at strengthening the régime of George III in a time of financial crisis. The goal had been to introduce administrative rationalization into the electoral domains. What Hardenberg sought was a state completely co-ordinated by central administrative organs, populated by industrious subjects, and thus a state militarily stronger than before. This total conception (presented in 1781) was not to be realized quickly in decentralized Kurhannover. Hardenberg was annoyed by the impossibility of carrying through a comprehensive administrative reform putting the large number of independent boards (potentially including the consistory) under tighter central control.[35]

Hardenberg entered the service of the Duke of Braunschweig-Wolfenbüttel in May of 1782 as president of the board administering cloisters and as a member of the privy council with ministerial rank. He aimed at the same administrative goal as formerly. On May 28, 1786 Hardenberg recommended a reorganization replacing the numerous independent boards in Braunschweig-Wolfenbüttel (potentially including the consistory, though since the reform was never carried out, the details are uncertain). In place of the independent boards would have come a centralized structure subordinate to three ministers (one each for finance and domains; matters of law, church, and school; and internal affairs) responsible to the duke. Thus as advisor to the duke Hardenberg favored a major administrative reorganization of the absolutist state designed to increase and broaden the powers of the absolute monarchy.[36]

---

[34] H. von Sybel, "Hardenberg," *Allgemeine Deutsche Biographie* (Leipzig, 1879), 10:572-90; Hans Hausherr, *Hardenberg* (Cologne, 1963); Otto Merker, "Karl August Freiherr von Hardenbergs Reformdenken," *Niedersächsisches Jahrbuch für Landesgeschichte* 43 (1976): 325-44.

[35] Merker, pp. 325-27, 343-45; Schmitt, 1:163-64; what these reforms would have meant for the consistory can be debated.

[36] von Sybel, p. 572; Schmitt, 1: 162-65. The precise ramifications for the consistory are hard to ascertain with certainty.

Existing structures were first to be reorganized in the area of school and church affairs—the logical place to begin since the prelates and the estates had in 1768 and 1775 themselves called for reform here. Hardenberg himself was critical of the traditional position and privileges of the church, even as he was critical of the estates. Hardenberg opposed the traditional administrative independence of the institutional church and favored greater temporal control of it. Specifically, he did not approve of supervision of schools by the consistory. He supported a secularizing reform of the schools and wished to finance it in Braunschweig-Wolfenbüttel by appropriating for this purpose a portion of the "excessive" incomes of congregations, cloisters, and pious foundations. Since under the Old Régime it was not easy to obtain a clear idea of such incomes, Hardenberg urged that centralized accounting measures be introduced to allow a redistribution of ecclesiastical incomes, thereby issuing as well a slap at the procedures of the consistory.[37]

Only against this backdrop of plans for secularization and centralization can one properly evaluate Campe's move to reform schools and with them the status of preachers and schoolteachers. Hardenberg supported Campe's plan for Philanthropist reform of schools and their teachers because it agreed with Hardenberg's own wishes. Hardenberg was of importance here, for his assumption of responsibility for school and university matters on October 15, 1785 coincided with the start of negotiations concerning the duke's proposed reform: from the start it was clear that a man of Hardenberg's status and views would be backing Campe's specific proposals. Co-operation between the two was facilitated by Campe's enthusiastic support of absolutist government as the best hope for intelligent reform.[38]

The duke began to negotiate with Campe in August of 1785. At this time Campe had already become known as an educator. The duke and Hardenberg quickly decided that Campe was the right man for what they wanted. In December, 1785 Campe returned to Braunschweig to submit to the duke proposals for school reform. Already at this stage Campe envisioned a reorganization encompassing a reform of theological studies which, if carried out, would be of the greatest significance for the future character of the clerical identity.[39]

One aim of the reform was to withdraw schools from the supervision of the ecclesiastical consistory and instead give it to a new, secular board

---

[37] Schmitt, 1: 120, 162-75, 370.
[38] Schmitt, 1: 29, 159-79, 296; Seel, pp. 51-52; up to some point in 1789 the Philanthropists all put their hopes on state reform and administration of schools (Jeismann, p. 133).
[39] Koldewey, pp. 98-103; Beste, p. 484.

(the *Schuldirektorium*) created by the duke in virtue of his episcopal rights. The *Schuldirektorium* was established on June 12, 1786. The head was Hardenberg. Other native members included a prominent clergyman, a member of the ducal government, and an educator. Ranged alongside were the forces of innovation: besides Campe himself, two of his associates in Philanthropist projects had been called. One of the two, Johann Stuve (1752-1793) had close connections with Prussian educational officials. The other, Ernst Christian Trapp (1745-1818) was known as a fanatical opponent of the clergy and as the author of a satire on the theological faculty at Halle.[40]

A detailed narrative of the difficulties faced by the reformers and the steps leading up to the abandonment of ducal reform plans and the dissolution of the Philanthropist *Schuldirektorium* in 1790 would be out of place here.[41] What concerns us is how the issue of the purpose and identity of the clerical estate became a part of the controversy surrounding the *Schuldirektorium*. Such an emphasis is all the more important here because the point has hitherto received inadequate attention.[42]

There is no doubt that a number of interlocked issues called forth determined opposition to Campe's plans: controversy is known to have surrounded the deistic leanings of the reformers, the legal status of the ducal attempts to restrict the consistory's traditional power to supervise schools, the nature of specific experiments in school reform, the theological character of proposed new textbooks, and the possibility that such reform might foster political radicalism.[43]

Yet this conventional summary of issues in controversy does not exhaust the list of matters up for discussion. From the start Campe also aimed at changes of far-reaching significance for the status, preparation, and purpose of the parish clergy in rural areas (that is, the bulk of the clergy). This conclusion emerges plainly from a glance at the proposals submitted by Campe to the duke at the outset in December of 1785. The

---

[40] Beste, pp. 484-85; Fooken, p. 146; Behrens, pp. 1-2; Herrmann, "Modell," p. 169, n. 17.

[41] See the account in Schmitt; for documentation, see Schmitt, 2: 97.

[42] It is neglected in the presentation of the controversy in Fooken and Herrmann. Schmitt consistently emphasizes general social reaction and theological conservatism, linking it with anti-Enlightenment ideological reaction. Cf. Schmitt, 1, 180, 281, 290, 305, 368; however, he exaggerates the orthodox character of North German ecclesiastics at this time.

[43] See in general Schmitt. On textbooks see Schmitt, 1: 190, 207, 283, 305 and the archival material in the Staatsarchiv Wolfenbüttel, Sig. 2 Alt 15884, fols. 1 recto—24 verso, illustrating opposition to possible radical deist influence on future school-books. For general background see Fritz Valjavec, *Die Entstehung der politischen Strömungen* (Munich, 1951); Klaus Epstein, *The Genesis of German Conservatism* (Princeton, 1966): Henri Brunschwig, *La Crise de l'État Prussien* (Paris, 1947).

radical character of these plans guaranteed a clash with the clerical leadership.

Campe emphasized the importance of attracting talented school-teachers and of improving the skills of those already employed. In order to do this, argued Campe, one should abolish the useless traditional curriculum in theology; in its place should come a curriculum based on the "excellent plans of Dr. Bahrdt." Furthermore "a man of Bahrdt's talents, insight, and energy" should be called to the theological faculty at Helmstedt to put these plans into effect by founding a pedagogical seminary.[44] (Bahrdt was, let it be said, never actually called to Helmstedt.) Campe then went on to propose changes in Riddagshausen, the Lutheran cloister which had traditionally trained the leadership of the clergy in Braunschweig-Wolfenbüttel. He contended that, since

> a true preparation for the estate of schoolteacher is also at the same time the best preparation for the clerical estate (which ... cannot be said the other way around)[45]

therefore the theological seminary at Riddagshausen ought to be transformed into a pedagogical institute that would provide theoretical and practical training on Philanthropist lines. The candidates studying in Riddagshausen were to be given special training in how to transform existing schools into industry schools.[46]

Joined to these plans were a number of proposals by Campe to make the career of schoolteacher more attractive—pay raises, more impressive titles for schoolteachers, and the foundation of a decoration (*Pro merito scholastico*) to reward "pedagogical merits."[47] So as to promote meritorious pedagogy even further, it was to be announced that

> the most esteemed and most profitable clerical positions will in future be conferred only on schoolteachers of outstanding merit.[48]

Campe had in mind an elevation of the status of schoolteachers accomplished at the expense of the clergy. He not only wanted to telescope the estate of pastors with that of schoolteachers by giving both an identical utilitarian training different from the traditional training given pastors in philology and metaphysical theology (Bahrdt's suggestion); Campe also urged that advancement to positions of clerical leadership be made dependent on adherence to Philantropist principles. Given the this–worldly orientation of Bahrdt's version of pastoral ministry and the

---

[44] Koldewey, p. 98.
[45] Koldewey, pp. 98.
[46] Koldewey, pp. 98, 100.
[47] Koldewey, pp. 98-99.
[48] Koldewey, p. 99.

far-reaching nature of Campe's plans for a reform of theological education at both the university and the post-university levels, one is safe in
concluding that Campe's plans constitute a comprehensive blueprint to
deprive the clergy of their traditional identity, purpose, leadership, and
institutional independency so as integrate them into the administrative
apparatus of the absolutist state. This impression is strengthened by the
fact that Campe's governmental superior and co-worker Hardenberg
made plans to finance the project of school reform by a redistribution of
the incomes of congregations and ecclesiastical corporations.[49] Part of the
institutional church's financial base of independence was to be diverted
to establish an estate of governmental functionaries very much like
Bahrdt's *Volkslehrer*.

Precisely the same term—*Volkslehrer*—was used by Campe himself to
describe what he had in mind. The concept of *Volkslehrer* is central to a
work published by Campe at Wolfenbüttel in 1786 as two *Fragments* (a
reminiscence of Lessing's Wolfenbüttel *Fragments*). The work presented a
full version of Campe's reform ideas.[50] Campe wanted to enlist public
opinion at a time when the struggle for reform was not going well in
Braunschweig-Wolfenbüttel. The *Fragments* were however dedicated to
Friedrich II's successor on the Prussian throne in the (vain) hope that
he might promote a program of pedagogical Enlightenment and thus
by example advance further reform in Braunschweig-Wolfenbüttel.[51]
Thus the program in the *Fragments* is not exclusively designed for the
dukedom but rather represents a general ideal which Campe recommends categorically.

In his *Fragments* Campe proposes six methods of promoting the public
prosperity:[52]

1. Transformation of the grammar schools into industry schools.
2. A more goal-oriented preparation of those destined to become country
   preachers.
3. Complete and general toleration.
4. Knowledge of the human heart [on the part of teachers and preachers]
   and attraction of such persons as have gained an outstanding possession
   of this knowledge by means of philosophy and the observation of people
   [sc.recruiting such persons as teachers].
5. Establishment of a patriotic society spread throughout the entire land.

---

[49] Schmitt, 1: 168-75.

[50] Joachim Heinrich Campe, *Über einige verkannte, wenigstens ungenützte Mittel zur
Beförderung der Indüstrie, der Bevölkerung und des öffentlichen Wohlstandes* (Wolfenbüttel, 1786)
(hereafter: *1.* or *2. Fragment*). Cf. Schmitt, 1: 273; Beste, p. 485.

[51] Cf. Schmitt, 1: 265; Rudolf Vierhaus, "Politisches Bewußtsein in Deutschland vor
1789," *Der Staat* 6 (1967): 188.

[52] Following the summary of Campe in Schmitt, 1: 267.

6. Greater care on the part of the state with regard to the education of young women.

Here only the first two suggestions require detailed consideration.

The necessity of transforming schools into industry schools is supported by Campe's charge that existing grammar schools are "schools of laziness, of stupidity and of uselessness for life."[53] The well-being of the nation demands that princes support the establishment of industry-schools on Sextroh's model staffed by *Volkslehrer*.[54] Here Campe goes further than Sextroh in promoting a utilitarian model of ministry, for Sextroh had not envisioned that the pastor would be directly involved in the industry-school in a capacity other than that of supervisor.

Campe then turns to the preparation of a suitable group of *Volkslehrer*.[55] His consideration of the preparation of those destined for a career in the rural clergy opens with a bow in the direction of Bahrdt. Campe then gives a critical presentation of the traditional activities of the rural clergyman. Those activities were conventionally limited to the following "onerous"[56] duties of the pastor, as Campe sees it:

1. [The pastor] baptized, married, heard confession, preached, and distributed the Lord's Supper.
2. He administered the parish lands ... and collected his tithes.
3. When requested, he visited the sick and fortified them, not with extreme unction, but with communion, to the strengthening of the general superstitious notion that this holy action (instituted for quite different purposes) was the means of suddenly wiping clean a whole life full of sin and shame and of obtaining eternal blessedness in exchange for nothing.
4. He visited ... the school of his village, not in order to teach there himself, but in order to see if the catechism was being properly learnt, and to remind the schoolteacher that he had a supervisor.
5. He prepared the catechumens for several months, that is, he examined them to see if they had learnt the catechism, and grafted onto the catechism learnt by rote a part of the dogmatics he had ... taken down at the university.[57]

Campe then argues that

if the rural clergyman were the proper man for the job, if he were spared superfluous studies quite useless to him, and on the other hand were prepared in a more appropriate way, he could be the father, the teacher, the physician, the counselor, and the model of his congregation, ...[58]

---

[53] *1. Fragment*, p. 7.
[54] *1. Fragment*, pp. 16-18, 6, 10.
[55] Cf. *1. Fragment*, pp. 18, 39, 44.
[56] *1. Fragment*, pp. 28-29.
[57] *1. Fragment*, pp. 29-30.
[58] *1. Fragment*, p. 32.

Indeed, there is little the country preacher could not do if differently trained:

> he could take care of the education and the reasonable practical instruction of the youth, he could disseminate an Enlightenment suited to the needs of the country dweller throughout his village and his area, he could improve the morals and manners of his parishioners, and help improve the home management, agriculture and other occupations of his congregation; ...[59]

But this does not exhaust the pastor's potential:

> he could lengthen the lives of many of his parishioners by helping the farmer to follow a better plan of life, by replacing superstitious quack medicines with truly effective remedies, and by giving prompt aid to those suffering from external lesions or wounds through his skill in the care of wounds; he could ... nip in the bud many useless and harmful legal actions; in short, he could be the most honored and most useful instrument for promoting true practical fear of God, appropriate Enlightenment, good morals, order, diligence, industry, increase of population, and public welfare.[60]

Achieving such a goal requires a change in the theological curriculum. Campe explains what this means:

> To begin with ..., in schools and in universities one must no longer strive to educate future rural clergy as learned men in the exact sense, least of all, though, to educate them as real theologians ... for the future country preacher has no time to become a scholar and a theologian, because he should become something better, learning something more useful than the wisdom of the school ...[61]

Indeed, if the clergy are to become "useful citizens of the state" it is necessary to eliminate from their training those academic studies which are positively harmful to the exercise of their office in a utilitarian and practical manner:

> The acquisition ... of school learning ... makes one ... stiff and pedantic: and the spiritual teacher of the people should neither the one nor the other, but rather be ... natural, straightforward, open, cordial, and without any learned pretensions.[62]

Campe then tries to give a better explanation of why the acquisition of traditional theology has this harmful effect; in so doing, he reveals that he has lost all belief in the real existence of the otherworldly objects with which traditional religion and theology had dealt:

> The acquisition ... of school learning removes people from the real world into the world of the school; weakens the concentration on that which really

---

[59] *1. Fragment*, pp. 32-33.
[60] *1. Fragment*, pp. 33-34.
[61] *1. Fragment*, p. 35.
[62] *1. Fragment*, pp. 36-37 and "citizens" on p. 34.

exists, on that which goes on around and beside us, and gradually fixes it upon vain bookish ideas; introduces ... a distaste for the customary business of life; causes our powers of imagination to cleave more to words than to things, more to desire learned than useful knowledge, becomes more interested in how this or that figures in a book or learned lecture, than in how it can be applied to the business and happiness of life: and the spiritual teacher of the people should be a man from the real world and for the real world, a man for life, not for speculation; ... nothing by means of which he can become useful should disgust him ...; he should ... pay ... attention, not to words and logomachies, but simply to things, not to learned abstractions, but rather to the thing itself, not to that which sparkles in a dissertation, but rather to that which can be applied to the life and purpose of his parishioners.[63]

Campe continues at length in this vein: abstract school learning makes the clergy intolerant and unable to speak in a fashion intelligible to ordinary people. The acquisition of learned theological training weakens the powers of perception, and moreover it

dries out the hearts ... in virtue of the increasing delicacy of life, softness, and weakening of humanity, attacks the muscles, especially those of the lower body and the powers of digestion, and thus makes one sickly, ill-tempered, and hypochondriacal.[64]

Campe then provides a list of the traditional studies which, because they are useless or harmful, must be eliminated from any future curriculum for training rural clergy. He begins by eliminating Greek, Hebrew, "and every other eastern language," for they contribute nothing to promoting the "real purpose" of the *Volkslehrer*, that is, the purpose of advancing their parishioners' well-being.[65]

Next to go must be hermeneutics, "or the art of interpreting the Old and New Testaments of the Bible on the basis of the original languages."[66] Here Campe is even more radical than Bahrdt. Campe argues that, since most parish pastors forget whatever of the ancient languages they may once have learnt, one must realize that it is perfectly possible to be a good country pastor using only the vernacular: learned theological argument is not the purpose of ministry.

Also to be eliminated is traditional dogmatics, which consists of mere human traditions, has nothing to do with the religion taught by Jesus, and is useless. In the same category are polemic and traditional logic and metaphysics.[67]

---

[63] *1. Fragment*, pp. 37-38.
[64] *1. Fragment*, pp. 41-42.
[65] *1. Fragment*, pp. 44-45.
[66] *1. Fragment*, p. 45; cf. pp. 46-49.
[67] *1. Fragment*, pp. 50-56.

Finally Campe wishes to do away with the greatest part, or even all, of the study of the Latin language and Latin literature, which he regards as useless for the rural clergy. Again Campe strikes a more radical note than Bahrdt.[68]

Campe now recommends his curriculum for rural clergymen. First he demands education to develop sound common sense. The goal is by familiarity with real life to produce a clergyman capable of promoting an Enlightenment fitted for rural life: the clergyman must be able to deal with simple, moral, practical religion, leaving out of consideration dogmatics and polemics as inappropriate for the laity. Furthermore the future *Volkslehrer* must be trained to aid parishioners in matters of agriculture and other affairs of daily life so as to stimulate industry and insure prosperity. Joined to this must be a knowledge of the religion "taught by Jesus Christ himself," uncorrupted by theological speculation and supplemented by "what human reason, even without supernatural instruction, can know concerning God, our duties, and our purpose." That is to say, the clergyman must learn "a system of the Christian religion" containing nothing that is not practical; he need learn only what can be applied immediately to the needs of his rural congregation.[69] This would amount to a system of deistic morality of the kind which had allegedly been taught by Jesus Christ. The clergyman must learn to teach the common people intelligibly by the socratic method. He must gain a critical acquaintance with the "true" history of the origin and alteration of religion so that he can distinguish the original shape of the Christian religion from its accretion of human traditions.[70]

Next, Campe recommends the acquisition of much knowledge of humanity as a prerequisite for effective work. Furthermore the future pastor must acquire

> much knowledge and skill in physical and mechanical matters, much theoretical and practical knowledge of economy, agriculture, the arts and crafts, especially those which the farmer cannot figure out for himself.[71]

Obviously, Campe argues, there will be time for this only if a good part of the traditional curriculum in theology be abolished; that is no problem, for it is useless anyhow. As Campe puts it: let one only consider the matter soberly, and then one can readily give the answer to the questions:

> of both, which is more ... important, fruitful, and useful ... for the con-

---

[68] *1. Fragment*, pp. 59-62.

[69] *1. Fragment*, pp. 64-71.

[70] *1. Fragment*, pp. 72-74; cf. Martin Schian, *Die Sokratik im Zeitalter der Aufklärung* (Breslau, 1900).

[71] *1. Fragment*, p. 77.

gregation and the state? Dogmatics or natural history? Oriental languages or physics? Polemical theology or mechanics? Classical literature or the knowledge of economic and technological matters?[72]

Besides the advantages to the state, one must also consider

that by means of the above-mentioned secular disciplines the rural clergyman can far more certainly than by means of any of the theological disciplines be put into a condition in which he can acquire the respect, trust, and love of the country dweller so as to have a real effect upon him.[73]

Finally, Campe recommends

as much medical knowledge and surgical skill as are necessary in order rightly to treat the most common ... diseases ... and in any necessity to carry out the business of a surgeon. To this end the future country parson must study dietetics and anatomy, gain practical experience in certain surgical matters, get to know the ... best medicines ..., undergo a pathological and clinical instruction designed especially for him, and in the last year of his academic career visit ... hospitals at the side of a skilled physician.[74]

With Campe we stand at the logical conclusion to a long development: the traditional metaphysical and philological elements of the pastor's stock-in-trade have been reduced to an absolute minimum—as it were, well below the fifty percent mark. The historic *raison d'être* of the clergy (that is, expounding the truths of a supernatural salvation drawn from revealed scripture) has in large measure given way to a new *raison d'être* derived from absolutist *raison d'état*: the pastor is chiefly concerned with the temporal welfare of his parishioners, and that in a fashion designed to benefit the state.

It was immediately clear that Campe's was no idle proposal; seen in context it was a blueprint for transforming the Lutheran clergy into state functionaries deprived of the financial or ideological basis for any purpose independent of that which the temporal government might dictate.

The serious nature of this possibility can be gauged by looking at the not insignificant support which Campe's proposals found both inside and outside the dukedom—though *not*, it should be noted, among indigenous churchmen.[75] Campe could not be ignored: at this point a decision had to be made. Either the erosion of the traditional concept of the pastoral ministry was to continue until the clergy in fact became simply functionaries of the state, or else this process of erosion was to be resisted in an effort to retain and perhaps even restore part of the ideological and

---

[72] *1. Fragment*, p. 78.
[73] *1. Fragment*, p. 79.
[74] *1. Fragment*, pp. 81-82.
[75] See Appendix D.

institutional independence historically characteristic of the traditionally constituted clerical estate.

2. *Resistance to the Radical Secularist Attack on Clerical Identity*

a. Sources of the Resistance Movement

The proposals of Campe and like-minded reformers posed a political question: was there to be allowed the further assimilation of one of the traditional estates into the apparatus of absolutist government? The dangers of this tendency had long since been pointed out: Mosheim as a spokesman for particularism and the mixed constitution had underlined the dangers inherent in the proposals of Thomasius; moreover, in his proposals for a reform of clerical training and professional functioning, Mosheim had provided an important example of how conservative or particularist reform plans could be used to counter secularizing tendencies.

In the struggle resulting from the proposals of Bahrdt and Campe, it was only to be expected that the clerical leadership would look for support where they could find it—also to lay spokesmen and lay allies. For by finding such assistance among lay leaders interested in the political consequences of the centralist challenge to traditional German society, the clerical leadership could show that their opposition to utilitarian reform plans arose from more than narrow self-interest: indeed, spokesmen for clerical particularism would eventually follow the example of political critics of enlightened centralism by invoking, not merely the principles of tradition and divine law, but as well the "rational" principles of natural law.

One important political writer pointing the way was Friedrich Carl von Moser (1723-1798), whose criticisms of clerical co-operation with absolutist policy were widely read. From a standpoint of Pietism Moser criticized Thomas Abbt and clerical propagandists for Prussian militarism. At the same time he attacked the servility characteristic of those dependent on absolutist princes, urging instead a reliance on the traditional political power of the various estates in society and the force of revealed religion: only these could provide protection against absolutism, cameralism, and "despotism."[76] Moser was particularly critical of the

---

[76] Notker Hammerstein, "Das politische Denken Friedrich Carl von Mosers," *Historische Zeitschrift* 212 (1971): 316-38; Karlfriedrich Eckstein, *Friedrich Carl von Moser (1723-1798)* (Diss., Rechtswiss., Giessen, 1973); Friedrich Carl Gottlob Hirsching, ed., *Historisch-litterarisches Handbuch* (Leipzig, 1804), 6: 176-77; F. C. von Moser, *Beherzigungen* (Frankfurt a.M., 1761), p. 462; F. C. von Moser, *Patriotische Briefe* (Frankfurt a.M., 1767), pp. 186-92.

willingness of some of the Lutheran clergy to serve as "helpers of despotism" by preaching passive obedience joined with one-sided concentration on the duties subjects owe their sovereigns.[77]

Moser's lengthiest and most trenchant criticisms of this kind were published in his *Reliquien* of 1766. He ridicules cameralism as an absolutist policy transforming subjects into beasts efficiently fattened for slaughter by immoral and war-mongering princes. With an obvious reference to the call for a variety of civil religion in the last chapter of the *Social Contract*, Moser condemns the Göttingen cameral theorist Justi, asserting that he is for "cameralistic moral doctrine" what Rousseau is in religion: for Justi, like Rousseau, contends that traditional Christian morality and the general welfare are in some points incompatible.[78]

Moser's wrath is reserved for attempts to use religion as a tool of statecraft. Stressing that prayer, comforting, and admonition constitute the duty of the clergy, and further that the clergy ought not to allow themselves to be used as "politicians," Moser criticizes Abbt for his propagandizing for clerical support of the Prussian army, which threatens to transform church services into centers for forcible recruiting.[79] Condemning Abbt's revival of the pagan civil religion of the ancient Romans, Moser goes on to pillory Abbt's absolutistic concept of merit.[80]

Thus Moser rejects the transformation of historic revealed Christianity into a reasonable religion on cameralistic principles.[81] This traditionalistic viewpoint accords well with his particularistic politics. Yet at one point Moser moves beyond this to employ for his purposes the terminology of Enlightenment natural law writers. This approach was to be developed more fully by subsequent opponents of clerical utilitarianism.

In attempting to refute the Enlightenment charge that traditional Christianity is inimical to the best interests of the state, Moser argues thus concerning the connection of religion with the state:

> Those [i.e. Enlightenment critics] who detect difficulties in the connection of civil society with religion attack the wisdom, goodness, mercy, and omniscience of God Himself directly. The *civic man* [*der bürgerliche Mensch*] and the *man created for immortality* [*der zur Unsterblichkeit erschaffene Mensch*] can never be in contradiction the one with the other without burdening God

---

[77] Moser, *Briefe*, pp. 192-95; *Beherzigungen*, pp. 441-42; F. C. von Moser,*Reliquien* (Frankfurt a.M. and Leipzig, 1776), pp. 182, 4-5, 107-8.

[78] Cf. n. 77 above; Moser, *Reliquien*, p. 108; cf. Karl Dietrich Erdmann, *Das Verhältnis von Staat und Religion* (Berlin, 1935); Robert Derathé, "La religion civile selon Rousseau," *Annales de la Société Jean-Jacques Rousseau* 35 (1959-62): 161-80; Ronald Grimsley, *Rousseau and the Religious Quest* (Oxford, 1968), pp. 84-85.

[79] Moser, *Reliquien*, pp. 176-79.

[80] Moser, *Reliquien*, pp. 239-41.

[81] Moser, *Reliquien*, pp. 205-9.

with the guilt for the cruelty of having put man into two relationships which cannot be united with each other, so that the well-being of the one constitutes the misfortune of the other, so that one must become an ever-worse citizen the more one attempts the more perfectly to fulfill one's commandments.[82]

Moser goes on to explain why this is the case:

Man is created for immortality, for an eternal blessedness; he is born for religion, which is to show him the way in which he is to live, how he is to live happy and content, in order to be able to contemplate his end with comfort and his coming to life again with joy. If then statecraft has as its highest and purest intention the production of contented and happy citizens, then religion has not only the same intentions, but rather leads still further; where politics stops, religion still continues to operate; thus it does not abandon man where civil society stops. ...[83]

Here Moser has stepped onto the territory of his Enlightenment opponents, the territory of natural law with its distinction between man and citizen. On the one side is "the civic man," but on the other is "the man created for immortality." As Moser insists that man is created for immortality and the religion that guides him to it, he can argue that religion must continue where the life of the citizen leaves off. Hence, though Moser couches his position in the language of the Enlightenment's natural law distinction between man and citizen, he nonetheless is in a position to imply that the interests of man as an immortal being are of greater import than those of man as citizen—even though, for apologetic purposes, he must deny that those interests could come into conflict.

Thus Moser the Pietist has taken the step of moving the defense of service to the religious needs of humanity onto the territory of the Enlightenment itself; he has adopted what Manfred Riedel terms "the theory of modern natural law," a theory which was to be "codified in the rights of man and citizen of the North American and French Revolution." Proponents of this view held, in Riedel's words, that

man as man was a member of the great society of the human race (*societas generis humani*), a place accorded him by reason itself; as citizen he belonged to civil society in the sense of the state (*civitas sive societas civilis*), to the valid positive laws of which he was subjected.[84]

---

[82] Moser, *Reliquien*, pp. 209-10.

[83] Moser, *Reliquien*, p. 210.

[84] For all this see Manfred Riedel, "Bürger, Staatsbürger, Bürgertum," *Geschichtliche Grundbegriffe*, ed. Otto Brunner, Werner Conze, and Reinhart Koselleck (Stuttgart, 1972), 1:706. For the dissociation of "civil society" from the state see Diethelm Klippel, *Politische Freiheit und Freiheitsrechte* (Paderborn, 1976), p. 137 and n. 9. Yet cf. Riedel, "Bürger," pp. 693-94 on *Bürger* in the sense of *citoyen* or *Staatsbürger* in the later eighteenth century.

This natural law distinction went back to Hobbes's separation of the public sphere from the private domain of religious belief, and had thus from the start an intrinsic connection with questions pertaining to religion. By the late eighteenth century it had become a commonplace that, just as the state existed to deal with external matters, so was it the case that religion and religious ideas as such pertained only to the man, not the citizen—a view taught explicitly by, for example, Schlözer at Göttingen.[85]

Obviously this natural law distinction was potentially of great interest to would-be defenders of the traditional or non-temporal version of the clerical *raison d'être*. For it established a sphere for religion independent of the state by connecting religion with the capacity for being fully human; furthermore, use of this distinction gave the appearance of an appeal to Enlightenment principles not given by the old-fashioned appeal to bald divine right.

The natural law distinction between man and citizen as a means of arguing for the priority of the non-temporal over the temporal function of the clergy could, however, become truly useful only once the initial con-notation of natural law thought in German-speaking Europe had begun to fade. For natural law thinking as a whole had originally been used by absolutist princes and their theoreticians as a way of breaking the authority and power of the traditional estates, including the clergy.[86] In this early period the "natural" basis for natural law and rights had been found in the primeval state of nature abolished by subsequent contract. In the later eighteenth century, however, and particularly beginning with the 1780's, there came about a change: the basis for argumentation was now located in a nature of the human individual held to remain constant over time. With this change in emphasis came a new concern with "natural freedom," for it now became possible to derive from the constant and personal human nature of the individual a variety of inalienable and unalterable rights. In German-speaking Europe this list of rights included freedom of religion and freedom of conscience.[87] Argumentation of this kind was, of course, intended to limit the demands of the central state and to defend the interests of a nonnoble group now

---

[85] August Ludwig Schlözer, *Allgemeines StatsRecht und StatsVerfassungsLere* (Göttingen, 1793), p. 21. For background see Reinhart Koselleck, *Kritik und Krise* (Frankfurt a.M., 1973), pp. 18-31 and p. 168, n. 75 with reference to Hobbes, *De hom.* XIII, 9; Jürgen Schlumbohm, *Freiheit* (Düsseldorf, 1975), pp. 119-21; Josef Bohatec, "Die Vorgeschichte der Menschen- und Bürgerrechte," in Roman Schnur, ed., *Zur Geschichte der Erklärung der Menschenrechte* (Darmstadt, 1964), pp. 268, 313-14; Samuel Pufendorf, *De officio hominis & civis* (Cambridge, 1682).

[86] Klippel, pp. 105-8.

[87] Klippel, p. 123.

desirous of more public influence—the late-Enlightenment ancestors of what was in the nineteenth century to become the *Bildungsbürgertum*.[88]

Once natural law argumentation had in the late Enlightenment been put to this antiabsolutist purpose, the usefulness of the man-citizen distinction as a way of subordinating the utilitarian definition of the clerical function to the nontemporal or "religious" definition of it would become increasingly apparent to those who wished persuasively to state the case for reaffirming that traditional subordination. For in so doing the spokesmen for the traditionalist or "religious" point of view on clerical identity could make common cause with progressive-appearing critics of enlightened absolutism and its attendant economic doctrines: there would be proposed a divorce of clerical self-interest from the self-interest of absolutist politicians and centralist economists, and a new marriage of clerical self-interest with that of the emergent proto-*Bildungsbürgertum*.

Another important influence on the Northwest German clergy was the defense of clerical particularist *raison d'être* made by the churchman Johann Gottfried Herder (1744-1803).[89] In his attack on clerical utilitarianism[90] Herder restated the traditionalist claim that the clergyman must be a servant of religion whose chief purpose is interpreting the divine revelation mediated through scripture. He even attempted to reconfer a positive connotation on the term "priest" (without however giving it a sacrificial connotation). In this connection Herder in

---

[88] Cf. Klippel, pp. 104-36; Rudolf Vierhaus, "Bildung," *Geschichtliche Grundbegriffe*, 1: 508-51; Hans Rosenberg, *Bureaucracy, Aristocracy and Autocracy* (Cambridge, Mass., 1958); Rosenberg, "Theologischer Rationalismus und vormärzlicher Vulgärliberalismus," *Historische Zeitschrift* 141 (1930): 497-541; Vierhaus, "Zur historischen Deutung der Aufklärung," in *Judentum im Zeitalter der Aufklärung* (Wolfenbüttel, 1977), pp. 39-54; Vierhaus, "Deutschland im 18. Jahrhundert," in *Aufklärung, Absolutismus und Bürgertum in Deutschland*, ed. Franklin Kopitzsch (Munich, 1976), pp. 173-91; Kurt von Raumer, "Absoluter Staat, korporative Libertät, personliche Freiheit," *Historische Zeitschrift* 183 (1957): 55-96; Hajo Holborn, "German Idealism in the Light of Social History," in his *Germany and Europe* (New York, 1970), pp. 1-32; Eckart Kehr, "Zur Genesis der preussischen Bürokratie und des Rechtsstaates," in *Moderne deutsche Sozialgeschichte*, ed. Hans-Ulrich Wehler (Cologne, 1966), pp. 37-54; Henri Brunschwig, *Enlightenment and Romanticism*, tr. Frank Jellinek (Chicago, 1974); Karl-Ernst Jeismann, *Das preußische Gymnasium in Staat und Gesellschaft* (Stuttgart, 1974); Werner Conze, "Staat und Gesellschaft in der frührevolutionären Epoche Deutschlands," *Historische Zeitschrift* 186 (1961): 1-34; Alexandria Schlingensiepen-Pogge, *Das Sozialethos der Lutherischen Aufklärungstheologie* (Göttingen, 1967); Johanna Schultze, *Die Auseinandersetzung zwischen Adel und Bürgertum* (Berlin, 1925); and Fritz Martiny, *Die Adelsfrage in Preußen vor 1806* (Stuttgart, 1938).

[89] Rudolf Haym, *Herder nach seinem Leben und seinen Werken*, 2 vols. (Berlin, 1877); Horst Stephan, *Herder in Bückeburg* (Tübingen, 1905).

[90] See Joseph Schollmeier, *Johann Joachim Spalding* (Gütersloh, 1967); Reinhard Krause, *Die Predigt der späten deutschen Aufklärung* (Stuttgart, 1965); Herder, *An Prediger. Funfzehn Provinzialblätter* (Leipzig, 1774) reprinted in *Herders Sämmtliche Werke*, ed. Bernhard Suphan (Berlin, 1884), 7:225-312.

the 1770's held that the clergyman is "the bearer of a divine gift to the people," and thus a

> teacher of revelation, propagator of the purest means toward cultivation—and insofar really a consecrated, chosen mediating person—a messenger and instrument of God

who is

> selected by the [common mass of people] and thus by God to bear God's word to them.[91]

At such points Herder early moved beyond attempts to defend the clergy on the basis of natural law in favor of a statement on ministry anticipating the later appropriation by Schleiermacher of the position of Ignatius of Antioch and Gottfried Arnold. Quite logically, then, Herder could defend as praiseworthy the fostering of a clerical *esprit de corps* despite Enlightenment criticism of clerical party spirit; for the clergy were for Herder praiseworthy because of their divine and revelatory purpose in the Kingdom of God.[92]

Equally logical was Herder's rejection of Rousseauesque attempts to establish the church on the rational and human basis of social contract, and with it the view that, since the church and clergy have no claim on divine right, they are matters of political convenience that can be abolished at will.[93] With this went Herder's repudiation of the absolutist policy of encouraging the clergy to read edicts from the pulpit and to occupy themselves with cameralism.[94] Explicitly condemned was the proposition that the clergy could be defended if they functioned as established teachers of morality and virtue, servants of civil society proclaiming a "political-Christian religion" consisting simply of expedient morality.[95] Against Hume's well-known charge that the inherent character of the clerical profession necessarily tends to corrupt the clergy and to turn them against the best interests of society, Herder set his counter-claim that it is the political estate which is responsible for the degeneration of the clerical estate.[96] Herder thus aimed at replacing this relative significance of the clergyman with an absolute significance: the preacher is to be a depository of a treasure of revelation rather than a depository of civic morality.[97]

---

[91] Suphan, 7: 290.

[92] Cf. Suphan, 7: 292, cf. for background Justus Möser, *Sämtliche Werke*, ed. Ludwig Schirmeyer (Oldenburg and Berlin, 1943), 4: 245, 246.

[93] Suphan, 7: 238-39, 294.

[94] Suphan, 7: 240-41.

[95] Suphan, 7: 239-41; 295; 305.

[96] Suphan, 7: 281-93. Cf. n. 23 above.

[97] Cf. Suphan, 7: 239, Johann Joachim Spalding, *Ueber die Nutzbarkeit des Predigtamtes* (Berlin, 1772), p. 54; Schollmeier, pp. 122-23.

All this does not mean that Herder in his defense of the uniquely religious function of the clerical task did not appeal to natural law. It will be recalled that the animating religious principle in Herder's scheme is panentheism linked with aestheticism and joined to an obscure theory of the efficacious power of poetic language to transmit effects from one soul to another. This substitute for the traditional notion of revelation serves Herder as a way of glorifying the historical basis for the ancient social importance of the clerical and priestly estate: for Herder utilizes the idea made current by English and Scottish critics according to which in primeval times poetry and theology had together been fostered by a single leadership group composed of priests. Thus for Herder the original and essential function of the clergy is a highly honorable one—the function of furthering the cultivation of the souls of people, of communicating a *Philosophie der Menschheit* (philosophy of humanity), and of thus contributing to the education (*Bildung*) of the world.[98]

At this point Herder makes an appeal to the natural law distinction between man and citizen. For by asserting that the religious task of the clergyman is at the same time a task of elaborating a *Philosophie der Menschheit* so that the clergy, far from simply serving their own self-interest, in fact constitute instead an estate of humanity (*Stand der Menschheit*), Herder readily moves into the linguistic domain of natural law terminology—that same terminology which could in the later eighteenth century be used by the proto-*Bildungsbürgertum* as a weapon against absolutist and centralist doctrines.[99] Thus Herder in 1774 clearly implies that, since the pastor's main responsibility is to the religious needs of the *Mensch* rather than to the *Bürger* as a citizen of this world, therefore the main clerical responsibility is to an eternal purpose far weighter than anything based on social contract or political convenience. Herder declares:

> But, if the priest were ... the bearer of a divine gift to the people—the teacher of revelation, propagator of the purest means of *Bildung*—and insofar really a consecrated, chosen mediating person—a messenger and instrument of God ... [then the clergy would be] chosen carriers-out of a sacred matter, the holiest matter on earth—*Bildung* of the soul by means of religion. As such we recognize neither citizens [Bürger], nor subjects, but

---

[98] Hirsch, *Geschichte der neuern evangelischen Theologie*, 4: 223-47; Klaus Scholder, "Herder und die Anfänge der historischen Theologie," *Evangelische Theologie* 23 (1962): 425-40; Hans W. Frei, *The Eclipse of Biblical Narrative* (New Haven, Conn., 1974), pp. 19-21; Suphan, 7: 290-300; F. McEachran, *The Life and Philosophy of Johann Gottfried Herder* (Oxford, 1939).

[99] Cf. Suphan, 7: 286-300.

rather men [Menschen], creatures of God, brothers of Jesus, members of revelation.[100]

The significance of this passage is clear: Herder envisions a ministry devoted not to the preparation of citizens trained for efficient and contented functioning in the machinery of absolutism, but rather to the propagation of a religious *Bildung* upon which society as a whole will place a high value.[101] The fullest statement of this view of ministry was to come in Schleiermacher's *Reden*, which move far more explicitly than Herder toward a reworking of the clerical role. That is, the pastor will for Schleiermacher become as agent of *Bildung* a sacral focus functioning in a way analogous to that envisioned by Ignatius of Antioch or Gottfried Arnold—the bearer of a word not, to be sure, divine in its derivation from supernaturally-efficacious scripture, but a word nonetheless worthy of reverence: for the claim to possess a social status founded on *Bildung* was after all a matter of ultimate concern to the *Bildungsbürgertum* fighting for recognition in the face of noble privilege. And it was the claims of a *Bildungsbürgertum* increasingly doubtful concerning its chances for further advancement within the absolutist framework which Herder and Schleiermacher represented.

Herder thus anticipates the way in which, in the last fifteen years of the eighteenth century, the educated bureaucracy, the clergy, and some of the nobility would increasingly turn against the ideal of the absolutist state, in the process taking its bureaucracy as it were captive for their own social purposes, or else turning in disgust from efforts to realize the ideals of church or school within a state-supported system.[102]

Herder's identification of the clerical task with service to the eternal needs of the *Mensch* rather than to the temporal duties of the *Bürger* signals then a proposal that the clergy identify themselves with the social goals of a newly-self-conscious *Bildungsbürgertum* no longer content with allowing their purposes to be defined by spokesmen for absolutist government, but instead determined to assert the claim that their considerable worth to society depended upon their acquisition of that mystic quality of intellectual and spiritual *Bildung* which could be got only by a demanding study of traditional texts.

The kind of position represented by Herder at the same time points to a renewed emphasis on ancient philology and the interpretation of sacred

---

[100] Suphan, 7: 290.
[101] Cf. Suphan, 7: 238.
[102] Vierhaus, "Bildung," pp. 511-25; Jeismann, pp. 132-48; Brunschwig; Friedrich Schleiermacher, *On Religion*, tr. John Oman (New York, 1958), p. 131; cf. Terry Hancock Foreman, "Religion as the Heart of Humanistic Culture: Schleiermacher as Exponent of *Bildung*" (Diss., Yale University, 1975).

and classical texts as a part of the religious and humanistic tradition: it is an anticipation of the movement later to be known as Neohumanism, a movement born at Göttingen and opposed to the utilitarian goals of the absolutist Enlightenment.[103]

Argumentation in these antiabsolutist circles at the close of the eighteenth century would stress Neohumanism in education, the importance of cultivation or *Bildung*, and (in the jargon of the day) the priority of pedagogical and clerical responsibility to the man as individual over responsibility for the citizen as a creature of the state. Such rhetoric had a definite appeal. It attracted those who found who found absolutism, cameralism, Philanthropism or national education, and the clerical reform plans of Bahrdt and Campe unacceptable—yet who, in their rejection of the exaggeratedly "practical," centralist emphases in general education advocated by the Philanthropist party (especially the de-emphasis of classical education and metaphysics for the nonnoble literate) still could not in this rejection of centralist utilitarianism return to pre-Enlightenment positions. Those who could not advocate pre-absolutist positions stressing the guiding role of the nobility or the unreconstructed supernaturalism of Lutheran Orthodoxy needed "progressive" anticentralist rhetoric of the kind provided by the language of Neohumanism and *Bildung*.

That is to say, the rhetoric of Neohumanism, *Bildung*, and the priority of *Mensch* over *Bürger* would appeal chiefly to the emergent *Bildungsbürgertum* and to the churchmen and theologians who, abandoning the proud claims of Lutheran Orthodoxy while also rejecting the counterproposals made by enlightened proponents of a clerical alliance with absolutism, sought instead toward the end of the eighteenth century a different alliance, one with the newly self-confident *Bildungsbürgertum*. For in proclaiming the "cultivating" power of the clerical message based on classic texts, the churchmen could hope to protect their traditional non-temporal *raison d'être* against further absolutist-inspired enlightened attrition: they could now stress how the educative role of the clergy as transmitters of religious and aesthetic *Bildung* could legitimate the demand of the nonnoble upper classes for a more influential role in society.[104] Already in the last part of the eighteenth century moves in this direction were made among the Northwest German churchmen as they repudiated the plans of Bahrdt and Campe.

---

[103] Holborn; Fritz K. Ringer, *The Decline of the German Mandarins* (Cambridge, Mass., 1969), pp. 85-90; and A. Reble, "Neuhumanismus. II. Pädagogisch," *RGG*, 3rd ed. (Tübingen, 1960), 4: cols. 1418-19.

[104] See Appendix E.

b. Clericalist Resistance to Campe and its Allies in Braunschweig-Wolfenbüttel

The reform plans sponsored by Campe in his capacity as educational advisor to the Duke of Braunschweig-Wolfenbüttel represented a kind of thinking inimical to the self-definition current among most of the leading churchmen in Northwest Germany at the time—a kind of thinking appealing to those who, like Bahrdt and Campe, had for one cause or another abandoned the active practice of Christian ministry. On the other hand, the clerical leadership opposed the plans put forward by Campe, and in so doing, drew certain conclusions about the limits to which theological Enlightenment in a centralist and utilitarian framework could be pushed without endangering the very existence of the clerical estate as conventionally conceived.[105]

In the long run, very little came of the Philanthropist reform plans for schools, teachers, and clergy put forward by Campe in his capacity as advisor to the duke. As a step toward realization of Campe's comprehensive reform plan, Duke Karl Wilhelm Ferdinand did indeed make a dramatic move on June 12, 1786. On that date the duke withdrew the supervision of schools from the consistory and put it in the hands of a body directly responsible to him. This new board or *Schulddirectorium* included Campe, Trapp, and Hardenberg as members. But by April 6, 1790 the duke had been forced to abolish the *Schuldirectorium* and to return the supervision of schools to the consistory, thereby admitting that the comprehensive reforms envisioned by Campe and Hardenberg were impossible of realization.[106] Both the social composition of the opposition mounted against the *Schuldirectorium* and the statements on the purpose of the clergy made by churchmen during this period must be taken into account if one is to gain an adequate idea of how the Northwest German churchmen were coming to understand themselves at the close of the Enlightenment.

Active and overt opposition to the ducal reform plans as articulated by Campe was localized in a variety of particularist institutions in Braunschweig-Wolfenbüttel. Lay opposition, in part under clerical influence, was to be found first in the estates—both in its standing committees and its convocation; and second in the government of the city of

---

[105] It should be emphasized that, though the leading Northwest German churchmen came to adopt positions akin to those of Moser and Herder, we are here not interested in assessing precisely the "influence" of particular figures on the churchmen. For a more conservative attack on utilitarianism than Herder's, see Daniel Joachim Köppen, *Der Hauptzweck des Predigtamts* (Leipzig, 1778).

[106] Schmitt, 1: 161-78; Herrmann, "Modell," p. 169; and in general Behrens.

Braunschweig.[107] Clerical opposition was centered in the clergy of the city of Braunschweig sitting as a corporation (the so-called *Geistliches Ministerium*) and in the so-called *Geistliches Gericht*, an anomalous body which functioned as a sort of sub-consistory with jurisdiction over scholastic and charitable matters and marital causes for the city of Braunschweig.[108] Though it is sometimes stated that the consistory was not involved in the opposition movement,[109] in fact the situation was not so simple. The consistory in Wolfenbüttel, it will be recalled, had for some time been the object of ducal attempts at temporal domination. This was the case insofar as the ducal government had succeeded in installing as president of the consistory a layman who was to a degree amenable to ducal policies; however, the *clergymen* in the consistory therefore strove all the more fiercely to arouse other particularist institutions to active opposition to the proposed ducal reforms of schools and of training for the clerical estate.[110] Their success was, in the long run, almost perfect.

The tactics used by the particularist opponents included prolonged negotiations aiming at delay, ignoring ducal orders, convocation of the assembly of estates, and the eventual threat of a suit against the duke in the imperial court (*Reichskammergericht*).[111] The last threat is of particular interest: on February 12, 1788, the general convocation of estates raised the possibility of such a suit; though it was rejected as an immediate option by majority vote, the action eventually taken on February 16, 1788 recommended such a suit if further attempts at compromise should fail.[112] In this attempt to preserve customary privilege, the estates (which, of course, included clerical members or "prelates") thus fully supported the clerical members of the consistory, who opposed the ducal creation of the *Schuldirectorium* as an attempt to reduce the consistory's supervisory powers over the schools. Though the estates sought an official opinion or *Gutachten* from the faculty of law at Jena, the decision, when it arrived, found in favor of the ducal power to create such a new body as the *Schuldirectorium*.[113] In view of this opinion and of the eventual capitulation by the duke, the estates did not go so far as actually to bring suit.

---

[107] Schmitt, 1: 179-90, 290-340; cf. Walther Lampe, "Grundsätzliches zur Frage der Prälatur," *JGNK*, 53 (1965): 264-71.

[108] Schmitt, 1: 262, 276-78, 290-343; Vitus Dettmer, "Das Geistliche Gericht der Stadt Braunschweig," *ZGNK* 34/35 (1929-30): 200-27.

[109] Vitus Dettmer, *Das Konsistorium zu Wolfenbüttel* (Braunschweig, 1922), p. 91.

[110] Schmitt, 1: 285.

[111] Schmitt, 1: 285-354.

[112] Schmitt, 1: 324, 335, 342.

[113] Fooken, p. 150.

The use of all these tactics by particularist forces—especially the threat of a lawsuit—is indicative of the political orientation of the leaders of active opposition. As Rudolf Vierhaus has recently recalled, at the close of the eighteenth century in Germany there stood opposed two political schools: the centralist school of enlightened absolutism and the particularist school stressing the need to limit central monarchy by means of revived assemblies of estates (and as well the ultimate desirability of reforming the Holy Roman Empire). According to Vierhaus, the continuing strength of the particularist party in Germany at this time was demonstrated by their skill at using the threat of a suit in the imperial courts as a means of achieving a favorable outcome in negotiations with monarchies in the effort to preserve traditional particularist privileges.[114] It has hitherto escaped notice that the opposition tactics in Braunschweig-Wolfenbüttel fit into the pattern discerned by Vierhaus.

Though these remarks suffice as a general characterization of the social basis for the active opposition to the proposed ducal reforms, they must not be taken as a total index of the forces hindering the accomplishment of Campe's plans. For the active opponents of reform (with their traditionalist arguments on the basis of revealed religion and customary privilege) carried the field only because the Philanthropist reformers failed to arouse energetic support among influential indigenous proponents of Enlightenment in Braunschweig-Wolfenbüttel: the powerful and educated in the territory, however attractive they might find moderate Enlightenment, failed to support Campe and the duke once particularist counterattacks were begun.[115] Though these enlightened moderates ordinarily did not go so far as to speak out against Campe and the duke, that—in view of the opposition from the traditionalist clergy and the estates—was scarcely necessary: the centralist reform was doomed by the silence of the educated class. Here we see a striking example of an anticentralist alliance between the traditional particularist estates, clergy, and other corporate bodies on the one hand, and the proto-*Bildungsbürgertum* newly determined to assert itself in the face of absolutist policy on the other. The rhetorical expression of this unlikely alliance of antiabsolutist forces was the coincidence of the traditional appeal to revealed religion and customary privilege with the new appeal to the principle that the task of the clergy as cultivators of humanity, since that task pertains chiefly to the eternal man rather than to the temporal

---

[114] Vierhaus, "Land, Staat und Reich in der politischen Vorstellungswelt deutscher Landstände im 18. Jahrhundert," *Historische Zeitschrift* 223 (1976): 40-60, esp. pp. 43, 48; cf. Geraint Parry, "Enlightened Government and its Critics in Eighteenth-Century Germany," *The Historical Journal* 6 (1963): 178-92.

[115] Schmitt, 1: 348.

citizen, must take precedence over purely temporal duties. In other words, in opposing Campe's reform plans for school and clergy, the Northwest German churchmen moved from arguing mostly on the simple basis of revealed religion and customary privilege to a more complex basis for argumentation that incorporated as well the newer appeal to natural law as a means for limiting the claims of absolutism. For by use of the latter they could appeal to the emergent *Bildungsbürgertum*.

Once the controversy surrounding Campe's proposed reforms is set into the context of the struggle between centralist and anticentralist approaches to government and administration, it becomes necessary to carry through a certain revision in the customary historiographical judgments concerning the aims of the anti-Philanthropist party that succeeded in blocking the plans supported by Hardenberg. Accounts such as that by the historian of education Ulrich Herrmann can now be seen not to supply an adequate picture of matters in describing the motives of Campe's opponents as simple fear of the possibility that political unrest in the lower orders might result from improved education plus fear that reforms carried out by deists and Rationalists might weaken the hold of revealed religion on the public.[116] Such a summary approach, betraying an uncritical allegiance to the pedagogical aims of Enlightenment Philanthropism, is scarcely characterized by sympathetic inquiry into the motives of the clerical opposition. In particular, it fails to give an adequate idea of the considerable degree to which clerical opposition to the ducal reforms was motivated by reaction to the threat which the *governmental* policies behind the reform plans of Campe posed for the basis for the traditional identity and functioning of the clerical estate. In fact, a close look at the sources confirms that one of the major concerns moving the clerical opposition was anxiety concerning the future function, status, and identity of the clergy should the full plans of Campe and Hardenberg be put into effect by a ducal government aiming at a secularizing transformation of the clerical estate. It is not surprising that the leading churchmen came quickly to the conclusion that, under these circumstances, a truly effective defense of the clerical estate might after all not be one chiefly based on its utility to civil society and the temporal government.[117]

Though it would be possible to dwell at length on the many indications that a central concern in the society of late Enlightenment Braunschweig-Wolfenbüttel was and for a time remained the question of the chief pur-

---

[116] Herrmann, "Modell," pp. 175-76; similar, though less differentiated, is Schmitt's account.

[117] For details of particularist opposition see Appendix F.

pose and the fundamental nature of the clerical estate,[118] it is advisable at this point to turn to a more detailed consideration of the fashion in which those churchmen who rejected Campe's views came to state their own conception of the nature and function of the clerical estate within society.

A thoroughly traditionalistic restatement of the clerical role was attempted in opposition to Campe by Johann Caspar Velthusen (1740-1814).[119] Velthusen studied at Göttingen, which later in 1775 awarded him the theological doctorate. In 1770 he became chaplain to the German court in London. In 1778 he accepted an appointment at Helmstedt. There as professor of theology he lectured on dogmatics, showing a special interest in the study of the Lutheran Confessions. At the same time he was named General Superintendent, inspector of schools, and *Abt* of the Lutheran cloister at Mariental. With these dignities went a seat in the estates, a position he was to put to good advantage as a tactician during the struggle against the reform plans of Campe and Hardenberg. In 1789 he became a professor at Rostock, and in 1791 he returned to Northwest Germany to take a post as Lutheran General Superintendent in Stade.

Velthusen was an extremely conscientious churchman, deeply interested in reviving the morale of the clerical estate. His theological position is not easily described, for it exhibits elements of Enlightenment influence as well as components of a moderate Lutheran Orthodoxy. Thus on the one hand his thought shows the influence of Rationalistic moralism and a considerable interest in Freemasonry; on the other hand, Velthusen takes a conservative stand on such matters as the significance of scripture, the real presence in the sacrament of the altar, the vicarious atonement, and the resurrection. This position of moderation can readily be seen to reflect the tradition of Mosheim's theology.[120]

Given this outlook, given his alarm at the spread of unbelief and immorality in his congregation, and given his longstanding faith in the value of a thorough classical education, one has no difficulty in imagining Velthusen in the role of traditionalist opponent. Velthusen's views are

---

[118] See esp. "Die Verhandlungen und Streitigkeiten wegen der Kirchenagenda im Herzogthum Braunschweig," *Blätter aus dem Archiv der Toleranz und Intoleranz, 1. Lieferung* (1797), pp. 21-114; *3. Lieferung* (1797), pp. 1-83; Niedersächsisches Staatsarchiv Wolfenbüttel, Sig. 2 Alt 15096, fols. 1 recto and verso; fols. 6-15.

[119] "D. Johann Caspar Velthusen," in H. Schlichthorst, ed., *Beyträge zur Erläuterung der ältern und neuern Geschichte der Herzogthümer Bremen und Verden* 2 (Hannover, 1797): 263-79; Rudolf Steinmetz, "Die Generalsuperintenden in dem Herzogtum Bremen-Verden," *ZGNK* 11 (1906): 29-38; Vitus Dettmer, "Abt D. Velthusen," *ZGNK* 23 (1918): 1-94.

[120] Steinmetz, "Bremen-Verden," pp. 34-35; Dettmer, "Velthusen," pp. 67, 84-89.

sketched in his *Ueber die nächste Bestimmung des Landpredigerstandes* (Helmstedt, 1787).[121]

Velthusen's position, though not unaffected by Enlightenment thought, represents in the main a reworking of the classic Lutheran Orthodox concept of the clergy as highly-educated proclaimers of a supernatural Gospel in principle independent of temporal government: his views constitute a truly conservative restatement of the function, authority, legitimation, and education of the clerical estate. To a degree he obviously intends to return to some of the views associated with the sixteenth and seventeenth centuries. The importance of this kind of traditionalist thinking ought not to be underestimated, especially as Velthusen himself was a leader of the active clerical opposition to Campe. However, since our prime interest here is not in the political maneuvering connected with Campe's defeat, and since Velthusen's position clearly offers little in the way of innovation, there is little point in considering it here.[122] More significant as an indicator of future developments is clerical thought among those less traditionalist churchmen who, though they did not actively oppose Campe and the ducal reforms, nonetheless by their silence insured the triumph of the conservative party. These more obviously "enlightened" or Rationalistic churchmen can stand as representatives of the proto-*Bildungsbürgertum* and its clerical spokesmen.

One instance[123] will suffice: the influential late Enlightenment theologian and churchman Heinrich Philipp Conrad Henke (1752-1809). He joined the Helmstedt faculty in 1778 and gained a name for himself as a church historian and as a Rationalist dogmatician. Though Henke was proposed for his post at Helmstedt by his friend Velthusen, his own theological position was far less conservative. Indeed, Henke is customarily cited by historians of dogma as a typical Rationalist because of his universalism and because of his criticism of the extreme veneration of Christ as superstitious. The rightness of this assessment of Henke as a true Rationalist is underlined by the fact that he numbered among his pupils the future radical Rationalist Wegscheider and further by the circumstance that his company was valued by Goethe.[124] Thus Henke,

---

[121] Dettmer, "Velthusen," pp. 67, 74-75; Johann Caspar Velthusen, *Ueber die nächste Bestimmung des Landpredigerstandes. Ein durch Herrn Campens Fragmente veranlaßter Beytrag zur Pastoraltheologie* (Helmstedt, 1787).

[122] For details on Velthusen's position see Appendix G.

[123] But see also August Christian Bartels, *Ueber den Werth und die Wirkungen der Sittenlehre Jesu*, 2 vols. (Hamburg, 1788).

[124] Georg Karl Bollmann and Heinrich Wilhelm Justus Wolff, *Heinrich Philipp Conrad Henke* (Helmstedt and Leipzig, 1816); Ernst Henke, "Henke," *PRE*, 3rd ed. (Leipzig, 1899), 7: 680-82; Hirsch, *Geschichte der neuern evangelischen Theologie* (Gütersloh, 1954), 5: 11-14; H. Henke, *Lineamenta institutionum fidei Christianae historico-criticarum* (Helmstedt,

with what his son delicately terms his recognition of the "godlikeness" rather than the "godhood" of Christ,[125] is the perfect example of the theologian of the emergent *Bildungsbürgertum*.

Henke, who was devoted to classical literature, served in the latter years of the eighteenth century as both director of the newly-reorganized theological seminary at Helmstedt and *Abt* of the seminary in the Lutheran cloister at Michaelstein.[126] Thus Henke was in an excellent position to exercise a substantial influence upon future pastors in Braunschweig-Wolfenbüttel.

Now as Henke numbered Campe among his friends, and as Campe was the publisher of Henke's church history beginning in 1788,[127] one would seek in vain for any sign that Henke was among the leaders of the active opposition to the reforms of Campe and Hardenberg. However, this fact does not mean that Henke found himself unable to adopt a negative attitude toward Campe's view of the ministry, or powerless to give expression to his views. On January 8, 1790, speaking at the installation of a new *Abt* of Riddagshausen, Henke discussed the situation of religion. While he found it alarming that some in his day rejected religion, he found

> far more a cause for concern ..., that in our days so many fail to display ill-will toward religion only because it is an indispensable instrument in the governing of the great machine of a civil society, and because without it the respect for the laws, good order, security, and prosperity in the commonwealth cannot be well preserved; ...[128]

Henke then explained why this attitude was unacceptable:

> for [those who hold to it] treat religion as a trade, and expose it to the danger of being perverted into hypocrisy, of being furthered by means of unnatural and forcible regulations, and of being mixed with superstitions and absurdities.[129]

He went on to explain the superior nature of religion as a matter pertaining to the man, rather than chiefly to the citizen:

> But the more humane the way in which ... the principles of statecraft are studied, the more certainly will one recognize that, since the affairs of the man are present in the order of nature sooner and last longer, than the af-

---

1795), pp. 11-14; Goethe, *Tag- und Jahres-Hefte 1805* = *Goethes Werke*, 1. Abth. (Weimar, 1892), 35: 233-38.

[125] E. Henke, p. 681.

[126] E. Henke, pp. 681-821; Bollmann, p. 97.

[127] Leyser, 2: 395.

[128] H. Henke, "Frohe Aussichten für die Religion in die Zukunft," in his *Predigten ...*, *2. Sammlung* (Braunschweig, 1803), p. 246. The "machine" imagery is drawn from physiocratic writers.

[129] H. Henke, "Aussichten," p. 246.

fairs of the citizen, since the man is equipped with capacities ... not simply for society, but rather also for himself, for, the more he trains these [capacities], the more those [affairs of the citizen] attain greater usefulness, and, as precisely to the degree in which he becomes a better man by means of the guidance of religion, he also becomes a better citizen—consequently religion is not a necessary evil, but rather furnishes the most natural and effective aid, and the most certain support for welfare both general and personal.[130]

Thus Henke refused to found the position of religion chiefly or simply upon its utility to the temporal good of society. Even more emphatic were his words later in the same year in speaking on the general theme of the clerical complaints concerning the low esteem in which the clerical estate was held. While the address concedes that not everyone has up to the present point learnt properly to appreciate the value of a reasonable instruction in religion "for the welfare of the man, the citizen, and the entire society,"[131] the force of the entire address is to urge sobriety gained from historical perspective and careful reflection when considering the ever-mounting clerical complaints that nothing but contempt was being poured upon a once-proud estate.[132] For, Henke fears, in the highly emotional condition characteristic of the Protestant clergy in the age of the Wöllner Edict and the political unrest in Europe, there is a real danger that the churchmen will pay too much heed to the opinions of those not in their own estate and become overly desirous of acquiring "merit" in the eyes of strangers to the clerical estate.[133]

The precise implications of this general position are then spelled out. Taking a stand on the principles of Rationalistic theology (that is to say, a theology, which, though based to a degree upon Kantianism, still is intended to uphold the value of the church and its clergy), Henke first traces the spread of the exaggeratedly negative view of Christianity which, as he sees it, has been spread by promoters of radical Enlightenment:

Thus it is ... understandable, how respect for the Christian teaching office ... has suffered from the fact that religion itself ... has been described as a thing altogether dispensable, which causes more harm than useful results, in that it indeed makes people interested in and workers for another, future world but not for this present [world]; and calls them away from the earthly affairs and business of civil life, and elevates them to leisurely contemplations and transports them into a higher and invisible kingdom.[134]

[130] H. Henke, "Aussichten," pp. 246-47.

[131] H. Henke, *Beurtheilung der Klagen über Geringschätzung des Predigerstandes* (Helmstedt, 1790), p. 27.

[132] Cf. H. Henke, *Beurtheilung der Klagen*, pp. 15-25.

[133] H. Henke, *Beurtheilung der Klagen*, pp. 16-17.

[134] H. Henke, *Beurtheilung der Klagen*, p. 31.

Such opinions, declares Henke, are

> prejudices concerning the essence and the goal of religion, which must tend to bring suspicion, disdain, and hateful decrying upon that office which was instituted to proclaim and inculcate this religion.[135]

Henke then turns to the harmful consequences of the utilitarian defense against such Enlightenment charges, a defense which he regards as ultimately mistaken and pernicious:

> In this connection it might be wise to consider that, in the well-meaning intention of securing for this estate a proper and appropriate honor, some have described it in our day as a part of the state service [einen Theil der Dienerschaft des Staats]. Now however true it is that genuine religion at the same time is of the most considerable influence for order, peace, and the welfare of the commonwealth, and that, the more its spirit is spread among all classes of people, the better off is the whole society; just as certain is it that religion is still not at all a concern of the person insofar as he is a citizen, but rather is concerned with his entire purpose and destiny [= Bestimmung] for the present and future world, with his immortal spirit, with his relation to his creator, with everything, by which and how he can ascend from one step of perfection and happiness to another within the immeasurable Kingdom of God.[136]

Thus religion according to Henke is chiefly concerned with the divine education of the person as man; and

> precisely on this account then the notion that the teachers of religion [= clergy] are simply nothing but state-instituted and empowered spokesmen for good morals, civic loyalty and order is very one-sided and incomplete. Their calling is a higher one; and the purpose of their labors extends further; they are speakers, interpreters, and heralds of the most important truths, guides, counselors, and companions of all their brothers in the striving after wisdom, virtue, and contentment, inner and eternal welfare.[137]

Henke continues with an exclamation:

> A calling, which is as much more elevated and divine than any civil utilitarian service, as the destining of man for those perfections is older and more important than all his social relationships, or as virtue is more than civic love for order, blessedness is more than civic welfare![138]

This does not mean, of course, that Henke denies the civil benefits of Christianity and the Christian ministry; but that aspect of ministry must remain peripheral and subordinate to the essential task:

---

[135] H. Henke, *Beurtheilung der Klagen*, p. 32.
[136] H. Henke, *Beurtheilung der Klagen*, pp. 32-33.
[137] H. Henke, *Beurtheilung der Klagen*, p. 33.
[138] H. Henke, *Beurtheilung der Klagen*, p. 34.

The more loyally and conscientiously, however, [the teachers of religion = pastors] fulfill this great calling, the more important and numerous will be the advantages which civil society in all its special areas, needs, and concerns derives from their efforts; the more can and will their services be salutary and beneficial for the state in a mediate fashion.[139]

Be that as it may, Henke cannot in this connection resist adding a final word of caution:

If however their [= the clergy's] office should merit respect only in the capacity and in the measure in which they are useful to the state, then it is to be feared that the fruit of their labors will at all times receive too little attention, and will appear too inconsiderable to those who do not look farther than to see things immediately present; consequently their office too will lose its dignity and prestige.[140]

c. Clericalist Resistance to Radical Secularization of the Pastoral Role in Electoral Hannover

At first glance it might seem that the traditionalist churchmen in Electoral Hannover had far less cause for alarm than did their colleagues in Braunschweig-Wolfenbüttel. Electoral Hannover was, after all, the classic example of a decentralized territory—the territorial lord absent in London, local affairs chiefly managed by a local aristocracy. Yet, though no plans comparable to those of Campe were sponsored by the Hannoverian government, the theologians and churchmen in the territory expressed themselves with comparable traditionalist vigor on the issue of professional identity in the years after 1785. This was the case for a number of reasons.

To begin with, the university at Göttingen diffused cameralist ideas—the case of Sextroh illustrates the effect of such ideas upon the clergy. Furthermore, the example of governmental pressure in a radical direction (revolutionary France) and in a conservative direction (Prussia) in the late eighteenth century served to bring attention to the entire question of church-state relations. The unrest in Electoral Hannover itself in the 1790's, resulting largely from events in France, eventuated in several notable instances of governmental pressure on the church and clergy. In addition, even in so decentralized a territory as Hannover, it was not *a priori* impossible that indigenous reform attempts might have posed a threat to the traditional status of the clergy. On the other hand, lending support to conservative clerical particularism was the very strong Han-

---

[139] H. Henke, *Beurtheilung der Klagen*, p. 34.

[140] H. Henke, *Beurtheilung der Klagen*, pp. 34-35. While Henke's words may reflect knowledge of the situation in France, it is safest to take them as chiefly a comment on German and territorial conditions.

noverian tradition of lay political anticentralism exemplified by such figures as August Ludwig Schlözer and August Wilhelm Rehberg; the latter well-known "reform conservative" political writer in 1788 sharply attacked the Philanthropist view of education and directly repudiated Philanthropistic plans for a radically utilitarian training of the parish clergy (that is, the plans of Bahrdt and Campe).[141]

In view of all this, it is not surprising that the influential churchmen and theologians in electoral Hannover took up their pens in defense of clerical particularism. For example, there was Johann Conrad Holscher, assistant pastor at Hannover's Neustadter Hof- und Stadtkirche St. Johannis. Holscher (1755-1840) later became General Superintendent of Hoya-Diepholz.[142]

Though Holscher was not unalterably opposed to a peripheral involvement of the clergy and teachers in the industry-school movement, he nonetheless took a strong stand against Campe's proposals. In a pamphlet published at Hannover in 1787, Holscher rejects the extreme utilitarian concept of clerical training advanced by Campe, pointing out that even Bahrdt had not gone so far.[143] Joined to these views are critical remarks on the heavy burden of bureaucratic statistical work of a civic character imposed on the clergy by the state.[144] Holscher's strongest criticism of Campe's proposals comes in the argument that such plans would harm other estates in society by providing jacks-of-all-trades who could not possibly be trained in mechanical and surgical skills necessary to do the job adequately. Furthermore, there would be a real risk that the clergy would soon come to consider their secondary occupations (i.e., temporal tasks) more important than their primary or religious task, a task which itself ought to be seen to provide sufficient opportunity for meritorious activity.[145] As Holscher viewed it, the pastor's "main business" was that of preserving the Christian religion in the world while caring for the needs of those he served,[146] a task which Holscher held to

---

[141] The work in question by August Wilhelm Rehberg is his "Sollten die alten Sprachen dem allgemeinen Unterricht ... zum Grunde gelegt ... werden," *Berlinische Monatsschrift*, ed. F. Gedike and J. E. Biester, 11 (1788): 105-31, 253-71. Cf. the anti-utilitarian sentiments in Ernst Brandes, *Ueber den Einfluß und die Wirkungen des Zeitgeistes*, 2. Abth. (Hannover, 1810), pp. 178-81. For details on the situation in Electoral Hannover at the close of the century see Appendix H.

[142] Philipp Meyer, ed., *Die Pastoren der Landeskirchen Hannovers* (Göttingen, 1941), 1: 438, 442, 408, 411; 2: 159, 321.

[143] Johann Conrad Achaz Holscher, *Versuche über den Landprediger* (Hannover, 1787), pp. 22-23, n. For background see *Göttingische Anzeigen von gelehrten Sachen*, Jg. 1791, pp. 2094-96.

[144] Holscher, *Versuche*, p. 16.

[145] Holscher, *Versuche*, fols. *7 recto and verso; fol. *8 recto.

[146] Holscher, *Versuche*, fol. *8 recto.

be intimately connected with biblical philology; for philological study of
the scriptural text must provide the basis for the pastor's personal
knowledge of that Christian religion which he is to preserve.[147] If the
clergy were to be educated without receiving training in Greek, it would
then appear to the public that they were completely without genuine interest in the Christian religion itself. Furthermore, the Protestant critical
principle demands philological competence in dealing with the original
texts; if the clergy cannot do this, argues Holscher, there will be a
substantial danger of undisciplined enthusiasm. Starting from this traditionalist conception of the clerical role and message, and adding the argument that theological candidates must be able to serve as tutors in the
classics for the children of wealthy households if they are to be employed
in the interim between completion of study and eventual parish placement,[148] Holscher can make a case for the traditional curriculum. He upholds the necessity of Latin, Greek, and Hebrew as the basis for scriptural interpretation; he also defends philosophy and classical literature.
In addition, contending that these studies are necessary so as to enable
one to become a good teacher and a competent apologist, Holscher insists
on the need for study of dogmatics, moral theology, polemical theology,
and church history, adding as well the opinion that even scholastic
theology is not useless.[149]

Interwoven with this traditional kind of argumentation is another,
newer strand—the strand of incipient Neohumanism. According to
Holscher, study of the classics is the one sure way of providing true
culture, *wahre Cultur*.[150] The study of the classics broadens one's perception and opens the heart, yielding an acquaintance with the "noble
simplicity of nature."[151] Study of the humanities, especially ancient
literature, is necessary for the parish clergy because it promotes the *Cultur
des Geistes*, the cultivation of the spirit. The final proof that Holscher is
completely caught up in the rhetorical universe of early Neohumanism is
given by the fact that he explicitly recommends study of the classics
according to the method of the Göttingen professor Heyne.[152]

Furthermore, this is no mere appropriation of rhetoric. Holscher
shows every awareness of the way in which the Neohumanistic claims to
possession of a superior cultivation could be used in the battle for social
status against claims of the nobility and other social groups. Without the

---

[147] Holscher, *Versuche*, pp. 35-38; fol. *8 recto.
[148] Holscher, *Versuche*, pp. 37-38, 41, 46, 26.
[149] Holscher, *Versuche*, pp. 21, 44-45, 26, 2-12, 51-86.
[150] Holscher, *Versuche*, p. 3.
[151] Holscher, *Versuche*, pp. 6-7.
[152] Holscher, *Versuche*, pp. 17, 19.

possession of a learned background, he contends, the pastor will be doomed to experience the contempt of the young landed nobility. This contempt will then spread to the peasantry, who observe how their superiors regard the local clergy. While Holscher renounces all claim to a superior status of the clergy in virtue of a supposed "immediate divine commission," this means that he will all the more strongly recommend the "innocent" source of respect in classical education as a way of guaranteeing the esteem in which the clergy are to be held.[153] Indeed, he goes so far as to insist that, if the parish clergy are in future to be deprived of any thorough *Geistes Cultur* of this kind, then it will become impossible to attract capable students for the clerical estate. In short, even the rural preachers must have "a learned education."[154]

Thus Holscher implicitly suggests that it is not by a simple alliance with the theoreticians of the utilitarian absolutist state that one can best acomplish the transformation of the pre-absolutist clerical estate so as to enable it to survive under post-Orthodox conditions. True, all claim to authority based on immediate supernatural sanctions must be abandoned; but the proper substitute for them is now seen to lie, not in the unlimited acquiescence of the clergy in the temporal demands made by centralist régimes, but rather in an alliance with the educated classes as a whole. By adopting the rhetoric of Neohumanism, Holscher in effect urges that clergy make common cause with the educated nobility, administrators, and other professionals—those who, as the *gebildete Stände*, the cultivated estates,[155] were beginning to ask for a larger place in the direction of social and even political affairs than that formerly assigned to them by the doctrines of enlightened absolutism. Holscher's tacit suggestion is that the mystique of cultivation acquired by study of classical literature can provide the clergy with a renewed claim to importance in society, one which can furnish a much-needed supplement to their now-dubious claim to carry out an essentially supernatural role.

Holscher has already begun to use that fuzzy boundary between traditional Christian doctrine and the domain of spiritual cultivation acquired by *Bildung* which the nineteenth-century religion of German Idealism was to utilize to such effect as an initial basis for its celebrated "overcoming" of the utilitarian Enlightenment.[156] It is noteworthy that with Holscher this process of repudiation of the strategy of clerical survival by assimila-

---

[153] Holscher, *Versuche*, pp. 29-31.

[154] Holscher, *Versuche*, pp. 33-34, 28.

[155] See the articles by Vierhaus cited above; also Manfred Baumotte, *Theologie als politische Aufklärung* (Gütersloh, 1973), pp. 90-120.

[156] Cf. Wilhelm Lütgert, *Die Religion des deutschen Idealismus und ihr Ende*, 4 vols. (Gütersloh, 1923-1930; reprint, Hildesheim, 1967, 3 vols.).

tion to absolutist utilitarianism and its replacement by appropriation of
the religion of *Cultur* as a tactic for clerical survival is already well
developed by 1787: one year in advance of Wöllner's Edict in Prussia,
two years before the outbreak of the revolution, and twelve years before
the publication of Schleiermacher's *Reden*, an event which has been taken
to mark some kind of "turning point" in the "overcoming" of the
Enlightenment.

Also characteristic of these tendencies is Gottfried Less (1736-1797).[157]
Educated at Halle under the Wolffian S. J. Baumgarten, Less, after
travels in Holland and England, returned to Germany to take a post as
professor of theology in 1765, having declined an offer to serve as
preacher to the Hamburg congregation in London. At Göttingen, where
Less became head of the theological faculty in 1784 while gaining a seat
in the Hannover consistory, he became known as a prolific moral
theologian and a specialist in moderately enlightened refutations of
Deism. A professor of homiletics despite his whining voice, Less published a number of volumes of sermons, including a series of twelve sermons
on chastity, and also found time to make a contribution to the Enlightenment discussion concerning the question whether venereal disease could
be transmitted by the common communion chalice. In 1791 Less moved
to Hannover to take a post as court preacher with a seat in the consistory,
a call which he gladly accepted, since by this time he had begun to lose
touch with a new generation of students affected by Kantianism.[158]

Less's standpoint was one of Orthodoxy mitigated by Wolffianism and
moving toward Rationalism despite Less's conservative inclinations.
Though in his early period Less was critical of Herder's theology,
ultimately Less came to adopt a view of scripture as a witness to progressive divine revelation in some respects akin to Herder's.[159]

The evolution of Less's views on the Christian ministry tended in the
same general direction as Holscher's. Before the controversy over Bahrdt
and Campe broke, Less, despite his strong basic commitment to some
variety of supernaturalism, nonetheless often espoused a moderately
utilitarian view of the ministry, renouncing in typical Enlightenment

---

[157] Johann Konrad Achaz Holscher, *Gottfried Less* (Hannover, 1797); Wagenmann and
Paul Tschackert, "Less," *PRE*, 3rd ed., 11: 404-6; Rudolf Steinmetz, "Die
Generalsuperintendenten von Calenberg," *ZGNK* 13 (1908): 201-11.

[158] Gottfried Less, *Die Lehre von der christlichen Mässigkeit und Keuschheit, in 12 Predigten*
(Göttingen, 1772; 2nd ed., 1780); [Less], "Ueber die Furcht vor der Mittheilung
ansteckender Krankheiten durch den Nachtmahlskelch," *Stats-Anzeigen*, ed. Schlözer,
Heft 21 (1783): 356-63; Wagenmann-Tschackert, p. 406.

[159] Wagenmann-Tschackert, pp. 404-6; Steinmetz, "Calenberg," pp. 201-10; Johannes Meyer, "Geschichte der Göttinger theologischen Fakultät," *ZGNK* 42 (1937): 33.

fashion any claim on a priestly or intermediary and sacrificial role for the Protestant clergy.[160]

Though Less did not abandon these views altogether as the century drew to a close, he did become increasingly aware of the desirability of *also* couching his definition of ministry in terms other than those of the mere proclamation of utilitarian Christian virtue; his new emphases differ little from those of Herder or Holscher. They are contained in his treatise on the Christian teaching office of the clergy published at Göttingen in 1790.[161]

The occasion for Less's book is, he explains, "the common lukewarm-ness and coldness toward Christianity and all religion."[162] He is alarmed by the attacks on the dignity of the clergy launched by critics such as Hume and the proposals to abolish the established clerical estate altogether.[163]

However, Less's anxiety is aroused even more by the condition of students of theology:

> From the schools ... there comes every semester a group of sluggish, ig-norant students, ... Unfortunately most of them are flung straight into theology. Youths from the lowest estate, without capability and without education, devoid of culture, poor and inexperienced in thinking and in morals; they want to become—teachers of Christianity.[164]

Other factors make matters worse:

> Then, too, the families of worthy preachers, especially in the country, which hitherto always provided the most capable material for the Christian teaching estate, are gradually closing themselves off. Their sons, in-timidated by the evernew mass of opinions with which theologians and ex-egetes confuse and ruin theology, scared away by the contempt into which (to a great extent precisely on this account) theology and theologians are ever deeper sinking, devote themselves to other disciplines which bring more fame and riches.[165]

For all these reasons Less exclaims:

> The ignorant and the half-baked, the puffed-up and the ranting, the base-thinking and the base-acting become ever more numerous among the

---

[160] Gottfried Less, *Rede bei der Ordination des Herrn Professor Koppe* (Göttingen, 1784), p. 19; Less, *Opuscula*, 2nd ed. (Göttingen, 1780), p. 109; cf. the repudiation of the pastor as priestly or sacrificial intermediary in J. J. Spalding, *Ueber die Nutzbarkeit des Predigtamtes*, 1st ed. (Berlin, 1772), p. 6.

[161] Gottfried Less, *Ueber Christliches Lehr-Amt* (Göttingen, 1790).

[162] Less, *Lehr-Amt*, p. vi.

[163] Less, *Lehr-Amt*, pp. 104, 34; cf. Stroup, "Protestant Churchmen," *Lessing Yearbook* 10 (1978): 154-55; also Appendix D.

[164] Less, *Lehr-Amt*, pp. vi-vii.

[165] Less, *Lehr-Amt*, p. vii.

preachers and the theologians! ... On this account the hatred of the teaching estate which one sees breaking out ... in so many lands, even among the common people.[166]

In his introductory remarks Less explains that he is publishing this treatise in the hope that it will move governments to take the necessary steps to reform existing conditions by providing more "temporal encouragement" to the clergy, who are more and more deprived of it. Comprehensive reform is necessary to avoid the "complete decline" of religion, a fate which now threatens.[167] In view of this grave situation, Less feels called upon to explain his view of Christian ministry so as to aid in a revival of the clerical estate.

Having emphatically rejected the proposal that the parish clergyman should become merely a *Volkslehrer* as suggested by Bahrdt and Campe, Less refuses to

> speak further about the assertions of certain innovators, which in the end would result in transforming the preacher into an artisan, economist [= agronomist and county agent] and village-physician. ... They refute themselves.[168]

Less here implies that these suggestions of Campe cannot stand up to the true ideal of ministry, which he has developed on the basis of both traditional supernaturalistic and quasi-Herderian or quasi-Neohumanistic grounds. Though Less is willing to recognize a certain value in the activities of the clergy for the temporal well-being of their congregations, his harsh words on rulers and courts show that he had a deep-seated aversion to overmuch willingness of the clergy to serve purposes defined by the temporal government.[169]

What then is Less's ideal of Christian ministry? According to Less, the Christian religion as reflected in the New Testament consists of the loftiest morality built upon "the most illuminated and spiritual theory"; its purpose is the imparting of "effective principles, divine disposition," the "formation" (*Bildung*) of "the most perfect character" and the "conduct of a life most beneficial to the common good."[170] Thus Christianity teaches the attainment of true felicity by the practice of a "wisdom of life"; it is a wisdom essentially non-temporal, in that it deals primarily with such non-temporal matters as God, virtue, immortality, and "the kingdom of spirits, especially of men." On that account Christianity is

---

[166] Less, *Lehr-Amt*, pp. viii-ix.
[167] Less, *Lehr-Amt*, pp. x-xi.
[168] Less, *Lehr-Amt*, p. 79n.; cf. pp. 17, 20.
[169] Less, *Lehr-Amt*, pp. 23-34.
[170] Less, *Lehr-Amt*, pp. 6-7.

"a profound philosophy." Its source is Jesus, a divine teacher,[171] and its record is the New Testament, a part of the divine Bible, God's word.[172] Thus, since Less mixes Orthodoxy with Enlightenment by describing Christianity as both divine revelation and a philosophy, it is not too surprising that he, in terms reminiscent of Lessing and Herder, also describes the New Testament as "God's educational institution" (*Erziehungs-Anstalt-Gottes*).[173]

What then of the clergy properly understood? In the true sense, the clergyman is a teacher of Christianity.[174] To this point Less adds a remark showing that he has begun to supplement the standard Enlightenment view with other ideas akin to those of Herder and anticipating the revival of clericalism characteristic of the nineteenth century. Less introduces the notion that, though in the New Testament there are no "corporeal priests" performing sacrifice as intermediaries, there are indeed clergy who are "priests in the spiritual, moral sense: priests, who present the spiritual offering, of high divine virtue, to God."[175] Though at this point Less quickly connects this with the notion of universal priesthood of believers, citing I Peter 2:5, he has at any rate reintroduced the notion of priesthood in some positive sense into an Enlightenment university theologian's discussion of ministry, thereby showing that he finds the grounding of ministry in simple *teaching* of virtue to be somehow inadequate.[176]

Less goes on to explain that the true theologian is a philosopher. Beyond this, the calling of the clergyman is divine in virtue and happiness; for the teacher of humanity (*Menschheit*) as a servant of the gospel functions simultaneously as an interpreter of the source of religion, the New Testament, a text of written revelation possessing divine authority.[177]

---

[171] Less, *Lehr-Amt*, pp. 41-42.

[172] Less, *Lehr-Amt*, pp. 21, 125-32.

[173] Less, *Lehr-Amt*, p. 11.

[174] Less, *Lehr-Amt*, p. 11.

[175] Less, *Lehr-Amt*, pp. 11-13.

[176] Less, *Lehr-Amt*, p. 13, provides an example of such thinking; for a more complete effort at reintroduction of irrationalistic defenses of the clergy by a Northwest German Enlightenment writer, see J. G. H. Feder, "Der Prediger und der Priester," *Beyträge zur Kenntniß und Verbesserung des Kirchen- und Schulwesens*, ed. J. C. Salfeld (Hannover, 1807), 7:499-522. Here we cannot consider efforts by late Enlightenment and early Romantic writers (many former students of theology) to accord a quasi-priestly, irrationalistically-grounded status to their ego-gratifying calling as *Erzieher des Menschengeschlechts*. See Diana Behler, "Lessing's Legacy to the Romantic Concept of the Poet-Priest," *Lessing Year-book* 4 (1972): 67-93; A. Leslie Willson, "Dichter-Priester," *Colloquia Germanica* 1/2 (1968): 127-36; Rohtraut Bäsken, *Die Dichter des Göttinger Hains und die Bürgerlichkeit* (Königsberg, 1937), pp. 46-47; Klaus Lindemann, *Geistlicher Stand und religiöses Mittlertum* (Frankfurt a.M., 1971). — See also *PRE* 12:305-306.

[177] Less, *Lehr-Amt*, pp. 8n., 16-23, 55-56; cf. Less, *Opuscula* p. 110.

Less's apologetic for the clergy weaves together a variety of elements: to the Enlightenment strand (the teacher of virtue) there is added a remnant of the Orthodox strand (with the stress on divine authority of the sacred text) and a newer strand (one emphasizing the responsibilities as an educator of humanity with the overtones of *Bildung* and of Lessing and Herder joined with the claim that Christianity is the true philosophy, an agent of culture and civilization).[178]

Not surprisingly, then, Less in his suggestions concerning theological education takes an antiutilitarian stand. He emphasizes the need for academic learning, especially ancient languages, dogmatics, and church law.[179] However, in his opinion, practical exercises in the activities later to be carried out in the parish ministry have lately been given too much weight in the course of study,[180] a slap at the exercise in pastoral care at the Göttingen hospital carried out under the supervision of Sextroh. Therefore, with regard to theological education, just as with his concept of the function of ministry, Less's later position clearly represents an attempt at a comprehensive restatement of traditional Lutheran views on ministry in late Enlightenment terms mixed with Neo-humanistic language.[181]

Less's overall aversion to according utilitarian activity by the clergy anything more than a subordinate and peripheral status may be taken as emblematic of the prevailing attitude at Göttingen even after his resignation. For the departure of Sextroh in 1789[182] meant that a powerful influence in a mitigated utilitarian direction was removed from the faculty. The rise of Kantianism helped confer a fresh prestige on occupation with the study of positive theology that in part lessened the earlier pressure to find a substitute for it in training for purely temporal activities.[183] Furthermore, the two leading theologians at Göttingen in the decade after Less's departure continued his crusade against radical utilitarianism. In 1794 the professor and consistorial councillor Gottlieb Jacob Planck

---

[178] Less, *Lehr-Amt*, p. 45; Bernard Plongeron, "Bonheur et 'civilisation chrétienne,'" paper at the Fourth International Congress on the Enlightenment, Yale University, July, 1975.

[179] Less, *Lehr-Amt*, pp. 63-96.

[180] Less, *Lehr-Amt*, pp. 81, 93.

[181] In line with Less's conservatism is his defense (against Enlightenment attack) of the practice of private confession by the laity to the Protestant clergy; see Less, *Lehr-Amt*, pp. 150-70.

[182] J. Meyer, "Geschichte der Göttinger theologischen Fakultät," p. 102.

[183] See in particular the comments of the Hannoverian pastor Christian Dassel, "Worin soll die Thätigkeit der Prediger bestehen," *Euusebia*, ed. H. P. C. Henke, 3 (Helmstedt, 1799-1800): 533-34, arguing that the rise of Kantian critical philosophy did in the credibility of Philanthropist projects designed to dispense the clergy from the necessity of any thorough training in academic matters.

(1751-1833) published an elaborate defense of the necessity of academic theology and classical philology even for those concerned with religious instruction of the uneducated;[184] in the following year the professor of homiletics Christoph Friedrich Ammon (1766-1850) published an attack on sermons concerning economic and medical topics, alleging the uselessness of such utilitarianism as a means of persuading the fallen-away to return to Christianity.[185]

The Northwest German theologians and churchmen, then, were moving toward a consensus on how a defense of the status of the non-temporal aspect of Christian ministry might effectively be made in the age of Kant. They were furthermore of the opinion that mere written defenses would not suffice to rescue the cause of religion from what seemed to Less to be the threat of complete collapse[186] and to encourage students of theology to have the proper regard for the duties and worth of their calling.[187] To Less more seemed required: nothing less than a complete program of institutional reforms of a kind that professors of theology alone could scarcely hope to carry out. As Less put it, the growing bitterness toward religion and the low state of the clergy constituted an evil

> which no professor, nor all the universities together, can help. Reforming the schools; reducing the number of students; and from the poor permitting only those to study who have unusual talents and who are adequately prepared: this must be done in order thoroughly to heal those drastic ills which threaten religion with nothing less than complete decline among us. This however is a matter for authorities and rulers. Professors can do nothing further than slow them down and somewhat mitigate them. And this is ... the purpose of my present work.[188]

As if in response to Less's words, the Northwest German churchmen in the decade after 1790 began to campaign for a set of institutional reforms that would provide a means of insuring that the emerging traditionalistic, antiutilitarian consensus on the primary purpose of the clergy would carry the field. To the programmatic statements of that consensus and their institutional manifestations we must now turn.

---

[184] Gottlieb Jacob Planck, *Einleitung in die Theologische Wissenschaften, 1. Theil* (Leipzig, 1794), pp. 53-56, 166; J. Meyer, "Geschichte der Göttinger theologischen Fakultät," p. 99.

[185] Christoph Friedrich Ammon, *Ideen zur Verbesserung der herrschenden Predigtmethode* (Göttingen, 1795), esp. p. 6.

[186] Less, *Lehr-Amt*, p. x; cf. Christoph Levin Heinrich Dedekind, *Die Zeichen der Zeit* (Wolfenbüttel, 1798).

[187] Less, *Lehr-Amt*, pp. x-xi.

[188] Less, *Lehr-Amt*, pp. ix-x.

CHAPTER FIVE

PROTESTANT CLERICAL IDENTITY IN NORTHWEST GERMANY ON THE EVE OF THE NAPOLEONIC INVASION

1. *Consolidation and Transformation*

By 1790 the leading churchmen and theologians in Northwest Germany had arrived at an anticentralist, antiutilitarian consensus on the chief purpose of Christian ministry: a clerical particularist reaction had begun. Chronicling the measures by which this consensus was given institutional expression ought to be easy: one could demonstrate how conservative particularist reform planning was advocated so as to insure the continued independency and revived *esprit de corps* of a clergy devoted chiefly to a nontemporal task proper to the clerical estate. In so doing one could show how the lead of Mosheim was followed in the area of planning for a particularist reform of theological training and clerical functioning, all the while noting the continuing usefulness to the churchmen of Mosheim's theology that mixed reason with revelation and Mosheim's collegialist view of church-state relations.

This task is rendered more challenging by the evidence. For after 1789 the self-understanding of the Northwest German churchmen underwent a subtle yet important transformation even as measures were taken to enforce the anticentralist consensus achieved in the struggle against Campe. Up to this point in our account the traditionalist churchmen have been seen facing the problem of how to preserve their relative autonomy and independency in the face of governmental threats to that independent functioning. The chief threat was one of transformation into temporal functionaries clad in clerical black: the occasional propagandistic call for disestablishment made in Enlightenment Germany had little chance of realization.[1] After 1789, and particularly after the Napoleonic invasion, however, the churchmen confronted the possibility of actual disestablishment or serious change in the status of the church and clergy.

The gravity of the situation must be borne in mind if we are to understand the mental universe of the churchmen. For in revolutionary Europe after 1790 there was demonstrated the possibility of fundamental

---

[1] Cf. "Ueber die Nothwendigkeit der moralischen Verbesserung des Predigerstandes," *Eusebia*, ed. H. P. C. Henke, 1 (Helmstedt, 1797): 68-69.

secularizing change, either by direct export of the French Revolution or by a domestic régime's imitation of its more extreme policies. The nationalization of church lands, state-supported paganism, the persecution of Christianity, and even the confiscation of incomes were now seen as eventualities capable of coming to pass.[2] The threat was in part realized by the central government of the Kingdom of Westphalia ruled by Jérôme Bonaparte in the years after 1807: it introduced parity among confessions and stripped the church in Braunschweig and Hannover of its privileges in civil society.[3]

As a result, among the Protestant clergy the years after 1789 saw a shift of emphasis from simple reassertion of independency to a concern with strategies for warding off disestablishment. These two emphases are distinct, yet closely related. They are distinct, in that the chronologically subsequent threat of disestablishment or radical secularization came chiefly from a foreign source with domestic support in some circles, whereas the earlier threat to clerical independency had come from domestic spokesmen for enlightened centralism intent on mere revision of clerical function.

Yet the régimes of the French Revolution and the anticlericalism characteristic of most of them were in considerable measure products of that same Enlightenment thought and administrative centralism that had earlier produced in Germany the domestic pro-absolutist threats to traditional clerical autonomy.[4] Therefore it is correct to say that the clerical particularist or anticentralist reaction already in progress in Northwest Germany at the time of the Bahrdt-Campe debate served as the first phase of an ongoing Protestant clericalist reaction that reached its second, more intense phase only during and after the Napoleonic era—at a time when clerical sentiment was to be directed, no longer against spokesmen for domestic centralist policies, but against the policies associated with revolutionary France and its allies in German-speaking Europe. For to the eyes of the churchmen, though secularizing anticlericalism emanated from thinkers both German and French who shared a common centralist perspective,[5] still events in the years of crisis

---

[2] On the French events and their effects in Germany see "Rede ... von B. Gregoire," *Eusebia* 2 (1798): 531-44; Isaac Haffner, "Erinnerungen," *Religions-Annalen*, ed. H. P. C. Henke 2 (Braunschweig, 1805): 583-604; Edward Dixon Junkin, *Religion versus Revolution* (Austin, Texas, 1974); Rudolf von Thadden, *Restauration und Napoleonisches Erbe* (Wiesbaden, 1972); Hedwig Hintze, *Staatseinheit und Föderalismus* (Stuttgart, 1928); Rudolf Vierhaus, ed., *Eigentum und Verfassung* (Göttingen, 1972).

[3] For details and documentation see Appendix I.

[4] Cf. Hedwig Hintze; also Helmut Berding, *Napoleonische Herrschafts- und Gesellschaftspolitik* (Göttingen, 1973); von Thadden, *Restauration*.

[5] This point and its significance escape Junkin.

showed where the greater threat lay. In retrospect the German central governments of the Enlightenment seemed to have been weaker than the movements and invasions generated by revolutionary France—which on the whole had kept no unshaken overt commitment to Christianity, unlike the outwardly Christian régimes of Enlightenment Germany. The churchmen, however caught up they might have been on the eve of invasion in the domestic struggle to preserve clerical self-interest and independency in the face of the tradition of Thomasius and Campe, would in the long run be forced by revolution to conclude that alliance with domestic Christian governments was preferable to the radical reorganization or virtual disestablishment promoted by the centralism of revolutionary imperialism in its more extreme phases. Domestic régimes of a traditional kind seemed far safer than the unpredictable swings of a revolutionary movement based to a degree on anti-Christian principles.

In a word, then, the clerical particularist or anticentralist reaction originally set in motion by opposition to pro-absolutist thinking (e.g., Abbt and Campe) led ultimately to a clerical anticentralist reaction that was eventually to identify France with Enlightenment and—in the course of the nineteenth century—to conclude an alliance between German thrones and Protestant pulpits that would have horrified Herder, Henke, and their colleagues.[6]

That unthinkingly reactionary alliance of throne and pulpit was, let it be emphasized, still scarcely dreamt of by most of the churchmen here discussed—even as late as 1806. For on the eve of invasion, even as they voiced ever-greater support for safe domestic régimes, the churchmen and theologians still continued to insist that bounds must be put on the obligation to the state.[7] The churchmen even in the period 1790 to 1806 continued in traditional clericalist fashion to uphold the priority of the nontemporal aspect of the clerical task, and furthermore, by the use of Neohumanistic and natural law language, to proclaim the continuing validity of their anticentralist alliance with the claims of the emergent *Bildungsbürgertum*.[8]

Yet one must not overlook as well the theme of transformation in evaluating the material on clerical purpose to be presented below. The

---

[6] Cf. Reinhard Wittram, "Kirche und Nationalismus in der Geschichte des deutschen Protestantismus im 19. Jahrhundert," in his *Das Nationale als europäisches Problem* (Göttingen, 1954), pp. 109-48.

[7] For the patriotic (anti-French) pressure forcing the more thoughtful churchmen to consider the bounds of their obligation to domestic governments, cf. *Aufklärung, größtentheils eine Grille* (Hannover, 1794); Werner Schneiders, *Die wahre Aufklärung* (Munich, 1974); Richard Nürnberger, *Die Lehre von der Politik an der Universität Göttingen während der französischen Revolution* (Göttingen, 1971).

[8] Cf. Appendix I. Continuing anticentralism will be documented below.

argumentation of the churchmen and theologians after 1789 places particular emphasis also on the defense of the traditional privileged position of the clergy as an estate supported by traditional incomes legally guaranteed by the state. In this argumentation the attempt is made above all to make this defense of privilege more effective by recalling the important (yet subordinate) role of the clergy as an aid to the state in a time of unrest—but the effort is also made to strengthen the case against disestablishment by pointing to the clergy's function as a helper of humanity. In these ways it was hoped that domestic governments could be persuaded to oppose the radical secularism represented by some phases of the French Revolution rather than letting it go unopposed or even emulating it.[9]

The situation of the Protestant churchmen at the close of the eighteenth century was, then, highly uncertain. Having rebuffed proposals that they rescue their estate by transforming it into an agency of the centralist régimes in the German states, the churchmen were then faced with the necessity of reaffirming their allegiance and usefulness to those same territorial régimes so as to insure the co-operation of the territorial régimes in countering the threat of disestablishment and secularization posed by the revolutionary central government in France and its allied movements. The German churchmen found themselves in precisely the same situation as the emergent *Bildungsbürgertum* with which they had allied themselves: though they might indeed assert themselves up to a point in search of expanded liberty within the framework of the autocratic state, once faced with a threat of the magnitude which Napoleonic Europe constituted, they would quickly confine their aspirations to those of "true" (i.e., politically innocuous) Enlightenment—hence underlining their allegiance to the territorial state, even as they sought with the help of bourgeoisie and bureaucracy to see to it that indigenous absolutist régimes did not have too free a hand.[10]

In the writings on the purpose and identity of the clergy to be examined below from the years 1789-1806, it is impossible to isolate a single theme. Rather is the position of the leading churchmen to be explained as the product of a variety of forces finding expression in the following contentions of the part of the churchmen:

1. The clerical estate must be supported at public expense above all because it benefits humanity—but also because it can serve politically useful ends.

---

[9] For background see the tendentious account in Junkin and also Felix Arndt, *Zur Publistik über Kirche und Staat* (Ph. D. Diss., Kiel University, 1918).

[10] Cf. the background in Volker Sellin, "Friedrich der Große und der aufgeklärte Absolutismus," in Ulrich Engelhardt et al., eds., *Soziale Bewegung und politische Verfassung* (Stuttgart, 1976), pp. 83-112.

2. Because the clergy exist chiefly to serve a nontemporal purpose, steps must be taken to protect the clergy from exploitation as tools of the state (i.e., from being transformed into mere temporal *Volkslehrer* and nothing else).[11]

3. In order to counteract propaganda for the disestablishment of the clergy or for reduction in the social or legal status of the clergy, any number of reforms are desirable so as to improve the functioning and reputation of pastors and students of theology.[12]

This list of *desiderata*, altogether characteristic of the Protestant churchmen of the 1790's and shortly thereafter, betrays an exceedingly unstable or ambiguous position.[13] In the underlying demand for social, financial, and professional independency of the clergy one can indeed detect a unifying element; but in the way in which that demand is worked out one can discern anticipations of more than one position that was to be characteristic of the nineteenth century. The demand for autonomy of the clerical profession and the concern for defense of clerical status or privilege even as they recall Lutheran orthodoxy and Mosheim simultaneously anticipate certain elements of the Neoconfessional revival of clerical ideology that was to flower in the course of the nineteenth century. The reserve with regard to the central state (whether German absolutist or French imperial) and the hesitation to commit oneself unthinkingly to its mercies anticipate both the difficulties of later extreme confessional groups (e.g., *Altlutheraner*) and the continuing claim of the *Bildungsbürgertum* to play a significant role in public life. Yet the emphasis on service to the patriotic and conservative aims of the territorial central government as a bulwark against French deistic radicalism and revolutionary expansionism foreshadows the kind of reaction which one associates with the post-1848 alliance of throne and altar in Germany.

Thus the debates, plans, programs, and reforms of this period of Rationalism anticipate the subsequent rebirth of what might be termed reactionary Protestant clericalist ideology in the course of the nineteenth cen-

---

[11] Some churchmen in this period by way of defending the religious task of the clergy introduce the concept of a "christlicher Volkslehrer"; cf. the Göttingen theologian J. G. Marezoll's *Ueber die Bestimmung des Canzelredners* (Leipzig, 1973), p. 147.

[12] Background in Alexandra Schlingensiepen-Pogge, *Das Sozialethos der lutherischen Aufklärungstheologie* (Göttingen, 1967), pp. 187-88.

[13] On the instability and ambiguity inherent in the "rational Supernaturalism" in theology in Northwest Germany at this time, cf. Emanuel Hirsch, *Geschichte der neuern evangelischen Theologie* (Gütersloh, 1954), 5:57; Luigi Marino, *I Maestri della Germania: Göttingen 1770-1820* (Turin, 1975); Hans W. Frei, *The Eclipse of Biblical Narrative* (New Haven, Conn., 1974), pp. 170-73; Johann Dietrich Schmidt, "Die theologischen Wandlungen des Christoph Friedrich von Ammon," (Theol. Diss., Erlangen University, 1953).

tury.[14] That is, these late Enlightenment measures from the period 1789-1806 or thereabouts can be regarded as a foreshadowing[15] of the later Romantic and Neoconfessional attempt at an unembarrassed reassertion of clerical claims of social function and status cast—as they were to be eventually in the nineteenth century—in frankly irrationalist terms. Such unabashed reaction would, of course, be possible only in the course of the nineteenth century, once it had become politically and socially possible to make the broader supernaturalist claim that the Enlightenment had finally been "overcome."

The years after 1790 represent then a *continuation and a consolidation* of the earlier campaign against clerical utilitarianism. However, they also constitute a *transformation* of that campaign resulting from a metamorphosis of the motives and methods behind the churchmen's reassertion of the distinctive *raison d'être* of their estate in the face of domestic political reaction and revolutionary propaganda for disestablishment. Both these aspects of clerical identity at the turn of the century must be kept in mind if one is to view with historical sympathy the debates on clerical purpose and the plans for institutional reform elaborated in this period.

2. *Electoral Hannover*

a. Introduction

The Göttingen theologians throughout the 1790's upheld the primacy of the nontemporal task of the clergy. The antiutilitarian stand of Less, Planck, and Ammon[16] led to an adoption of Neohumanistic rhetoric. Thus the Göttingen theologian Carl Friedrich Stäudlin agreed in 1799 that the purpose of the clerical estate was bound up closely with the goals of humanity.[17] This tendency to conceptualize the pastoral role as one in which nontemporal, nonutilitarian tasks of educating humanity predominate occurs often. Even when it was recognized that the Protestant clergy had customarily co-operated closely with the government in temporal matters, this Neohumanistic conceptualization is found. For example, a manual for beginning preachers published at Hannover in

---

[14] Holsten Fagerberg, *Bekenntnis, Kirche und Amt in der deutschen Konfessionellen Theologie des 19. Jahrhunderts* (Uppsala, 1952).

[15] Thus demonstrating anew the rightness of the unconventional judgment by Emanuel Hirsch that theological Rationalism at the close of the German Enlightenment itself constituted an extremely potent force for "cautious ecclesiastical renewal"; see Hirsch, 5:56, in pointed contrast to such church historians as Christian Tischhauser and Gustav Ecke.

[16] See nn. 160-185 to Chapter 4 above.

[17] Comments in Carl Friedrich Stäudlin's review of F. H. C. Schwarz, *Der christliche Religionslehrer* (Gießen, 1798), in the *Göttingische Bibliothek der neuesten theologischen Literatur*, ed. Stäudlin, 4 (Göttingen, 1799): 834-50.

1802 recognized the fact of such temporal duties, yet carefully adopted the rhetoric of *Bildung* to describe the task of the clergy in preparation for eternal life:

> They as preachers should form [bilden] the hearts of their listeners by teaching, make good citizens of the state out of them and prepare them for their eternal destiny. Quite exclusively must this be done by Christian doctrine. ...[18]

In other words, though clerical activity of a temporal variety could be recognized as legitimate so long as it retained a peripheral character, no radically utilitarian revision of the clerical task was to be allowed.[19]

The attempt to accord a revived dignity to the nontemporal *raison d'être* of the pastorate can be discerned as the major theme in a variety of measures from this period pertaining to students of theology and pastors. In these measures one can also detect efforts to enhance the social prestige of the clerical estate and efforts to defend the civic utility of the clergy against charges that they were harmful to the state and the general welfare. How closely these themes intertwine will become apparent below.

b. Educational Reforms

The last years of the eighteenth century and the period preceding the Napoleonic invasion saw a redoubling of efforts to strengthen the training of future clergy. These measures built upon earlier efforts. The basis was provided first of all by a royal edict of September 27, 1735, that is, of roughly the same period in which the university at Göttingen had been founded, during which the government in Hannover had hoped to attract students of theology of higher social background so as to increase the prestige of the Protestant clerical estate as a means of furthering the Protestant cause in the Holy Roman Empire. The edict of 1735 is of a piece with these general plans, aiming at a more rigorous process of screening before admission of students to the parish clergy. The edict provided for four examinations in a student's career, two of which were to be carried out by the consistory; it also called for yearly reports from spiritual and temporal authorities concerning the conduct of students of theology. In addition, stimulated by the demands for post-university practice in preaching and pastoral care uttered by Molanus, Spener, Seckendorff, and Löscher, the authors of the edict attempted to set up "Seminaria" under the leadership of local clergy, in which candidates awaiting a call

---

[18] Heinrich Wilhelm Rotermund, *Handbuch für Candidaten* (Hannover, 1802), p. 7.

[19] Cf. Christoph Friedrich Ammon, *Anleitung zur Kanzelberedsamkeit* (Göttingen, 1799), pp. 9, 37-38.

could obtain practice in preaching, teaching, and pastoral care. Though these measures were not in all respects strictly enforced, nonetheless the principles of steady observation, periodic examination, and supervision in the period between leaving the university and receiving a parish call had been established as a goal toward which churchmen could in future work.[20]

The years after the edict of 1735 provided other anticipations of the concerns to be voiced later as the century was drawing to a close. For example, we find the consistory in Hannover complaining in 1751 concerning the low level of proficiency in Latin among students and candidates and urging measures to correct this. Though in 1771 a royal order of September 20 required that in future all those planning to seek a post in Electoral Hannover spend three years at the university, the consistory continued to be dissatisfied with the abilities of students and candidates. It complained on February 6, 1776 that the number of candidates of ability had decreased; furthermore, the number of pastors encouraging their sons to enter the clerical estate was declining. This latter complaint was uttered in even stronger language in 1790. In explanation the consistory pointed to the general contempt for religion and made a number of recommendations: better recruitment of students and clearer preliminary announcements of the nature of the questions to be asked by the consistory so as to avoid scaring away competent students.[21]

Similar concerns were voiced by a group of professors from the theological and philosophical faculties at Göttingen. Their memorandum, directed to the Privy Council in Hannover and dated February 4, 1788, was signed by some of the most noted professors at Göttingen—Ludwig Timotheus Spittler and Christian Gottlob Heyne, as well as J. G. H. Feder and Christian Meiners; the theologians signing were the aged Johann Peter Miller, Gottfried Less, and the young Planck. In view of the significance of this document as an expression of opinion on the part of both the theologians and the Neohumanist Heyne, and because only a few lines of it have been published,[22] it is desirable to reproduce a few passages from the manuscript here. It opens:

---

[20] Text of the edict in Christian Hermann Ebhardt, ed., *Gesetze, Verordnungen und Ausschreiben* (Hannover, 1845), 1:583-85; cf. Philipp Meyer, "Die theologischen Prüfungen in den lutherischen Kirchen Calenberg-Göttingens und Lüneburgs," *ZGNK* 53 (1955): 75-79; Reinhardt Wittram, *Die Universität und ihre Fakultäten* (Göttingen, 1962), p. 7.

[21] P. Meyer, "Prüfungen," 53:81-83; J. Meyer, "Geschichte der Göttinger theologischen Fakultät," *ZGNK* 42 (1937): 26; cf. n. 165 to Chapter 4 above.

[22] Universitäts-Archiv Göttingen, Kurat.-Akten, 4 II a 31, fol. 15 recto (cited hereafter as Kur.-Akten); excerpts in P. Meyer, "Prüfungen," 53:85.

The condition of theological studies at our university has occasioned the undersigned to meditate concerning the noticeable decline of the same and concerning the means of arresting the further progress of that decline. As the matter ... is of the greatest importance, in that the decline proceeds apace so that religion together with the spiritual estate must be deprived of their dignity: therefore they [the undersigned] request by gracious leave to lay their thoughts most humbly before Your ... Excellencies.[23]

The faculties then attempt to explain why this decline has come about, concluding that the chief source of the decline in theological studies as well as the remedy is to be found among the "students themselves." For

experience teaches us that for some years the students have come to us ever worse prepared: that most of them are unbelievably deprived of the necessary preliminary education; therefore one can expect no zeal in their studying, for so little capacity for participating in courses with profit is present. In theological studies this observation is all the more striking, since study of the ancient languages ... constitutes the basis [for them].[24]

The faculty continues with a cut at the plans advocated by such reformers as Bahrdt and Campe:

For some years the neglect of exegetical courses, especially of oriental ones, has visibly increased. The way of thinking of this age, prevailing opinions about the dispensability or uselessness of Hebrew and Greek for a theologian contribute to it; but even more is this the case because in this way one finds an excuse and a cover-up for one's ignorance.[25]

The faculty then turns to another cause:

Then too comes the fact that mostly only the poorest devote themselves to theological study, those among whom early instruction was ordinarily still worse, the capacities ... still less ... sharpened. They are thus all the less capable of following the teacher in his lecture, so soon as learned knowledge is requisite: therefore they leave and neglect this kind of lecture, and rather flock only to such classes where they can hope to grasp something without learned knowledge of languages.

In this way are trained immature candidates deprived of all knowledge of languages and the Bible.[26]

In searching for the underlying causes of this, the faculty finds them to be two in number: bad teaching in schools below the university level, and excessive numbers of students.[27] The remedy is to be found in a program of school reform of a decidedly elitist nature: the faculty recommends that many of the small Latin schools be transformed into trade schools so that

---

[23] Kur.-Akten, fol. 7 recto.
[24] Kur.-Akten, fol. 7 verso.
[25] Kur.-Akten, fol. 7 verso.
[26] Kur.-Akten, fol. 8 recto.
[27] Kur.-Akten, fol. 8 verso.

only the most able of the poor will be encouraged to seek further study at the university. Examinations in Latin schools are to be stricter.[28] Students in Latin schools are to be supervised more closely, and the Latin schools are to be reorganized so that their activities can be co-ordinated by a member of the consistory in Hannover working with the Göttingen faculty. Curricular reforms are urged so as to make sure that only poor students of extraordinary gifts are attracted to the university and to insure that more well-off students will be persuaded to study theology. Arrangements are suggested whereby four gifted students of theology can be encouraged to remain in study after completing the basic theological curriculum at Göttingen in hope of providing financial incentive to undertake advanced theological careers.[29]

One cannot regard as novel such plans to improve the status of the clerical estate by screening out all but the most able of the poor and by attracting those of higher social station (well-to-do nonnobles, one must suppose, since the number of Protestant clergy of noble background was minuscule.)[30] In fact such elitist and exclusivistic thinking—bolstered by the oversupply of theological candidates awaiting a call in Electoral Hannover—was commonplace in clerical circles in Northwest Germany. Thinking of this kind was the result of a traditionalistic, estate- or corporation-oriented, conservative tendency; thinkers of this school wanted to arrest the growth of social pressure from the peasantry and the artisan class. The goal of this kind of thinking was the preservation of the traditonal order of estates in society as it had been adjusted to the situation of the Old Régime in the age of Enlightenment.[31] Across Germany it was the theologians who were the most vehement defenders of the traditional proposition that the right to study ought to be closely guarded, since it constituted something akin to a "feudal" privilege.[32]

Thus—despite the adoption of liberal, Neohumanistic, and antiabsolutist natural law rhetoric in token of the clerical alliance with the Bildungsbürgertum—the unified way in which the Northwest German theologians sought to limit access to theological study by the lower orders indicates with unmistakable certainty their continuing allegiance to the notion of society divided into unequal estates: to the end, despite

---

[28] Kur.-Akten, fols. 11 recto and verso; 12 recto.

[29] Kur.-Akten, fols. 12 verso—15 recto.

[30] W. H. Bruford, Germany in the Eigteenth Century, 2nd ed. (Cambridge, 1971), p. 247; Gerd Heinrich, "Amtsträgerschaft und Geistlichkeit," in Günther Franz, ed., Beamtentum und Pfarrerstand 1400-1800 (Limburg/Lahn, 1972), pp. 179-238; Georges Pariset, L'État et les Églises en Prusse (Thèse, Paris, 1896), pp. 253-62.

[31] On the background to this kind of thinking and the figures on unemployment of candidates see Appendix J.

[32] Hans-Georg Herrlitz, Studium als Standesprivileg (Frankfurt a.M., 1973), pp. 66-69.

Enlightenment opposition to noble privilege and to absolutistic "despotism," the churchmen remained clearly conscious of themselves as an estate within the social framework of what we now describe as the Old Régime, an unequal society of privilege and of legal corporations.

In view of this traditionalistic orientation it was to be expected that the churchmen, theologians, and consistory in Electoral Hannover would take some measures to insure a closer supervision of theological students. These measures reflect the double situation of the leading churchmen at this time: first as representatives of a traditional *Stand* fighting for its life, and second as allies of a newly-emergent *Bildungsbürgertum* determined to assert itself against pressure from nobles, upwardly mobile elements, and spokesmen for absolutist policies that would have restricted "bourgeois" access to wealth and status in favor of allowing a greater share of both to landed and service nobility. This double situation of the churchmen is reflected in the way measures tightening theological education stress first traditional theology (i.e., remnants of Lutheran Orthodoxy adjusted to the demands of Enlightenment in a way precisely analogous to the way in which the clerical estate, though adjusted to the changed world of the eighteenth century, still attempted to maintain continuity with its historic identity) and second the classical education favored at Göttingen (i.e., Neohumanism as a rejection of the utilitarian ideal of pro-absolutist cameralism).

In the first measures taken toward the close of the century, the emphasis falls clearly on continuity with earlier efforts to upgrade theological education. In a directive of January 28, 1796 the consistory in Hannover demanded more detailed reports than hitherto on what theological students actually were learning. The list of questions shows that concern was with insuring that students acquire a thorough acquantaince with Biblical philology and with the literary sources for a good style in the pulpit—here betraying as well a concern with linguistic form essential to meeting the requirements of the *Bildungsbürgertum*.[33]

A rescript from the territorial government to the Göttingen theological faculty of October 11, 1799 went even further in demanding supervision of studies. Professors were ordered to institute regular examinations for students aiming at a parish in the Electorate.[34]

The next step was a comprehensive royal order of August 21, 1800, placing all theological students from the Electorate under supervision as they studied at Göttingen. The supervisor, the theologian Gottlieb Jacob

---

[33] "Ausschreiben" (January 28, 1796), in Ebhardt, ed., 1:591-93.

[34] Rescript of October 11, 1799 in *Beyträge zur Kenntniß und Verbesserung des Kirchen- und Schulwesens in den Königl. Braunschweig-Lüneburgschen Churlanden*, ed. Johann Christoph Salfeld 2 (1801): 220-22. (Hereafter cited as *Beyträge*.)

Planck, was to direct their studies and oversee their morals. He was to submit to the consistory reports on students. Furthermore, those planning to seek a parish in the Electorate were required to spend the last two years of their academic life at Göttingen.[35]

This royal order also specified the content of the examination for those concluding university study. Those planning a pastoral career in the Electorate were to be examined in four areas: (1) interpretation of Latin or Greek authors (a test of fitness to become a tutor in a noble household while waiting for the first parish); (2) Biblical exegesis; (3) dogmatic and moral theology (thus demonstrating continuity with the tradition of Lutheran Orthodoxy); (4) catechetical instruction and preaching.[36]

Furthermore, in 1801 a remedial course in the reading and interpretation of classical literature was set up for the Göttingen theological students. Conducted free of charge, it included readings in Hesiod, Lucian, Cicero, and Horace. Instruction in the Latin authors was carried out by the very father of Neohumanism, Heyne himself. The consistory gave its full approval to this course; indeed, it was virutally required of all theological students from the Electorate. The consistory announced through the supervisor that the results of this course would be taken into account in future consistorial examining of theological candidates.[37]

Looking back on the way in which this matter had developed, the knowledgeable Johann Christoph Salfeld traced the origin and success of this effort on the part of professors and consistory at reviving enthusiasm for the humanities and the classics:

> Loud and general, but only too correct, had long been the complaint that the study of the classical languages of antiquity was extraordinarily neglected, not only by law and medical students, but even by theologians, who in earlier times though had rightly placed a high value upon this splendid means of forming [Bildungsmittel] the spirit and the taste. ...[38]

This was, in the churchman Salfeld's opinion, all the more regrettable in view of the long-standing pre-eminence of classical studies at Göttingen; but nonetheless

> in the last decades of the previous [i.e., eighteenth] century, ... almost all feeling for the classical languages of antiquity and almost all taste for the humanities seemed to be wanting among the students, even among young

---

[35] "Verordnung" of August 21, 1800, in Ebhardt, ed., 1:782-91.

[36] P. Meyer, "Prüfungen," 53: 86-87. Also required were more explicit testimonials for entering students of theology concerning background in classics (Ebhardt, ed., 1:790-91).

[37] [J. C. Salfeld], "Beförderung der humanistischen Studien," in *Neue Beyträge zur Kenntniß und Verbesserung des Kirchen- und Schulwesens*, ed. J. C. Salfeld and J. P. Trefurt, 2 (1810): 1-55 (hereafter cited as *Nene Beyträge*); cf. P. Meyer, "Prüfungen," 53:85.

[38] Salfeld, "Beförderung," p. 1.

theologians, who could however scarcely do without them for their immediate occupation as private tutors.[39]

The decline was general:

> So long as biblical exegesis remained a prime study of the theological students, there remained a place of honor for philological and classical studies. As however the dominant opinion declared them to be useless, they fell from honor.[40]

Heyne the classics professor was alarmed by the lack of students interested in classics:

> Not without sorrow did the worthy Privy Justice Councillor Heyne see where the wind was blowing. As much as in him lay, he tried to give it another direction.[41]

At last, Salfeld reports, as a result of the measures taken to reorganize theological study at Göttingen, there occurred at the turn of the century a rebirth of interest in classical philology and literature. Concerning the response to the official measures, Salfeld writes:

> The success corresponded to [prior] expectation ... Soon more thorough study habits became visible among the young theological students, and they began to be less indifferent to the related disciplines—philological studies.[42]

In the same period there were taken measures to give a more systematic and supervised character to the training of future leaders for the church at Kloster Loccum. Although in this period Loccum seems at times to have housed only three candidates at any one time, nonetheless these measures may be noted as indicative of the desires of the leading churchmen.[43] The chief impulse to reorganization and better supervision of academic and practical studies and exercises came from the *Abt* himself, Johann Christoph Salfeld (1750-1829), though the new measures built upon earlier regulations. The details of the provision for more rigorous supervision and organization of academic studies and practical exercises need not concern us here; they are to be found in a document prepared at the instigation of the *Abt*, the "Instruktion für das Hospitium zu Loccum und den zur Dirigirung der Studien und praktischen Uebungen desselben committirten Conventual."[44] It will suffice to

---

[39] Salfeld, "Beförderung," p. 13.

[40] Salfeld, "Beförderung," p. 14.

[41] Salfeld, "Beförderung," p. 14.

[42] Salfeld, "Beförderung," p. 21; on this success, see Appendix K.

[43] Cf. Friedrich Düsterdieck, *Das Hospiz im Kloster Loccum* (Göttingen, 1863), p. 27.

[44] See "Instruktion für das Hospitium zu Loccum," in *Beyträge* 1 (Hannover, 1800): 465-81; Marahrens, "Instruktion für das Hospitium," *ZGNK* 29/30 (1924/25): 72-82; Düsterdieck, pp. 25-33; "Kirchliche Ankündigung bei dem Todesfalle des Abtes zu Loccum, Dr. Joh. Chr. Salfeld," *Hannoversches Magazin*, Jg. 1830, pp. 25-29; Fr. Schultzen

remark that the "Instruktion" of 1800 is particularly forceful in reiterating the importance of academic theology and philosophy, in providing for exegesis on the basis of Hebrew and Greek carried out in Latin, and in encouraging those studying in the cloister to use the time as an opportunity to gain an acquaintance with learned theological scholarship.

In view of the growing consensus that a revival of academic theology was desirable at all levels, the attempt was made at Loccum to see to it that future leaders of the church might be trained, as the "Instruktion" put it, "to be sure not as real scholars, but certainly however to be trained as learned theologians ... insofar as the estate of preachers, especially in our times, needs such in so many a regard."[45] Here again the old ideal of an estate with its own leadership and its own facilities for training such leaders shows itself even at the very close of the Old Régime.

c. Reforms Directed at the Entire Clergy

At the same time voices were raised in favor of a program of systematic reform designed to enhance the status and effectiveness of the entire pastorate. One of the most interesting of the proposals from the turn of the century was made by Christian Konrad Jakob Dassel (1768-1845), formerly a teacher in Hannover, and from 1796 preacher at Schloss Rücklingen near Hannover.[46] Dassel's ideas appeared in 1800 in a journal devoted to the advancement of Enlightenment religion, worship, and the institutional church published by Henke at Helmstedt.[47]

Dassel begins by calling into question the value of excessive concern of the parish clergy with what he terms "außerdienstlichen Beschäftigungen," that is, such peripheral matters as agriculture (in particular, increase of their own income thereby), the founding of schools, and the like; Dassel condemns the frequent consequence, namely, that "the theological discipline becomes alien" to the pastor.[48] Indeed, Dassel will recognize the legitimacy of writing on learned topics by clergymen only when it has an application to the clerical estate and theology—i.e., "moral theology, exegesis, dogmatics, pedagogics, philosophy, etc.," but not "economics, politics, medicine, and mechanics."[49]

and G. Müller, *Zum Jubiläum des Klosters Loccum* (Hannover, 1913); H. C. Heimbürger, *Carl Georg Schuster* (Celle, 1849); and the "Vorschlag zu einem Studienplan in Loccum" by Carl Georg Schuster (Archiv Kloster Loccum Signatur VIII,6) kindly made available to me by Dr. Ernst Berneburg.

[45] "Instruktion," in *Beyträge*, 1:467-68; cf. pp. 469-81.
[46] Kelchner, "Dassel," *Allgemeine Deutsche Biographie* (Leipzig, 1876), 4:760-61.
[47] Christian Dassel, "Worin soll die Thätigkeit der Prediger bestehen," *Eusebia*, ed. H. P. C. Henke, 3 (Helmstedt, 1800): 530-59.
[48] Dassel, pp. 530-33.
[49] Dassel, p. 533.

Dassel goes on to deal with hindrances to the pastor's ability to operate as a theologian, rejecting the attempts of absolutist spokesmen to deprive the clergy of a traditional grounding in philosophy, theology, and philology, remarking that such proposals have come to seem less plausible since the rise of the Kantian philosophy. He defends the necessity of a systematic study of theology even for parish pastors, explaining that, whereas the secular functionary can operate according to a few simple rules requiring little systematic thought, the clergyman must constantly assemble new truths and first look at them from a variety of angles before applying them. Therefore systematic and theoretical study of theology is necessary even for the parish clergy. Finally, though poverty and lack of books certainly contributes to the low level of concern with theological scholarship, in Dassel's view this is to be attributed chiefly to the quality of the clergy themselves.[50]

Dassel then turns to a positive presentation of the elements which he values in the pastoral role. First the clergyman is simply a "spiritual functionary, whose calling is the service of the church."[51] Though this is the pastor's first duty, the mere formal fulfillment of the requirements of service to the institutional church is not enough.

Second come the pastor's duties as *Volkslehrer*. Remarkable here is the fashion in which Dassel reinterprets what it means to be a *Volkslehrer*: for Dassel this consists in being an "educator of the people chiefly in the intellectual and moral capacity."[52] Here Dassel cautions against teaching the future pastor every conceivable kind of knowledge:

> To the theologian there can and may be from the start to the finish of his career nothing holier than theology. It alone is his discipline. Every step which he takes beyond it into the area of an alien discipline should be for him only a means, never an end.[53]

Dassel then proceeds with the reinterpretation of the concept of *Volkslehrer* in a sense removed from the usage of Bahrdt and Campe and rather transported into the realm of *Bildung* and *Kultur*:

> To the activity of the *Volkslehrer* belong instruction and *Bildung* of the congregation entrusted to him by means of public lectures and by his conduct. This is easily said, but truly not ... so easily done. Aside from the fact that many natural capacities pertain to this, and that it presupposes a constant cultivation [Kultur] of the entire exterior, especially of the organs of sense, so also must the necessary disciplines, which with the steadily progressing Enlightenment of the human race are extending into infinity, be precisely

---

[50] Dassel, pp. 533-38.
[51] Dassel, p. 539.
[52] Dassel, p. 539.
[53] Dassel, p. 540.

known, ... and the truths contained therein ... be extracted ... Every pause in the striving after one's own perfection [as a clergyman] brings with it a standstill in the culture of the people.[54]

Third for Dassel comes the clergyman's role as a man of learning:

> The preacher works as does the philosopher in an area of scholarship in which more depends upon thoroughness and connectedness in thought than on amount of factual knowledge. The study of moral theology ... necessarily presupposes a sound intellect and a cultivated faculty of judgment. All the more necessary do these requirements appear if the moral fundamentals are to be applied to the man [den Menschen].[55]

In particular Dassel recommends an acquaintance with Kantianism, and he reiterates the need for every student of theology to gain familiarity with philosophy.[56]

Clearly Dassel propagandizes for a concept of the clerical office which blends the strictly traditional and ecclesiastical duties of pastoral ministry (e.g., preaching, administration of the sacraments) with a more general form of moral and intellectual service to humanity. In this respect, the pastor is not simply a functionary of the institutional church; he is regarded in his capacity as man (i.e., as an ally of the *Bildungsbürgertum*):

> In his quality as man, and as one should indeed assume, as a cultivated man [gebildeten Menschen], the preacher is certainly and readily allowed to speak up for truth and morality.[57]

Dassel then passes in review the means by which this kind of pastoral activity (in particular, the literary cultivation of the pastor as theologian) can be advanced. He recommends first of all a revival of synods (or pastoral conferences under the leadership of the Superintendents) giving an opportunity for the reading of papers and articles. Tighter supervision is advised, along with the formation of reading clubs to defray the cost of books and journals. More detailed reports should be demanded by ecclesiastical superiors. The requirement of the consistory in Hannover in 1798 that pastors seeking transfer submit to the consistory examples of their preaching and teaching also meets with Dassel's approbation. Consistories must advance to more desirable parishes only those pastors who demonstrate true competence. In identifying such competence consistories must take into account ability and progress in homiletics, liturgics, catechics, moral theology, popular dogmatics and philosophy. Finally, Dassel urges that a professional journal for all the clergy of the

---

[54] Dassel, pp. 540-41.
[55] Dassel, p. 541.
[56] Dassel, p. 542.
[57] Dassel, p. 545.

territory be founded, one which would stimulate the exchange of ideas by printing both official announcements from the consistory and articles by pastors—especially proposals for the improvement of the schools and of the clerical estate.[58]

In a footnote at the close Dassel remarks that after the text had gone to print he learned that the *Consistorialrath* and *Abt* of Loccum Johann Christoph Salfeld had founded such a journal at Hannover.[59] Thus Dassel's ideas accurately reflect the kinds of proposals being seriously entertained by the consistory in Hannover. The way in which semi-official reflection on these matters proceeded can be gauged by glancing at an article which appeared in the following year (1801) in the second volume of Salfeld's quasi-official professional journal. The author was Carl Georg Schuster, who had recently helped to reorganize the training institute for clergy at Kloster Loccum, of which he was the *Studiendirektor*.[60]

Schuster takes as his theme "the necessity of a teaching-and-preaching-estate in every more perfect state." His intention is to provide apologetic for the traditional established church and clergy that will meet the attacks on public support of the clergy and counter the example of newly-organized states abroad which have dispensed with established church and clergy. By the "necessity" of the clerical estate Schuster understands a necessity which will legitimate public support of it.[61] It must, then, be seen as all the more striking that (despite his arguments against disestablishment) Schuster carefully puts limits on what the state may require of the clergy.

Schuster follows Herder and Henke in taking up the defense of the nontemporal chief purpose of ministry on the basis of the natural law distinction between service to the citizen and service to humanity, and at last links that defense with a specific demand that the state define and delimit its claim on the pastor.[62]

Schuster aims to prove that the state must support the clerical estate because of moral necessity, *not* just because that estate can aid the state in advancing its immediate political goals. Writing from a Kantian and Neohumanistic perspective, he first argues that the state on the basis of its own goals and presuppositions must recognize the legitimacy of public

---

[58] Dassel, pp. 545-59.

[59] Dassel, p. 558.

[60] Cf. Heimbürger.

[61] Carl Georg Schuster, "Ueber die Nothwendigkeit eines Lehr- und Predigerstandes in jeden vollkommneren Staate," in *Beyträge* 2 (Hannover, 1801): 274-335, esp. pp. 275-86.

[62] Cf. Schuster, pp. 276-78; Johann Georg Jonathan Schuderoff, *Beyträge zur Beförderung zweckmäßiger Kanzelvorträge* (Braunschweig, 1796).

support for an estate of preachers and teachers because it is necessary that there be instruction in law and morality. A similar necessity arises from the need for "public institutions of instruction and education," which require preachers and teachers as a distinct estate.[63] Schuster then provides a third argument for the necessity of the clerical estate, one which reveals how strongly he sees a need to delimit the claims of the state on society and the clerical estate.

In the final analysis, argues Schuster, the state itself is intended to function as a "servant of humanity"; it must stand in the "Dienst der Menschheit."[64] This claim is grounded in the priority of man over citizen:

> As a principle it is uncontestably to be recognized in every state that its members were men earlier than they were citizens, and that they in no way ceased to be the former when they became the latter; indeed, that they became the latter in the higher intention of being able to become the former ever more and better. To be sure, the first contractors of the state may not have thought on this last intention as the final end of the state ... indeed could not think thereon. For unquestionably an awakening of reason to a certain degree, which can be attained to only gradually, is required, in order that one become clearly and fully conscious of one's humanity in all of its capacities for perfection. However, once this consciousness be brought to expression in us—and that this be the case in the current state of cultivation [Policirung] is indeed certain enough—then one cannot and may not without denying one's peculiar human essence reject the imperative demand of humanity, the highest possible perfection to which one can attain according to all of the physical, intellectual and moral forces and capacities of one's human nature.[65]

One recognizes readily enough the earnest tone of incipient German Idealism mingling as it does with undertones of the notions to be given expression in Goethe's *Wilhelm Meister*.[66] For such a view the priority of man over citizen is beyond argument. What then becomes of the attempt to realize the state's own true goal, that of fostering morality for the benefit of humanity? According to Schuster, the state left to itself does exactly the opposite in practice. Invoking Kant's opinion, Schuster asserts that the state, by causing people to live too close together, overstimulates the passions. This causes the Principle of Evil to "wound" humanity's moral condition in a way that the state itself cannot avoid.[67] Indeed, the

---

[63] Schuster, p. 304; cf. pp. 287-399.
[64] Schuster, pp. 308, 310.
[65] Schuster, pp. 308-9.
[66] Cf. H. A. Korff, *Geist der Goethezeit* (Leipzig, 1923-57), 2:341-44.
[67] Schuster, pp. 319-21; cf. Friedrich Theodor Rink, ed. *Sammlung einiger bisher unbekannt gebliebener kleiner Schriften von Immanuel Kant* (Königsberg, 1800), pp. 50-52.

state is a "cause of the worsening of the human condition of its citizens."[68]

Schuster insists that this process of moral deterioration must be stopped, since "humanity is above the state" and since it is not permissible to harm humanity by any such sacrificing (*aufopfern*) of *Mensch* to *Bürger*.[69] Therefore the state is obligated "before the judgment seat of humanity"[70] to provide humanity with a compensation for damage done (*Schadenersatz*).[71] This compensation is the clerical estate, whose purpose is to help humanity attain by religious means to that morality made unattainable in practice by the state. In short, because the state's influence on human life is a "poison" (*Gift*), it is the clergyman's task to provide the "antidote" (*Gegengift*) to this evil influence.[72]

Having established that the clergy protect the interests of humanity (i.e., the *Bildungsbürgertum*) against the state's evil influence, Schuster is consequently able to give a satisfactory explanation for the relationship of the clergy to the state. According to Schuster, the pastor in his capacity as carer for souls is supported by his congregation for the purpose of providing moral and religious instruction. This capacity, that of the clergyman as *Seelsorger*, is to be distinguished from the capacity in which the state has any claim on him, for that capacity is to be regarded as distinct from and subordinate to the primary and nontemporal task.[73]

The state, in Schuster's scheme, makes two claims on the pastor. First, it entrusts the administrative aspect of ecclesiastical affairs to him so as to encourage religion. Second, it can under certain circumstances also ask the pastor to act as a *Volkslehrer* responsible for instructing the people about their civic and temporal welfare—but only under definite conditions. The state must plainly declare that the pastor is to be considered one of its functionaries (*Beamten*) in this connection, and in so doing it should issue a *Pastoralinstruction* enumerating in specific detail the exact extent of the pastor's administrative and civic duties to the state.[74] Citing the opinion of Luther, Schuster holds furthermore that such duties in service to the state should be discharged on clearly defined occasions separate from actual divine worship so that piety not be disturbed.[75] In so

---

[68] Schuster, p. 321.

[69] Schuster, p. 321.

[70] Schuster, p. 322; for the background to this expression, which implies that the *Bildungsbürgertum* is the representative of humanity before which the state is to be justified, see Reinhart Koselleck, *Kritik und Krise* (Frankfurt a.M., 1973), Chapter 2.

[71] Schuster, pp. 319, 321.

[72] Schuster, p. 329.

[73] Schuster, pp. 316-17.

[74] Schuster, pp. 313-18; cf. W. A. Teller, ed., *Neues Magazin für Prediger*, 7:305, cited by Schuster, p. 315.

[75] Schuster, p. 316.

doing, the clergyman is not simply delivered up to the whims of the secular authority, but is rather permitted to undertake this civic activity only insofar as the state itself must recognize the supremacy of humanity and itself in the service of the same.[76]

For Schuster the clergyman's responsibility to the individual members of humanity with respect to the formation of their eternally developing souls as tokens of their human qualities consistently overshadows the pastor's distinct and supplemental role as a state functionary. Indeed, for Schuster the state has a part in bringing about the realization of spiritual and moral culture ("the highest thing" for humanity) only insofar as it makes its own the goals of humanity itself, and thus by sanctioning the traditional support of the clergy at public expense thereby provides humanity with the clerical estate as a *Schadenersatz*, as a means of undoing the damage inflicted on humanity by the state.[77]

In the same period appeared official signs that the consistory in Hannover was prepared to take steps to put into effect measures for the clergy closely akin to those favored by Dassel and Schuster. First, in a pair of orders dated February 1, 1798 and January 15, 1799, the consistory stressed that theological learning of an academic sort was henceforth to be a criterion for advancement to more desirable parishes, a policy intended to encourage pastors to keep up with the latest developments in theology.[78]

Second, amid the chaos of voices arguing for different ways of reforming the Protestant clergy, the Hannoverian consistory spoke very clearly, and in accents much like those of Schuster. On July 1, 1800 it issued a new "Pastoral-Instruction," intended, it is true, chiefly for beginning pastors, but also making clear to all where the consistory stood on the issue of the clergyman's identity and function.[79] This document carefully reasserts a moderately traditionalistic position on ministry, making plain that the clergyman's main task must remain that of promoting a religion and a morality grounded in learned biblical exegesis, a task seen as service to humanity in good Neohumanistic fashion. The *Pastoral-Instruction* clearly eliminates any possibility of interpreting this-worldly elements in ministry as primary. At the same time, it itemizes the administrative and

---

[76] Schuster, p. 335.
[77] Schuster, pp. 319-20.
[78] *Beyträge* 2 (1801): 195-202.
[79] Text with introductory "Ausschreiben," followed by the "Pastoral-Instruction für die unter dem Hannoverschen Consistorio stehenden Prediger" in Ebhardt, 1:819-35. One cannot simply describe this document as a statement "composed in the spirit of the age of Enlightenment," as is done in Philipp Meyer, "Der Quellenwert der Kirchen- und Schulberichte," *ZGNK* 19 (1914): 84. Rather must one note the mix of Kantian Enlightenment with conservative and Neohumanistic elements.

civic duties which pastors owe the state. In so doing, it fulfills the demand for a clear demarcation of the clergyman's religious from his civic responsibilities, thus reasserting the official primacy of the pastor's purely otherworldly role while providing a subordinate and distinct place for temporal and civic tasks.

According to its introduction, the *Pastoral-Instruction* of 1800 is addressed above all to pastors beginning their ministry (i.e., those most likely to be affected by radical ideas). This statement of the goals and duties of the clerical estate is intended to build on what is contained in the traditional church orders of the territories. It emphasizes the importance of preserving the reputation of the clergy by making certain that proper morality and decorum are observed.[80]

The body of the *Pastoral-Instruction* is divided into four sections. The first deals with the pastor's duties to the entire congregation and is particularly rich in Neohumanistic rhetoric. Only at the very end of this first section does the emphasis shift from service to the religious and moral needs of humanity to service to the temporal and civic needs of the citizen.[81]

The first section leaves no doubt that the "main matter" and "real goal" of the clerical calling is a moral and religious one deriving from study of scripture, and one nontemporal in nature.[82] This first section opens with the directive that "the Christian preacher should ... become a practical teacher of religion," and in consequence "as such, the promoter of true religiosity and of a morality in the congregation entrusted to him. ..."[83] In this connection the need for the pastor to continue to progress in his study is stressed so that he can adequately take account of "the spirit of the age" and the "true needs of humanity" in his private instruction of the more "cultivated" (*gebildeteren*) members of his congregation.[84]

Specific measures mentioned as ways of encouraging this kind of continuing education are the formation of theological reading societies and the requirement of 1798 that pastors seeking transfer submit written proof of the effect of their studies on their sermons.[85] The pastor must study the Bible, seeking the "spirit and content of the holy documents of religion," so that by proper acquaintance with the "genius of the language" he can

---

[80] Ebhardt, 1:819.

[81] Ebhardt, 1:821, 825.

[82] Ebhardt, 1:822; of course, a Christianity active in the world is affirmed as a subordinate or peripheral concern; cf. pp. 834-35.

[83] Ebhardt, 1:820.

[84] Ebhardt, 1:821.

[85] Ebhardt, 1:821-22.

apply its content to practical needs.[86] The closeness to Herder's world of thought is sufficiently clear to need no comment.

Furthermore, the pastor "as a member of the more cultivated society" is to promote "correct Enlightenment" by extending his studies to include something besides theology—e.g., "philosophy, natural science, natural history, Oriental, or Latin philology." Here it is emphasized that this peripheral study must not separate him from his proper theological task, but rather be carried out so as to have some immediate connection with "the real goal of his calling."[87]

There follow miscellaneous instructions, making clear that while the pastor's *Hauptsache* (main task) is "edification" executed by means of preaching and administration of the sacraments, nonetheless he is expected to conduct special Bible studies and instruction in the catechism. [88] The pastor is explicitly warned that, though he should not neglect to give advice and help where needed, nonetheless he ought not to meddle in affairs which properly speaking belong to the "physician, judge, lawyer, etc." Thus the ideas of Bahrdt and Campe are formally repudiated.[89]

The second section, which concerns the pastor's work as a supervisor of schools, is noteworthy in that it contains no explicit mention of industry schools as such and devotes most of its attention to the pastor's work in seeing to it that religious and moral instruction are provided.[90] In this section there is clear linguistic evidence that the churchmen had begun to conceptualize the pastor's task in Kantian terms. The adoption of Kantian language (in contrast to utilitarian terminology) leaves no doubt that the primary tasks of the clergyman are here conceived as being directly concerned with service to the Kantian ideals of the providential God, the moral law, and the hope of the perfectibility of the world.[91]

The third section of the *Pastoral-Instruction* stresses the importance of the pastor's serving as a good administrator of ecclesiastical property—a necessity if the basis for the independent existence of future generations of clergy was to be preserved. The opening of this section brings out the importance of the pastor's services to the state, but at the same time affirms the principle met with in Schuster that the church within the

---

[86] Ebhardt, 1:822.

[87] See Ebhardt, 1:822-23, citing earlier orders to this effect as early as September 15, 1684.

[88] Ebhardt, 1:823-24.

[89] Ebhardt, 1:825. At the same place, however, the pastor is instructed to act as an exemplary father and citizen.

[90] Ebhardt, 1:826-29.

[91] Cf. Ebhardt, 1:820, 826; for the Kantian background, see Appendix L.

framework of the state exists in order to serve the purpose of "religious and moral *Bildung*."[92]

The fourth section provides what had come to seem increasingly necessary, namely, an itemized list of the capacities in which the pastor is to serve the state.[93] Itemized are the supervision of schools, reports on the conduct of the pastoral office and on the state of the schools, the reading of governmental orders, care for the poor, the keeping of various statistical records and parish property records, and various matters of marriage law. Yet in this work of co-operating with other constituted authorities the principle is admitted that all this is distinct from the "great goal of [the pastor's] real calling" and that such co-operation for the common good should ultimately support that properly nontemporal goal.[94]

The last point is underscored in the concluding paragraph of the consistory's *Pastoral-Instruction*. It recalls that the document is designed to provide beginning preachers with an occasion for "serious consideration" of the "great and real purposes of their calling" with the expectation that the consequences will be

> the advancement of the general good in real aiding and satisfaction of so many essential needs of humanity and in the spread of ... feeling for truth and virtue, or of an active Christianity, and the greater general welfare, which is connected with them inseparably.[95]

Thus, despite the repudiation of radical utilitarianism and the adoption of Kantian and Neohumanistic rhetoric, the consistory still sensed a need to recall that the nontemporal work of the pastor would nonetheless serve to advance temporal well-being. It may thus be said that the conception of pastoral ministry in the *Instruction* of 1800, since it is the product of a long evolution during the decades of Enlightenment, represents a compromise: the need to characterize Christianity as useful to state and society is felt, but the overwhelming emphasis throughout the document falls rather upon the role of the pastor as an agent of religious and moral *Bildung* with a special relationship to the educated classes.

At the same time the consistory attempted to tighten its supervision of pastors in the field so as to insure that they did a more creditable job and one more in keeping with the goals outlined in the *Pastoral-Instruction*. This effort is symbolized by the appearance in 1800 of a massive new handbook for superintendents giving detailed instructions on how pastors should be supervised. This two-volume work was written by

---

[92] Ebhardt, 1:828; cf. 829.
[93] Ebhardt, 1:829-35.
[94] Ebhardt, 1:831.
[95] Ebhardt, 1:835.

Campe's old opponent Holscher, by now the Superintendent of Ronnenberg.[96] The work underscores the identification of the clergy with "the true and eternal interest of humanity"[97] and, while covering every imaginable aspect of the pastoral office as a matter for supervision, gives particular emphasis to the necessity for careful study and observation of the *Pastoral-Instruction*; for only in this fashion, argues Holscher, can one be so permeated by the "goals of the calling" that one receives a proper "conviction of the worth and dignity of the practical teaching office."[98]

In this period there also appeared numerous signs that the leading churchmen and their lay allies in the consistory were determined to defend the incomes, privileges, and marks of status traditionally enjoyed by the Protestant clergy. This "clericalist" reaction points up the willingness of late Enlightenment churchmen to adopt a fundamentally condemnatory attitude toward the dissolution of traditional institutional Christianity as an element in the Old Régime.[99] Defense of clerical incomes and rights had become necessary in view of their imperiling by attrition, anticlerical propaganda, litigation, pressure for commutation into fixed cash payments, and the example of disestablishment and secularization in revolutionary France. In response the Hannoverian consistory around 1799 instituted a special legal counsel to represent parish clergy in all actions at law; one of its members versed in church law also brought out in 1801 a five-volume codification of historic clerical privilege.[100]

In addition, the step was taken of making sure that future pastors would be equipped with the legal knowledge necessary for them to defend their incomes and rights. A new textbook of pastoral theology adopted at Göttingen in 1803-1804 served this purpose. The author was Johann Friedrich Christoph Gräffe (1754-1816), a local pastor and Director of

---

[96] Johann Conrad Achaz Holscher, *Praktisches Handbuch für Ephoral- und kirchliche Geschäfte*, 2 Theile (Hannover, 1800, 1805).

[97] Holscher, *Handbuch*, 2:5.

[98] Holscher, *Handbuch*, 2:192; cf. in the same volume "Zweytes Capitel. Moralischreligiöse Bildung durch Prediger-Geschäfte. I. Kenntniß und Studium der Pastoral-Instruction," pp. 191-93.

[99] On concern with the place of the clergy in tables of ranks for use at court and clerical social status, see "Haben die Prediger ... einen bestimmten bürgerlichen Rang?" in *Annalen der Braunschweig-Lüneburgischen Churlande*, 8. Jg. (Hannover, 1794): 310-12; Johann Friedrich Christoph Gräffe, *Die Pastoraltheologie nach ihrem ganzen Umfange* (Göttingen, 1803), 2:150-51; "Fürst-Bischöffliche Preisfrage und die Wirzburgische Landgeistlichkeit," *Journal von und für Deutschland*, ed. Siegmund Freyherr von Bibra, 6. Jg. (Fulda, 1789): 364-67; Martin Hasselhorn, *Der altwürttembergische Pfarrstand im 18. Jahrhundert* (Stuttgart, 1958), pp. 56-92.

[100] Details on these measures (including codification of church law) and the background to them will be found in Appendix M; cf. also nn. 166-178 below.

the Royal Pastoral Institute at Göttingen.[101] Gräffe's textbook proceeds from a Neohumanistic concept of the distinctive function of the clergy and from the notion of religion as a matter pertaining to the *Mensch* to a defense of the traditional privileges of the clerical estate.

In his first volume Gräffe begins with a bald assertion of the autonomous worth of religion in the state:

> Religion is no invention of politics; for it was there earlier then politics was ever thought of; rather is it a plant that grows immediately out of the essence and out of the soil of humanity. ... religion must be recognized as an essential, inner need of human nature ... Religion opens a prospect on eternity, ... religion comforts man [den Menschen], lightens his burden, and gives him the power of overcoming his inclinations. Only by means of religion can the man become that which he should become.[102]

The extent to which Gräffe has adopted the Neohumanistic conception of the pastoral responsibility to the man can be seen from the way in which he includes aesthetics as a topic in catechetical training and from the way in which he treats moral and religious training as a special form of *Bildung*.[103]

However up-to-date this version of clerical identity may have seemed, Gräffe nonetheless saw good cause to provide his students as well with the means for a juridical defense of the traditional rights and privileges of the clerical estate. He devotes 29 of his second volume's 354 pages to the administration of parish property and 131 pages to Protestant ecclesiastical law in Germany.[104] In the preface to the second volume, he feels called upon to justify his lengthy treatment of such matters:

> On several grounds I have thought it necessary to treat Protestant ecclesiastical law ... What disadvantages arise, if the pastor has lagged behind in this area of his professional training! ... Often ... he will keep silent ... when he is bound to defend the rights of his estate, his parish, and his church with decisive manly courage. Again, in other causes he will carelessly allow that which may not be allowed at all.[105]

The efforts of the leading churchmen to revive the self-consciousness and self-esteem of the clerical estate in this period are also well attested in the measures to insure the regular holding of conferences and synods of the clergy at which learned and practical topics of professional interest could be discussed.[106] Perhaps more important still was the periodical.

---

[101] Cf. n. 99 above and J. Meyer, "Geschichte der Göttinger theologischen Facultät," p. 92.

[102] Gräffe, 1:3-4.

[103] Gräffe, 1:190-92, 230-32.

[104] Gräffe, 2:111-40 (administration) and 2:223-54 (church law).

[105] Gräffe, 2:viii; cf. Appendix M.

[106] See Appendix N.

The general significance of the periodical as a means for the diffusion of Enlightenment in Germany has been underscored by Paul Raabe.[107] In the late Enlightenment the churchmen naturally turned to the periodical as a means of raising the *esprit de corps* of their estate.[108]

The most important journal for the clergy as a whole in Electoral Hannover was one founded at Hannover in 1800. The editor was Johann Christoph Salfeld, a member of the consistory and *Abt* of Loccum.[109] The journal's aim was to improve the functioning, morale, and reputation of the clerical estate in Electoral Hannover. This journal in its first issue listed 462 subscribers, over 95 percent of whom appear to have been churchmen and schoolteachers in Electoral Hannover.[110] These subscribers could read in it official notices such as the instruction for Loccum; discussions of liturgical and educational reforms; debates on the nature, purpose, and morale of the clergy and the means of raising that morale; and articles on matters of practical concern such as the issue of the preservation of traditional incomes.[111] Thus in Salfeld's journal, as elsewhere, the synthesis of traditional clerical identity (as a function of its status as an estate privileged in the Old Régime)[112] with the new identity of the clergy (as spokesmen for the cause of the *Bildungsbürgertum*) was to be observed.[113]

---

[107] Paul Raabe, "Die Zeitschrift als Medium der Aufklärung," *Wolfenbütteler Studien zur Aufklärung*, ed. Günter Schulz, 1 (Wolfenbüttel, 1974): 99-136.

[108] Cf. for example the *Magazin für Religions- Moral- und Kirchengeschichte*, ed. Carl Friedrich Stäudlin (Hannover, 1801—); also *Beyträge zum Bau des Reiches Gottes*, ed. Johann Christoph Friedrich Gieseler, 1 (Hannover, 1803), esp. pp. 98-105: "Ist das Christenthum hauptsächlich nur ein Bedürfniß des Pöbels, oder auch der höhern und gebildetern Stände."

[109] See Salfeld's *Beyträge* and *Neue Beyträge* and the continuation as *Viertheiljährige Nachrichten von Kirchen- und Schulsachen* (Hannover, 1809ff.).

[110] Rough computations from the "Verzeichniß der Pränumeranten," in *Beyträge*, 1 (1800): fols. *1 recto—*7 recto.

[111] See for example in Salfeld's *Beyträge*: "Instruktion für das Hospitium zu Loccum," 1 (1800): 465-81; "Die akademischen Studia iunger Theologen betreffend," 2 (1801): 216-55; C. G. Schuster, "Ueber die Nothwendigkeit eines Lehr- und Predigerstandes in jedem vollkommneren Staate," 2 (1801): 272-335; J. F. Jacobi, "Die Beichthandlung vor dem heiligen Abendmahl betreffend," 3 (1802): 19-60; "Ueber Prediger-Synoden," 5 (1804): 56-96; J. G. H. Feder, "Der Prediger und der Priester," 7 (1807): 499-522; G. F. Reinhold, "Ueber den absoluten Begriff des Geistlichen," in *Neue Beyträge*, 1 (1810): 334-78; "Zur Geschichte der Abschaffung der Prediger-Accidenzien," in *Viertheiljährig Nachrichten*, Jg. 1809, pp. 120-28.

[112] See for example "Sollte nicht billig in einer jeden Pfarr-Registratur eine bestimmte Instruction vorhanden seyn, welche die Geschäfte, Jura und Verhältnisse des Predigers enthielte," *Viertheiljährige Nachrichten*, Jg. 1809, pp. 114-20; and to a degree of course "Pastoral-Instruction," in *Beyträge* 1 (1800): 62-103.

[113] See the articles by Schuster and Reinhold cited in n. 111 above; also "Die akademischen Studia iunger Theologen betreffend," in *Beyträge* 2 (1801): 216-55; and [Salfeld], "Beförderung der humanistischen Studien," in *Neue Beyträge* 2 (1810): 1-55.

Yet it would be an inadequate statement of the themes in Salfeld's publications were we to leave out of account another current in clerical thought at the time. Already remarked upon is the tendency toward transformation—the tendency of the churchmen after 1789 to counter propaganda for disestablishment by stress on what Schuster termed the "necessity" of the preaching estate. In this period one rightly expects to find specific attempts to demonstrate the utility of the clergy to the temporal government.

Such demonstrations are not absent from Salfeld's journals. For example, in 1802 the *Beyträge* carried an article showing in detail how "ecclesiastical activities" could be used for furthering the "spread of moral-religious knowledge in all classes of people by promoting a closer acquaintance with the content and spirit of the Bible."[114] In 1802 we find as well a lengthy article on the use of poorhouses "for the purpose of promoting greater religiosity and morality in the lower classes of the people" written by a superintendent.[115] Again, the journal's continuation in 1814 published fulsome outpourings of patriotic sentiment on the occasion of the restoration of the pre-Napoleonic government, including the consistory's thanks for the action of "divine providence" in restoring the "glorious and much-loved" government in Hannover and London.[116] Nor were such patriotic effusions isolated occurrences after 1789.[117]

There is, then, ample reason to find in this period not simply a continuation of the previous effort on the part of the churchmen to preserve their historic identity by effecting a synthesis with Neohumanism that would provide an additional rationale supporting their privileges; also present are signs of an incipient alliance between throne and altar that was to become so firm in the course of the nineteenth century that earlier tensions between temporal government and established clergy would be forgotten.

3. *Braunschweig-Wolfenbüttel*

a. Introduction

We turn to Braunschweig-Wolfenbüttel without the expectation of finding so fully developed a positive program for the defense of

---

[114] "Kirchliche Einrichtungen zu mehrerer Verbreitung sittlichreligiöser Kenntnisse," in *Beyträge* 3 (1802): 1-18.

[115] Superintendent Hoppenstedt, "Ueber Armenanstalten und ... Moralität," in *Beyträge* 4 (1802): 1-66, 112-253.

[116] *Viertheiljährige Nachrichten*, Jg. 1814: 19, 21-22.

[117] Cf. Johann Georg Fock, *Zwey öffentliche Religionsvorträge über die ächte Bürgertreue*, ed. Johann Caspar Velthusen (Stade, 1793); Velthusen, ed., *Christliches Trostbuch in Kriegszeiten: Taschenbuch für christliche Soldaten* (Hannover, 1795).

autonomous clerical identity as in Electoral Hannover. For in Braunschweig the power of absolutist ideology and the power of its particularist opposition were well matched. While the traditionalist forces were able to sabotage ducal plans for secularization of clerical training, it was scarcely to be expected that in a situation of this kind the traditionalist forces would have sufficient strength to impose positive measures for the furthering of the particularist identity of the clergy—at any rate, hardly to the degree possible in more decentralized Electoral Hannover. Here there holds an analogy with the paralysis characteristic of other areas of ecclesiastical reform in Braunschweig.[118] The absence of any *coordinated* reform program for a revival of clerical *esprit de corps* on the Hannoverian model can then be attributed to this deadlock resulting from the nearly equal strength of absolutist and anticentralist tendencies.

Nonetheless, careful inspection discloses that most of the features of clericalist revival (and subsequent transforming accommodation to the changed conditions after 1789) are to be found in rudimentary (though not programmatic) form in Braunschweig-Wolfenbüttel as well. Here we can only list the similarities to the program in Electoral Hannover.

The same consensus and the same transformation of the consensus can be found in statements concerning clerical identity from this period in Braunschweig-Wolfenbüttel. One extended example will suffice; it is drawn from an address concerning the "Dignity and Purpose of the Christian Preaching Office" delivered in 1799 by the Helmstedt Professor Heinrich Philipp Conrad Henke.[119] As Henke was the most important theologian at Helmstedt and directly involved in the training of future pastors, we may safely take this example as indicative of the official line of the churchmen in Braunschweig-Wolfenbüttel at the time.

To begin with, Henke emphasizes the divine institution of the ministry by Jesus Christ, and with it the divinity of the call extended to the individuals in the ministry. The precise nature of the clergyman's relationship to the state may vary according to the accident of historical circumstance, allows Henke; but that accident pales into unimportance beside the fact that the "real business" of the clergy, that is, their "divine mission," is that of preaching and explaining "the doctrines of Christianity."[120] In this sense the clergy are the "ambassadors for Christ," through whom God makes the appeal on behalf of Christ to be "reconciled to God."[121] That is, the clergy are "successors of the

---

[118] Cf. Johannes Meyer, *Kirchengeschichte Niedersachsens* (Göttingen, 1939), p. 186.
[119] Heinrich Philipp Conrad Henke, "Würde und Bestimmung des christlichen Predigtamts," in his *Predigten*, 2. Sammlung (Braunschweig, 1803), pp. 32-78.
[120] Henke, "Würde," pp. 44-47.
[121] Henke, "Würde," pp. 48-49 with reference to 2 Cor. 5:20.

apostles"; moreover, the preachers of this message are "equipped" by Jesus Christ, that most perfect teacher of religion and virtue.[122]

These claims do not mean that Henke backs off from the Rationalistic refusal to see in the clergy "special, holy people, ... so-called priests and representatives of God, or ... keepers of the keys of heaven." For this would, in Henke's view, be to misapply to the person of the preacher the divine promises concerning the ministry, rather than rightly limiting them to the calling and the office, which are indeed of God, and of which may be said—no less than of secular government—that they are part of the authority instituted of God (Rom. 13).[123] Thus Henke claims for the church and clergy a legitimation at the least equal to that accorded the state.

The fuller dimensions of this claim become evident as Henke then turns to the nature of what the ministry seeks to accomplish by the "application" of Christian doctrines "to the spirit and morals of men."[124] In good Neohumanistic fashion Henke claims for the clergy a unique significance in their use of eternal truths to improve the man as man;

> ... this good differs markedly from the good promoted by other estates and kinds of business in that it concerns the man as *man*. All other useful works and services concern either the man and his well-being with regard to his senses and his animal part, or they are connected with his social and civic affairs.[125]

The clergy however serve a higher purpose:

> We [human beings] are not merely members of a world of the senses, and not merely members of an external society; we have, as men, in the differentiating, peculiar marks and traits of our nature, in our reasonable and moral free being, a higher dignity, a higher goal, ... more important duties and expectations. This our relation takes precedence over all others, and reaches higher than all others in which we may be placed by our temporal life.[126]

By all this Henke understands the human relationship to divine law, which

> extends further than all human laws. ... before this court must finally be spoken decisively and impartially concerning our value, and eternity must develop and justify everything.[127]

It is furthering of such development of the person in its eternal aspect which the clergy serve; therefore

---

122 Henke, "Würde," pp. 51, 53.
123 Henke, "Würde," pp. 54-55.
124 Henke, "Würde," pp. 56-57.
125 Henke, "Würde," p. 58.
126 Henke, "Würde," p. 58.
127 Henke, "Würde," p. 59.

there can be conceived no more noble and beneficent institution of human love [than the Christian preaching office]; the man, as *man*, as a free spirit, accountable to himself, immortal, as citizen of the kingdom of God, this is the field upon which we work. ...[128]

Furthermore, claims Henke, the good which is in this way to be promoted by the clergy is in a unique way "the Good in itself":

All results which are sought and won by means of other kinds of business and strivings of men, however valuable and indispensable they may be, are always subordinate to another and higher goal. Health of body, preservation, relaxation, ... peace, order, and happiness in the commonwealth—all that is no good in and for itself, but rather a means and help to some other higher good. Wisdom and virtue, however, and the satisfaction and happiness of the man contained therein, are not further means to a higher goal.[129]

Thus the clergy serve the ultimate good, one higher than that served by the state. In this connection Henke explicitly repudiates the view of Campe and like-minded critics, according to which Christianity was too much concerned with the unreal world. On the contrary, insists Henke, the activity of the clergy

in no way removes and transports the man out of the real into an alien and self-created, or merely imaginary world. It rather can ... instruct, advise, and equip man for all circumstances and relations in which he may be or into which he may get.[130]

But Henke quickly protects himself against misinterpretation:

To be sure Christian preachers ... do not have the task and the office of educating good citizens, but rather good men; therefore they are not so much servants of the state, as of humanity.[131]

Having thus carefully observed the typical Neohumanistic distinction (reaching back to Herder) between service to the man and service to the citizen, and having thereby subordinated the temporal activity of the clergy to a nontemporal *raison d'être*, Henke then goes on to accomplish the transformation of the clerical consensus which we have earlier seen to be typical of this period: in the face of the threat represented by radical secularism in France and elsewhere, he moves toward an argument in

---

[128] Henke, "Würde," p. 60.

[129] Henke, "Würde," p. 61.

[130] Henke, "Würde," p. 64. On continuing limited interest in peripheral utilitarian pursuits among clergy in Braunschweig-Wolfenbüttel, see the brief remarks in Johann Georg Justus Ballenstedt, *Beitrage zur Geschichte unsers Landes* (Schönigen, 1809), p. 157; these observations in no way alter the conclusion that an antiutilitarian consensus emerged and was maintained among the leading churchmen.

[131] Henke, "Würde," pp. 64-65.

favor of continued establishment of church and clergy on the grounds of the utility of the church to the state *despite* his careful insistence on the essentially nontemporal purpose of church and clergy. After a lengthy disquisition on the way in which by the church's activity the man becomes as well a better citizen,[132] Henke moves to the point:

> Thus the more human and the more cosmopolitan [weltbürgerlicher] a state apparatus is, the more certainly ... will its ... administrators [care for] men and human rights [Menschenrechte]—not indeed by ostentatious activity, but rather treasure and honor them, ... out of the effort to educate men, not merely for external honor and civil righteousness, but rather also for the proper disposition, for fixed and tender conscientiousness, for the best of the people, for general peace and welfare ...; all the more gladly and seriously will they seek to raise and increase the usefulness and the effectiveness of an institution [i.e., the ministry] which has so close a connection with their own purpose. ... Such an institution for the common good is the Christian preaching office, and such a one can it become even more.[133]

This leads to the conclusion:

> ... O you rulers and authorities, encourage and promote the blessings of this institution [i.e., the ministry], by means of all kinds of stimulation and help, especially by your own example, by public proofs of esteem and participation.[134]

b. Educational Reforms

There was no lack of official efforts in Braunschweig to provide stimulation and encouragement for the clerical estate. The measures taken are of the same general type as those in Hannover.

First we find a reform of theological studies reasserting the nontemporal chief purpose of minstry coupled with efforts to enhance the status of the clerical role by apeals to the canons of Neohumanism. There was in Braunschweig-Wolfenbüttel already existing a receptivity toward Neohumanism.[135] The *Abt* Jerusalem, the most respected proponent of Enlightenment in the territory, had toward the end of his life in 1788 restated his ideas on the education of the clergy. It will be recalled that at this time—in the midst of the Campe controversy, though the revision saw print only in 1793—Jerusalem had advocated a classical and traditionalist approach to education anticipatory of Neohumanism, stressing the humanistic curriculum and the importance of religious and moral instruction; Jerusalem had in particular emphasized the place of Greek and

---

[132] Henke, "Würde," p. 65.

[133] Henke, "Würde," pp. 66-67.

[134] Henke, "Würde," p. 67.

[135] Playing a part here was the tendency toward elitism in educational policy favored by such figures as Jerusalem and Velthusen—as well as reverence for the classics. Cf. Appendix J.

Latin in training a clergy that could serve as "the true general school of humanity" (*Menschheit*).[136] This receptivity to Neohumanism among the churchmen was further enhanced by the circumstance that the two chief theologians at Helmstedt in its last days, Henke and the Göttingen-trained Anton August Heinrich Lichtenstein (1753-1816; professor at Helmstedt from 1799) were both leading classicists.[137]

Were one to search for a counterpart to the plans for a reform of theological study at Göttingen and Loccum at the turn of the century, the logical place for Braunschweig-Wolfenbüttel would be among the proposals for reviving the dying university at Helmstedt. Here one might well find a counterpart to the Göttingen ventures in Neohumanistic reform of theological training. Yet printed accounts make no specific mention of such a theological reform plan.

It will be recalled that Heinrich Philipp Sextroh, who began his career as a propagandist for the industry school at Göttingen, accepted a call to the Helmstedt faculty in 1789, where he remained until taking a post in Hannover in 1798.[138] Sextroh underwent a theological evolution of a kind not uncommon at the time: in his case, as in so many others, the influence of Kantianism led to a revival of interest in positive theology and a gradual de-emphasis on utilitarianism, so that by the time of his career at Helmstedt he was holding Latin lectures on dogmatics. This revival of interest in aspects of the traditional is not surprising in view of Sextroh's close ties with the Neohumanist Heyne.[139] Thus we see Sextroh moving from the borderline of radical utilitatianism in 1785-86 to a position more in line with that of the mainstream of the Northwest German churchmen.

In the mid-1790's the sinking attendance at Helmstedt brought about a number of efforts by the duke, the estates, and the professors to revive the university. Reform plans were circulated. Sextroh sat on the commission charged with evaluating these schemes, and more than once delivered himself of his opinions.[140] One must then ask what kinds of plans for the reform of theological study might have been circulated during the last years before Helmstedt's dissolution by Jérôme Bonaparte in 1810.

This question can now be answered, for Sextroh's papers from this period have been located in the *Landeskirchenamt* in Hannover.[141] Among

---

[136] Johann Friedrich Wilhelm Jerusalem, *Nachgelassene Schriften*, 2. Theil (Braunschweig, 1793), pp. 162-63; cf. pp. 178-230, 262.

[137] Friedrich Koldewey, *Geschichte der klassischen Philologie auf der Universität Helmstedt* (Braunschweig, 1895), pp. 180-81, 168-69.

[138] Friedrich Rupstein, *Dr. Heinrich Philipp Sextro* (Hannover, 1839), pp. 34, 50.

[139] Rupstein, pp. 37-39, 31.

[140] Rupstein, pp. 43-45.

[141] See in the archive of the Landeskirchenamt, Hannover, "Ordnung des Nachlaßes des Oberkonsistorialrates und Abtes Dr. H. P. Sextro in Hannover, soweit dieser auf Erichsburg vorliegt."

them is a plan for the reorganization of Helmstedt University running to one hundred fifty-eight folio pages.[142]

The plan obviously originated in the mid-1790's in the course of Sextroh's deliberations on the future of Helmstedt University. As this plan has not been dealt with elsewhere, and as it is indicative of what would probably have been done had not political developments precluded reform, a few remarks concerning the plan are in order.

Sextroh's proposal contains general remarks on the situation, observations on the training to be expected of incoming students whatever their field,[143] and a revised plan for theological study at Helmstedt.[144] Sextroh's point of view is similar to that of Planck and Heyne at Göttingen. In discussing requirements for incoming students, pride of place is given to the ancient languages: the "Greek and Roman languages have ever been regarded as the best possible aid" to the "acquisition of a thorough and genuine learning" according to Sextroh. Moreover, their necessity for students of theology appears to Sextroh to be beyond question.[145]

Sextroh's view of the theological curriculum ca. 1795 shows that he has clearly distanced himself from the projects of Bahrdt and Campe. He differentiates between the education of those who are to become preachers and those destined to become school-teachers. The student of theology must in future study, among other subjects, logic and metaphysics, Hebrew grammar, philological exegesis of scripture, dogmatics, even Aramaic.[146] The mere recital of this proposed list of studies illustrates what point of view had triumphed with Sextroh: utilitarianism had been abandoned.

c. Reforms Directed at the Entire Clergy

Among measures carried out we find attempts to improve the functioning and the reputation of the parish clergy. An order of 1788 urges the clergy to be more faithful in carrying out their duties and requires reports in greater detail.[147] Indicative of the renewed importance given by the leading churchmen to a well-educated parish clergy is an order from the

---

[142] See in the archive of the Landeskirchenamt, Hannover, "Nachlaß des Oberkonsistorialrates und Abts Dr. H. Ph. Sextro. II. 16. (12): Entwurf eines Studienplans für Beförderung eines wohlgeordnete Fleißes auf der Julius Carls Universität in Helmstädt." (Herafter cited as Sextroh, "Entwurf,".)

[143] Sextroh, "Entwurf," fols. 30-74.

[144] Sextroh, "Entwurf," fols. 75-112.

[145] Sextroh, "Entwurf," fols. 32-33; quotation, fol. 32.

[146] Sextroh, "Entwurf," fols. 104, 84-85, 90, 95-96.

[147] Landeskirchliches Archiv Braunschweig, Signatur V 1229 = von Münchhausen for the duke to the consistory, November 21, 1788; precise motivation unclear.

consistory in Wolfenbüttel of November 7, 1801 requiring the formation of reading clubs and libraries for the parish clergy in each district.[148] This order provides for regular financing of reading clubs for clergy under the supervision of the consistory.[149]

At the same time we find efforts to revive and make more effective the traditional synods of the clergy.[150] Simultaneously we also find efforts similar to those in Electoral Hannover to use periodicals for the clergy so as to aid them in increasing their effectiveness and social status. These efforts are centered around Henke at Helmstedt, who issued a number of journals. Several of them are devoted to the academic study of religion, comparative religion, exegesis, and the chronicling of current developments in ecclesiastical affairs.[151]

More significant for the parish clergy was Henke's journal *Eusebia*, published at Helmstedt from 1796 or 1797 to 1800.[152] Although Henke's *Eusebia* was a direct outgrowth of the movement for liturgical reform,[153] the journal was in fact far more than a forum for the discussion of problems of worship. For, since the question of liturgical reform brought with it the issue of the legal status of the traditional liturgies, and thus questions of principle in church-state relations, discussion of such matters brought about reflection on the relation of the clergy to state and society. This reflection is announced in the preliminary advertisement for the journal:

> *Eusebia* is no magazine for preachers, and no Sunday paper for private edification. Its general theme is religion as an important affair in civil society. It contains therefore wishes, proposals, attempts for promoting in such fashion as can be done under the prevailing way of thought in our time the honor and dignity, the power and beneficence of that higher authority and support which the precepts of morality receive from religion. ...[154]

Beyond this, the journal would touch on the theme of the utility of religion in a time of international crisis, concentrating on the

---

[148] "Reglement, die ... Inspections-Lesegesellschaften und Bibliotheken betreffend" = Landeskirchliches Archiv Braunschweig, Signatur Consistorial Verordnungen 1803-1813.

[149] On such "Fachlesegesellschaften" see Marlies Prüsener, *Lesegesellschaften im 18. Jahrhundert* (Frankfurt a.M.,, 1972), col. 524; cf. Landeskirchliches Archiv Braunschweig, Signatur XXII C 4.

[150] See Appendix N.

[151] See for example *Magazin für Religionsphilosophie, Exegese und Kirchengeschichte*, ed. Henke (1794ff.); *Archiv für die neueste Kirchengeschichte*, ed. Henke (1795ff.); *Reliogionsannalen*, ed. Henke (1800ff.); and *Commentarii de rebus novis literariis*, ed. Henke (1780ff.).

[152] There seems to be some uncertainty about when the first volume of Henke's journal was printed. Cf. Johannes Beste, *Geschichte der Braunschweigischen Landeskirche* (Wolfenbüttel, 1889), p. 546.

[153] Johannes Beste, *Geschichte der Braunschweigischen Landeskirche*, pp. 543-51.

[154] Reprinted in the "Vorrede," *Eusebia* 1 (1797): fol. 2 recto.

"unavoidable" necessity of religion for the security of the commonwealth.[155] From this point of view, then, the journal would contain

> debates about religious education in schools; about social awakening to
> religion in churches; about training [Bildung] of the estate devoted to the
> perpetuation of religion; about principles and prejudices, aids and hin-
> drances that must be taken into account with all this; about catechisms,
> liturgy, preaching; about church order, consistories, and other institutions
> and arrangements which are in the Protestant Church either already present
> or still to be desired, which have the goal of preserving and increasing
> morality and religion.[156]

The discussion in *Eusebia* reflects exactly the subtly transformed consensus on clerical identity resulting from the uncertain situation of the
churchmen after the outbreak of the French Revolution and after the first
retreat of Enlightenment after the death of Friedrich II in Germany. The
debates in *Eusebia* focus on the relation of the church to the existing order,
and particularly on the prestige and effectiveness of the clergy in a time of
propaganda for disestablishment. For example, the opening article in the
first number of *Eusebia* is an anonymous plea for governmental backing
for reform of the clergy.[157] Yet the author operates on the premise that
the "chief business" of the clergyman is "to teach religion," affirming
the corollary that the clergy are by no means civic functionaries.[158] He
condemns the custom of requiring the clergy to read governmental orders
from the pulpit, arguing that this lowers the dignity of the clergy and
disturbs public worship. Such matters are "obviously opposed" to the
"goal of [the] ministry"; and, as they "in no way" belong to the
preaching office, the clergy are not obliged to tolerate such practices.[159]

The author's perspective is thus by no means one of radically
utilitarian subservience to the goals of the temporal state. All the more
striking, then, is the author's repeated insistence on the political and
social utility of religion and the established clergy as a means of giving
training in good morality, furthering the public welfare, and promoting
good order in a time of unrest.[160] The author's predilection for this kind
of argumentation in the face of his strongly-developed sense for the
priority of the nontemporal element in the clerical task can be rendered

---

[155] "Vorrede," *Eusebia* 1 (1797): fol. *2 recto.
[156] "Vorrede," *Eusebia* 1 (1797): fols *2 recto and verso.
[157] "Ueber die Nothwendigkeit der moralischen Verbesserung des Predigerstandes,"
Eusebia 1 (1797): 1-141. The article is anonymous; there is no reason to suppose that it was
written by Henke, or that he approved of every detail of the reforms therein proposed.
(Hereafter cited as "Nothwendigkeit,".)
[158] "Nothwendigkeit," p. 70; cf. p. 66: "Prediger sind keine Polizeybediente; ..."
[159] "Nothwendigkeit," pp. 65-67.
[160] "Nothwendigkeit," pp. 13-16 and elsewhere.

explicable only if it be seen as a stratagem for enlisting the financial and organizational support of temporal governments for reform programs designed to benefit the clerical estate. This kind of argument could be made plausibly in an age of anticlericalism and propaganda against the established clergy only by suggesting in the strongest possible terms that a respected, effective, and well-trained clergy was indispensable to the promotion of good civic order in a time of revolutionary unrest. Precisely that is what the author does: stress the civic utility of the clergy and outline a reform program which, if implemented, would have had the ultimate effect of *strengthening* the basis for the independency of the clergy as an estate supported at public expense.

The nature of the reforms suggested tells the whole story: in order to counteract the fact that, compared with what has been done to modernize and aid other estates, almost nothing has hitherto been done for the clergy,[161] the anonymous author makes a variety of suggestions designed, as he puts it, to insure that the "clerical estate" merits as much "esteem and attention" as do other estates.[162] Measures must be introduced with the help of governments to screen out worthless students of theology. Students and their selection of studies must be better supervised. A whole new kind of seminary for preachers must be devised and established at public expense.[163] Theological examinations must be reformed. A more professional and more efficient sytem of advancement for clergy in the field must be introduced. Supervision over clergy in the field must be tightened, all the while taking care that the pastor's "freedom in thought and action" not be restrained, and without disturbing the traditional arrangement whereby ecclesiastical consistories retain the right of supervison.[164] A carefully-thought-out system of rewards and encouragements, both financial and intangible, must be put into effect so that ability will be rewarded. Pay must be raised to keep pace with rising costs. Finally, discipline among clergy in the parish must be tightened if esteem for the estate is to be raised.[165]

This is a program to elevate the public respect for the clergy while at the same time insuring that the clergy themselves maintain higher standards—all to be accomplished at public expense through the aid of the temporal government. This tactic was no new one: we recall that precisely the same had been attempted by Mosheim in his plans to raise the prestige and morale of the clergy by a governmental reform of clerical

---

161 "Nothwendigkeit," p. 32.
162 "Nothwendigkeit," p. 68.
163 "Nothwendigkeit," p. 72.
164 "Nothwendigkeit," pp. 88-89, 100-103.
165 "Nothwendigkeit," pp. 112-13, 120, 135.

education and placement. The turn of the century saw, then, a revival of efforts such as Mosheim's to put the resources of the central government behind the self-interest of the clergy as a particularist body. The fact that this effort was supported by lengthy argumentation concerning the advantages which would accrue to the central government (e.g., contented subjects, political stability) should in no way prove surprising, nor should it mislead us into thinking that the proposers of such clerical reforms intended to turn the clergy into mere black-garbed temporal functionaries. Rather does such argumentation show how the churchmen exhibited a respect for political and financial reality.

Mosheim's concern for the status of the clergy and the independency of the institutional church received renewed means of diffusion with the publication in 1800 of a reworking of his textbook on church law, an edition prepared by the Helmstedt law professor Christian August Günther.[166] Günther tries to present the ideas of Mosheim in a better order,[167] yet he preserves the view of church-state relations in Mosheim's first edition. The collegial system is upheld by Günther against Thomasius' denial that the church can constitute a particular society within civil society.[168] The clerical members of consistories are held to represent the congregations, the secular members the prince. Princes are held to exercise the collegial rights of the church only insofar as they have the consent of the congregations;[169] furthermore, the congregational right to reclaim delegated rights (*jus retrahendi*) is again affirmed.[170]

Thus Günther retains Mosheim's stress on preserving the rights of the church within the framework of the existing system. In some respects Günther makes modifications to take account of changed conditions. For example, his explicit argument for the propriety of deriving from the consent of the congregations the collegial rights that may be exercised by the prince can be taken as an atttempt to defend the social contract aspect of the collegial system against possible reactionary charges that such views were too dangerous in view of the democratization and disestablishmentarianism let loose in revolutionary Europe. Striking is Günther's use of the late phase of natural law thought so as to argue for the inalienability of rights pertaining to freedom of conscience.[171] While both these kinds of argumentation represent an outgrowth of Mosheim's earlier views, Günther goes beyond Mosheim in his desire to secure the independency

---

[166] Johann Lorenz von Mosheim, *Allgemeines Kirchenrecht der Protestanten ... neu bearbeitet ... von D. Christian August Günther* (Leipzig, 1800). (Hereafter cited as Günther.)
[167] Günther, fol. *3 verso.
[168] Günther, pp. 548, 536-37.
[169] Günther, pp. 540-51.
[170] Günther, p. 541.
[171] Günther, pp. 551, 556; cf. nn. 84-88 to Chapter 4 above.

of religion and the institutional church without shaking the foundations of the system of established churches.

Deserving remark is the way in which Günther, like Mosheim, pleads for enhancing the basis for clerical autonomy. After criticizing the views of Thomasius for their pernicious effect on the esteem accorded the clergy,[172] Günther's version of Mosheim goes on to express two wishes. First,

> ... It would be desirable that the proper rights of the church be better preserved. For it cannot be denied that in some places these rights are much repressed: and the authority of the territorial government is little short of being extended also over consciences.[173]

The latter represents for Günther-Mosheim a departure from the normative practice of the Reformation wherever it may occur; in particular, the situation in some territories is criticized whereby congregations under governmental patronage are forced to install pastors they do not desire, with the pernicious result that such are necessarily regarded as "mere creatures of the princes."[174]

The second wish is that

> the esteem and the incomes of our preachers be increased. The preacher must necessarily have a certain esteem in the congregation so that the respect for religion itself can be preserved.[175]

Here, as in the area of congregational rights, is a domain in which the government can help the clergy. Similarly, the government can increase clerical incomes, thus raising the public esteem of the clergy—a step of "political importance"

> because in this way the esteem of religion is preserved, and this is the strongest remedy against despotism.[176]

For, holds Günther's reworking, by so raising the public esteem and the income of the clergy, one pays allegiance to the principle long ago invoked by Mosheim in citing "what the English say":

> Our bishops must be respected; our religion and church must resist the king, so that he does not acquire all the power; for this the clergy need esteem and incomes; they should sit in Parliament; they should do more charitable works than others; but then for this they must have greater income.[177]

---

[172] Günther, p. 567.
[173] Günther, p. 571.
[174] Günther, p. 571.
[175] Günther, p. 572.
[176] Günther, p. 575.
[177] Günther, p. 573.

Thus, despite the "transformation" of clerical identity in the light of increasing desire for co-operation with the state, the preservation of the particularist rights of the clerical estate remained a vital concern in Northwest Germany.

This concern is illustrated again by the fact that in the same year (1800) a pastor published a comprehensive survey of the church law pertaining to Braunschweig-Wolfenbüttel. This work[178] systematically catalogues the incomes, privileges, and immunities traditionally due the church and clerical estate in Braunschweig-Wolfenbüttel under the Old Régime: again we see how the clergy remained conscious of their privileged condition as an estate (despite their alliance with the *Bildungsbürgertum*), and how determined the clergy remained in their resolution to uphold by any means their traditional status. Only a military invasion representing a new form of social and political organization would have sufficient strength fundamentally to alter that historic privileged status.

---

[178] Johann Christoph Stübner, *Historische Beschreibung der Kirchenverfassung in den Herzogl. Braunschweig-Lüneburgischen Landen* (Goslar, 1800).

CONCLUSION

The preceding pages have demonstrated the necessity of revising our picture of Enlightenment churchmen. The clerical response to secularizing pressures proves to have been more complex than previously suspected. What formerly seemed to be unthinking capitulation now appears as a deliberate policy of camouflage undertaken for apologetic and conservative purposes. This assimilation or camouflage was, to be sure, fraught with dangers—but dangers of which the churchmen were aware and which they sought to avoid by refusing to let this-worldly duties become the chief element in the clerical *raison d'être*.

In the territories under consideration the churchmen do not seem even to have divided into pro- and anticentralist parties corresponding to the two chief factions in political thought;[1] rather they seem almost without exception to have espoused some variant on traditionalist particularism. Above we studied the use to which the tradition of both antisecularist reform and particularist reform planning for the clerical profession was put; as a result, we conclude that the churchmen pursued anticentralist or antisecularist goals in practice as well as in theory. Finally, the decay of traditional dogma hampered the protection of the interests of the church and clergy less than formerly supposed: though the assumption[2] has proven correct that a belief system or ideological structure is required for an effective defense of group self-interest, in truth, the ideological place formerly taken by supernaturalist Orthodoxy was filled with surprising effectiveness by a blend of the rhetorics of humanism, natural law, and Idealism.[3]

---

[1] Cf. p. 9 above.

[2] Cf. pp. 9-11 above.

[3] Left out of consideration here is the justified question (which was repeatedly posed in the nineteenth and twentieth centuries) whether so great a stress on the clergyman as agent of *Bildung* could allow for a truly distinctive *raison d'être* of the clergy. The problematical nature of *Bildung* as a substitute for theology gradually became apparent and is today witnessed to by the contempt in which ecclesiastical writers hold *Kulturprotestantismus*. The ideological significance of Neohumanistic and natural law (e.g., the man-citizen distinction) rhetoric as pointed out in the works by Vierhaus and Jeismann cited above emerges from a larger project of investigating the use of language in situations of social conflict during the transition from the Old Régime to "modern" society. See for example Reinhart Koselleck, "Einleitung," *Geschichtliche Grundbegriffe*, ed. Otto Brunner et al. (Stuttgart, 1972—), 1:xiii-xxvii; Koselleck, ed., *Historische Semantik und Begriffsgeschichte* (Stuttgart, 1979); Helmut Berding, "Begriffsgeschichte und Sozialgeschichte," *Historische Zeitschrift* 223 (1976): 98-110; J. B. Metz and Trutz Rendtorff, eds., *Die Theologie in der interdisziplinären Forschung* (Düsseldorf, 1971); Joachim Ritter, "Leitgedanken und Grundsätze des Historischen Wörterbuchs der Philosophie," *Archiv für Begriffsbeschichte* 11 (1967): 75-80; Hans-Georg Gadamer, *Die Begriffsgeschichte und die Sprache der Philosophie*

What then are we to make of this very real defense of professional and institutional independence among the Enlightenment churchmen during the last years of the Old Régime? Depending on one's perspective one may see here an instance of any of several larger tendencies. This clerical movement can appear as one reactionary chapter in the continuing effort (in progress since late medieval times) to impose upon the clerical estate the responsibilities of citizenship in the commonwealth.[4] It can represent the German clerical variant of that "closing of the ranks" held to have been a general phenomenon in the privileged bodies of the dying Old Régime.[5] Again, here one can discern habits of mind favoring the institutional church and clergy so strongly ingrained that these attitudes survived from seventeenth-century Orthodoxy down into the era of nineteenth-century ecclesiastical Restoration. Such a set of attitudes remained intact despite Enlightenment secularism; those sharing them attempted to legitimate the pursuit of ecclesiastical and clerical interests even as Enlightenment critics attacked such pursuit by invoking the "general welfare" as a good forever opposed to the well-being of the clergy as a particular body.

Much can be said for each of these views; but the last of them is of greatest interest to the church historian, who must ask how the church subject to time has managed to survive the changes and chances of this mortal life. Having realized that Enlightenment secularism and centralism did not fully extinguish clerical efforts to preserve the institutional church and the unique *raison d'être* of its servants, one can even see in the spread of clerical resistance to co-operation with utilitarianism an anticipation of Schleiermacher's repudiation of eudaemonism or utilitarianism. The last phase of ecclesiastical Enlightenment then appears as a step leading to the nineteenth-century effort to establish the worth of the clergy and church upon other than rational foundations.[6]

(Opladen, 1971); and James J. Sheehan, "Begriffsgeschichte: Theory and Practice," *Journal of Modern History* 50 (1978): 312-19.

[4] Some would term this process "secularization."—Cf. Bernd Moeller, "Kleriker als Bürger," *Festschrift für Hermann Heimpel* (Göttingen, 1972), 2:195-224; Moeller, *Pfarrer als Bürger* (Göttingen, 1971).

[5] Contributions towards such a view might be taken from an interpretation of parts of such works as Franklin L. Ford, *Robe and Sword* (reprint ed., New York, 1965); and R. R. Palmer, *The Age of the Democratic Revolution* (Princeton, N.J., 1959), 1:439-65. Cf. D. D. Bien, "La réaction aristocratique avant 1789." *Annales E.S.C.* 29 (1974): 23-48, 505-34.

[6] Cf. for example Paul Seifert, *Die Theologie des jungen Schleiermacher* (Gütersloh, 1960); Martin Daur, *Die eine Kirche und das zweifache Recht* (Munich, 1970); Klaus Lindemann, *Geistlicher Stand und religiöses Mittlertum* (Frankfurt a.M., 1971); Emanuel Hirsch, *Geschichte der neuern evangelischen Theologie* (Gütersloh, 1954), 5:145-231; Joachim Heubach, *Die Ordination zum Amt der Kirche* (Berlin, 1956); Ludwig Adolph Petri, *Die Bedürfnisse und Wünsche der protestantischen Kirche im Vaterlande* (Hannover, 1832); Hansjörg Bräumer, *August von Arndswaldt 1798-1855* (Göttingen, 1972).

With these points in mind, one should ask why historians have customarily portrayed the Protestant churchmen and theologians of the German Enlightenment as mere tools of temporal government. Clearly such a view suited the needs of profane and sacred historians remarkably well. To secular historians (whether German or Anglo-Saxon) these churchmen necessarily appeared as mere creatures of government, for that view was required by one of the premises of historiography after Troeltsch: that the German preference for the ideas of 1914 over those of 1789 could in large measure be accounted for by the political passivity and public servility unvaryingly characteristic of the Lutheran clergy from Luther down to modern times. There was thus no incentive to look more closely—especially since nationalistic historians saw particularism as having retarded progress toward liberalism.[7]

Ecclesiastical historians likewise lacked the incentive to look more closely.[8] Viewing Enlightenment churchmen as promoters of unchecked secularism allowed these clergymen and theologians to serve as arguments in favor of the anti-Enlightenment attitudes favored by nineteenth-century advocates of a restoration of the institutional church and its ministerial office.[9] Nineteenth-century theologians of ecclesiastical rebuilding had every reason to overlook signs that the Enlightenment churchmen had been unhappy with the policies of absolutism and utilitarianism, for taking note of such signs could only have weakened the nineteenth-century campaign against the rational theology associated with the Enlightenment. Any evidence that Rationalist theologians might have been able to defend (or even perceive) the interests of the church and the unique *raison d'être* of the clergy[10] could have

---

[7] See for example Ernst Troeltsch, *Die Bedeutung des Protestantismus für die Entstehung der modernen Welt*, 2nd ed. (Munich, 1924), pp. 55-56; Gerhard Ritter, "Die Ausprägung deutscher und westeuropäischer Geistesart im konfessionellen Zeitalter," *Historische Zeitschrift* 144 (1934): 240-52; and George H. Sabine, *A History of Political Thought*, 3rd ed. (London, 1963), pp. 354-85. Cf. however Hajo Holborn, "Machtpolitik und lutherische Sozialethik," *Archiv für Reformationsgeschichte* 57 (1966): 23-32. On the pejorative connotations of particularism see Theodor Schieder, "Partikularismus und nationales Bewußtsein im Denken des Vormärz," in Werner Conze, ed., *Staat und Gesellschaft im deutschen Vormärz 1815-1848*, 3rd ed. (Stuttgart, 1978), pp. 9-38.

[8] See the citation of Ecke and Tischhauser and other writers in the Introduction above.

[9] See in general Martin Werner, "Die Korruption der historischen Forschung durch die kirchlich-theologische Restauration," in his *Der protestantische Weg des Glaubens*, 2 vols. (Bern, 1955-62), 1:456-90;—Cf. Franz Overbeck, *Über die Christlichkeit unserer heutigen Theologie*, 2nd ed. (Leipzig, 1903; reprint ed., Darmstadt, 1963); Karl Löwith, *From Hegel to Nietzsche*, trans. David E. Green (London, 1964), pp. 377-88; E. Saurer, "Kirchengeschichte als historische Disziplin?" in F. Engel-Janosi et al., eds., *Denken über Geschichte* (Vienna, 1974), pp. 157-69.

[10] Yet with reference to France note the remark of Alexis de Tocqueville, *L'ancien régime et la révolution = Oeuvres complètes* (Paris, 1887), 4:165-66: "Les prêtres, qu'on a vus souvent depuis si servilement soumis dans les choses civiles au souverain temporel ... et ses plus

been taken as disconfirming the post-Enlightenment claim that such interests and professional purpose could be defended only by those who had
overcome the claims of human reason. Twentieth-century ecclesiastical
writers have on the whole persisted in upholding the same negative view
of the Enlightenment churchmen and theologians, ignoring evidence that
calls out for a more differentiated and nuanced assessment.

Those who write on this topic in our own day would do well to ask
themselves whether such facile caricatures of early efforts to come to
terms with the problems of modernity do not obscure the extent of
current difficulties: by making the condition of the church and theology
look so bad in eighteenth-century Germany, such writers imply that
twentieth-century solutions are without serious flaw. Yet today the chief
issues facing the church are the same as they were in the eighteenth century—the difficulty of defining the uniqueness, legitimacy, and necessity
of the Christian message; and the search for ways of insulating the clergy
from pressures threatening to transform them into mere tools enabling
society and state to realize purely this-worldly aims. To the historian the
pressures exerted on the church look much the same whether they derive
from the eighteenth-century *summus episcopus* or the twentieth-century articulators of the *vox populi*. Karl Barth had good reason to single out the
period introduced by Rousseau, Lessing, and Schleiermacher as one "all
too pressingly related to our own time."[11]

This study has shown that the eighteenth-century churchmen knew
what issues accompanied the emergence of a society and a state freed
from clerical tutelage so that it became possible to assert a largely secular
ideal of life. The eighteenth-century theologian took little comfort in this
situation; of him, Karl Barth wrote:

> The theologian of the period is ... a very earnest, fluent and clever man, but
> at the same time he is evidently gloomy, worried, not to say oppressed and
> desperate. This is so even when, as often happened, he pretended to be very
> cheerful and self-confident. One can see that everywhere he is on the
> retreat, that he is vexed and sorry that things are so and that he cannot
> change them. He obviously fears that he will not long remain free from at-
> tack in any of these positions that he has chosen. He sees that he will con-
> stantly have to deal with new opponents. He is not certain where his retreat
> will take him in the end. His is rather the mood of a general staff which feels
> that the initiative has been taken out of its hands and lies with the enemy,
> not to mention that of an Indian tribe slowly dying out in the territory that
> has been provisionally allotted to it.[12]

---

audacieux flatteurs ... formaient alors l'un des corps les plus indépendants de la nation.
... Je n'entreprends point de juger cette ancienne constitution de l'Église; je dis seulement
qu'elle ne préparait point l'âme des prêtres à la servilité politique."

[11] Karl Barth, *Protestant Theology in the Nineteenth Century* (Valley Forge, 1973), p. 18.
[12] Barth, p. 138.

Such was the frame of mind of the Enlightenment churchmen as they tried to defend the independent worth and outward status of their estate, seeking allies wherever they could be found. Some servants of the church made common cause with the absolutist state (though in the Welf territories they were not numerous); others, once, they had seen where they could expect to be led by the plans devised by former clergymen now in the pay of the power of this world, joined with the emergent *Bildungsbürgertum* in its attacks on centralism. Those tempted today to sit in ecclesiastical judgment on these churchmen should ask themselves how free they themselves are from the pressures of state and society, remembering Barth's insistence that the "problems, questions, and answers" of the era of Lessing and Schleiermacher "reach all too openly into our own."[13] Indeed, the theological and ecclesiastical struggles of the age inaugurated by Lessing and Schleiermacher seemed to Barth so compelling in their closeness to the issues of the twentieth century that in introducing his history of those struggles he cited the words of Horace: *mutato nomine de te fabula narratur.*[14]

---

[13] Barth, p. 18.
[14] Q. Horatius Flaccus, *Sermonum*, I.1., lines 69-70; cf. Barth, p. 19.

APPENDIX A

THE TEMPORAL FRAMEWORK:
ECONOMIC, POLITICAL, AND SOCIAL CONDITIONS IN ELECTORAL HANNOVER AND BRAUNSCHWEIG-WOLFENBÜTTEL

The core territories of Electoral Hannover under the Old Régime—Lüneburg, Calenberg and Grubenhagen, the Harz, Hoya, Diepholz, and Hohnstein, but without such later and peripheral acquisitions as Bremen-Verden—covered an area of approximately 6,973 square kilometers. Its total population at the turn of the eighteenth to the nineteenth centuries numbered between 900,000 and 1,000,000. Here, as elsewhere in Lower Saxony, the peasantry worked under a relatively mild condition of *Grundherrschaft* exercised by temporal or spiritual lords: eviction of the peasantry was difficult, and the peasant enjoyed considerable freedom in the routine process of cultivation.[1]

Hannover was not a wealthy land, and only by the greatest diligence could a decent standard of living be maintained. The sale of wool and the manufacture of linen were important; also significant were dairy farming, mining in the Harz area shared with Braunschweig-Wolfenbüttel, diversified agricultural enterprises, the production of timber and salt, and the breeding of horses for export.[2]

Electoral Hannover and its neighbor the dukedom of Braunschweig-Wolfenbüttel were ruled by branches of the Welf or Guelph dynasty, a German house dating back to Carolingian times. The history of this family and its possessions is extremely complex: the narrative involves numerous extinctions of lines and divisions and exchanges of territories within Northwest Germany. By the eighteenth century the situation was clear: the Elector of Hannover, simultaneously king of England, ruled the territories around the city of Hannover and those around Göttingen; the duke of Braunschweig-Wolfenbüttel ruled the territories north of the

---

[1] Georg Schnath, *Geschichte Hannovers im Zeitalter der neunten Kur* (Hildesheim, 1976), 2:359; Friedrich Thimme, *Die inneren Zustände des Kurfürstentums Hannovers* (Hannover and Leipzig, 1893), 1:1, for population figures including Bremen-Verden; Waldemar Fischer, "Die ländliche Verfassung Niedersachsens im 18. Jahrhundert," *Niedersachsen* 26 (1920-21): 182-83.
[2] "Denkschrift von Ernst Brandes an Edmund Burke ... (October 29, 1796)," Niedersächsisches Hauptstaatsarchiv Hannover, MS Q, Nr. 010, pp. 7-8, 12, 22-25.

Harz. The older possessions around Lüneburg and Celle had by this time passed to the Elector of Hannover.[3]

The departure in 1714 of the Hannoverian Elector Georg Ludwig for London had considerable results for the course of events in the Electorate. For with the departure of the Elector the local impetus for centralization on the absolutist model disappeared; however close the ties between the governments in London and Hannover might be, the management of the affairs in the Electorate inevitably fell ever more tightly into the hands of a local aristocracy composed of nobles and highly-educated functionaries of non-noble origin: the *Deutsche Kanzlei* in London was unable to carry out an independent policy, and the government in Hannover was staffed with indigenous nobles and with an exclusive group of nonnobles known as the "Sekretariokratie."[4]

The structure of the government surviving in Hannover from the days of Electoral residence falls into a common pattern: Privy Council for government and affairs of state; Chamber of Finance for revenues and domains; Chancery of Justice; Consistory for ecclesiastical and school affairs; and Chancery of War.[5] The existence of additional agencies for particular territories need not concern us so long as we keep in mind that the Electorate consisted of a patchwork of states, not all of them uniformly governed by the agencies in the city of Hannover which were enumerated above.

This patchwork character is of significance for understanding the role of the assemblies of estates and the limits of centralization in the Electorate. The constitutions of the various Hannoverian principalities varied considerably, agreeing only in ways that show how the power of the prince was restrained. As Brandes wrote to Burke:

> the Sovereign can not levy any taxes, without the consent of the States [sc. assemblies of estates], and that the legislative power, in the restricted sense of the word, excluding all what belongs to the police [sc. routine local administration], is to be exercised conjointly by the Prince and the States.[6]

Each of the territories within the Electorate had, for most of the period under discussion, its own assembly of estates; only in 1801 were the estates of Calenberg and Grubenhagen united.[7] In all the provinces ex-

---

[3] "Welfen," *Der Grosse Brockhaus*, 17th ed. (Wiesbaden, 1953-57), 12:419; and in the same work "Braunschweig," 2:309-11 and "Hannover," 5:255-57.

[4] Rudolf Vierhaus, "Die Landstände in Nordwestdeutschland im späteren 18. Jahrhundert," in *Ständische Vertretungen in Europa im 17. und 18. Jahrhundert*, ed. Dietrich Gerhard (Göttingen, 1969), p. 79.

[5] Schnath, 2:319-26; Brandes, "Denkschrift," pp. 15-22.

[6] Brandes, "Denkschrift," p. 32.

[7] Vierhaus, "Landstände," pp. 79-80.

cept Hoya, Bremen, and Lauenburg (where the clergy no longer attended) the assemblies of estates were composed of landholding representatives of the three social estates: clergy, nobility, and magistrates of the cities. That the nobility were dominant during the eighteenth century is axiomatic.[8]

The estates in the Electorate, like those elsewhere, had by this point fallen into the custom of leaving the management of their routine affairs in the hands of standing committees, in most cases reserving convocation of the plenary estates for times of crisis. This fact in no way diminished the considerable power of the estates in the Electorate after the Elector's departure. The estates had a real voice in the levying of taxes; in concession of loans on the domains; over financial support of the army, court, and the university of Göttingen; and over the administration of courts of law.[9]

The neighboring and historically related territory of Braunschweig-Wolfenbüttel extended over approximately 3,690 square kilometers.[10] Its total population in 1799 numbered 200,164.[11] Besides farming and the cultivation of fruit and hops, the production of cattle, horses, and wool was economically significant; the sale of dairy products was of importance.[12]

Throughout the eighteenth century Braunschweig-Wolfenbüttel differed significantly from Electoral Hannover in that the rulers remained resident, and hence were able consistently to pursue an absolutist policy of subjecting to central control the pre-existing elements in traditional society. In consequence the dukes in their economic policy followed the maxims of mercantilism or cameralism.[13] As the dukes of Braunschweig-Wolfenbüttel are hardly so familiar to the English reader as the Hanoverian monarchs, a few lines must go toward characterizing them. In our period an example had been set by Anton Ulrich (co-regent from 1685; sole ruler 1707-1714). He spent his life and his people's treasure in a vain competition with Louis XIV. Money was spent, not only on wars against the French, but as well on the operation of a costly late baroque court complete with churches, opera house, country palaces, and a new building for the famous ducal library in Wolfenbüttel once directed by

---

[8] Brandes, "Denkschrift," p. 32; Vierhaus, "Landstände," p. 80.

[9] Vierhaus, "Landstände," pp. 80-81.

[10] Hanno Schmitt, "Leistungen, Widersprüche und Grenzen pädagogischer Reformarbeit," (Diss. Erziehungswissenschaften, Marburg University, 1977), 1:13.

[11] Carl Venturini, *Das Herzogthum Braunschweig in seiner gegenwärtigen Beschaffenheit* (Helmstedt, 1826), p. 19.

[12] Schmitt, 1:14-15.

[13] Joseph König, "Landesgeschichte," in *Braunschweigische Landesgeschichte im Überblick*, ed. Richard Moderhack (Braunschweig, 1977), p. 82.

Leibniz.[14] Especially worthy of mention are two subsequent dukes, Karl I (1735-80) and his son Karl Wilhelm Ferdinand (1780-1806). In their policies they emulated those of the Prussian Friedrich II, and the connection was strengthened by both ties of marriage with the Hohenzollerns and shared devotion to cameralism and militarism.[15] The reign of Karl I was marked by numerous state-led industrial and agricultural ventures as well as by heavy expenses for court and army. In the wake of the Seven Years' War a severe financial crisis developed requiring the convocation of the assembly of estates. The result was measures by the estates to restore financial stability—not least important of which was the estates' extracting of a promise by the duke to limit governmental expenditures. This incident increased tension between the central government and particularist bodies within the territory.[16]

Karl Wilhelm Ferdinand, though just as devoted to enlightened absolutism as his father, pursued on the whole a more cautious course. By administrative reorganization before his accession he had already in 1773 succeeded in obtaining personal control over the financial affairs of the territory. He moved toward putting the finances in order. Remembered today as the patron of Lessing, Karl Wilhelm Ferdinand will be of interest to us on account of his abortive plans for more complete administrative reorganization involving new measures for the training of schoolteachers that were of immediate interest to the ecclesiastical establishment in the territory. Simultaneously a General Field Marshal in the Prussian forces, Karl Wilhelm Ferdinand suffered setbacks in the War of the First Coalition against France (1792-97); he was mortally wounded at Auerstedt in 1806.[17]

The government and institutions of Braunschweig-Wolfenbüttel, which were like those of the Electorate to be swept away by the Napoleonic invasion, presented a somewhat more centralized version of the pattern familiar to us from Hannover. Here we find the Privy Council, Consistory, Chamber of Finances, Chancery of Justice, and from 1769 a War Board. Peculiarities include the so-called *Finanzkollegium*, created in 1773 to give the heir closer control over finances; the *Klosterratstube*, with rights of inspection over cloisters; and the *Collegium Medicum*, created in 1747 to supervise physicians, surgeons, apothecaries, and midwives. One sign of trouble ahead was the existence of the so-called *Generalschulinspektoren*, a group responsible to the duke (created 1648; abolished 1756). They were given rights of inspection over the

---

[14] König, pp. 79-81.
[15] König, pp. 82-84.
[16] König, pp. 82-83.
[17] König, pp. 83-84.

schools; that right was in consequence for the time being withdrawn from the ecclesiastical consistory. Though these rights were restored to the latter in 1756, the issue was to come up again in 1786. As for local affairs, their administration remained in the hands of locals caught up in the web of traditional society, just as in Hannover. However, Braunschweig-Wolfenbüttel was more centralized in affairs of justice, for in 1688 the duke had created a new official (the *Justizamtmann*) responsible for such matters.[18]

The estates in Braunschweig-Wolfenbüttel were by no means an insignificant factor; however, at the start of our period it appeared that they were less powerful than in the Electorate. Co-operation between standing committees and the ducal government had become customary. From 1682 until the financial crisis of 1768 no general assembly of estates had been convoked; but once again convoked, the estates did insist on ducal reconfirmation of their old rights, including co-operation in exercise of the legislative power and recognition of their rights concerning approval and collection of taxes.[19]

Concerning the social and financial structure of the area, we are best advised to attempt generalizations simultaneously about both territories under consideration. This was an agrarian society, one in which the peasantry constituted the great majority of the population. Country nobles still played an important part, though the aristocracy was to a growing degree absent from its lands, resident rather in cities.[20] Despite the importance of court society and the rise of cities, one could equally well say of Braunschweig-Wolfenbüttel what Joachim Lampe has said of the Electorate:

> In the Hannover of the eighteenth century the norms of life are still altogether those of the medieval-corporative [ständisch] world of the old European nobility. The principle of order according to which the state is formed and inwardly arranged is the aristocratic-oligarchic: the nobility as the measure of all things. ...[21]

In this society more than 80 percent of the population was engaged in some form of agriculture—including a fair number of the parish clergy, though increasingly they preferred to lease out, wondering all the while whether the income therefrom derived would keep pace with inflation. The importance of agrarian society is underscored by the fact that even a

    [18] König, pp. 84-86 (ignoring here the Country of Blankenburg).
    [19] König, pp. 86-87.
    [20] Wilhelm Treue, *Niedersachsens Wirtschaft seit 1760* (Hannover, 1964), pp. 8, 10; on the contrast between courtly or urbanized nobility and landed nobility see Joachim Lampe, *Aristokratie, Hofadel und Staatspatriziat in Kurhannover* (Göttingen, 1963).
    [21] Lampe, 1:3.

city like Hannover had at the middle of the eighteenth century only about 10,000 inhabitants.[22]

By the turn of the eighteenth to the nineteenth century a relatively independent and well-off peasantry had established itself: by this point in Northwest Germany only about 8 percent of arable land was managed by domains, cloisters, and church; the nobles cultivated perhaps 7 percent; the peasantry under light feudal dues and with a favorable usufruct cultivated about 80 percent of the land.[23]

The nobility, enjoying tax exemption and trial in special courts, was increasingly familiar with the ways of court and city. Those who stayed on the land remained tenaciously faithful to the norms and religion of their forefathers; those who moved into cities or those who served at court were increasingly receptive to the hostility toward traditional religion characteristic of radical Enlightenment.[24] Despite tensions between the nobles and nonnobles that ought not to be minimized, and despite the notoriously closed character of the Northwest German nobility as a social group, that nobility tended on the whole to co-operate with enlightened nonnoble functionaries serving the government.[25]

Finally a word is necessary concerning those who were of neither peasant nor noble origin. Though a certain number of artisans and clergymen lived on the land,[26] the greatest number of artisans lived in urban areas. If we take as our example the city of Braunschweig in the middle of the eighteenth century, we can provide certain statistics to illustrate the situation:

A lower class consisting of day laborers, the indigent, soldiers, and single women constituted 54 percent of the inhabitants. Moving up on the social scale we find a lower middle class composed of artisans, small tradesmen, cantors, and schoolteachers; they made up 34 percent of the urban population. Next we detect an upper middle class composed of well-to-do artisans, brewers, leading tradesmen, apothecaries, academics, and bureaucrats (including a fair number of clergy); these made up 8 percent of the population. Finally an upper stratum was composed of court and administrative functionaries, wealthy merchants, and nobles; they numbered a bit over 4 percent. With the spread of

---

[22] Treue, p. 8.

[23] Treue, pp. 8-11.

[24] Lampe, 1:ix, 9, 45-, 85-91, 153-55, 200, 215.

[25] Schmitt, 1:32; cf. Wilhelm von Hassel, *Das Kurfürstentum Hannover vom Baseler Frieden bis zur preußischen Occupation* (Hannover, 1894), pp. 94-97; Thimme, 1:28-34. On tensions in general: Johanna Schultze, *Die Auseinandersetzung zwischen Adel und Bürgertum* (Berlin, 1925); Fritz Martiny, *Die Adelsfrage in Preußen vor 1806* (Stuttgart, 1938); Helmuth Kiesel and Paul Münch, *Gesellschaft und Literatur im 18. Jahrhundert* (Munich, 1977), pp. 42-67.

[26] Rural artisans: Schmitt, 1:19.

Enlightenment and egalitarian ideas, there was finally to be noted a movement toward social interaction between the upper level of the non-nobles and nobles; this occurred in clubs and lodges and ought not to be taken as a sign of true coalescence.[27]

---

[27] On all this see Schmitt, 1:30-50.

APPENDIX B

JOHANN FRIEDRICH JACOBI

The economic difficulties after the Seven Years' War led to all manner of cameralistic and physiocratic proposals for improvement. One of the leading churchmen to be affected by this movement was Johann Friedrich Jacobi (1712-91). Widely respected, highly thought of at Göttingen University, Jacobi became General Superintendent of Celle in 1758, a post that carried with it a seat in the consistory in Hannover.[1]

Jacobi's theological standpoint was consistently held throughout his life: reason and revelation agreed with each other. Thus he rejected strict Lutheran Orthodoxy and affirmed a mild supernaturalistic Pietism open to incipient Enlightenment but closed to more radical deism or naturalism.[2] In the 1780's he even felt called upon to defend miracles, supernatural revelation, and the historicity of the resurrection; at another time he upheld in vivid terms the doctrine of eternal bodily torments in hell.[3]

Nonetheless Jacobi (who precisely because of his moderation was respected among the churchmen) took the lead in propagating a marketable version of clerical utilitarianism among the clergy in Electoral Hannover. His motives and goals emerge from the section of his obituary dealing with his work as an educator, champion of liturgical reform, and advocate of modern agronomy:

---

[1] See "Lebensnachrichten von dem verstorbenen Consistorialrath, D. Johann Friedrich Jacobi," *Annalen der Braunschweig-Lüneburgischen Churlande* 6 (Hannover, 1792): 417-42 (hereafter: "Lebensnachrichten"); and Gottlieb Franz Münter, ed., *Ausfuhrliche Beschreibung aller Feyerlichkeiten ... D. Joh. Friedr. Jacobi* (Hannover, 1789); also cf. Philipp Meyer, ed., *Die Pastoren der Landeskirchen Hannovers und Schaumburg-Lippes seit der Reformation* (Göttingen, 1941), 1:161.

[2] "Lebensnachrichten," p. 421; K. Knoke, "Der lutherische Bekenntnisstand der Prediger an der Universitätskirche zu Göttingen," *ZGNK* 23 (1918): 95-112; Johannes Meyer, "Geschichte der Göttinger theologischen Fakultät," *ZGNK* 42 (1937): 7-107; E. Beyreuther, "Halle und die Herrnhuter in den Rezensionen der Göttingischen Zeitungen von gelehrten Sachen," *ZGNK* 73 (1975): 109-34; K. Knoke, "Lectiones asceticae an der Gottinger Universität," *ZGNK* 25 (1920): 73-80; Münter, pp. 131-34.

[3] Johann Friedrich Jacobi, "Nähere Entdeckung eines neuen Lehrgebäudes," in his *Sämtliche Schriften, Dritter Theil* (Hannover, 1784), pp. 125-92; Jacobi, *Leichter und uberzeugender Beweis von Gott* (Celle, 1787): Jacobi, "Kurze und zur Erbauung eingerichtete Einleitung in die Christliche Glaubens- und Sittenlehre," in his *Sämtliche Schriften, Ersten Theils erste Abtheilung* (Hannover, 1781), pp. 599-601; cf. the dedication to Jacobi in Johann Conrad Eggers, *Ueber das Aergerniß an Christo* (Hannover, 1788). I am indebted to the late Prof. Dr. Ludwig Deike for many suggestions concerning Jacobi.

By means of several kinds of efforts at making the spiritual estate more worthy of respect and more useful, he tried to make religion itself better loved.[4]

As Jacobi explains in detail, pressure from the educated laity caused him to make such reforms: not the pressure of the theologians, but the complaints of the laity moved him to eliminate the older dogmatic terminology and modernize the texts of sixteenth-century chorales. He recounts the instance of a layman who, in order to avoid being disturbed in his piety by antiquarian intrusions in conventional public worship, had his personal pew equipped with curtains so that he could isolate himself when the traditional hymns, preaching, and liturgy struck him as so antiquatedly absurd as to make devotion impossible.[5]

Jacobi's obituary enumerates the areas in which he tried by reform to revive the prestige of clergy and religion: he brought out a new hymnal and catechism and school textbooks; above all, he helped found the Agricultural Society at Celle in 1765.[6] The Celle group was one of the most important societies for promoting prosperity and the public good founded during the German Enlightenment. Instrumental in adapting English advances in agronomy to local needs and in evolving new approaches, it was equally effective in disseminating this information throughout Northwestern Germany because its network of influential members reached throughout the landed nobility and the literate public (e.g., Albrecht Thaer). These men put into deed the ideal of heightening domestic prosperity by encouraging citizen participation in reform under government sponsorship so as to realize what was then understood by "patriotism."[7]

The Celle Society, though a volunteer enterprise, was founded on the initiative of a group of Hannoverian ministers around Georg III in an effort to improve economic conditions in Electoral Hannover after the Seven Years' War.[8] Though the statutes adopted by the society in 1764 indicate that its "first law" was to be "subjection and loyalty to the king and loyalty toward the fatherland,"[9] under Jacobi's directorship from 1764 to 1791 the society did not limit itself to noncontroversial matters such as the development and diffusion of better agricultural techniques (though Jacobi's editing of a journal devoted to agriculture took up much

---

[4] "Lebensnachrichten," p. 426.

[5] Jacobi, *Beytrag zu der Pastoral-Theologie* (Hannover, 1766), fols.) (3 verso fff.

[6] Cf. "Lebensnachrichten," pp. 425-30.

[7] Hans-Joachim Braun, *Technologische Beziehungen zwischen Deutschland und England* (Düsseldorf, 1973), pp. 117-22; Hans Hubrig, *Die patriotischen Gesellschaften des 18. Jahrhunderts* (Weinheim/Bergstraße, 1957).

[8] *Festschrift zur Säcularfeier der königlichen Landwirthschafts-Gesellschaft zu Celle am 4. Juni 1864* (Hannover, 1864), pp. 3-4, 16-18 (hereafter cited as *FS 1864*).

[9] *FS 1864*, p. 24.

of his time). Equally important in Jacobi's eyes was the elimination of legal hindrances to modern agriculture such as enclosure of the common, burdening of the peasantry with tithes and feudal services, and irrational distribution of land that made modern cultivation impossible. Jacobi tried to persuade the assemblies of estates to abolish these hindrances.[10]

That the Celle Society encouraged clergymen within and outside the Electoral territories to become more interested in projects for augmenting temporal welfare is evident. This is suggested by the fact that nearly 12 percent of the 487 foreign and domestic members enrolled between 1764 and the Napoleonic invasion were Protestant clergymen.[11]

In another way Jacobi pointed the way by introducing a topic that later would be widely debated—namely, an attack on part of the traditional theological curriculum. In 1761 Jacobi published an argument that most theology students should no longer be required to study Greek, Hebrew, other ancient Oriental languages, or the historical details of dogmatic and polemical controversies. Students, he claimed, lacked the time to acquire adequate training as exegetes working in Greek and Hebrew. What they learnt they forgot in the parish; furthermore, too much study led to "hypochondria." Jacobi took this as ground for denying that most pastors should be trained as learned exegetes, holding instead that limited numbers should study at the most one of the ancient languages at a time.[12]

The essay, reprinted in 1764, 1774, and 1783, aroused controversy.[13] Undoubtedly Jacobi helped to prepare the way for the later attack on all study of ancient philology in the theological curriculum—an attack that within a few years was joined with an extreme utilitarian demand that the training of parish pastors should focus on this-worldly tasks to the exclusion of activities using traditional philological and metaphysico-theological skills. Jacobi himself, though, by no means went so far. His recommendations and his theoretical statement of the nature of ministry do *not* necessarily lead to the later demand that the clergy be trained primarily for this-worldly tasks.

---

[10] *FS 1864*, pp. 24-27, 72, 120-21.

[11] See the table in *FS 1864*, pp. 55-63.

[12] Jacobi, "Gedanken über die Gewöhnliche Erziehung junger Geistlicher," *Hannoversche Beyträge zum Nutzen und Vergnügen*, Jg. 1761, cols. 665-724; I have used the text reprinted in Jacobi, *Sämtliche Schriften, Zweyter Theil* (Hannover, 1783), pp. 300-42 (hypochondria, p. 311; languages, pp. 316, 334-35).

[13] Philipp Meyer, "Die theologischen Prüfungen in den lutherischen Kirchen Calenberg-Göttingens und Lüneburgs bis zum Jahre 1868," *JGNK* 53 (1955): 84; Jacobi, "Vorrede zu der zweyten Auflage," in his *Beytrag zu der Pastoral-Theologie*, 3rd ed. (Hannover, 1774), fols. **recto through ****2 verso; cf. Philipp Meyer, "Die Entwicklung der Fürsorge für die Fortbildung der Geistlichen in den Braunschweig-Lüneburgischen Kurlanden während der Aufklärungszeit," *ZGNK* 34/35 (1929): 324.

This is the case for several reasons. Jacobi in fact favors the mastering of the ancient languages by those able, and suggests that preference in professional advancement be given to those who do so; his objection is to philological study by students who have yet to acquire basic skills in ministry. He does not recommend reduced philological study to make room for this-worldly training—but rather to give more time for training in preaching, religious teaching, and pastoral counseling.[14] Jacobi's book-length treatment of pastoral duties leaves no doubt that for him the pastor's chief duty is by means of teaching revealed doctrine and by administration of the sacraments to prepare souls for heaven.[15] Jacobi's personal intention was not to make the pastor more secular; nor was it to capitulate before the demand that the clergy cease to constitute an economically independent estate functioning according to its own purposes in relative autonomy. Jacobi rather intended to make the clergy more effective in their traditional way of operating.

---

[14] Jacobi, "Gedanken," pp. 334-40; cf. Jacobi, *Sämtliche Schriften, Zweyter Theil*, pp. 343-86.

[15] Jacobi, "Gedanken," pp. 333, 340. Cf. Jacobi, *Beytrag zu der Pastoral-Theologie* (Hannover, 1766), pp. 1-2, 16, 20. His pastoral theology includes no section on "this-worldly" activities.

HELMSTEDT THEOLOGY AT THE TIME OF CAMPE

Helmstedt University had entered a decline with the departure of Mosheim. At the time of Campe's arrival in 1765 the university was disturbed because of radical theology, or rather on account of the declining enrollment resulting from such theology. In 1764 the young Helmstedt professor Wilhelm Abraham Teller (1734-1804) had published at Halle and Helmstedt his *Lehrbuch des christlichen Glaubens*, a work so thoroughgoing in its rejection of Christian dogma that it was publicly condemned by the author's own brother and officially confiscated in Electoral Saxony. For a time the reputation of the book caused other territorial governments to forbid the sons of their inhabitants to study at Helmstedt. As a result the city government of Helmstedt petitioned Duke Karl to remove Teller from his post. The duke was a liberal in such matters and successfully temporized until 1767, when there was arranged a call to Berlin for Teller in the capacity of *Oberkonsistorialrath* and *Propst*.[1]

The cause of Lutheran Orthodoxy was championed at Helmstedt by Teller's critic Benedict Carpzov (1720-1803). Born at Leipzig and professor at Helmstedt since 1748, Carpzov was descended from an eminent and prolific line of conservative Lutheran theologians and jurists in Saxony. The greatest luminary in the family had been the Orthodox Lutheran lawyer Benedikt Carpzov II (1595-1666); one of the founders of German criminal law, a pioneer in Protestant church law, noted in his day as a model of piety for having read the Bible from cover to cover fifty-three times and for having received the sacrament monthly throughout his life, celebrated throughout Europe for his defense of the reality of sorcery and the witches' Sabbat in the face of the "frivolous" objections raised by sceptics, renowned as a jurist for having refined and promoted the use of torture in judicial investigation and for having signed 20,000 death warrants, and still recalled today for his pronouncement that the practice of homosexuality results in divinely-ordained punishment in the form of "earthquakes, famine, pestilence, Saracens, floods, and very fat, voracious field mice."[2]

---

[1] Johannes Beste, *Geschichte der Braunschweigischen Landeskirche* (Wolfenbüttel, 1889), pp. 441-42; Paul Gabriel, *Die Theologie W. A. Tellers* (Gießen, 1914); Jakob Anton Leyser, *Joachim Heinrich Campe* (Braunschweig, 1896), 1:11-12.

[2] G. Müller and F. Tholuck, "Carpzov," *PRE*, 3rd ed. (Leipzig, 1897), 3:726-31; H. R. Trevor-Roper, *The European Witch-Craze of the Sixteenth and Seventeenth Centuries and Other Essays* (New York, 1969), p. 121-22, 159 (though the figure for the number of death war-

The Carpzov at Enlightenment Helmstedt, a great-grandson of the afore-mentioned jurist's brother, remained true to the conservative principles of his family and of Saxon Lutheranism. Alarmed by the decline in Helmstedt's enrollment, he published at Braunschweig in 1767 his *Liber doctrinalis theologiae purioris ut illa in academia Helmstadiensi docetur*. This work, composed in the traditional format, contains a solemn repudiation of the heretical doctrine espoused by Teller and at the same time constitutes the last new presentation of Lutheran Orthodoxy to be written before the onset of nineteenth-century attempts at repristination in the face of revolutionary ideology and political upheaval.[3]

The young Campe at first studied with Carpzov but soon rejected the conservative approach, turning instead to study with Teller. From Teller Campe received a thorough philological grounding and training in biblical exegesis on Enlightenment principles.[4] So great was Campe's attachment to Teller and his method that already as a student Campe was rumored to be heterodox. In consequence he was plunged into financial distress, for his scholarship from the assembly of estates was withdrawn. As the estates communicated to him at the time:

> we are not disposed to squander the charity of the Fatherland on a frivolous youth who allows himself to be seduced by notorious false teaching.[5]

In consequence Campe continued his studies under Semler at Halle.

---

rants signed may be exaggerated, it unquestionably represents the spirit, if not the letter, of Carpzov's jurisprudence); and Helmut Thielicke, *The Ethics of Sex*, trans. John W. Doberstein (New York, 1964), citing Carpzov's *Practica Rerum Criminalium*.

[3] Beste, p. 442; F. Lau, "Orthodoxie, altprotestantische," *RGG*, 3rd ed. (Tübingen, 1960), 4: col. 1724.

[4] Beste, pp. 11-12.

[5] Leyser, 1:12, n. 2.

APPENDIX D

SUPPORT FOR THE PLANS OF CAMPE AND LIKE-MINDED WRITERS

The plausibility attaching to the plans of Bahrdt and Campe, and the support they found in some circles, cannot be understood unless one first examines the background. Already in 1773 Karl Christoph Reiche, later a book-dealer in the Philanthropist center of Dessau, had called for the abolition of the paid clergy and their replacement by lay preachers.[1] In 1782 it was sarcastically argued in the *Deutsches Museum* that the paid clergy should be abolished since they hindered the spread of natural religion and social harmony.[2]

The proponents of the Berlin variety of Enlightenment were not to be left behind in urging radical reform of this area of society. For example, in 1783 Moses Mendelssohn argued for direct state compensation of the clergy, a proposal tending toward greater state control over pastors.[3] In the same year Johann Erich Biester urged in the *Berlinische Monatsschrift* that the state, not the clergy, should solemnize marriages, and then went on to contend that in future "politics and religion" should become identical so that "all laws would have the sanctity of religious precepts."[4]

Furthermore, one can find many plans akin to Bahrdt's—plans suggesting that the estate of preachers and the estate of schoolteachers ought to be telescoped, sometimes with the variant that existing schoolteachers should in time be replaced by theological interns; or again, plans pointing in a utilitarian direction. A few examples will illustrate the situation.

The Prussian *Oberkonsistorial-* and *Oberschulrat* Gotthelf Samuel Steinbart (1738-1809), whose name was invoked with approval by Bahrdt, argued in some detail in his *Vorschläge zu einer allgemeinen Schulverbesserung* (Züllichau, 1789) that in villages the traditionally distinct posts of schoolmaster and pastor should be combined, and that a whole new

---

[1] Karl Christoph Reiche, *Ueber das Schädliche des Predigerordens und desselben Abänderung* (Halle, 1773); cf. Johann Georg Meusel, *Lexikon der vom Jahr 1750 bis 1800 verstorbenen teutschen Schriftsteller* (Leipzig, 1811), 11:111-12.

[2] "Nachricht von U-Pang," *Deutsches Museum*, Jg. 1782, no. 2 (1782): 220-36. Cf. Friedrich Germanus Lüdke, *Gespräche über die Abschaffung des geistlichen Standes* (Berlin and Stettin, 1784).

[3] Moses Mendelssohn, *Jerusalem* (Philadelphia, Penn., 5612), p. 30.

[4] Johann Erich Biester, "Vorschlag, die Geistlichen nicht mehr bei Vollziehung der Ehen zu bemühen," in *Was ist Aufklärung? Beiträge aus der Berlinischen Monatsschrift*, ed. Norbert Hinske (Darmstadt, 1973), pp. 99, 102.

category of persons should be trained for this work—all the while making certain that they would not waste so much time on polemical theology as had their Orthodox predecessors.[5] Similar ideas were expressed at the turn of the eighteenth to the nineteenth century by a number of other persons, including Julius Eberhard von Massow (1750-1816), the head of the Prussian *Oberschulkollegium* and of the Lutheran *Kirchendepartement*; he favored requiring all preachers to serve for a time as teachers.[6] Ideas of a like nature were put forward in this general period as well by Johann Friedrich Zöllner (1753-1804), the Lutheran *Propst* of Berlin and a member of the Prussian *Oberkonsistorium* from 1788; Zöllner favored requiring theological candidates to work as teachers.[7] Again in 1799 the Prussian *Oberkonsistorial-* and *Oberschulrat* F. S. G. Sack (1738-1817) proposed an austerity program for rural areas, according to which the post of schoolteacher and preacher were to be combined; in case of need, he hinted, the resulting all-purpose official could even take over the work (and income) of the sexton.[8]

Other examples from the period could readily be cited from Protestant territories.[9] Equally significant of the climate, though, is the circumstance that similar policies were followed for the Roman Catholic Church in the Habsburg territories. As Ferdinand Maas, the authority on "Josephinism" points out, under Maria Theresia and Joseph II, the Habsburgs carried out a series of ecclesiastical reforms which, joined to a reorganization of theological studies, were calculated to enable the state the better to regulate its subjects. The goal was to make more efficient use of ecclesiastical institutions as a means of manipulating both the economic power and public spirit of the country in the service of the dynasty.[10] That the independence of the church was sacrificed to dynastic interests is beyond serious question.[11] The Habsburg policy in these matters during the Enlightenment was summed up by Joseph von Sonnenfels, who wrote that

---

[5] Enno Fooken, *Die geistliche Schulaufsicht* (Wiesbaden, 1967), p. 96; cf. Carl Friedrich Bahrdt, *Ueber das theologische Studium auf Universitäten* (Berlin, 1785), p. 36.

[6] Fooken, p. 97.

[7] Karl Ernst Jeismann, *Das preußische Gymnasium* (Stuttgart, 1974), p. 433; Fooken, p. 97.

[8] Fooken, p. 99.

[9] J. H. P. Seidenstücker, *Ueber Schulinspection* (Helmstedt, 1797); cf. Johann Jakob Wilhelm von Münnich, *Gedanken und Vorschläge* (Leipzig, 1791); cf. Johann Georg Meusel and Georg Christoph Hamberger, *Das gelehrte Teutschland* (Lemgo, 1797), 3:351-52.

[10] Ferdinand Mass, "Josephinismus," *Lexikon für Theologie und Kirche*, 2nd ed. (Freiburg i. Br., 1960), 5: cols. 1137-39; cf. Elisabeth Bradeler-Rottmann, *Die Reformen Kaiser Josephs II* (Göppingen, 1973).

[11] E. N. Williams, *The Ancien Régime in Europe* (Harmondsworth, Sussex, 1972), p. 466.

religion is the most effective instrument to further moral conditions. Secular legislation will be insufficient on several points if not supported by the bond of religion and its "punishments" ... Therefrom it follows that it is the concern of the sovereign as secular authority that his subjects should be well instructed in religious matters.[12]

In the Habsburg territories, as in the Protestant lands, "religious matters" in this period was defined in an ever-broader fashion to embrace an ever-growing list of temporal concerns.

It is hardly surprising, then, that in some circles (mostly lay) the plans of Campe found support among some educated North Germans. One such supporter was Jacob Mauvillon, an instructor in military tactics at Braunschweig's Collegium Carolinum and an advocate of physiocratic economic reform as a means of strengthening the state.[13] Mauvillon advised the state to set up a totally new group of teachers (distinct from the traditional clergy) which would be specifically established in order to propagate natural religion and political virtue.[14] At the same time he argued that the church needed no clergy and that the government's support of the clergy was completely unnecessary.[15] In supporting these recommendations Mauvillon argued from the familiar Enlightenment premise that true Christianity was a completely internal matter; he also utilized a set of arguments beginning with the familiar Enlightenment claim that priests remain eternally the same, and that, because of the self-interest and *esprit de corps* of their estate, they inevitably tend to revert to the propagation of superstition and the promotion of persecution despite occasional interludes of Enlightenment.[16] Criticizing the existing Protestant clergy for their lack of efforts to promote economic well-being (especially in the countryside), Mauvillon went on to suggest that the traditional Christian clergy were beyond any hope of reform.[17] The hopelessness of any real reform of the established clergy combined with the fact that many people were no longer moved to virtue by argumentation drawn from revealed Christianity led Mauvillon to urge instituting a new kind of teacher to spread the knowledge of the "true relation" of man and citizen so as to promote the welfare of the state.[18]

---

[12] The opinion of Sonnenfels as given by Edith Murr Link, *The Emancipation of the Austrian Peasant, 1740-1798* (New York, 1949), p. 143 and reproduced by Williams, p. 466.

[13] Leser, "Mauvillon," *Allgemeine Deutsche Biographie* (Leipzig, 1884), 20:715-16; Jacob Mauvillon, *Physiokratische Briefe* (Braunschweig, 1780); cf. Heinz Holldack, "Der Physiokratismus und die absolute Monarchie," *Historische Zeitschrift* 145 (1932): 517-49.

[14] Mauvillon, *Das einzige wahre System der christlichen Religion* (Berlin, 1787), pp. 1-3, 110-11, 304-5, 332-39, 357-58, 455-57, 527-28, 548-49, 552-69, 572-84.

[15] Mauvillon, *System*, pp. 527, 549-50.

[16] Mauvillon, *System*, pp. 1-3, 334.

[17] Mauvillon, *System*, p. 297, with special reference both to Campe and bee-keeping.

[18] Mauvillon, *System*, p. 334.

Voices were raised in support of Campe outside Braunschweig as well. An anonymous pamphlet published at Hamburg in 1787 defends Campe's entire concept of education for the pastoral ministry, arguing that the duty of the rural clergyman was

> to make civic happiness the chief characteristic of his efforts. If he is only to care for the well-being of the souls in his congregation: nonetheless, as has been seen, this is so inseparable from civic happiness that

the one cannot exist without the other.[19] Indeed, in this author's opinion, it was of no consequence if the minister should designate as the ultimate goal of pastoral care either temporal or eternal welfare, for:

> to me the citizen of earth and the citizen of heaven are the same person.[20]

Though this was perhaps the most eloquent defense of Campe published outside Braunschweig-Wolfenbüttel, there were others. A pastor named Christoph Johann Rudolph Christiani published a milder defense of Campe at Schleswig in 1789. Yet Christiani as a clergyman continued to place a high value on Biblical revelation and the symbolical books of the Lutheran Church—a view not customarily held by the proponents of a radically secular reform of the clergy, most of whom were themselves no longer active as churchmen.[21]

---

[19] *Kommentar über einige Stellen in Campe's Fragmenten und die Beurtheilung der Schrift Campe's, von Velthusen* (Hamburg, 1787), p. 73.

[20] *Kommentar*, p. 74. Cf. Ernst Christian Trapp, *Ueber die Gewalt protestantischer Regenten in Glaubenssachen* (Braunschweig, 1788), pp. 60-61.

[21] See Christoph Johann Rudolph Christiani, *Ueber die Bestimmung, Würde und Bildung christlicher Lehrer* (Schleswig, 1789), pp. 11-19, 102-20; also Martin Ehlers, *Winke für gute Fürsten* (Kiel and Hamburg, 1786-87), 2:389, 405, 497; Felix Kelle, *Martin Ehler's pädagogische Reformbestrebungen* (Phil, Diss., Leipzig University, 1907).

THE SOCIO-POLITICAL FUNCTION OF THE CONCEPT OF "BILDUNG"

The notion of *Bildung* or cultivation and the closely associated concept of *Kultur* were important weapons for the nonnobles seeking more influence on state and society—ideological tools that could be used to suggest a superiority both inherent and laboriously acquired, a superiority of a kind ultimately more valuable than that acquired by noble birth.

Concerning the transformation of the term *Bildung* in the later eighteenth century, so that the original Pietist shape of the term was altered, Fritz Ringer writes (with regard to the pedagogical model here envisioned):

> ... much more is involved than the transmitting of information and the development of analytical capabilities. Cultivation reflects and originates in religious and neohumanist conceptions of "inner growth" and integral self-development. The starting point is a unique individual. The materials which are "experienced" in the course of learning are "objective cultural values." ... [For example, in the neohumanist's relationship to his classical sources:] He does not only come to know them. Rather, the moral and aesthetic examples contained in the classical sources affect him deeply and totally. The whole personality is involved in the act of cognition. If the materials to be learned are properly selected, their contemplation can lead to wisdom and virtue. They can attract, elevate, and transform the learner. He can thus acquire an indelible quality, also called *Bildung*, which is a potential rival to the characteristics of the aristocrat.[1]

In the later eighteenth century, the German term *Kultur*, which according to Ringer was adapted by Samuel Pufendorf and by Herder from Cicero's *cultura animi*, "remained very closely related to the concept of Bildung":

> It had the meaning of "personal culture"; it referred to the cultivation of the mind and spirit. Then gradually, it was used in German learned circles in its more general sense to epitomize all of man's civilized achievements in society.[2]

Important steps toward the elaboration of this set of ideas were taken by Herder, who put forward the idea that the *Bildung* of the person to full humanity was accomplished by the quasi-mystic powers of language.

---

[1] Fritz Ringer, *The Decline of the German Mandarins* (Cambridge, Mass., 1969), p. 87; quoted by kind permission.

[2] Ringer, p. 87.

Under the influence of Winckelmann, Wieland, Goethe, and others, a new impetus was given to the notion that in language, philosophy and art the ancient Greeks had reached the summit of attainment.[3] In consequence Greek and Latin could plausibly be put forward as the best aids in attaining true cultivation of the personality.

This entire emphasis, which was to culminate in the movement of Neohumanism associated with German Idealism, provided an alternative to the educational approach of the Philanthropists linked as it was with cameralism and state centralism as the best means of furthering human well-being. For the Philanthropist writers had stressed "practical" instruction for the future estate which children were to occupy in the society directed by the state officials during the later phase of absolutism,[4] whereas writers favoring the approach of "Neohumanism" tended to stress the need to limit and direct the influence of the state upon the means of education so that the state did not become the end which all else served. In particular, it thus became possible to argue against the exaggeratedly utilitarian or practical emphasis (training in trades, manufactures, administration at an early stage of education) associated with Philanthropism. Since this anti-Philanthropistic view was closely connected with the ideas advanced by the Northwest German churchmen in their reaction against Campe, it is necessary to look at these ideas in more detail.

For the Philanthropists and their allies it was axiomatic that only by educational training for a place in the industries or bureaucracies of the absolutist state could one hope to provide for a fully human life. In view of the troubled economic and political situation at the close of the eighteenth century, and in view of the increasingly anti-Enlightenment position adopted by the Prussian government after 1786, many writers began to question this centralist premise. The issue was phrased variously—should the perfection of the man be sacrificed to the usefulness of the citizen? should the man be sacrificed to the citizen? Discussions of this kind, which began to appear in the mid-1780's,[5] first provided an affirmative answer to the question on the part of the Philanthropists; but after the failure of the reform program in Braunschweig-Wolfenbüttel, and after the onset of religious and political reaction in Prussia, even the Philanthropists began to waver, and many of them eventually joined their critics in the conclusion that the state could scarce-

---

    [3] Vierhaus, "Bildung," *Geschichtliche Grundbegriffe*, ed. Otto Brunner et al. (Stuttgart, 1972), 1:516-19.

    [4] Cf. Vierhaus, "Bildung," p. 513.

    [5] Vierhaus, "Bildung," pp. 513-15; Jeismann, *Das preußische Gymnasium* (Stuttgart, 1974), pp. 132-48, 263-65.

ly be relied on.[6] Though many continued to see an important role for the state in the supervision of education, that role was now seen as part of a duty to provide a humanizing education: the man must after all *not* be sacrificed to the citizen.

Holding such views was the educator Peter Villaume in Berlin (1746-1825).[7] In 1785 he declared that the individual had a right to expect an education to his greatest possible perfection, so that the government was as little justified in robbing him of such "ennobling" education as it would be justified in the name of utilitarianism in robbing him of one of his inherent human rights—though in the end Villaume had to admit that some kind of compromise was necessary.[8] Similarly, in opposition to those who wished to subordinate the goals of education to the needs spelled out by the state for society as whole, Pestalozzi in 1779-80 proclaimed that "education for professions and estates" was to be subordinated to "the general goal of educating men [Menschenbildung]."[9]

Perhaps the fullest statement of this position was given by the Neohumanist Wilhelm von Humboldt (1767-1835) in his *Ideen zu einem Versuch die Gränzen der Wirksamkeit des Staats zu bestimmen* of 1792.[10] As Vierhaus has pointed out, Humboldt identified "Menschen bilden," the formation of men, with the refusal to educate them for purposes external to themselves.[11] The practical effect of this was that Humboldt began to evaluate the state according to the extent to which it promoted an education that would allow the individual to unfold the character of his own personality.[12] But Humboldt must speak for himself:

> Certainly it is beneficial, if the relationships of man and citizen should coincide as much as possible; but it remains so only so long as the relationships of the citizen demand so little of properties peculiar to them, that the natural form of the man can be preserved without sacrificing anything —simultaneously the single goal toward which all the ideas that I dare to develop here tend. But it completely ceases to be healthy if the man is sacrificed to the citizen. For although the disadvantageous consequences of the disequilibrium [for the state] disappear: then the man loses as well precisely that which he had by means of his joining together in a state

---

[6] On the role of Wöllner and the failure in Braunschweig-Wolfenbüttel, see Jeismann, pp. 135-46.

[7] Jeismann, p. 432.

[8] Details in Jeismann, p. 136.

[9] Johann Heinrich Pestalozzi, *Die Abendstunde eines Einsiedlers* (1779-80) in his *Sämtliche Werke* (1927), 1:270, as cited in Vierhaus, "Bildung," p. 520, n. 60.

[10] See Vierhaus, "Bildung," p. 520, n. 65, citing Wilhelm von Humboldt, *Gesammelte Schriften*, ed. Preußische Akademie der Wissenschaften (Berlin, 1903), 1:143-45; 101-6; 158, 175.

[11] Vierhaus, "Bildung," p. 520.

[12] Vierhaus, "Bildung," p. 520.

striven to secure. On this account, in my opinion, the most liberal education of the man ... should in all respects precede education directed toward civic relationships. A man so educated should then enter the state and as it were ... test the constitution of the state. Only by means of such a struggle would I have any sure hope of a true improvement of the constitution by the nation, and only by such would I not fear the harmful influence of the civic structure [Einrichtung] upon the man.[13]

Thus for Humboldt the special value of training in the ancient languages, philosophy, and history lay in the distance of these studies from present concerns: only in this way could the man be so educated as to have any hope of clearly seeing through to a proper exercise of his faculties as citizen.

Humboldt and the other founders of Neohumanism, like a number of the disappointed Philanthropists,[14] viewed the state as anything but the determining principle in education. Similar positions were to be adopted in the early nineteenth century by Schleiermacher, who sharply criticized any attempt to employ learned schools or universities for immediately utilitarian or governmental purposes,[15] a position fully in accord with Schleiermacher's earlier declaration in 1799 that "the state pollutes religious fellowship" by exploiting it for the state's own interests[16] and that the capacity for religion in people has suffered from "the paternal eudaimonistic politics which has supplanted rude despotism" with the result that many had come to advocate "the extreme of utilitarianism."[17] Here Schleiermacher, like Herder before him, repudiates the use of cameralist theory and the absolutist variety of natural law to put religion at the service of the state.

In the Neohumanistic educational plans circulating at the close of the eighteenth century one finds, of course, the ideal that full cultivation should be provided to every person; but in point of fact the discussions on the function of education had to do first of all with the social role of the educated classes: were they to continue to carry out roles assigned by the absolutist state and its bureaucracy,[18] or were they to assert themselves through the bureaucracy? Thus, as Vierhaus observes, in these plans

---

[13] Humboldt in the year 1792 as cited according to his *Gesammelte Schriften*, 1:144 in Jeismann, pp. 142-43.

[14] Cf. Jeismann, pp. 144-46 for details on projects for private rather than public education by Philanthropists disappointed with what could be obtained by the aid of the absolutist state.

[15] Jeismann, pp. 263-69.

[16] Friedrich Schleiermacher, *On Religion: Speeches to its Cultured Despisers*, trans. John Oman (New York, 1958), p. 169.

[17] Schleiermacher, p. 131.

[18] Cf. Hans Rosenberg, *Bureaucracy, Aristocracy, and Autocracy* (Cambridge, Mass., 1958).

there is detectable above all "the social interest of the educated themselves," which took specific shape in the hope of reaching the political goal of a greater influence upon the ordering of society. It is not surprising that the anti-Philanthropist writers all ascribe to the "cultivated" a very important place in the state, either as Vierhaus notes, "as representatives of progress," or as "guarantors of order."[19] The later eighteenth century in Germany saw then, the coalescence of the trained nobility with the university-trained into a social group at once distinct from the pre-Enlightenment learned estate and from the people.[20] In this group it was axiomatic that, as one writer put it shortly after the turn of the century, every "cultivated state" must recognize that "the boundary of its power is there where the spiritual [das Geistige] begins."[21] Equally axiomatic in these circles at the close of the eighteenth century was the notion that, since reform of the existing states was necessary, and since the number of people capable of carrying out rational reform was limited, therefore the state must rely to an increasing degree upon those who possessed *Bildung* as the only hope for the reorganization of the state.[22] Clearly any set of ideas based on these axioms would prove of interest to the post-Orthodox churchmen desirous of reasserting the social importance of a clerical estate chiefly devoted, not to the application of cameralistic principles, but to the pursuit of a nontemporal purpose of giving meaning to human life.

The Neohumanistic educational philosophy, with its search for the well-rounded, balanced personality, with its rejection of mere training of the intellect coupled with early specialization for job training in the service of the absolutist state, and with its stress on the achievement of a general education and *Bildung* by the study of the classics of Greece and Rome, was early associated with the Göttingen philologists. Important here were Johann Matthias Gesner (1691-1761) and Wilhelm von Humboldt's teacher Christian Gottlob Heyne (1729-1812).[23] It was then only to be expected that the Neohumanistic program would profoundly affect the churchmen in the Welf territories.

---

[19] Vierhaus, "Bildung," p. 525.

[20] Vierhaus, "Bildung," p. 525.

[21] Henrik Steffens, *Die Idee der deutschen Universität* (Darmstadt, 1956), p. 324, cited in Vierhaus, "Bildung," p. 529.

[22] Vierhaus, "Bildung," pp. 532-33.

[23] A. Reble, "Neuhumanismus. II. Pädagogisch," *RGG*, 3rd ed., 4: cols. 1418-19; Walter Nissen, *Göttinger Gedenktafeln* (Göttingen, 1962), pp. 59-60, 79-80, 86; Götz von Selle, *Die Georg-August-Universität zu Göttingen* (Göttingen, 1937), pp. 152-56.

APPENDIX F

PARTICULARIST OPPOSITION TO CAMPE'S PLANS IN BRAUNSCHWEIG-WOLFENBÜTTEL

An analysis of the protests made by the standing committee of the estates at the outset of the negotiations between duke and estates on July 18, 1786, shows that the issue was not simply supervision of schools as such. The issue was broadened by the estates to encompass the legal conclusions that could potentially be drawn from the duke's creation of the *Schuldirectorium*: that is, the legal point at issue was whether the duke could at will alter the ecclesiastical constitution of the territory in view of the fact that the valid church orders for the territory clearly and repeatedly put supervision of schools into the hands of the consistory.[1] At the same time concern was voiced over the ducal government's claim to be able independently to create new components in government. The prime previous controversial case was the ducal establishment of a medical board in 1747—a matter brought up by the consistory and its noble allies in the assembly of estates of 1768-1770, and again alluded to at this point.[2] For if such creative powers were conceded to a duke so devoted to thorough-going Enlightenment, who could predict the eventual legal and social consequences for the clerical estate?

The clergy of the city of Braunschweig, sitting with certain lay officials to compose the *Geistliches Gericht*, had already expressed similar concerns in a complaint issued to the duke on June 30 of the same year.[3] This rambling document went on to protest against the Enlightenment and Philanthropist charge that the clergy and the city governments were ignorant of proper educational methods, terming it "a great injury" should the clergy and city officials of Braunschweig be subordinated to the new officials.[4] Then the natural law and collegialist principles of Daniel Nettelbladt[5] were invoked to defend the rights of the subject

---

[1] *Hofrath* Rham to Duke Karl Wilhelm Ferdinand, July 18, 1786, in F. Behrens, ed. *Das Fürstliche Schuldirektorium* (Braunschweig, 1888), p.3.

[2] Cf. Behrens, p. 8.

[3] See *Geistliches Gericht* to Karl Wilhelm Ferdinand, June 30, 1786, in Hanno Schmitt, "Leistungen, Widersprüche und Grenzen pädagogischer Reformarbeit" (Diss. Erziehungswissenschaften, Marburg University, 1977), 2:32-45, citing Niedersächsisches Staatsarchiv Wolfenbüttel Sig. 2 Alt 15886, fols. 2-16.

[4] Schmitt, 2:33-34.

[5] Nettelbladt flourished in the mid- and late-eighteenth century period; see Klaus Schlaich, *Kollegialtheorie* (Munich, 1969), p. 308.

against the claims of the monarch.[6] This group of clergy then challenged
the basic principle of Campe and the Philanthropists that the highest goal
of life was the promotion of human welfare, thereby implicitly calling into
question Campe's attempt at a governmentally-executed redefinition of
the ministry in a utilitarian direction:

> *Religion!*—the thought of it makes us tremble. Is it true that the whole life of
> man ought to be a preparation for eternity? Is it unquestionably certain that
> this preparation carries within itself an active inclination to encourage ...
> the good of civil society during earthly life? Is it finally an admitted conclu-
> sion that man must be educated for all for which he should be, and that a
> godpleasing, Christian purpose and conversation ought to be the chief trait
> of man if he is to become capable [fähig] of his great destiny? If so, then it is
> also clear enough, that mere Enlightenment is far from sufficient for this.[7]

After this the clergy went on to defend revealed religion against the principles of Bahrdt and the Philanthropists, expressing indignation at the attacks made on the clergy by unbelieving writers such as Hume.[8] Particular anxiety was aroused by the possible irreligious character of new
textbooks proposed since the consistory had hitherto had the right of cen-
sorship over textbooks.[9]

It is thus once again made clear that one of the chief issues in controversy was the purpose and status of the established clerical estate as a
component of society. Equally clear is that, from an early point,
defenders of the traditional understanding of the purpose of the clergy
were ready to invoke custom, divine right, the law of the territory, and
enlightened principles of natural law in order to oppose the plans of
Campe and Hardenberg; for they were seen as an implicit governmental
threat to the continued existence of the established clerical estate in its
conventional form.

The joining of this group of concerns with argumentation from such a
mixture of traditionalist and natural law principles emerges clearly as
well from a communication of the standing committee of the estates to the
duke of November 10, 1786.[10] The concern about textbooks is repeated,
but the chief issue is made out to be the principle that the supervision
over religion and schooling has been fixed by agreement and custom.[11]
Early on it is argued that no change in the religious constitution can be

---

[6] Schmitt, 2:34-35.
[7] Schmitt, 2:39-40.
[8] See for example Schmitt, 2:42.
[9] Schmitt, 2:43.
[10] *Schatz-Collegeium* to Karl Wilhelm Ferdinand, November 10, 1786, in Behrens, pp. 13-22.
[11] This is a recurrent theme; for the textbooks, see Behrens, p. 14.

made in view of the confirmation of the religious *status quo* made by the
duke at his installation.[12]

In another place it is argued that it is to the consistory that jurisdiction
over both the person and the affairs of clergy and schoolteachers belongs
(and especially jurisdiction over religious instruction). The basis adduced
is on the one hand the confirmation of privileges made by Duke Karl at
the assembly of estates in 1770; and on the other hand Duke Karl
Wilhelm Ferdinand's assurance to the estates at his accession in 1780 that
no changes in religious matters would be made. This assurance is then
interpreted to imply the promise that there would be no changes in the
existing arrangement regulating the boundary between the collegial
rights retained by the church as a society, and those collegial rights
delegated to the territorial lord—the conclusion being that supervision
over scholastic and religious matters and over the affairs and persons of
clergy and schoolteachers has been solemnly determined to lie within the
purview of the consistory. Thus positive and customary law as a basis for
argumentation supporting the inviolable nature of the legal status of the
clerical estate mingles with the basis in Enlightenment natural law of the
anticentralist variety signaled by the use of the terminology of collegialism.[13]

Finally, the document stresses the importance of the peculiar function
of the consistory and superintendents as supervisors of religious doctrine,
a function as it were vitiated by the ducal establishment of the *Schuldirectorium* composed of persons not bound by oath to the symbolical books of
the Lutheran Church. The implicit argument is that such a change constitutes an illegal alteration in the established and traditional religious
constitution of the territory.[14]

Even clearer evidence that a major concern motivating the clerical opposition was anxiety about the potential governmental threat to clerical
status under law comes from the transcript of a session of the clergy of the
city of Braunschweig (*Geistliches Ministerium*) held on January 28, 1787.[15]
As the issue was put early in the session, specific concerns included the
ridiculing of Christian doctrine by the Philanthropist reformer Trapp and
the general spread of unbelief among the new school officials in the territory.[16] One clergyman then complained that both in writings (i.e.,

---

[12] Behrens, p. 14.
[13] Behrens, pp. 19-20.
[14] Behrens, pp. 20-21.
[15] See Schmitt, 2:52-58: Transcript of sessions of the *Geistliches Ministerium* of
Braunschweig = Stadtarchiv Braunschweig CVIII, Nr. 58, Acta varia 1671-1825,
Verhandlungen des geistlichen Ministerii, fols. 337-66, January 28, 1787.
[16] Schmitt, 2:52.

those of Campe) and by word of mouth it was being declared that the official acts of the clergy were burdensome and that the preachers were
merely stupid priests.[17] It was then asked

> Whether it were permissible to tolerate [hinnehmen] the said injuries to us
> and our estate in both Campe's *Fragments* and as they circulate orally.[18]

In the course of discussion on this point, one Braunschweig city pastor
urged that an appeal be made to the duke to depose Campe and the other
reformers on the juridical ground that, according to the valid church
order in the territory, no one who publicly repudiated the Lutheran
religion should be allowed to remain in a position of supervision over the
schools.[19] Campe's opposition looked for ways to thwart his pedagogical
reform plans because they were alarmed by the potential legal implications of both his more general criticisms of the purpose and identity of the
Christian clerical estate and his proposals for utilitarian reform of the
rural clergy.

In this connection there spoke up the Superintendent Johann Wilhelm
Breithaupt (1738-1818), who is remembered as "Braunschweig's
Goeze" for his conservative opinions in a controversy about the actual
existence of the devil.[20] No less conservative in matters concerning traditional clerical status, Breithaupt favored issuing a joint printed declaration condemning "the places in Campe's *Fragments* that are injurious to
our estate."[21] His colleague August Christian Bartels (1749-1826),
recommended a less militant approach as being in the long run a more effective strategy.[22]

After the opinions of all had been heard, another pastor again suggested that it might be advisable after all to issue a joint condemnation of
the "foolishness" in Campe's *Fragments*. In answer to this, another pastor

> proposed that to this end one should make an extract from Spalding's *Nuz-*
> *barkeit des Predigtamts* [sic], and could insert it in the newspaper here. But
> there was no one who wanted to make such an extract. ...[23]

Thus the clergy decided instead to deal directly with the duke.[24]

---

[17] Schmitt, 2:52.
[18] Schmitt, 2:53.
[19] Schmitt, 2:53.
[20] Schmitt, 2:54, n. 5; and "Braunschweigs Göze," *Evangelisch-lutherische Monatsblätter
für Kirche, Schule und innere Mission im Lande Braunschweig*, 5, nos. 7-9 (1885): 23-31.
[21] Schmitt, 2:54.
[22] Schmitt, 2:54-55.
[23] Schmitt, 2:57.
[24] Schmitt, 2:58.

Particularly significant is the churchmen's reluctance to issue an abridgment of the Berlin churchman Johann Joachim Spalding's moderate utilitarian defense of the clergy: it would appear that utilitarian principles, once pushed to their logical extreme by writers such as Bahrdt and Campe, had now begun to make even a moderate utilitarian defense of the clerical estate suspect to the pastors.

APPENDIX G

VELTHUSEN'S CAMPAIGN AGAINST CAMPE

The militancy with which Velthusen intends to carry out his polemical campaign in defense of clerical autonomy is signalled by the fact that on the very title page of his pamphlet against Campe Velthusen reproduces a quotation to the effect that one would do well to avoid meddling in all manner of affairs not directly pertaining to the religious purpose of the clerical office. The source of the quotation is there identified as the rueful *Oberhofprediger* Johann Funck, an advisor to Duke Albrecht of Prussia who had eventually been decapitated in 1566 on juridical complaint of the Lutheran estates in the course of a long and bitter struggle to protect their traditional authority and doctrinal integrity against the encroachments of the duke.[1]

Velthusen's position throughout[2] is that the chief concern of the clergy—also the rural clergy—must be to follow the command of Jesus in Matthew 28:19f. to preach the gospel to every creature. This is the principal goal, purpose, and calling of the clergy.[3]

Indeed, insists Velthusen, on the basis of his own experience it appears likely that the peasantry would not look kindly upon attempts by the clergy to abandon the cure of eternal souls for technological and this-wordly tasks,[4] nor would parents look with favor upon the transformation of schools into industry schools if they suspected that their children were being exploited under the guise of job training.[5] Nevertheless, Velthusen is willing to allow that, as a purely peripheral and subordinate matter, distinct from the pastor's chief and religious responsibility for the cure of souls, the pastor may do much to make himself useful to the state.[6]

---

[1] See the title page to Johann Caspar Velthusen, *Ueber die nächste Bestimmung des Landprediger standes. Ein durch Herrn Campens Fragmente veranlaßter Beytrag zur Pastoraltheologie* (Helmstedt, 1787); Johannes Beste, *Geschichte der Braunschweigischen Landeskirche* (Wolfenbüttel, 1889), p. 489; and Wilhelm Bofinger, "Zur Rolle des Luthertums in der Geschichte des deutschen Ständeparlamentarismus," in *Geist und Geschichte der Reformation* (Berlin, 1966), pp. 404-5; also the echo of Velthusen in Ernst Brandes, *Ueber den Einfluß und die Wirkungen des Zeitgeistes*, 2. Abtheilung (Hannover, 1810), p. 180. Velthusen himself had hoped to write a conservative catechism revising that of Jacobi for use in schools; thus his bitterness toward Campe the educator. Cf. Niedersächsisches Staatsarchiv Wolfenbüttel, Sig. 2 Alt 15884, fol. 11 recto.

[2] Velthusen, *Bestimmung*, pp. 3, 36-38.
[3] Velthusen, *Bestimmung*, pp. 11, 26-28.
[4] Velthusen, *Bestimmung*, pp. 9-10.
[5] Velthusen, *Bestimmung*, pp. 22-23, n.
[6] Velthusen, *Bestimmung*, pp. 15, 8-9, 11-12.

However, this is best done by the pastor's working to enlighten further the schoolteacher who in non-Philanthropist fashion remains subordinate to him.[7] For furthering the education and the temporal well-being of the population is the task, either of the schoolteacher and his wife,[8] or else of the purely temporal functionary of the government, who is the "real civil father of the country population" ("den eigentlichen bürgerlichen Vater des Landvolkes").[9] Thus according to Velthusen, one must be careful to distinguish "what the country preacher on the side [nebenher], apart from his real calling" can do for the "civil welfare [die bürgerliche Wohlfahrt]" on the one hand, and on the other hand the pastor's true calling of preaching and the cure of souls.[10] Furthermore, cautions Velthusen, if the pastor does not leave the principal concern with such temporal matters to the "bürgerliche Landvolkslehrer," to the civil teacher of the peasantry,[11] then the pastor will be in danger of becoming an example of the *allotriepiskopos* of 1 Peter 4:15, an obscure term which Velthusen takes to mean a meddler who neglects his own proper duty.[12] Rather one should consider, suggests Velthusen, that the pastor's total efforts constitute a "quiet merit" (*stille Verdienst*), a term which in Velthusen's usage implies that the benefits conferred on society by the traditional variety of Christian ministry are worthy of respect in their own right.[13]

It is noteworthy that in all this Velthusen takes his stand upon the traditional command of scripture to preach the gospel; he does not follow the example of Herder in evoking the image of the clergyman as a means of *Bildung* serving the needs of the *Mensch* for divine *Erziehung*. In fact, in the course of the controversy with Campe, Velthusen does not employ the dichotomy *Mensch-Bürger*. His customary polarity is rather spiritual-civil (*geistlich-bürgerlich*), which he uses to signify those "civic matters" (*bürgerliche Angelegenheiten*) such as the advancement of industry and the discouraging of excessive litigation in which clergymen do well not to meddle; for, contends Velthusen, pastors ought rather principally to concern themselves with "the welfare of the souls" of their congregation (*das Seelenheil ihrer Zuhörer*).[14] Thus Velthusen relies far more upon a simple assertion of divine right that had for example even Mosheim, who in his

---

[7] Velthusen, *Bestimmung*, p. 15.
[8] Velthusen, *Bestimmung*, pp. 15-17.
[9] Velthusen, *Bestimmung*, p. 18.
[10] Velthusen, *Bestimmung*, p. 25.
[11] Velthusen, *Bestimmung*, p. 25.
[12] Velthusen, *Bestimmung*, pp. 41n.; Walter Bauer, *A Greek-English Lexicon of the New Testament*, ed. William F. Arndt and F. Wilbur Gingrich (Chicago, 1957), pp. 39-40.
[13] Velthusen, *Bestimmung*, p. 8.
[14] For all this see Velthusen, *Ueber Absichten und Tendenz* (Helmstedt, 1787), p. 14.

arguments with Thomasius had employed the natural law opposition between the rights of the church as a society and the claims of *die bürgerliche
Gesellschaft*.[15] However, as is evident, the use of natural law argumentation in this connection was by no means neglected in ecclesiastical circles
in Braunschweig-Wolfenbüttel at this time.

Velthusen goes on to underscore the dangers that would threaten if the
rural clergy were to be trained according to the plans of Campe. Deprived of the traditional training, they would, he argues, be unable to
discharge their prime responsibility as preachers. For, since they would
lack the traditional acquaintance with philosophy and metaphysical
theology as the basis for dogmatics, they would be unable correctly to
discern the interconnection of the teachings they are called to proclaim.[16]
Furthermore, deprived of the philological basis for a critical exegesis of
the text in the original languages, the clergy would according to Campe's
plans tend readily to become uncritical enthusiasts.[17] Finally, deprived of
a divine message, the clergy prepared according to Campe's proposals
would be stripped of their true dignity, for they would be forced to derive
their value, not from the gospel of Christ, but from human esteem, and
would be reduced to proclaimers of the merely human opinions of their
governmental superiors—a situation which Velthusen condemns as a
return to the "hierarchy" characteristic of pre-Reformation Europe.[18]

On this basis Velthusen can readily defend the traditional curriculum
in theology, arguing for the necessity of Latin, Greek, and Hebrew[19] as
the basis for proper exegesis.[20] Velthusen also defends the necessity of
doctrinal and dogmatic theology[21] and the advantage of a study of church
history designed to give apologetic demonstration of the good effects
Christianity has conferred on humanity.[22]

---

[15] Johann Lorenz von Mosheim, *Allgemeines Kirchenrecht der Protestanten*, ed. Christian
Ernst von Windheim (Helmstedt, 1760), p. 577.
[16] Velthusen, *Bestimmung*, p. 28.
[17] Velthusen, *Bestimmung*, pp. 39-40, n.
[18] Velthusen, *Bestimmung*, pp. 40-41.
[19] Velthusen, *Bestimmung*, pp. 19, 29.
[20] Velthusen, *Bestimmung*, pp. 29-33.
[21] Velthusen, *Bestimmung*, pp. 30-31.
[22] Velthusen, *Bestimmung*, p. 36.

APPENDIX H

PRESSURES TOWARD PARTICULARIST REACTION IN ELECTORAL HANNOVER

The university at Göttingen provided a source of cameralist ideas in the tradition of Justi.[1] The effect of this on practical-minded theologians such as Sextroh, and upon the circle of students around him, should not be underestimated. For, though Sextroh's ideas stopped well short of those of Bahrdt and Campe, they still represented a considerable concession to utilitarian pressures, and hence a potential cause for alarm by the traditionally-minded.

Then again the times were exceedingly unstable, and governmental centralism with resultant pressure upon the clerical estate was a theme demanding repeated attention in this period. The conservative reaction in Prussia after the death of Friedrich II stimulated a far-reaching discussion of church-state relations, the political role of the clergy, and the political function of theological Enlightenment.[2]

This instability of the times was not without its effect on local conditions. The spread of irreligion at Göttingen and the decay of orthodoxy among the students of theology, already noted, accelerated toward the close of the century. Tensions were not eased by the events in France. The situation was aggravated by the adoption of the Civil Constitution of the Clergy in July of 1790, with its transfer of clerical pay to the sphere of state activity, its reorganization of the clergy, and its institution of nonclerical election of the clergy. This set of measures brought with it a heightened awareness of the question of the interrelation of the civic and religious roles of the clergyman: for, as one speaker put it in France at the time, the issue was not the character received by the priest at ordination, but only the cleric considered as a citizen.[3] The discussion about the Civil Constitution and the resulting schism in the French clergy served to focus German attention on the issues of principle involved.[4]

---

[1] Götz von Seele, *Die Georg-August Universität zu Göttingen* (Göttingen, 1937), pp. 106-7; cf. F. Frensdorff, "Die Vertretung der ökonomischen Wissenschaften," in *Festschrift zur Feier des hundertfünfzigjährigen Bestehens der Königlichen Gesellschaft der Wissenschaften zu Göttingen* (Berlin, 1901), pp. 495-65.

[2] Cf. Paul Schwartz, *Der erste Kulturkampf in Preußen* (Berlin, 1925); Hans Beyer, "Niederdeutsche Kirchenkämpfe im ausgehenden 18. Jahrhundert," *JGNK* 53 (1955): 104-27; Werner Schneiders, *Die wahre Aufklärung* (Munich, 1974).

[3] See "Lutherische Priester-Reform in Frankreich," *Stats-Anzeigen*, ed. A. L. Schlözer, 15, no. 60 (1791): 386-93.

[4] See the one-sided account in Edward Dixon Junkin, *Religion versus Revolution* (Theol. Diss., Basel University, 1968; Austin, Texas, 1974).

Throughout the decade, as unrest mounted, so did local concern with the political consequences of religion. For example, in 1792, in the face of peasant unrest in one part of Electoral Hannover, a local official blamed a new Enlightenment catechism.[5] Again, in 1794, local authorities in another town complained that students on vacation from the teachers' seminary in Hannover were fomenting unrest with speeches critical of traditional religious truth in the local tavern, an activity which was severely punished.[6] Matters went so far that, by 1799, one conservative member of the consistory managed to have banned by royal decree the *Philosophisches Journal* co-edited by Fichte for fear of general harm resulting from its atheistic tendencies—an abandonment of the rather relaxed policy in these matters traditionally characteristic of the territory.[7] The climate, in short, was one in which journalists could sum up the content of patriotism in the formula: "Fear God, honor the King!"[8] Amid such circumstances, it is not surprising that local authorities could propose (as one did in 1794) that the clergy and the schoolteachers become active as propagandists for the conservative policies of the government.[9]

Despite the absence of the territorial lord, it should not be thought that Electoral Hannover was free from indigenous reform attempts of a kind that, if carried out, might have proved a threat to the status of the clergy. The very existence of projects of reform on Enlightenment lines served to underscore the possibility that sooner or later thorough-going reforms might be carried out. Thus, for example, Friedrich Esajas Pufendorf's draft law code of 1772 would have carried out secularizing reforms in marriage law and would have greatly lessened the traditional severity of punishment for the crime of offending against the dignity of the clergy.[10] Again, Hardenberg's proposed administrative reforms for Electoral Hannover of 1780, though they would have kept religious affairs within the purview of the consistory, would have centralized administration as a whole and would have seen to it that no official of ministerial rank would in future have served as president of the consistory, thereby illustrating the subordinate rank of this board.[11] The possibility of Enlightenment

---

[5] Cf. Carl Haase, "Obrigkeit und öffentliche Meinung in Kurhannover 1789-1803," *Niedersächsisches Jahrbuch für Landesgeschichte* 39 (1967): 192-294, esp. p. 215.

[6] Haase, "Obrigkeit," pp. 249-50.

[7] Johannes Meyer, *Kirchengeschichte Niedersachsens* (Göttingen, 1939), p. 184.

[8] Haase, "Obrigkeit," p. 245. Cf. 1 Pet. 2:17.

[9] Haase, "Obrigkeit," p. 255, citing Niedersächsisches Staatsarchiv Hannover, Sig. Z. F. Hann. 74, Celle, Fach 279, Nr. 9.

[10] Wilhelm Ebel, ed., *Friedrich Esajas Pufendorfs Entwurf eines hannoverschen Landrechts (vom Jahre 1772)* (Hildesheim, 1970), pp. xxii-xxv.

[11] Ernst von Meier, *Hannoversche Verfassungs- und Verwaltungsgeschichte, 1680-1866* (Leipzig, 1899), 2:612.

reform of clerical affairs was not *a priori* to be excluded even in Electoral Hannover: a proposal made elsewhere to abolish certain traditional incomes of the Protestant clergy seemed dangerous enough to evoke a lively rebuttal in Göttingen.[12] A number of minor incidents in the course of the 1790's show the mere geographical absence of the Elector did not mean friction between him and particularistic forces (including the clerical leadership) was necessarily excluded.[13] The issue of clerical obligations to the state and the whole problem of church-state relations was then of more than academic interest in Electoral Hannover.

If we turn to the way in which the political environment in Electoral Hannover helped to condition the response of the churchmen to the issue raised by Campe, we can see how the tradition of political particularism fostered at the same Göttingen which had taught the centralist cameralism of Justi and Beckmann could help to provide a theoretical matrix for reassertion of clerical self-interest. The famous political publicist August Ludwig Schlözer of Göttingen, a forerunner of the school of Hannoverian particularist political conservatism,[14] seems to have taken a sympathetic interest in the financial plight of the Lutheran clergy.[15]

However, this kind of "conservative" thinking was not purely reactionary; as Epstein himself points out, it included a certain emphasis on reform of existing institutions.[16] Particularly with regard to pedagogical theory and its connection with social policy is it the case that a position of mere reaction cannot be ascribed to the Hannoverian particularist thinkers—a point of immediate interest in assessing the churchmen's view of radical utilitarian reform plans. For to a considerable degree it was in late Enlightenment Electoral Hannover that the innovative steps of assembling a doctrine of *Bildung* and with it the program of Neohumanism had been taken as one means of promoting the influence of the educated class (especially the clergy) on the state.[17]

---

[12] "Ueber die Mecklenburgische Preisaufgabe," in *Stats-Anzeigen*, ed. A. L. Schlözer, 6 (1784): 99-112, cf. "Aermlicher Zustand vieler Geistlichen," *Stats-Anzeigen* 15 (1791): 393-430; and J. J. B. Trinius, *Ueber Accidenzien und Predigergebühren* (Halle, 1803).

[13] F. Schultzen and G. Müller, *Zum Jubiläum des Klosters Loccum* (Hannover, 1913), pp. 156-57, on tensions with George III; cf. Heiko Leerhoff, *Friedrich Ludwig von Berlepsch (1749-1818)* (Hildesheim, 1970), p. 94.

[14] Klaus Epstein, *The Genesis of German Conservatism* (Princeton, N.J., 1966), p. 548.

[15] See the article "Aermlicher Zustand" cited in n. 12 above, esp. p. 412, asserting that the figures for clerical income are "die waren Pudenda manches Landes, die man sorgfältig verdeckt zu halten bemüht ist."

[16] Epstein, pp. 585-88.

[17] Cf. Ringer (cited in n. 1 to appendix E); Vierhaus, "Bildung" (cited in n. 3 to Appendix E); Eckart Kehr, "Zur Genesis der preussischen Bürokratie und des Rechtsstaates," in *Moderne deutsche Sozialgeschichte*, ed. Hans-Ulrich Wehler (Cologne, 1966), pp. 37-54.

Altogether in accord with this variety of "conservative" thought is the criticism of the utilitarian or philanthropist approach to education as it was expressed by the Hannoverian administrator and "reform conservative" political writer August Wilhelm Rehberg.[18] Rehberg is well known today as a spokesman for the traditionalist and particularist point of view: a critic of the uniformity brought about by absolute political measures based on an inflexible application of "reasonable" principles, he also advocated gradualist reform.[19]

In an essay published in the *Berlinische Monatsschrift* in 1788, Rehberg took sharp issue with the claim of the Philanthropists that in preparation for all the professions immediate practical training ought to take the place of a grounding in the classics and humanities.[20] Rehberg countered with a variety of arguments supporting the need for all those planning to enter the professions to gain an acquaintance with the ancient languages and the humanities. He stressed the utility of the classics as a means for inculcating good morals,[21] the usefulness of the classics as a means for the *Bildung des Geistes*, and went on to suggest that these studies were of such foundational importance that of all the professions only the military could go without such an education.[22] Rehberg defended the importance of giving members of each profession the means for acquiring the theoretical knowledge necessary to meet the challenges posed by an ever-changing diversity of situations, instead of simply furnishing them with the knowledge of technique and specialized professional detail advocated by the Philanthropists.[23]

These pedagogical views were linked by Rehberg to a criticism of the political and philosophical position underlying the Philanthropist view. He criticized the attempts of educational planners to determine in advance the profession which students would later follow (an implicit criticism of Campe's plan to give future country pastors a specialized training from the start).[24] This attempt laid too much stress on the mere increase of national wealth without taking account of the problem of the quality of people in the territory.[25] Such plans verged on slavery:

---

[18] F. Frensdorff, "Rehberg," *Allgemeine Deutsche Biographie* 27 (Leipzig, 1888): 571; Epstein, pp. 547-94.

[19] Epstein, pp. 550-94.

[20] August Wilhelm Rehberg, "Sollten die alten Sprachen dem Allgemeinen Unterricht der Jugend in den höhern Ständen zum Grunde gelegt, oder den eigentlichen Gelehrten allein überlassen werden," *Berlinische Monatsschrift*, ed. F. Gedike and J. E. Biester, 11 (1788): 105-31, 253-75; for his presentation of the Philanthropist position, see pp. 114-15.

[21] Rehberg, p. 253.

[22] Rehberg, p. 274.

[23] Rehberg, pp. 116-18.

[24] Rehberg, pp. 119-20.

[25] Rehberg, pp. 120-21.

> Is the individual man the slave of his fellow-citizens, and are then all citizens
> slaves of the ruler? or are not rather all the institutions of civil society only
> existent in order to assure and to further everyone's greatest possible free
> enjoyment of all his capacities?[26]

In urging that as many students as feasible be given by means of
linguistic and textual study the means of developing their faculties,
Rehberg declared:

> Utility for a prescribed profession can therefore never be prescribed as a
> final purpose and on its own account for the man ... The calling is ... always
> only the means to one's own enjoyment, one's activity.

> The greatest possible extending of this, one's enjoyment and activity of the
> mind, is the great final purpose of every man who perceives in himself in-
> tellectual capacities.[27]

From this basis—one closely related to Neohumanism, as will have
become obvious—Rehberg as a layman can make certain specific
criticisms of the Philanthropistic plans for a radically utilitarian training
of the parish clergy (e.g., Bahrdt and Campe). Against them, Rehberg
argues that the clergy must continue to master the ancient languages so
as to carry on the Reformation's work of criticism on the sources for
religion; otherwise the general population will quickly fall into dependen-
cy on a dead formalism of the kind Protestant polemic usually associated
with the Middle Ages. In such a situation the population would be reduced to blind obedience in matters of religion.[28] Furthermore, in Rehberg's
view, the pastor, like any learned person exercising a profession in a
practical capacity, needs the theoretical and general knowledge conferred
by a study of the humanities, for he must be ready to face an infinite
variety of new problems requiring a knowledge of the general rules of
proceeding. Such knowledge and such a spirit of critical observation is,
according to Rehberg, only imparted by study of the humanities; that
this had not been seen by the Philanthropists resulted from their failure to
see that theology is not merely a formula which can be dispensed from
any necessity of being critically tested and examined anew.[29]

---

[26] Rehberg, p. 121.
[27] Rehberg, p. 122.
[28] Rehberg, pp. 111-12.
[29] Rehberg, pp. 117-18.

CONDITIONS IN THE "KINGDOM OF WESTPHALIA" AFTER THE FRENCH INVASION

Church courts after 1807 were deprived of their jurisdiction. Ecclesiastical administration of schools was curtailed. Civil marriage was introduced. The clergy were required to serve as civil functionaries collecting demographic statistics for a civil register. Traditional clerical exemption from taxation was abolished. Since the state now claimed complete sovereignty over the church, the boundaries of consistories were forcibly redrawn. Members of the consistory were required to serve without pay. The parish clergy were now named by Jérôme Bonaparte himself, who took careful note of their political sympathies. In the search for wartime revenue Helmstedt University was closed despite the frantic efforts of Henke.[1]

Göttingen escaped a like fate, though the worst was at first expected when Jérôme declared that "All your universities are good for nothing; I shall burn them all; I want only soldiers and ignoramuses."[2] Notwithstanding rumors of plans to reform Göttingen on the model of the French *écoles* by eliminating the theological faculty, a carefully executed propaganda campaign succeeded in saving Göttingen University, and with it the theological faculty.

In this period the churchmen nonetheless continued to press for ecclesiastical autonomy of a sort. This enduring stress on clerical independency (linked however with apologetic directed against propaganda for disestablishment) emerges especially plainly from the defense of the Göttingen theological faculty published by one theologian in 1809 in a succesful effort to save the theological faculty from dissolution by the French. The theologian begins by arguing that, since the well-being of the state requires a trained professional clergy, therefore a theological faculty is required for the good of the state. Yet at the same time he defends the necessity of revealed theology and goes on to argue that the

---

[1] Johannes Meyer, *Kirchengeschichte Niedersachsens* (Göttingen, 1939), pp. 180-82; Dieter Henkel, *Staat und Evangelische Kirche im Königreich Hannover 1815-1833* (Göttingen, 1938), pp. 10-11; Götz von Selle, *Die Georg-August-Universtät zu Göttingen* (Göttingen, 1937), p. 217; "Salfeld, Abt zu Loccum," in *Allgemeine hannoversche Biographie* (Hannover, 1916), 3:384; Helmut Berding, *Napoleonische Herrschafts- und Gesellschaftspolitik im Königreich Westfalen 1807-1813* (Göttingen, 1973).

[2] von Selle, p. 217.

theological faculty did not take its origins from the state in order to serve mere temporal purposes; furthermore, in his view it has never been

> the opinion of rulers, that the faculties should teach nothing except that which was prescribed to them; that they should serve only political goals, and should not rather cultivate scholarship itself and extend it.[3]

Stäudlin's target must be understood as being, not simply régimes supported by Napoléon, but as well any régime desirous of controlling the clergy.

---

[3] Carl Friedrich Stäudlin in the German version of his (now vanished) pamphlet *De Facultate theologica in Universitatibus litterariis*, as printed in the *Göttingische gelehrte Anzeigen*, Jg. 1809, pp. 974-75.

"ELITIST" TENDENCIES IN
SCHOOL ADMINISTRATION

At an early point (in the 1730's) the government in Hannover had vainly hoped to attract the well-to-do to theological study at the new university at Göttingen. Less had also complained in 1790 that the abilities and social status of theological students were very low.[1] Similarly in 1768 the famous Göttingen orientalist Johann David Michaelis (1717-91) had thus defended himself against the charge that by wishing to require of theological students world history in addition to Latin, Greek and Hebrew he would incur the risk that too many would be scared away:

> If one fears that this would diminish the number of those who study theology, and especially might scare off the poor: now, indeed, I do not think that it will happen, but I could however conceive of no consequence more to be desired. For so long as those who have ended their theological studies at the university must wait several years without a job, so long is it clear that there are too many of those who study theology. ... From the reduction of [the number of] the poor who study theology there would come the advantage, that all the more from a somewhat better estate and of some means would devote themselves to it: and indeed they are certainly, all things otherwise being equal, the students most to be desired, since they have the means of learning something properly.[2]

A similar exclusivist spirit breathes throughout Heyne's plans for reform of a Latin school in Ilfeld from the year 1770, plans in response to which the *Abt* Jerusalem wrote as follows to the government in Hannover:

> If also some were by this [increase in academic rigor] altogether frightened away, this would be a desirable side effect for scholarship and for the territory ...[3]

Like sentiments concerning the excessive number of theological students were expressed in 1794 by Velthusen, who by this time was in Bremen; he recommended giving financial support only to the most able, since in his area there already existed an oversupply of unemployed can-

---

[1] Cf. Reinhardt Wittram, *Die Universität und ihre Fakultäten* (Göttingen, 1962), pp. 7, 32; and p. 143 above.

[2] Johann David Michaelis, *Raisonnement über die protestantische Universitäten in Deutschland* (Frankfurt and Leipzig, 1768), 1: 207-8.

[3] Holstein, "Zwei Schriftstücke," *Mitteilungen der Gesellschaft für deutsche Erziehungs- und Schulgeschichte*, ed. Karl Kehrbach, 4 (Berlin, 1894): 84.

didates equal in number to one-fourth of the total number of parish positions.[4] (Another knowledgeable source reports that in Electoral Hannover at the turn of the century there were candidates still awaiting a parish who had attained the thirty-sixth year.)[5]

Such exclusivistic thinking led as well to a great mass of propagandistic writings condemning the "mania for study" (*Studiersucht*) during the late eighteenth century,[6] and in some areas, such as Württemberg, eventuated in governmental regulations attempting to insure that the sons of artisans, schoolteachers, and peasants be admitted to theological study only if they could demonstrate the most extraordinary gifts and preparation[7]—though earlier orders of this kind in Württemberg had exempted the sons of poor clergymen from the efforts to eliminate the children of the poor from the ranks of theological students.[8] As Herrlitz has shown, the theoretical basis for this policy lay in the persistence of mercantilistic concepts according to which society was divided into the producing (i.e., uneducated, working) class and the consuming class (the learned and artists).[9]

---

[4] Johann Caspar Velthusen, "Einige Bemerkungen über die zu grosse Anzahl der Studirenden," in *Neues Magazin für Schullehrer*, ed. G. A. Ruperti and H. Schlichthorst, 2 (Göttingen and Bremen, 1793-94): 347-52.

[5] Ernst Brandes, "Ueber den gegenwärtigen Zustand der Universität Göttingen," *Neues Hannöversches Magazin*, Jg. 1802, cols. 161-240, 241-332, 333-448, esp. col. 235; cf. col. 231; "Die Verminderung der Zahl der Studirenden überhaupt ist kein Uebel, sondern ein Glück, ..." Background: Carl Haase, *Ernst Brandes 1758-1810*, 2 vols. (Hildesheim, 1973-74).

[6] Hans-Georg Herrlitz, *Studium als Standesprivileg* (Frankfurt a.M., 1973), pp. 66-67.

[7] Herrlitz, p. 59, citing from Württemberg the "General-Reskript. betr. die Abhaltung vom Studium der ev. Theologie" of March 30, 1780.

[8] Herrlitz, p. 57, with reference to an order in Württemberg from the year 1749.

[9] Cf. Herrlitz, e.g., pp. 66-69 and elsewhere. Herrlitz's work must be used with caution.

APPENDIX K

TRADITIONALIST SUCCESS AT GÖTTINGEN

The success of leading churchmen, consistorial officials, and theologians in winning young converts for the synthesis of Neohumanism with the defense of academic and nontemporal elements in the theological task can be judged by glancing at publications at Göttingen by students of theology and younger pastors on the eve of the Napoleonic invasion. Shortly after the reform measures at the turn of the century, a number of theological students at Göttingen founded with the encouragement of Henke at Helmstedt a theological society with a journal of its own.[1] During the unsettled years 1804-05 this circle of students tried to advance the prestige of academic theology by their activities; their society constituted an imitation of Enlightenment learned societies such as the Lateinische Gesellschaft in Jena, the famous Göttingen Königliche Gesellschaft der Wissenschaften with its even more famous *Anzeigen von gelehrten Sachen*, or the Physicalische Gesellschaft of Gmelin in Göttingen.[2]

The journal of the young society was edited by Dr. Johannes Horn and published at Hannover.[3] Entitled *Göttingisches Museum der Theologie und Literatur*, it was published not at Göttingen, but at Hannover, that is, at the seat of the consistory, and in its first number bore a dedication to the Hannoverian *Canzlei-Secretair* and Göttingen University administrator Ernst Brandes.[4] This fact many serve to alter the judgment of Brandes' biographer that there is no evidence of friendships between Brandes and theologians,[5] and may even suggest that Brandes helped to find financing for the publication of the journal.

The content of the journal itself constitutes a reaffirmation of the understanding of Christanity then current among the leading churchmen

---

[1] Repetent Dr. Johannes [von] Horn, "Ankündigung," *Göttingisches Museum der Theologie und Literatur*, ed. Johannes Horn (Hannover, 1804), 1, no. 1:1-30, esp. pp. 27-28.

[2] On the *Anzeigen* see Gustav Roethe, "Göttingische Zeitungen von gelehrten Sachen," in *Festschrift zur Feier des hundertfünfzigjährigen Bestehens der Königlichen Gesellschaft der Wissenschaften zu Göttingen* (Berlin, 1901), pp. 567-675. See also Johannes Horn, "Verfassung der Göttingischen Societät für theologischen Wissenschaften," *Neues Hannöversches Magazin* 14 (1804): cols. 129-36; Horn, "Ankündigung"; Horn, "Fernere Nachrichten," *Neues Hannöversches Magazin* 14 (1804): cols. 1087-88.

[3] On Horn see Heinrich Wilhelm Rotermund, *Das gelehrte Hannover* (Bremen, 1823), 2:411.

[4] See *Göttingisches Museum*, ed. Horn, 1, no. 1 (Hannover, 1804): dedication page.

[5] Carl Haase, *Ernst Brandes 1758-1810* (Hildesheim, 1974), 2:429.

and theologians of Northwest Germany: the conceptual systems of
Lutheran dogmatics, biblical theology, and philosophy of religion are affirmed as distinct and each of its peculiar value.[6] Despite the inclination
toward Rationalist theology,[7] still the journal's editor remained true to
the moderate tradition of the Göttingen theologians. Christianity, argued
Horn, had been from its inception supernaturalistic, not originally a
form of mere naturalism lacking belief in the supernatural.[8] As these examples indicate, the circle of young theologians around Horn provides
ample proof that the "danger" had been averted that the Göttingen
theological students might fall prey either to the radical utilitarianism of
Bahrdt and Campe or to the "atheism" of Fichte, the latter threat having
been something very much on the minds of Hannoverian officials.[9] Further evidence of the concern of this circle with upholding clerical independence comes from its defense of the traditional occasional incomes
of the parish clergy, which had long been under attack by Enlightenment
writers.[10]

---

[6] Horn, "Ankündigung," esp. pp. 9-10.

[7] Cf. Georg Konradt Horst, "Bemerkungen über die Geschichte der sogenannten
Himmelfahrt Jesu," *Museum*, ed. Horn, 1, no. 1 (1805): 1-70.

[8] Horn, "Ankündigung," p. 19.

[9] Cf. Johannes Meyer, *Kirchengeschichte Niedersachsens* (Göttingen, 1939), p. 184.

[10] D. Busse, "Ehrenrettung der Prediger-Accidenzien," *Museum*, ed. Horn, 1, no. 2
(1805): 143-60. Cf. "Ueber die Territorial-Abgaben in Helvetien," *Helvetische
Monathschrift* 1 (Bern, 1800): 70-112.

APPENDIX L

THE KANTIAN BACKGROUND TO THE HANNOVERIAN "PASTORAL—INSTRUCTION"

In the first paragraph to the second section of the Hannoverian *Pastoral-Instruction* it is stated that "the Christian preacher is ... required ... to be moral (not merely technical) religion-teacher of the youth in the congregation entrusted to him."[1] This offers a formal parallel to the opening of section one:

> The Christian preacher should ... become a practical religion-teacher, consequently as such the promoter of true religiosity and of a morality in the congregation entrusted to him. ...[2]

In both cases the terminology would seem to reflect clear knowledge and adaptation of the Kantian distinction between "moral-practical" and "technical-practical" action: the former, which is here advocated, refers to actions directed to unconditional or infinite moral goals, whereas the (rejected) pair "technical-practical" refers in Kant to actions connected with the means to the goals of an action (e.g., "technisch-praktische Vernunft").[3] This terminology, which is not unrelated to that of the *Critique of Judgment*,[4] is significant because it shows how the entire concept of the pastoral role has begun to move into the realm of service to the Kantian ideals of the providential God, the moral law, and the hope for improvement of the world.

---

[1] Christian Hermann Ebhardt, ed., *Gesetze, Verordnungen und Ausschreiben* (Hannover, 1845), 1:826.

[2] Ebhardt, 1:820.

[3] Rudolf Eisler, ed., *Kant-Lexicon* (Berlin, 1930; reprint ed., Hildesheim, 1961), p. 528.

[4] Cf. Immanuel Kant, *Critique of Judgment*, trans. J. H. Bernard (New York, 1972), section 88, p. 306 and elsewhere.

APPENDIX M

THE JURISTIC COUNTERATTACK IN ELECTORAL HANNOVER

Especially indicative of the increasingly defensive and assertive mood of the churchmen were the steps taken to defend the incomes and rights of the Protestant clergy. These incomes and rights, it will be recalled, were complex and bewildering in their diversity, but nonetheless subject to attack by spokesmen for Enlightenment absolutism. As examples of these incomes and privileges one may list: substantial incomes, paid in fixed yearly amounts of money, in kind, or in services (e.g., cash payments from congregations or from properties, income from parish properties either managed or leased, interest, tithes, the use of the parsonage, yearly collections, and various services owed by the peasantry); accidental incomes paid on the occasion of a special ecclesiastical rite or service (e.g., weddings, funerals, filing of certificates); and financial and other immunities too numerous to catalogue.[1]

At the close of the eighteenth century the financial situation of the parish clergy was universally acknowledged to be miserable and constantly deteriorating. Gradual inflation had replaced the deflation which had followed the events of 1763, but famines and shortages continued to be prevalent even once the era of Friedrich II's deflationary policies had ended. Thus pastors suffered from a variety of financial problems.[2] Though no study of the financial problems of the pastorate in Electoral Hannover at this time exists, it is nonetheless clear that basic cash payments to the clergy remained fixed at levels set long before, perhaps as far back as the seventeenth century. In Hannover the annual income of over half the pastors amounted to no more than 300 *Thaler*, if not less.[3]

Worse still, perhaps, was the loss of income by attrition. The congregationally-elected committee which administered parish property is reported in many places throughout Protestant Germany to have misused capital funds, with disastrous results for preachers and teachers.[4]

---

[1] Johann Friedrich Christoph Gräffe, *Die Pastoraltheologie*, 2 vols. (Göttingen, 1803), 2:113.

[2] On pastors: Gräffe, 2:111-40; on the economic situation: Helen Liebel, "Der aufgeklärte Absolutismus und die Gesellschaftskrise in Deutschland im 18. Jahrhunderts," in *Absolutismus*, ed. Walther Hubatsch (Darmstadt, 1973), pp. 488-544.

[3] Christian Tischhauser, *Geschichte der evangelischen Kirchen Deutschlands* (Basel, 1900), p. 132.

[4] Tischhauser, p. 131.

Pastors everywhere seem to have had difficulty in leasing parish lands to peasants at a rate high enough to provide themselves with a living if they themselves did not wish to farm.[5] There is reason to believe that for decades in Electoral Hannover an increasing number of parishes had begun to curtail or to ignore the payment of the various dues and services on which pastors were partially dependent for their livelihood.[6] Furthermore, pastors were inexperienced in legal matters and often had no success in recovering or defending parish incomes in court.[7] In addition, from the inception of Pietism a century before the Protestant clergy had been forced to contend with an organized and ever-stronger movement which demanded abolition of accidental incomes or their commutation into fixed regular cash payments in amounts bound to be disadvantageous to the clergy in a period of inflation.[8] Finally, of course, there was the sobering example of what had happened to the established clergy in revolutionary France.

In the face of all this, the Hannoverian ecclesiastical establishment acted to defend the historic incomes and privileges of the clerical estate. The first step came from the consistory late in the eighteenth century, perhaps around 1799.[9] The consistory instituted a special legal counsel to represent parish clergy in all actions at law,[10] however trivial. Formerly pastors had been forced to represent themselves in all but the most important cases, with the result that they usually lost the privilege or income at issue with the laity. This one change, it was later reported, contributed substantially to preserving pastoral incomes and privileges from loss through attrition and litigation.[11]

---

[5] Tischhauser, p. 134; cf. Gräffe, 2:111-40.

[6] A. L. Mirow, *Der Prediger in seinen Verschiedenen Verhältnissen* (Hannover, 1808), pp. 242-43.

[7] Johann Karl Fürchtegott Schlegel, *Kirchen- und Reformationsgeschichte von Norddeutschland und den Hannoverschen Staaten*, 3 vols. (Hannover, 1828, 1829, 1832), 3:505-6.

[8] Helmut Obst, *Der Berliner Beichtstuhlstreit* (Witten, 1972); Busse (see n. 10 to appendix K); Heinrich Moritz Gottlieb Grellmann, *Kurze Geschichte der Stolgebühren* (Göttingen, 1785); "Ueber Einführung der öffentlichen Beichte," *Annalen der Braunschweig-Lüneburgischen Churlande* 6 (Hannover, 1792): 364; "Die Beichthandlung," *Beyträge*, ed. Salfeld, 3 (1802): 19-60; Mirow, "Zur Geschichte der Abschaffung der Prediger-Accidenzien," *Viertheiljährige Nachrichten*, ed. Salfeld, Jg. 1809, pp. 120-22; Lüders, "Ueber die Abschaffung des Beicht- und Leichengeldes in Hameln," *Neues Hannöversches Magazin*, Jg. 1804, cols. 193-208; cf. Kurt Aland, "Die Privatbeichte im Luthertum," in his *Kirchengeschichtliche Entwürfe* (Gütersloh, 1960), pp. 452-522.

[9] Schlegel, *Kirchen- und Reformationsgeschichte*, 3:506.

[10] For a specimen of such litigation, see Niedersächsisches Hauptstaatsarchiv Hannover, Sig. Hann. 83 IV 317, fols. verso - 286 recto = "Register zu Schlegels Collectaneen." An inventory of this material should be made if further reserach on this topic is to be carried out.

[11] Schlegel, *Kirchen- und Reformationsgeschichte*, 3:505-6.

The next step was the publication of handbooks designed to acquaint parish clergy with the full extent of existing law pertaining to pastors, pastors' rights, and pastors' duties. The most important work here, and one demanding monographic study in its own right, is the neglected, massive *Churhannöversches Kirchenrecht*, a five-volume codification of historic clerical privilege published from 1801 to 1806 by the *Consistorial-Secretär* Johann Karl Fürchtegott Schlegel.[12] Though Schlegel's interest in history and his family connection as yet another of the famed Schlegel brothers mark him as what one customarily terms a Romantic, nonetheless the Semi-Rationalist clergymen in Electoral Hannover seem not to have scrupled at utilizing his work for the defense of their incomes. Another book along the same lines, though taking a wider geographical perspective, is Georg Wiese's *Grundsätze des gemeinen in Teutschland üblichen Kirchenrechts*, which by 1805 had gone through three editions at Göttingen.[13] This renewal of activity in the area of church law represents a revival of the kind of defense of clerical privilege advocated half a century before by Mosheim.

---

[12] Johann Karl Fürchtegott Schlegel, *Churhannöversches Kirchenrecht*, 5 vols. (Hannover, 1801-1806).

[13] I have consulted the first edition: Georg Wiese, *Grundsätze des gemeinen in Teutschland üblichen Kirchenrechts* (Göttingen, 1793).

APPENDIX N

SYNODS OF THE CLERGY

The most important late-eighteenth-century Hannoverian regulation concerning synods built on earlier orders in the eighteenth century. It was a consistorial order of September 16, 1802 pertaining to the regular holding of synods of the clergy.[1] As was remarked at the time, such synods were seen as a means of reversing the "Verfall" of the parish clergy and of promoting the cause of *Bildung* throughout the clerical estate by means of occupation with both academic and practical topics.[2] This general impression is confirmed by a glance at the topics discussed at some of the turn-of-the-century synods in Northwest Germany—issues such as the financial condition of corporations for pious purposes,[3] or broader issues such as "How should the preacher become teacher and moral improver ... of those who feel far superior to him in culture?",[4] or again such topics as "Is the office or the estate of Protestant preachers so constituted that from it a harmful influence upon their character ought to be feared?"[5]

We find a similar situation with regard to the revival of interest in synods if we turn to Braunschweig-Wolfenbüttel. In the period of late Orthodoxy the synods of the clergy had largely been taken up with syllogistical disputations in Latin concerning various points of dogmatics and the Lutheran Symbols.[6] Though the drive to increase the effectiveness of synods of the clergy as a means for growth and discipline can

---

[1] "Consistoral-Ausschreiben vom 16ten September 1802, die Haltung der Synoden in den Fürstenthümern Lüneburg u. Grubenhagen, auch in den Grafschaften Hoya und Diepholz betrf.," *Beyträge*, ed. Salfeld, 5 (1804): 66-68.

[2] "Ueber Prediger-Synoden," *Beyträge*, ed. Salfeld, 5 (1804): 56-96, esp. p. 58.

[3] "Ueber Prediger-Synoden," p. 95.

[4] Cited in Philipp Meyer, "Die Entwicklung der Fürsorge für die Fortbildung der Geistlichen in den Braunschweig-Lüneburgischen Kurlanden während der Aufklärungszeit," *ZGNK* 34/35 (1929): 314-40, with ref. to p. 329, citing material from ca. 1804.

[5] Georg Wilhelm Jäger, "Synodalrede über die Frage: Ist das Amt oder der Stand protestantischer Prediger so beschaffen, daß davon ein nachtheilger einfluß auf ihren Charakter zu fürchten wäre? auf der Synode in Selsingen am 3ten May 1793 gehalten," *Bremische und Verdensche Synodalbeyträge*, ed. Johann Kaspar Velthusen, Zweytes Heft (Stade, 1793), pp. 5-19.

[6] "Die Predigersynoden im Herzogthume Braunschweig. Geschichte derselben bis zum Anfange des gegenwärtigen Jahrhunderts." *Braunschweigisches Magazin*, Jg. 1866, pp. 209-24, esp. pp. 212-13.

be detected as early as 1750,[7] the truly significant attempts in this direction date from the 1770's. In that decade arose the custom of adding to the Latin disputations as well debates in the German language on more general questions pertaining to moral theology, apologetics, and pastoral practice.[8] By the 1790's it had become customary to discuss in these synods theological points of a distinctively Neological or Rationalistic character.[9]

In view of changing conditions, the two clerical members of the consistory in Wolfenbüttel proposed to the duke a number of alterations in the arrangement of synods.[10] The result was a ducal order of 1801.[11] The document takes cognizance of the need to arrive at a kind of synod more suited to current conditions so as to give better encouragment to an improvement of both scholarly study and practical effectiveness among the parish clergy.[12] Discussions are henceforth to concern issues of doctrinal, moral, apologetic, or historical theology, rather than the polemical theology that had once formed a staple of discussion.[13] Exegetical and practical or pastoral matters were also to be discussed.[14] The older syllogistical form was to be replaced by longer, freer discussions. Recent theological literature was also to be treated.[15] The wishes and concerns of the parish clergy concerning matters of pastoral care, education, and liturgical improvements were to be considered.[16] Special financial provision was to be made for establishing theological libraries in each district and for encouraging the formation of reading clubs for the clergy so that they might stay abreast of the latest theological publications.[17]

---

[7] Cf. "Serenissimi erneuertes Reglement ratione der jährlichen Colloquiorum und Zusammenkünfte der Prediger auf dem Lande" from the year 1750 in Landeskirchliches Archiv Braunschweig under Signatur S 1405.

[8] "Die Predigersynoden," p. 218.

[9] "Die Predigersynoden," pp. 219-20.

[10] "Die Predigersynoden," p. 221.

[11] "Serenissimi erneuerte Verordnung die jährlichen Synoden der Prediger auf dem Lande und in den Landstädten des Herzogthums Braunschweig Wolfenbüttelschen Theils betreffend. d. d. Braunschweig, den 9ten Oktober 1801" in Landeskirchliches Archiv Braunschweig under Signatur S 1396. Text reproduced as "Herzoglich-Braunschweigische Verordnung, die bessere Einrichtung der Prediger-Synoden betreffend," in *Religionsannalen*, ed. H. P. C. Henke, 2 (Braunschweig, 1805): 117-23. (Cited below as "Verordnung 1801".)

[12] "Verordnung 1801," p. 117.

[13] "Verordnung 1801," pp. 118-19.

[14] "Verordnung 1801," pp. 119, 121.

[15] "Verordnung 1801," pp. 120-21.

[16] "Verordnung 1801," p. 121.

[17] "Verordnung 1801," pp. 122-23.

BIBLIOGRAPHY

PART ONE: PRINTED AND MANUSCRIPT MATERIAL
CONSULTED IN ARCHIVES

Niedersächsisches Staatsarchiv Wolfenbüttel

Signatur
2 Alt 15096   fols. 1-15 (duke and consistory in case of Consistorial Councillor
                         Petersen, 1795).
2 Alt 15884   (material concerning Velthusen's reaction to Campe).

Landeskirchliches Archiv, Landeskirchenamt Braunschweig

Signatur
S 1396   "Serenissimi erneuerte Verordnung die jährlichen Synoden der
                         Prediger auf dem Lande und in den Landstädten des Her-
                         zogthums Braunschweig Wolfenbüttelschen Theils betreffend.
                         d.d. Braunschweig, den 9ten Oktober 1801."

S 1405   "Serenissimi erneuertes Reglement ratione der jährlichen Collo-
                         quiorum und Zusammenkünfte der Prediger auf dem Lande"
                         (1750).

V 1177   (collection of ducal orders to be read from the pulpit at regular in-
                         tervals; cf. that of June 27, 1774, concerning control of pet dogs
                         and that of December 8, 1776, concerning mulberry trees).

V 1226   (von Münchhausen for the duke to the consistory, November 21,
                         1788).

Consistorial Verordnungen 1803-1813
                         "Reglement, die ... inspections-Lesegesellschaften und
                         Bibliotheken betreffend."

XXII C 4   "Lesegesellschaften"

Niedersächsisches Hauptstaatsarchiv Hannover

Signatur
Hann. 83 IV 317   fols. 285 verso-286 recto ("Register zu Schlegels Collectaneen").

MS Q Nr. 010   "Denkschrift von Ernst Brandes an Edmund Burke über Ver-
                         fassung Verwaltung und Landesnatur des Kurfürstentums Han-
                         nover (October 29, 1796)."(Transcript by Stephen Skalweit of a
                         MS in the Central Library in Sheffield, Acc. 4 157).

Landeskirchenamt, Hannover

"Nachlaß des Oberkonsistorialrates und Abts Dr. H. Ph. Sextro. II. 16. (12): Entwurf
eines Studienplans für die Beförderung eines wohlgeordneten Fleißes auf der Julius Carls
Universität in Helmstädt."

Universitäts-Archiv Göttingen

Signatur
Kurat.-akten 4 II a 31
                         fols. 7-42 (begins "Königl. Großbrit. ... Landesregierung. ...").

Archiv Kloster Loccum
Signatur
VIII, 6   "Vorschlag zu einem Studienplan in Loccum" (by Carl Georg
                           Schuster).

PART TWO: PRINTED MATERIAL AVAILABLE OUTSIDE ARCHIVES

Note: Ordinarily, when more than one title by the same author is entered, arrangement of
titles is by date of publication.

A. *Works Composed Before 1830*

Abbt, Thomas. *Vermischte Werke, 1. Theil welcher die Abhandlung vom Verdienste enthält.*
   Berlin, 1768.
"Aermlicher Zustand vieler Geistlichen." *Stats-Anzeigen*, edited by A. L. Schlözer, 15
   (1791): 393-430.
"Die akademischen Studia iunger Theologen betreffend." *Beyträge zur Kenntniß und
   Verbesserung des Kirchen- und Schulwesens in den Königl. Braunschweig-Lüneburgschen
   Churlanden*, edited by Johann Christoph Salfeld, 2 (Hannover, 1801): 216-55.
Allgemeine Encyclopädie. Edited by J. S. Ersch and J. G. Gruber. Leipzig, 1818.
Ammon, Christoph Friedrich. *Ideen zur Verbesserung der herrschenden Predigtmethode als
   Ankündigung einer neuen Königlichen Prämie für die beste vom einem der hier zu Göttingen
   studierenden Theologen in der Universitätskirche iährlich zu haltende Predigt.* Göttingen,
   1795.
Ammon, Christoph Friedrich. *Anleitung zur Kanzelberedsamkeit.* Göttingen, 1799.
"Anzahl der Pfarren in den Churhannoverschen Landen." *Magazin für die Geschichte und
   Statistik und das Territorialstaatsrecht von Niedersachsen*, 1:no. 1 (Lemgo, 1787): 59-63.
"Anzahl der sämmlichen evang. Prediger in Sr. Königl. Majestät von Groß-Brittanien
   und Kurfürstl. Durchl. von Braunschweig-Lüneburg Deutschen Landen, nebst
   einer Anzeige, wie viel davon auf Königlichen, und wie viel auf Patronat-Pfarren
   stehen." *Journal von und für Deutschland*, edited by Siegmund Freyherr von Bibra,
   6ter Jg., 1.-6. Stück (1789). p. 131.
Aufklärung, größtentheils eine Grille. Hannover, 1794.
Bahrdt, Carl Friedrich. *Ueber das theologische Studium auf Universitäten.* Berlin, 1785.
Bahrdt, Carl Friedrich. *"Rechte und Obliegenheiten der Regenten und Untertanen in Beziehung
   auf Staat und Religion." System der moralischen Religion zur endlichen Beruhigung für
   Zweifler und Denker*, 3:251-300. Riga, 1792.
Ballenstedt, Johann Georg Justus. *Beiträge zur Geschichte unsers Landes. Zweites Stück.
   Geschichte des Klosters Riddagshausen bei Braunschweig.* Schöningen, 1809.
Bartels, August Christian. *Ueber den Werth und die Wirkungen der Sittenlehre Jesu. Eine Apologie
   derselben gegen das sogenannte einzige wahre System der christlichen Religion.* 2 vols.
   Hamburg, 1788.
Bayle, Pierre. *Commentaire philosophique sur ces paroles de Jesus-Christ: "Contrains les
   d'entrer".* Amsterdam, 1686.
Bege, Karl Friedrich. *Uebersicht der Verordnungen, welche im Herzogthume Braunschweig in
   Ansehung der weltlichen Geschäfte der Prediger ergangen sind.* Helmstedt, 1828.
"Die Beichthandlung vor dem heil. Abendmahl betreffend." *Beyträge zur Kenntniß und
   Verbesserung des Kirchen- und Schulwesens in den Königl. Braunschweig-Lüneburgschen
   Churlanden*, edited by Johann Christoph Salfeld, 3 (Hannover, 1802): 19-60.
Beyträge zum Bau des Reiches Gottes. Edited by Johann Christoph Friedrich Gieseler, 1.
   Hannover, 1803.
Biester, Johann Erich. "Vorschlag...'" *Was ist Aufklärung?* Beiträge aus der Berlinischen
   Monatschrift, edited by Norbert Hinske. Darmstadt, 1973.
Bollmann, Georg Karl and Wolff, Heinrich Wilhelm Justus. *Heinrich Philipp Conrad Henke.*

Denkwürdigkeiten aus einem Leben und dankbare Erinnerungen an seine Verdienste. Helmstedt and Leipzig, 1816.

Brandes, Ernst. "Ueber den gegenwärtigen Zustand der Universität Göttingen." *Neues Hannöverisches Magazin,* Jg. 1802, cols. 161-240, 241-332, 333-448.

Brandes, Ernst. *Ueber den Einfluß und die Wirkungen des Zeitgeistes.* 2. Abtheilung. Hannover, 1810.

Busse, D. "Ehrenrettung der Prediger-Accidenzien und Stolgebühren, gegen die mancherlei Angriffe neuerer Schriftsteller und Prediger." *Göttingisches Museum der Theologie und Literatur,* edited by Johannes Horn, 1, no. 2:143-60. Hannover, 1805.

Calixt, Georg. *Gründliche Widerlegung eines unwarhafften Gedichts unterm Titul: Crypto-papismus Novae Theologiae Helmstadiensis.* 2 vols. Lüneburg, 1641.

Campe, Joachim Heinrich. *Über einige verkannte, wenigstens ungenützte Mittel zur Beförderung der Indüstrie, der Bevölkerung und des öffentlichen Wohlstandes.* Wolfenbüttel, 1786.

Chalotais, Ludwig Renatus de Caradeuc de la. *Versuch über den Kinder-Unterricht aus dem Französischen Übersetzt.* Göttingen and Gotha, 1771.

Christiani, Christoph Johann Rudolph. *Ueber die Bestimmung, Würde und Bildung christlicher Lehrer.* Schleswig, 1789.

Claville, M. Le Maitre de, ancien Doyen du Bureau des Finances à Rouen. *Traité du vrai mérite de l'homme.* Frankfurt [a.O.?], 1755.

"Consistorial-Ausschreiben vom 16ten September 1802., die Haltung der Synoden in den Fürstenthümern Lüneburg u. Grubenhagen, auch in den Grafschaften Hoya und Diepholz betrf." *Beyträge zur Kenntniß und Verbesserung des Kirchen- und Schulwesens in den Königl. Braunschweig-Lüneburgschen Churlanden,* edited by Johann Christoph Salfeld, 5 (Hannover, 1804): 66-68.

"Controversie wegen des Rangs der Geistlichen." *Unschuldigen Nachrichten Von alten und Neuen theologischen Sachen,* edited by Valentin Ernst Löscher, pp. 860-862. Jg. 1709. Leipzig, 1707 [*sic*].

Dassel, Christian. "Worin soll die Thätigkeit der Prediger bestehen, und wie kann man dieselbe befördern?" *Eusebia,* edited by H. P. C. Henke, 3 (Helmstedt, 1799-1800): 530-559.

Dedekind, Christoph Levin Heinrich. *Die Zeichen der Zeit, am Ende des 18. Jahrhunderts.* Erstes und Zweytes Stück. Wolfenbüttel, 1798.

Ehlers, Martin. *Winke für gute Fürsten.* Kiel and Hamburg, 1786-87.

"Empfohlne theologische Examinatoria. Rescript Königl. Landesregierung an die theologische Facultät zu Göttingen am 11ten Octb. 1799." *Beyträge zur Kenntniß und Verbesserung des Kirchen- und Schulwesens in den Königl. Braunschweig-Lüneburgschen Churlanden,* edited by J. C. Salfeld, 2 (Hannover, 1801): 220-22.

Erneuerte Kirchen-Ordnung Unser Von Gottes Gnaden Anthon Ulrichs Hertzogen zu Braunschweig und Lüneburg. 2 vols. Braunschweig, 1709. Reprint. Braunschweig, 1862.

Ersch, Johann Samuel and Gruber, Johann Gottfried. *Allgemeine Encyclopaedie.* In 3 sections of 99, 43, and 25 vols. (incomplete). Leipzig, 1818-92.

Feder, J. G. H. "Der Prediger und der Priester, oder von der religiösen Wirksamkeit des Geistlichen ausser der Kirche." *Beyträge zur Kenntniß und Verbesserung des Kirchen- und Schulwesens in den Königlich Braunschweig-Lüneburgschen Churlanden,* edited by J. C. Salfeld, 7 (Hannover, 1807): 499-522.

Fock, Johann Georg. *Zwey öffentliche Religionsvorträge über die ächte Bürgertreue.* Edited by Johann Caspar Velthusen. Stade, 1793.

Francke, August Hermann. *Pädagogische Schriften,* edited by G. Kramer. Langensalza, 1885.

"Fürst-Bischöffliche Preisfrage an die Wirzburgische Landgeistlichkeit. Eingeschickt von einem protestantischen Geistlichen." *Journal von und für Deutschland,* edited by Siegmund Freyherr von Bibra, 6. Jg. (Fulda, 1789), pp. 364-67.

Gerhard, Johann, *Loci Communes Theologici.* Edited by Johann Friedrich Cotta. 20 vols. Tübingen, 1762-81.

Gerling, Christian Ludwig. *Nachricht von seinen Vorlesungen über die Practische Theologie.* Göttingen, 1771.

Gesenius, Justus. *Fest-Predigten. Erster Teil*. Helmstedt, 1664.

Goethe, Johann Wolfgang von. *"Tag- und Jahres-Hefte 1805." Goethes Werke*, 1. Abth., 35: 233-38. Weimar, 1892.

Göttingische Anzeigen von gelehrten Sachen unter der Aufsicht der königl. Gesellschaft der Wissenschaften. Jg. 1791.

Göttingische Bibliothek der neuesten theologischer Literatur. Edited by Carl Friedrich Stäudlin. Göttingen, 1799.

Gräffe, Johann Friedrich Christoph: *Die Pastoraltheologie nach ihrem ganzen Umfange*. 2 vols. Göttingen, 1803.

Grellmann, Heinrich Moritz Gottlieb. *Kurze Geschichte der Stolgebühren oder geistlichen Accidenzien, nebst andern Hebungen*. Göttingen, 1785.

"Haben die Prediger im Churfürstenthum Hannover einen bestimmten bürgerlichen Rang?" *Annalen der Braunschweig-Lüneburgischen Churlande*, 8. Jg., pp. 310-12. Hannover, 1797.

Haffner, Isaac. "Erinnerungen an die leidensvollen Schicksale, welche das Christenthum und die Lehrer desselben in Frankreich. ... betroffen haben." *Religions-Annalen*, edited by H. P. C. Henke, 2 (Braunschweig, 1805): 583-604.

Hagemann, Johann Georg. *Oratio secularis de beneficiis coenobio Riddagshusano praesertim per reformationem divinitus collatis sub auspiciis serenissimi Principis ac Domini Augusti Wilhelmi ... d. 4. Novemb. 1717 habita a Joh. Georgio Hagemanno, Colleg. Ridd. Subseniore et Bibliothec*. Braunschweig, ca. 1717.

Heilmann, Johann David. *Traites de parallèle entre l'esprit d'irreligion d'aujourdhui et les anciens adversaires de la religion chrétieene dédiés à ... Monsieur Baumgarten ...* n.p., 1750.

Heilmann, Johann David. *Der Prediger und Seine Zuhörer in ihren wahren Verhältnis betrachtet. Eine Abhandlung womit die theologische Facultät zu Göttingen die Erneuerung des unter ihrer Aufsicht stehenden homiletischen Seminarii öffentlich anzeiget*. Göttingen, 1763.

Helvétius, Claude Arien. *De L'Esprit*. Paris, 1759.

Helvétius, Claude Arien. *De L'Homme, de ses facultés et de son éducation*. n.p., 1772.

Henke, Heinrich Philipp Conrad, ed. *Commentarii de rebus novis literariis*. 1780 ff.

Henke, Heinrich Philipp Conrad. *Beurtheilung der Klagen über Geringschätzung des Predigerstandes. Eine Rede, bey der Einführung eines neuen Priors des Kloster Michaelstein am achten Sonntage nach Trinitatis 1790*. Helmstedt, 1790.

Henke, Heinrich Philipp Conrad, ed. *Magazin für Religionsphilosophie, Exegese und Kirchengeschichte*. 1794 ff.

Henke, Heinrich Philipp Conrad. *Lineamenta institutionum fidei christianae historico-criticarum*. 2d ed. Helmstedt, 1795.

Henke, Heinrich Philipp Conrad, ed. *Eusebia*. Helmstedt, 1797-1800.

Henke, Heinrich Philipp Conrad, ed. *Religionsannalen*. 1800 ff.

Henke, Heinrich Philipp Conrad. *Predigten größtentheils an Bußtagen und Festtagen wie auch bey feyerlichen Gelegenheiten gehalten, 2. Sammlung*. Braunschweig, 1803.

Herder, Johann Gottfried. *An Prediger. Funfzehn Provinzialblätter*. Leipzig, 1774. Reprinted in *Herders Sämmtliche Werke*, edited by Bernhard Suphan, 7: 225-312. Berlin, 1884.

Hirsching, Friedrich Carl Gottlob, ed. *Historischlitterarisches Handbuch*. 7 vols. Leipzig, 1794-1804.

Hobbes, Thomas. "Leviathan." In his *English Works*, edited by William Molesworth, vol. 3. 1889. Reprint. Aalen, 1962.

Holscher, Johann Conrad Achaz. *Versuche über den Landprediger. Für einige Leser der Fragmente des Herrn Raths Campe. Erstes Stück*. Hannover, 1787.

Holscher, Johann Conrad Achaz. *Gottfried Less. Ein biographisches Fragment*. Hannover, 1797.

Holscher, Johann Conrad Achaz. *Praktisches Handbuch für Ephoral- und kirchliche Geschäfte*. Erster Theil, Hannover, 1800, Zweyter Theil, Hannover, 1805.

Holstein. "Zwei Schriftstücke zur Hebung des Pädagogiums zu Ilfeld." *Mitteilungen der Gesellschaft für deutsche Erziehungs- und Schulgeschichte*, edited by Karl Kehrbach, 4: 65-84 Berlin, 1894.

Hoppenstedt, (Superintendent). "Ueber Armenstalten und deren Benutzung für den Zweck der Beförderung mehrerer Religiösität und Moralität in den untern Volksklassen." *Beyträge zur Kenntniß und Verbesserung des Kirchen- und Schulwesens in den Königl. Braunschweig-Lüneburgschen Churlanden.* edited by J. C. Salfeld, 4 (Hannover, 1802): 1-66, 112-253.

Horn, Johannes von. "Ankündigung." *Göttingisches Museum der Theologie und Literatur,* edited by Johannes Horn, 1, no. 1: 1-30. Hannover, 1804.

Horn, Johannes. "Fernere Nachrichten von der Göttingischen Societät der theologischen Wissenschaften." *Neues Hannöversches Magazin* 14 (1804); cols. 1087-88.

Horn, Johannes. "Verfassung der Göttingischen Societät für theologischen Wissenschaften," *Neues Hannöversches Magazin* 14 (1804), cols. 129-36.

Horst, Georg Konrad. "Bemerkungen über die Geschichte der sogenannten Himmelfahrt Jesu." *Göttingisches Museum der Theologie und Literatur,* edited by Johannes Horn, 1, no. 2: 1-70. Hannover, 1805.

Hume, David. "Of National Characters." In his *Essays Moral, Political and Literary,* pp. 202-20. Oxford, 1963.

"Instruktion für das Hospitium zu Loccum und den zur Dirigirung der Studien und praktischen Uebungen desselben committirten Conventual." *Beyträge zur Kenntniß und Verbesserung des Kirchen- und Schulwesens in den Königl. Braunschweig-Lüneburgschen Churlanden,* edited by Johann Christoph Salfeld, 1 (Hannover, 1800): 465-81.

Jacobi, Johann Friedrich. "Gedanken über die Gewöhnliche Erziehung junger Geistlicher." *Hannoversche Beyträge zum Nutzen und Vergnügen,* Jg. 1761, cols. 665-724.

Jacobi, Johann Friedrich. *Beytrag zu der Pastoral-Theologie.* Hannover, 1766.

Jacobi, Johann Friedrich. "Kurze und zur Erbauung eingerichtete Einleitung in die Christliche Glaubens- und Sittenlehre." In his *Sämtliche Schriften, Ersten Theils erste Abtheilung,* pp. 599-601. Hannover, 1781.

Jacobi, Johann Friedrich. "Nähere Entdeckung eines neuen Lehrgebäudes der Religion." In his *Sämtliche Schriften,* 3. Theil, pp. 125-92. Hannover, 1784.

Jacobi, Johann Friedrich. *Leichter und überzeugender Beweis von Gott.* Celle, 1787.

Jacobi, J. F. "Die Beichtandlung vor dem heiligen Abendmahl betreffend." *Beyträge zur Kenntniß und Schulwesens in den Königl. Braunschweig-Lüneburgschen Churlanden,* edited by J. C. Salfeld, 3 (Hannover, 1802): 19-60.

Jäger, Georg Wilhelm. "Synodalrede über die Frage: Ist das Amt oder der Stand protestantischer Prediger so beschaffen, daß davon ein nachtheiliger Einfluß auf ihren Charakter zu fürchten wäre? auf der Synode in Selsingen am 3ten May 1793 gehalten." *Bremische und Verdensche Synodalbeyträge,* edited by Johann Kaspar Velthusen. Zweytes Heft, pp. 5-19. Stade, 1793.

Jerusalem, Johann Friedrich Wilhelm. *Zwey Predigten bey der Eröffnung und dem Beschluß des Landtages.* Braunschweig, 1770.

Jerusalem, Johann Friedrich Wilhelm. *Nachgelassene Schriften, Zweiter und letzter Theil.* Braunschweig, 1793.

Kant, Immanuel. *Critique of Judgment.* Translated by J. H. Bernard. Hafner Library of Classics, no. 14. New York, 1972.

Kant, Immanuel. *Religion within the Limits of Reason Alone.* Translated by Theodore M. Green and Hoyte H. Hudson. Reprint. New York, 1960.

"Kirchliche Ankündigung bei dem Todesfalle des Abtes zu Loccum, Dr. Joh. Chr. Salfeld." *Hannoversches Magazin* Jg. 1830, (Hannover, 1830), pp. 25-29.

"Kirchliche Einrichtungen zu mehrerer Verbreitung sittlichreligiöser Kenntnisse in allen Volksklassen durch Beförderung einer näheren Bekanntschaft mit dem Inhalte und Geiste der Bible." *Beyträge zur Kenntniß und Verbesserung des Kirchen- und Schulwesens in den Königl. Braunschweig-Lüneburgschen Churlande,* edited by Johann Christoph Salfeld, 3 (Hannover, 1802): 1-18.

Köppen, Daniel Joachim. *Der Hauptzweck des Predigtamts.* Leipzig, 1778.

Kommentar über einige Stellen in Campe's Fragmenten. Hamburg, 1787.

Koppe, Johann Benjamin. *Genauere Bestimmung des Erbaulichen im Predigen. Zur Ankündigung des von Sr. Königl. Majestät auf der Georg Augustus Universität gnädigst gestifteten Prediger Seminariums.* Göttingen, 1778.

"Lebensnachrichten von dem verstorbenen Consistorialrath, D. Johann Friedrich Jacobi." *Annalen der Braunschweig-Lüneburgischen Churlande* 6 (Hannover, 1792): 417-42.

Less, Gottfried. *Die Lehre von der christlichen Mässigkeit und Keuschheit (in 12 Predigten).* Göttingen, 1772. 2d ed., 1780.

Less, Gottfried. "Ueber die Furcht vor der Mittheilung ansteckender Krankheiten durch den Nachtmahlskelch." *Stats-Anzeigen,* edited by August Ludwig Schlözer, Heft 21 (1783): 356-63.

Less, Gottfried. *Rede bei der Ordination des Herrn Professor Koppe als berufenen Ober-Konsistorial-Rath und General-Superintendent des Herzogthums Gotha.* Göttingen, 1784.

Less, Gottfried. *Ueber Christliches Lehr-Amt Dessen würdige Fürung, Und die Schikliche Vorbereitung dazu. Nebst einem Anhange von der Privat-Beichte.* Göttingen, 1790.

Lüders, Stadtsyndicus. "Ueber die Abschaffung des Beicht- und Leichengeldes in Hameln." *Neues Hannöversches Magazin.* Jg. 1804, cols. 193-208.

Lüdke, Friedrich Germanus. *Gespräche über die Abschaffung des geistlichen Standes.* Berlin and Stettin, 1784.

Lünig, Johann Christian. *Theatrum ceremoniale historico-politicum.* 2 vols. Leipzig, 1719-20.

"Lutherischen Priester-Reform in Frankreich." *Stats-Anzeigen,* edited by A. L. Schlözer, 15, no. 60 (1791): 386-93.

Magazin für Religions- Moral- und Kirchengeschichte. Edited by Carl Friedrich Stäudlin. Hannover, 1801—.

Mandeville, Bernard. *Free Thoughts on Religion, the Church, and National Happiness.* London, 1720.

Mandeville, Bernard. *An Enquiry into the Origin of Honour and the Usefulness of Christianity in War.* London, 1732.

Marezoll, J. G. *Ueber die Bestimmung des Canzelredners.* Leipzig, 1793.

Mauvillon, Jacob. *Physiokratische Briefe.* Braunschweig, 1780.

Mauvillon, Jacob. *Das einzige wahre System der christlichen Religion.* Berlin, 1787.

Meusel, Johann Georg and Hamberger, Georg Christoph. *Das gelehrte Deutschland.* 23 vols. Reprint, Hildesheim, 1965-66.

Meusel, Johann Georg. *Lexikon der vom Jahr 1750 bis 1800 verstorbenen teutschen Schriftsteller.* 15 vols. Leipzig, 1802-16.

Michaelis, Johann David. *Raisonnement über die protestantischen Universitäten in Deutschland.* Erster Theil. Frankfurt and Leipzig, 1786.

Miller, Johann Martin. *Briefwechsel drey Akademischer Freunde.* 2 vols. 2d ed. Ulm, 1778-79.

Miller, Johann Peter. *Grundsätze eines Blühenden christlichen Staates.* Leipzig, 1773.

Miller, Johann Peter. *Ausführliche Anleitung zur weisen und gewissenhaften Verwaltung des evangelischen Lehramts.* Leipzig, 1774.

Miller, Johann Peter. *Systematische Anleitung zur Kenntnis auserlesener Bücher in der Theologie und in den damit verbundenen Wissenschaften.* 2d ed. Leipzig, 1775.

Mirow, A. L. *Der Prediger in seinen verschiedenen Verhältnissen: Ein Beytrag zur Beförderung der nützlichen Führung des Predigtamtes. Mit besonderer Hinsicht auf den hannöverschen Landprediger.* Hannover, 1808.

Mirow, A. L. "Zur Geschichte der Abschaffung der Prediger-Accidenzien." *Viertheiljährige Nachrichten von Kirchen- und Schulsachen,* edited by J. C. Salfeld, Jg. 1809 (Hannover, 1809), pp. 120-22.

Möser, Justus. *Sämtliche Werke.* Edited by Ludwig Schirmeyer. Oldenburg and Berlin, 1943.

Moritz, Karl Philipp. *Anton Reiser: Ein Psychologischer Roman.* Edited by Wolfgang Martens. Reclams Universal-Bibliothek, no. 4813-18. Berlin, 1785. Reprint. Stuttgart, 1972.

Moser, Friedrich Carl von. *Beherzigungen.* Frankfurt a.M., 1761.

Moser, Friedrich Carl von. *Reliquien.* Frankfurt a.M. and Leipzig, 1766.

Moser, Friedrich Carl von. *Patriotische Briefe.* Frankfurt a.M., 1767.

Mosheim, Johann, Lorenz. *Heilige Reden,* Erster Theil. Hamburg, 1732.

Mosheim, Johann, Lorenz von. *Sitten-Lehre Der Heiligen Schrift.* 3d ed. Helmstedt, 1742.

Mosheim, Johann Lorenz von. *De Odio theologico commentatio.* Göttingen, ca. 1747.

Mosheim, Johann Lorenz von. *Kurze Anweisung, die Gottesgelahrtheit vernünftig zu erlernen, in academischen Vorlesungen vorgetragen*. Edited by Christian Ernst von Windheim. Helmstedt, 1756.

Mosheim, Johann Lorenz von. *Elementa theologica dogmatica in academicis qvondam praelectionibus proposita et demonstrata*. Edited by Christian Ernst von Windheim. Nürnberg, 1758.

Mosheim, Johann Lorenz von. *Allgemeines Kirchenrecht der Protestanten*. Edited by Christian Ernst von Windheim. Helmstedt, 1760.

Mosheim, Johann Lorenz von. *Anweisung erbaulich zu predigen*. Edited by Christian Ernst von Windheim. Erlangen, 1763.

Mosheim, Johann Lorenz von. *Pastoral-Theologie von denen Pflichten und Lehramt eines Dieners des Evangelii*. 2nd ed. Leipzig and Ansbach, 1763.

Mosheim, Johann Lorenz von. *Auserlesene akademische Abhandlungen*. Edited by Johann Peter Miller. Leipzig, 1766.

Mosheim, Johann Lorenz von. *Allgemeines Kirchenrecht des Protestanten. Zuerst mit Anmerkungen herausgegeben von Christian Ernst von Windheim. Nun neu bearbeitet und fortgesetzt von D. Christian August Günther*. Leipzig, 1800.

Mosheim, Johann Lorenz. *Institutes of Ecclesiastical History*. Translated by James Murdock. New York, 1861.

Münnich, Johann Jakob Wilhelm von. *Gedanken und Vorschläge*. Leipzig, 1791.

Münter, Gottlieb Franz, ed. *Ausführliche Beschreibung aller Feyerlichkeiten ... D. Joh. Friedr. Jacobi*. Hannover, 1789.

"Nachricht von U-Pang." *Deutsches Museum*, Jg. 1782, no. 2 (1782): 220-36.

Nicolai, Friedrich. *Ehrengedächtniß Herrn Thomas Abbt. An Herrn D. Johann George [sic] Zimmermann*. Berlin and Stettin, 1767.

"Pastoral-Instruction für die unter dem Hannöverschen Consistorio stehenden Prediger." *Beyträge zur Kenntniß und Verbesserung des Kirchen- und Schulwesens in den Königl. Braunschweig-Lüneburgschen Churlanden*, edited by Johann Christoph Salfeld, 1 (Hannover, 1800): 62-103.

Der patriotische Landprediger. Erstes Stück. Mit einer Vorrede herausgegeben vom Herrn Doktor Miller. Edited by Johann Heinrich Ress. Leipzig, 1779. *Zweites Stück*, 1780. *Drittes Stück*, 1781. *Viertes und letztes Stück*, 1783.

Pertsch, Johann Georg. *Recht der Beicht-Stuhle, Darinnen Der Ursprung und Fortgang Der Geheimen Beichte Aus denen Kirchen-Geschichte gezeiget*. 2d ed. Wolfenbüttel, 1738.

Pertsch, Johann Georg. *Recht des Kirchen-Bannes, worinnen der Ursprung und Fortgang desselben kürtzlich gezeiget*. 2d ed. Wolfenbüttel, 1738.

Planck, Gottlieb Jacob. *Einleitung in die Theologische Wissenschaften*. Erster Theil. Leipzig, 1794.

Pütter, Johann Stephen. *Versuch einer academischen Gelehrten-Geschichte von der Georg-Augustus-Universität zu Gottingen, Zweiter Theil von 1765 bis 1788*. Göttingen, 1788.

Pufendorf, Samuel. *De officio hominis & civis, Juxta legem naturalem libri duo*. Cambridge, 1682.

"Rede über die Freyheit des Gottesdienstes ... von B. Gregoire." *Eusebia*, edited by H. P. C. Henke, 2 (Helmstedt, 1798): 583-604.

Rehberg, August Wilhelm. "Sollten die alten Sprachen dem allgemeinen Unterricht der Jugend in den Höhern Ständen zum Grunde gelegt, oder den eigentlichen Gelehrten allein überlassen werden." *Berlinische Monatsschrift*, edited by F. Gedike and J. E. Biester, 11 (1788): 105-31; 253-75.

Rehtmeyer, Philip Julius. *Historiae ecclesiasticae inclytae urbis Brunsvigae, Pars. V. Supplementa*. Braunschweig, 1720.

Reiche, Karl Christoph. *Ueber das Schädliche des Predigerordens und dessen Abänderung*. Brandenburg, 1773.

Reinhold, G. F. "Ueber den absoluten Begriff des Geistlichen." *Neue Beyträge zur Kenntiß und Verbesserung des Kirchen- und Schulwesens, vorzüglich im Hannoverschen*, edited by J. C. Salfeld and J. P. Trefurt, 1 (Hannover, 1810): 334-78.

Rink, Friedrich Theodor, ed. *Sammlung einiger bisher unbekannt gebliebener kleiner Schriften von Immanuel Kant*. Königsberg, 1800.

Rotermund, Heinrich Wilhelm. *Das gelehrte Hannover*. 3 vols. Bremen, 1823.

Rotermund, Heinrich Wilhelm. *Handbuch für Candidaten, die ins Predigtamt treten*. Hannover, 1802.

Salfeld, Johann Christoph, ed. *Sammlung zur Geschichte des Königl. Churfürstlichen Consistorii zu Hannover, und zur Biographie des zeitigen ersten Raths in demselben, Hrn. Geh. Just. Rth. Dr. E. A. Heiliger*. Hannover, 1803.

Salfeld, Johann Christoph, ed. *Viertheiljährige Nachrichten von Kirchen- und Schulsachen*. Hannover, 1809 ff.

Salfeld Johann Christoph. "Beförderung der humanistischen Studien unter den auf der Universität zu Göttingen Theologie studierenden Landeskindern." *Neue Beyträge zur Kenntniß und Verbesserung des Kirchen- und Schulwesens in den Königl. Braunschweig-Lüneburgschen Churlanden*. Edited by J. C. Salfeld and J. P. Trefurt, 2 (Hannover, 1810): 1-55.

Salfeld, J. C. and Trefurt, J. P., eds. *Neue Beyträge zur Kenntniß und Verbesserung des Kirchen- und Schulwesens*. Hannover, 1810 ff.

Scharf, Christian Barthold. *Der Kirchen-Staat des Churfürstentums Braunschweig-Lüneburg*. Hannover, 1776.

Schlegel, Johann Karl Fürchtegott. *Churhannöversches Kirchenrecht*. 5 vols. Hannover, 1801-1806. Schlegel, Johann Karl Fürchtegott. *Kirchen- und Reformationsgeschichte von Norddeutschland und den Hannoverschen Staaten*. 3 vols. Hannover, 1828, 1829, 1832.

Schleiermacher, Friedrich. *Sämmtliche Werke*. 1. Abtheilung. Berlin, 1843.

Schleiermacher, Friedrich. *On Religion: Speeches to its Cultured Despisers*. Translated by John Oman. New York, 1958.

Schlichthorst, H., ed. *Beyträge zur Erläuterung der ältern und neuern Geschichte der Herzogthümer Bremen und Verden*. Hannover, 1797.

Schlözer, August Ludwig. *Allgemeines StatsRecht und StatsVerfassungsLere*. Göttingen, 1793.

Schuderoff, Johann Georg Jonathan. *Beyträge zur Beförderung zweckmäßiger Kanzelvorträge*. Braunschweig, 1796.

Schuster, Carl Georg. "Ueber die Nothwendigkeit eines Lehr und Predigerstandes in jedem vollkommneren Staate." *Beyträge zur Kenntniß und Verbesserung des Kirchen- und Schulwesens in den Königlich Braunschweig-Lüneburgschen Churlanden*, edited by Johann Christoph Salfeld, 2 (Hannover, 1801): 274-335.

Schwarz, Friedrich Heinrich Christian. *Der christliche Religionslehrer in seinem moralischen Daseyn und Wirken*. Gießen, 1798.

Sehling, Emil, ed. *Die evangelischen Kirchenordnungen des XVI. Jahrhunderts. 6. Band, Niedersachsen, 1. Halfte. Die Welfischen Lände, 1. Halbband*. Tübingen, 1955.

Seidenstücker, J. H. P. *Ueber Schulinspection*. Helmstedt, 1797.

Sextroh, Heinrich Philipp. *Ueber Materialien zum Religionsvortrage an Kranke*. Göttingen, 1782.

Sextroh, Heinrich Philipp. *Ueber praktische Vorbereitungsanstalten zum Predigtamt. Nebst einer Nachricht vom Königlichen Pastoralinstitut in Göttingen*. Göttingen, 1783.

Sextroh, Heinrich Philipp. *Abriß der Geschichte Jesu aus den Evangelien des Matthäus, Markus, Lukas und Johannes. Ein Entwurf zum Gebrauch in Vorlesungen über die Harmonie der Vier Evangelisten*. Göttingen, 1785.

Sextroh, Heinrich Philipp. *Ueber die Beförderung des Praktischen Studiums der Geschichte Jesu zu Vorbereitung auf das Predigtamt. Nebst einer Anzeige seiner Vorlesungen*. Göttingen, 1785.

Sextroh, Heinrich Philipp. *Über die Bildung der Jugend zur Indüstrie*. Göttingen, 1785.

Sextroh, Heinrich Philipp. *Ueber Pflicht, Beruf und Verdienst des Predigers. Tabellarischer Entwurf einer encyclopädischen Einleitung in die ganze Pastoraltheologie, zum Gebrauch in Vorlesungen*. Göttingen, 1786.

"Sollte nicht billig in einer jeden Pfarr-Registratur eine bestimme Instruction vorhanden seyn, welche die Geschäfte, Jura und Verhältnisse des Predigers enthielte." *Viertheiljährige Nachrichten von Kirchen- und Schulsachen*, edited by J. C. Salfeld, Jg. 1809 (Hannover, 1809), pp. 114-20.

Spalding, Johann Joachim. *Ueber die Nutzbarkeit des Predigtamtes und deren Beförderung*. Berlin, 1772.

Specht, Christian, Pfeffer, Johan Georg, and Overbeck, Adolph Theobald. *Augustana Confessio brevibus Aphorismis illustrata.* Braunschweig, 1695.

Specht, Christian. *Christliche Leich-Predigt ... Bey Christlicher Bestattung Des ... Herrn Johannis Lucae Pestorfen.* Braunschweig, 1695.

Stäudlin, Carl Friedrich. *"De Facultate theologica in Universitatibus litterariis."* Göttingische gelehrte Anzeigen, Jg. 1809, pp. 974-75.

"Stand, Zustand, Stand der Menschen, oder Personen." Johann Heinrich Zedler, ed., *Großes vollständiges Universal-Lexicon aller Wissenschaften und Künste,* 68 vols., 39: cols. 1093-1103. Halle and Leipzig, 1732-54; reprint, Graz, 1961-64.

Stübner, Johann Christoph. *Historische Beschreibung der Kirchenverfassung in den Herzogl. Braunschweig-Lüneburgischen Landen seit der Reformation.* Erster und zweiter Theil. Goslar, 1800.

Sturm, Christoph Christian and Feddersen, Jacob Friederich. *Gesellschaftliche Bemühungen, der Welt die christliche Religion anzupreisen.* 1 vol., 2 parts. Göttingen and Gotha, 1772-73.

Thiess, J. O. *Ist die Einführung der Allgemeinen Beichte oder die Beibehaltung des Beicht-Stuhls rathsamer?* Hamburg, 1788.

[Thiry, Paul Henri, Baron d'Holbach?]. *Ethocratie ou le gouvernement fondé sur la morale.* Amsterdam, 1776.

Thomasius, Christian. *Bedencken über die Frage: Wieweit ein Prediger gegen seinen Landes-Herrn Welcher zugleich Summus Episcopus mit ist sich des Bindeschlüssels bedienen könne?* Wolfenbüttel, 1706. 2d ed. 1707.

Toland, John. *Letters to Serena.* Edited by Günter Gawlick. London, 1704. Reprint. Stuttgart-Bad Cannstatt, 1964.

Trapp, Ernst Christian. *Ueber die Gewalt protestantischer Regenten in Glaubenssachen.* Braunschweig, 1788.

Trinius, J. J. B. *Ueber Accidenzien und Predigergebühren.* Halle, 1803.

"Ueber die Mecklenburgische Preisaufgabe." *Stats-Anzeigen,* edited by A. L. Schlözer, 6 (1784): 99-112.

"Ueber die Nothwendigkeit der moralischen Verbesserung des Predigerstandes." *Eusebia,* edited by H. P. C. Henke, 1 (Helmstedt, 1797): 1-141.

"Ueber die Territorial-Abgaben in Helvetien." *Helvetische Monathschrift* 1 (Bern, 1800): 70-112.

"Ueber Einführung der öffentlichen Beichte in einzelnen Orten." *Annalen der Braunschweig-Lüneburgischen Churlande* 2 (1788): no. 2: 171; no. 3: 181; 3 (1789): no. 3: 710; 6 (1792): no. 2: 364.

"Ueber Prediger-Synoden." *Beyträge zur Kenntniß und Verbesserung des Kirchen- und Schulwesens in den Königl. Braunschweig-Lüneburgschen Churlanden,* edited by Johann Christoph Salfeld, 5 (Hannover, 1804): 56-96.

Uffenbach, Zacharias Conrad von. *Merkwürdige Reisen durch Niedersachsen Holland und Engelland.* 3 vols. Ulm and Memmingen, 1753-54.

Ulrich, Friedrich. *Ueber den Religionszustand in den preußischen Staaten.* Leipzig, 1778-80.

Velthusen, Johann Caspar. *Ueber Absichten und Tendenz.* Helmstedt, 1787.

Velthusen, Johann Caspar. *Ueber die nächste Bestimmung des Landpredigerstandes. Ein durch Herrn Campens Fragmente veranlaßter Beytrag zur Pastoraltheologie.* Helmstedt, 1787.

Velthusen, Johann Caspar. *"Einige Bemerkungen über die zu grosse Anzahl der Studirenden."* Neues Magazin für Schullehrer, edited by G. A. Ruperti and H. Schlichthorst, 2 (Göttingen and Bremen, 1793-94): 347-52.

Velthusen, Johann Caspar, ed. *Christliches Trostbuch in Kriegszeiten: Taschenbuch für christliche Soldaten.* Hannover, 1795.

Venturini, Carl H. C. *Ideen zur Philosophie über die Religion und den Geist des reinen Christenthums.* Altona, 1794.

Venturini, Carl. *Das Herzogthum Braunschweig in seiner Gegenwärtigen Beschaffenheit.* Helmstedt, 1826.

"Verzeichniß der Pränumeranten." *Beyträge zur Kenntniß und Verbesserung des Kirchen- und Schulwesens in den Königlich Braunschweig-Lüneburgschen Churlanden,* edited by J. C. Salfeld, 1 (Hannover, 1800): fols. *1 recto—*7 recto.

Voetius, Gisbert. *Politica Ecclesiastica.* 4 vols. Amsterdam, 1663-76.
Walch, Johann Georg. *Historische und Theologische Einleitung in die Religions-Streitigkeiten Der Evangelisch-Lutherischen Kirchen.* 5 vols. Jena, 1730-34.
Weidemann, Christoph Erich. *Geschichte des Klosters Loccum,* edited by Friedrich Burchard Köster. Göttingen, 1822.
Wiese, George. *Grundsätze des gemeinen in Teutschland üblichen Kirchenrechts.* Göttingen, 1793.
"Zur Geschichte der Abschaffung der Prediger-Accidenzien." *Viertheiljährige Nachrichten von Kirchen- und Schulsachen,* edited by J. C. Salfeld, Jg. 1809, (Hannover, 1809), pp. 120-28.

B. *Works Composed After 1830*

Aalders, G. J. D. *Die Theorie der gemischten Verfassung im Altertum.* Amsterdam, 1968.
Adam, Alfred. *Lehrbuch der Dogmengeschichte.* 2 vols. Gütersloh, 1965.
Aland, Kurt. "Die Privatbeichte im Luthertum von ihren Anfängen bis zu ihrer Auflösung." In his *Kirchengeschichtliche Entwürfe,* pp. 452-522. Gütersloh, 1960.
Aner, Karl. "Die Historia dogmatum des Abtes Jerusalem." *Zeitschrift für Kirchengeschichte* 47 (1928): 76-103.
Aner, Karl. *Die Theologie der Lessingzeit.* Halle/Saale, 1929.
Antoni, Carlo. *Der Kampf wider die Vernunft.* Translated by Walther Goetz. Stuttgart, 1951.
Aretin, Karl Otmar Freiherr von, ed. *Der Aufgeklärte Absolutismus.* Neue Wissenschaftliche Bibliothek, Geschichte. Köln, 1974.
Arndt, Felix. *Zur Publizistik über Kirche und Staat vom Ausgang des 18. bis zum Beginn des 19. Jahrhunderts.* Ph.D. Dissertation, Kiel University, 1918.
Bäsken, Rohtraut. *Die Dichter des Göttinger Hains und die Bürgerlichkeit: eine literarsoziologische Studie.* Schriften der Albertus-Universität, Geisteswissenschaftliche Reihe, 6. Königsberg, 1937.
Barth, Hans-Martin. *Atheismus und Orthodoxie: Analysen und Modelle christlicher Apologetik im 17. Jahrhundert.* Forschungen zur systematischen und ökumenischen Theologie, no. 26. Göttingen, 1971.
Barth, Karl. *Protestant Theology in the Nineteenth Century* (Valley Forge, 1973).
Batany, Jean. "Des 'Trois Fonctions' aux 'Trois États'?" *Annales. Économies, Sociétés, Civilisations* 18 (1963): 933-38.
Battestin, Martin C. *The Moral Basis of Fielding's Art.* Middletown, Conn., 1959.
Bauer, Walter. *A Greek-English Lexicon of the New Testament.* Edited by William F. Arndt and F. Wilbur Gingrich. Chicago, 1957.
Baumotte, Manfred. *Theologie als politische Aufklärung. Studien zur neuzeitlichen Kategorie des Christentums.* Studien zur evangelischen Ethik, no. 12. Gütersloh, 1973.
Baur, G. "Campe." *Allgemine Deutsche Biographie,* 3: 733-37. Leipzig, 1876.
Behler, Diana. "Lessing's Legacy to the Romantic concept of the Poet-Priest." *Lessing Yearbook,* 4 (1972): 67-93.
Behrens, F., ed. *Das Fürstliche Schuldirektorium in Herzogthum Braunschweig vom Jahre 1786.* Braunschweig, 1888.
Die Bekenntnisschriften der evangelisch-lutherischen Kirche. Edited by Hans Lietzmann et al. 2d ed. Göttingen, 1952.
Bender, Annie. *Thomas Abbt. Ein Beitrag zur Darstellung des erwachenden Lebensgefühls im 18. Jahrhundert.* Bonn, 1922.
Berding, Helmut. *Napoleonische Herrschafts- und Gesellschaftspolitik im Königreich Westfalen 1807-1813.* Kritische Studien zur Geschichtswissenschaft, No. 7. Göttingen, 1973.
Berding, Helmut. "Begriffsgeschichte und Sozialgeschichte." *Historische Zeitschrift* 223 (1976): 98-110.
Berney, Arnold. "August Ludwig von Schlözers Staatsauffassung." *Historische Zeitschrift* 132 (1925): 43-66.
Berney, Arnold. "Reichstradition und Nationalstaatsgedanke (1789-1815)." *Historische Zeitschrilft* 140 (1929): 57-86.

Bertheau, Carl. "Gesenius, Justus." *PRE*, 6:622-24. 3rd ed. Leipzig, 1899.

Beste, Johannes. *Geschichte der Braunschweigischen Landeskirche von der Reformation bis auf unsere Tage*. Wolfenbüttel, 1889.

Beste, Johannes. "Das Predigerseminar zu Riddagshausen." *ZGNK* 10 (1905): 197-230.

Beyer, Hans. "Niederdeutsche Kirchenkämpfe im ausgehenden 18. Jahrhundert." *JGNK* 53 (1955): 104-26.

Beyreuther, Erich. "Halle und die Herrnhuter in den Rezensionen der Göttingischen Zeitungen von gelehrten Sachen auf dem Hintergrund niedersächsischer Religionspolitik zwischen 1739 und 1760." *JGNK* 73 (1975): 109-34.

Biehringer, Frieda. *Herzog Karl I von Braunschweig*. Quellen und Forschungen zur Braunschweigischen Geschichte, 11. Wolfenbüttel, 1920.

Bien, D. D. "La réaction aristocratique avant 1789." *Annales E.S.C.* 29 (1974): 23-48, 505-34.

Bienert, Walther, *Die Glaubenslehre des Christian Thomasius*. Dissertation. Halle, 1934.

Bigler, Robert M. *The Politics of German Protestantism: The Rise of the Protestant Church Elite in Prussia, 1816-1848*. Berkeley, Calif., 1972.

Birtsch, Günter. "Zur sozialen und politischen Rolle des deutschen, vornehmlich preussischen Adels am Ende des 18. Jahrhunderts." *Der Adel vor der Revolution*, edited by Rudolf Vierhaus, pp. 77-95. Göttingen, 1971.

Bizer, Ernst. "Coccejus." *RGG*, 1: cols. 1841-42. 3d ed. Tübingen, 1957.

Blumenberg, Hans. *Die Legitimität der Neuzeit*. Frankfurt a.M., 1966.

Bofinger, Wilhelm. "Zur Rolle des Luthertums in der Geschichte des deutschen Ständeparlamentarismus." In *Geist und Geschichte der Reformation: Festgabe Hans Rückert*. Arbeiten zur Kirchengeschichte, no. 38, pp. 397-417. Berlin, 1966.

Bohatec, Josef. "Das Territorial- und Kollegialsystem in der holländischen Publizistik des XVII. Jahrhunderts." *Zeitschrift der Savigny- Stiftung für Rechtsgeschichte, Kanonistische Abteilung* 35 (1948): 1-149.

Bohatec, Josef. "Die Vorgeschichte der Menschen- und Bürgerrechte in der englischen Publizistik der ersten Hälfe des 17. Jahrhunderts." *Zur Geschichte der Erklärung der Menschenrechte*, edited by Roman Schnur, pp. 267-331. Wege der Forschung, no. 11. Darmstadt, 1964.

Bonin, Henning von. "Adel und Bürgertum in der höhern Beamtenschaft der preußischen Monarchie 1794-1806." *Jahrbuch für die Geschichte Mittel- und Ostdeutschlands* 16 (1966): 139-74.

Bonwetsch, Nathanael. "Johann Lorenz von Mosheim als Kirchenhistoriker." *Festschrift zur Feier des hundertfünfzigjährigen Bestehens der Königlichen Gesellschaft der Wissenschaften zu Göttingen*, pp. 235-61. Berlin, 1901.

Bradeler-Rottmann, Elisabeth. *Die Reformen Kaiser Josephs II*. Göppingen, 1973.

Bräumer, Hansjörg. *August von Arndswaldt 1798-1855*. Studien zur Kirchengeschichte Niedersachsens, 20. Göttingen, 1972.

Braun, Hans-Joachim. *Technologische Beziehungen zwischen Deutschland und England*. Düsseldorf, 1973.

"Braunschweig." *Der Grosse Brockhaus*, 2:309-11. 12 vols. 17th ed. Wiesbaden, 1953-57.

"Braunschweigs Göze." *Evangelisch-lutherische Monatsblätter für Kirche, Schule und innere Mission im Lande Braunschweig*, 5, nos. 7-9 (1885): 23-31.

Broecken, Karl Heinz. "Mensch und Bürger bei Rousseau und den Philanthropisten." *Pädagogischen Rundschau* 32 (1978): 739-63.

Brödel, Hermann. "Die Arbeits- und Industrieschulen vor Ferdinand Kindermann." *Zeitschrift für Geschichte der Erziehung und des Unterrichts* 21 (1931): 308-19; 22 (1932): 35-49.

Brödel, Hermann. "Braunschweigische Industrieschulpläne um 1750." *Zeitschrift für Handelsschulpädagogik* 3 (1931): 245-315.

Brück, Gertrud. *Die Bedeutung Justus Mösers für das Leben und Denken Thomas Abbts*. Phil. dissertation. Munich University, 1937.

Brüggemann, Fritz, ed. *Der Siebenjährige Krieg im Spiegel der zeitgenössischen Literatur*. Deutsche Literatur. Sammlung literarische Kunst- und Kulturdenkmäler in Entwicklungsreihen, Reihe Aufklärung, 9. Leipzig, 1935.

Bruford, W. H. *Germany in the Eighteenth Century: The Social Background of the Literary Revival.* 2d ed. Cambridge, 1971.

Brunschwig, Henri. *La crise de l'état Prussien à la fin du XVIIIᵉ siècle et la genèse de la mentalité Romantique.* Paris, 1947.

Brunschwig, Henri. *Enlightenment and Romanticism in Eighteenth-Century Prussia.* Translated by Frank Jellinek. Chicago, 1974.

Büchsel, Jürgen. *Gottfried Arnold: Sein Verständnis von Kirche und Wiedergeburt.* Arbeiten zur Geschichte des Pietismus, no. 11. Witten, 1970.

Burmeister, Friedrich-Karl. *Der Merkantilismus im Lande Braunschweig-Wolfenbüttel im 16. bis 18. Jahrhundert.* Dissertation. Frankfurt a.M. University, 1928.

Campenhausen, Hans von. *Ecclesiastical Authority and Spiritual Power in the Church of the First Three Centuries.* Translated by J. A. Baker. Stanford, Calif., 1969.

Carsten, F. L. "The Defeat of the Estates of Prussia." In his *The Origins of Prussia.* pp. 202-28. Oxford, 1954.

Cattaneo, Mario A. "Hobbes Théoricien de l'Absolutisme Eclairé." *Hobbes-Forschungen,* edited by Reinhart Koselleck and Roman Schnur, pp. 199-210. Berlin, 1969.

Christern, Herman. *Deutscher Ständestaat und englischer Parlamentarismus am Ende des 18. Jahrhunderts.* Munich, 1939.

Claus, Oskar. *Die historische-politischen Anschauungen Thomas Abbts.* Phil. dissertation. Leipzig University, 1905.

Conze, Werner. "Staat und Gesellschaft in der frührevolutionären Epoche Deutschlands." *Historische Zeitschrift* 186 (1961): 1-34.

Conze, Werner, ed. *Staat und Gesellschaft im deutschen Vormärz 1815-1848.* Industrielle Welt. Schriftenreihe des Arbeitskreises für moderne Sozialgeschichte. Stuttgart. 1962.

Cranz, F. Edward. *An Essay on the Development of Luther's Thought on Justice, Law, and Society.* Harvard Theological Studies, no. 19. Cambridge, Mass., 1959.

Crisis in Europe 1560-1660. Edited by Trevor Aston. New York, 1965.

Dauer, Martin. *Die eine Kirche und das zweifache Recht: Eine Untersuchung zum Kirchenbegriff und der Grundlegung kirchlicher Ordnung in der Theologie Schleiermachers.* Jus Ecclesiasticum. Beiträge zum evangelischen Kirchenrecht und zum Staatskirchenrecht, vol. 9. Munich, 1970.

Demandt, Karl E. "Amt und Familie: Eine soziologisch-genealogische Studie zur hessischen Verwaltungsgeschichte des 16. Jahrhunderts." *Hessisches Jahrbuch für Landesgeschichte* 2 (1952): 79-133.

Depperman, Klaus. *Der hallesche Pietismus und der preussische Staat unter Friedrich III. (I).* Göttingen, 1961.

Derathé, Robert. "La religion civile selon Rousseau." *Annales de la Société Jean-Jacques Rousseau* 35 (1959-62): 161-80.

Dettmer, Vitus. "Abt K. Velthusen, Pastor prim., General-superintendent und Professor in Helmstedt. 1778 bis 1789." *ZGNK* 24 (1918): 1-94.

Dettmer, Vitus. *Das Konsistorium zu Wolfenbüttel.* Braunschweig, 1922.

Dettmer, Vitus. "Das Geistliche Gericht der Stadt Braunschweig." *ZGNK* 34/35 (1929/30): 200-27.

Dilthey, Wilhelm. "*Leben Schleiermachers: Erster Band.*" edited by Martin Redeker. In Dilthey's *Gesammelte Schriften,* 13:1. 1870. Reprint. Göttingen, 1970.

Doerr, Hildegard. *Thomasius Stellung zum Landesherrlichen Kirchenregiment.* Phil. dissertation, Bonn University, 1917.

Dörries, Hermann. *Geist und Geschichte bei Gottfried Arnold.* Abhandlungen der Akademie der Wissenschaften in Göttingen, 3. Folge, no. 51. Göttingen, 1963.

Dörries, Hermann. "Geschichte der vocatio zum kirchlichen Amt." In his *Wort und Stunde,* 3: 347-86. 3 vols. Göttingen, 1970.

Dorn, Walter L. "The Prussian Bureaucracy in the Eighteenth Century." *Political Science Quarterly* 46 (1931): 403-23; 47 (1932): 75-94, 259-73.

Dorwart, Reinhold August. *The Administrative Reforms of Frederick William I of Prussia.* Cambridge, Mass., 1953.

Drews, Paul. "Der Rückgang der Kommunikanten in Sachsen." *Zeitschrift für Theologie und Kirche* 10 (1900): 148-66.

Düsterdieck, Friedrich. *Das Hospiz im Kloster Loccum.* Göttingen, 1863.

Ebel, Wilhelm, ed. *Friedrich Esajas Pufendorfs Entwurf eines hannoverschen Landrechts (vom Jahre 1772).* Hildesheim, 1972.

Ebhardt, Christian Hermann, ed. *Gesetze, Verordnungen und Ausschreiben für den Bezirk des Königlichen Consistorii zu Hannover, welche in Kirchen- und Schulsachen ergangen sind.* 2 vols. Hannover, 1845.

Ecke, Gustav. *"Die theologische Schule Albrecht Ritschls und die evangelische Kirche der Gegenwart." Die evangelischen Landeskirchen Deutschlands im 19. Jahrhundert,* vol. 2. Berlin, 1904.

Eckstein, Karlfriedrich. "Friedrich Carl von Moser (1723-1798): Rechts- und Staatstheoretisches Denken zwischen Naturrecht und Positivismus." Dissertation, Rechtswissenschaft. Giessen University, 1973.

Eisler, Rudolf, ed. *Kant-Lexikon.* Berlin, 1930. Reprint. Hildesheim, 1961.

Elert, Werner. *Morphologie des Luthertums.* 2 vols. 1931. Reprint. Munich, 1965.

Epstein, Klaus. *The Genesis of German Conservatism.* Princeton, N.J., 1966.

Erdmann, Karl Dietrich. *Das Verhältnis von Staat und Religion nach der Sozialphilosophie Rousseaus (Der Begriff der "Religion civile").* Historische Studien, no. 271. Berlin, 1935.

Eulenburg, F. *Die Frequenz der deutschen Universitäten. Von ihrer Gründung bis zur Gegenwart.* Abhandlungen der Königlichen Sächsischen Gesellschaft der Wissenschaften, Philologisch- Historischen Klasse, 24: no. 2. Leipzig, 1904.

Euler, Friedrich Wilhelm. "Entstehung und Entwicklung deutscher Gelehrtengeschlechter." *Universität und Gelehrtenstand 1400-1800,* edited by Hellmuth Rössler and Günther Franz, pp. 183-232. Deutsche Führungsschichten in der Neuzeit, no. 4. Limburg/Lahn, 1970.

Evans, Eric J. "Some Reasons for the Growth of English Rural Anti-Clericalism c. 1750-c. 1830." *Past and Present* no. 66 (February, 1975): 84-109.

Fagerberg, Holsten. *Bekenntnis, Kirche und Amt in der deutschen Konfessionellen Theologie des 19. Jahrhunderts.* Uppsala Universitets Årsskrift, 1952, no. 9. Uppsala, 1952.

Feltrup, J. "Zur Geschichte des Predigerseminars Hannover-Erichsburg." *ZGNK* 29-30 (1924-25): 1-47.

Festschrift zur Säcularfeier der königlichen Landwirthschafts-Gesellschaft zu Celle am 4. Juni 1864. Hannover, 1864.

Fischer, Hermann. "Luther und seine Reformation in der Sicht Ernst Troeltschs." *Neue Zeitschrift für systematische Theologie und Religionsphilosophie* 5 (1963): 132-72.

Fischer, Waldemar. "Die ländliche Verfassung Niedersachsens im 18. Jahrhundert." *Niedersachsen* 26 (1920-21): 182-83.

Fleisch, Paul. "Hannoversche 'Vorsicht' in kirchenregimentlichen Äußerungen (1576-1866)." *Evangelische Wahrheit* 31 (1940): 74-76.

Flitner, A. "Bildung." *RGG,* 1: cols. 1278-81. 3d ed. Tübingen, 1957.

Flygt, Sten Gunnar. *The Notorious Dr. Bahrdt.* Nashville, 1963.

Foerster, Erich. *Die Entstehung der Preußischen Landeskirche unter der Regierung König Friedrich Wilhelms des Dritten.* 2 vols. Tübingen, 1905-7.

Fooken, Enno. *Die geistliche Schulaufsicht und ihre Kritiker in 18. Jahrhundert.* Probleme der Erziehung, 5. Wiesbaden-Dotzheim, 1967.

Ford, Franklin L. *Robe and Sword: The Regrouping of the French Aristocracy after Louis XIV.* Cambridge, Mass., 1953; reprint, New York, 1965.

Foreman, Terry Hancock. "Religion as the Heart of Humanistic Culture: Schleiermacher as Exponent of *Bildung.*" Dissertation. Yale University, 1975.

Frank, Gustav. *"Dr. Karl Friedrich Bahrdt." Historisches Taschenbuch,* edited by von Raumer, 3. Folge, 7 Jg., pp. 207-370. Leipzig, 1866.

Frank, Gustav. "Bahrdt." *Allgemeine Deutsche Biographie* 1: 772-74. Leipzig, 1875.

Frank, Gustav. *"Geschichte des Rationalismus und seiner Gegensätze." Geschichte der Protestantischen Theologie, 3. Theil.* Leipzig, 1875.

Frei, Hans W. *The Eclipse of Biblical Narrative: A Study in Eighteenth and Nineteenth Century Hermeneutics.* New Haven, Conn., 1974.

Frensdorff, F. "Rehberg." *Allgemeine Deutsche Biographie* 27:571. Leipzig, 1888.

Frensdorff, F. "Die Vertretung der ökonom. Wissenschaften." In *Festschrift zur Feier des hundertfünfzigjährigen Bestehens der Königlichen Gesellschaft der Wissenschaften zu Göttingen,* pp. 495-565. Beiträge zur Gelehrtengeschichte Göttingens. Berlin, 1901.

Fuhrmann, M. and Reble, A. "Neuhumanismus." *RGG,* 4: cols. 1416-19. 3d ed. Tübingen, 1960.

Gabriel, Paul. *Die Theologie W. A. Tellers.* Gießen, 1914.

Gadamer, Hans-Georg. *Die Begriffsgeschichte und die Sprache der Philosophie.* Arbeitsgemeinschaft für Forschung des Landes Nordrhein-Westfalen, no. 170. Opladen, 1971.

Gagliardo, John C. *From Pariah to Patriot: The Changing Image of the German Peasant 1770-1840.* Lexington, Ky., 1969.

Gawlick, Günter. "Cicero and the Enlightenment." *Studies on Voltaire and the Eighteenth Century* 24-27 (1963): 657-82.

Gay, Peter. *"The Rise of Modern Paganism."* In his *The Enlightenment: An Interpretation,* vol. 1. New York, 1966.

Gensichen, H. W. "Die Lehrverpflichtung in der Hannoverschen Landeskirche." *JGNK* 48 (1950): 98-108.

Gerhard, Dietrich. "Regionalismus und ständisches Wesen als ein Grundthema europäischer Geschichte." *Historische Zeitschrift* 174 (1952): 307-37.

Gerhard, Dietrich. "Periodization in European History." *The American Historical Review* 61 (1955-56): 900-13.

Gerhard, Dietrich. "Amtsträger zwischen Krongewalt und Ständen — ein europäisches Problem." *Europa und die moderne Gesellschaft: Festschrift für Otto Brunner,* edited by Alexander Bergengruen and Ludwig Deike, pp. 230-47. Göttingen, 1963.

Gilman, Sander L. "The Anti-clerical Novel and its Offshoots." In his *The Parodic Sermon in European Perspective.* Beiträge zur Literatur des XV. bis XVIII. Jahrhunderts, no. 6, pp. 60-5. Wiesbaden, 1974.

Glawe, Walther. *Die Hellenisierung des Christentums in der Geschichte der Theologie von Luther bis auf die Gegenwart.* Neue Studien zur Geschichte der Theologie in der Kirche, no. 15. Berlin, 1912.

Graf, Georg. "Der vom Himmel gefallene Brief Christi. (Nach Cod. Monac. arab. 1067)." *Zeitschrift für Semitistik und verwandte Gebiete* 6 (1928): 10-23.

Graff, Paul. *Geschichte der Auflösung der alten gottesdienstlichen Formen in den evangelischen Kirchen Deutschlands.* 2d ed., 2 vols. Göttingen, 1937.

Greschat, Martin. "Der Bundesgedanke in der Theologie des späten Mittelalters." *Zeitschrift für Kirchengeschichte* 81 (1970): 44-63.

Greschat, Martin. *Zwischen Tradition und neuem Anfang. Valentin Ernst Löscher und der Ausgang der lutherischen Orthodoxie.* Untersuchungen zur Kirchengeschichte, no. 5. Witten, 1971.

Grimm, Harold J. "Luther's Contributions to Sixteenth-Century Organization of Poor Relief." *Archive for Reformation History* 61 (1970): 222-33.

Grimsley, Ronald. *Rousseau and the Religious Quest.* Oxford, 1968.

Grossmann, Walter. *Johann Christian Edelmann: From Orthodoxy to Enlightenment.* Religion and Society, no. 3. The Hague, 1976.

Gruber, Otto. *Herder und Abbt.* Phil. dissertation. Marburg University, 1934.

Grüneberg, Horst. "Die Anfänge des Göttinger beruflichen Schulwesens und der geistige Anteil von Professoren der Universität an dieser Entwicklung." *Göttinger Jahrbuch,* pp. 163-99. Jahrgang 1966, edited by Walter Nissen. Göttingen, 1966.

Haase, Carl. "Obrigkeit und öffentliche Meinung in Kurhannover 1789-1803." *Niedersächsisches Jahrbuch für Landesgeschichte* 39 (1967): 192-294.

Haase, Carl. *Ernst Brandes.* Veröffentlichungen der historischen Kommission für Niedersachsen und Bremen, no. 32. 2 vols. Hildesheim, 1973.

Haase, Yorck Alexander. "Theater." *Braunschweigische Landesgeschichte im Überblick,* edited by Richard Moderhack, pp. 301-12. Quellen und Forschungen zur Braunschweigischen Geschichte, no. 23. 2d ed. Braunschweig, 1977.

Hammerstein, Notker. "Das politische Denken Friedrich Carl von Mosers." *Historische Zeitschrift* 222 (1971): 316-38.

"Hannover." *Der Grosse Brockhaus.* 12 vols. 17th ed. Wiesbaden, 1953-57, 5: 255-57.

Harnack, Adolf. *Lehrbuch der Dogmengeschichte.* 3 vols. 5th ed. Tübingen, 1931.

Harnack, Adolf. *History of Dogma.* Translated by Neil Buchanan. 1900. Reprint (7 vols. in 4). New York, 1961.

Hassel, Wilhelm von. *Das Kurfürstentum Hannover vom Baseler Frieden bis zur preußischen Occupation im Jahre 1806.* Hannover, 1894.

Hasselhorn, Martin. *Der altwürttembergische Pfarrstand im 18. Jahrhundert.* Veröffentlichungen der Kommission für Geschichtliche Landeskunde in Baden-Württemberg, Reihe B, no. 6. Stuttgart, 1958.

Hausherr, Hans. *Hardenberg. 1. Theil 1750-1800.* Cologne, 1963.

Havemann, Wilhelm. *Geschichte der Land Braunschweig und Lüneburg.* 3 vols. Göttingen, 1857.

Haym, Rudolf. *Herder nach seinem Leben und seinem Werken.* 2 vols. Berlin, 1877.

Heckel, Martin. "Staat und Kirche nach den Lehren der evangelischen Juristen Deutschlands in der ersten Hälfte des 17. Jahrhunderts." *Zeitschrift der Savigny-Stiftung für Rechtsgeschichte. Kanonistische Abteilung* 42 (1956): 117-247, and 43 (1957): 202-308.

Heckel, Martin. *Staat und Kirche nach den Lehren der evangelischen Juristen Deutschlands in der ersten Hälfte des 17. Jahrhunderts.* Jus Ecclesiasticum, no. 6. Munich, 1968.

Heimbürger, H. C. *Carl Georg Schuster ... nach seinem Leben und Wirken.* Celle, 1849.

Heinemann Otto von. *Geschichte von Braunschweig und Hannover.* 3 vols. Gotha, 1892.

Heinrich, Gerd. "Amtsträgerschaft und Geistlichkeit: Zur Problematik d. sekundären Führungsschichten in Brandenburg-Preussen 1450-1786." *Beamtentum und Pfarrerstand 1400-1800,* edited by Günther Franz, pp. 179-238. Deutsche Führungsschichten in der Neuzeit, no. 5. Limburg/Lahn, 1972.

Hellmuth, Eckhart. *Naturrechtsphilosophie und Bürokratie in Preussen im späten Absolutismus.* Phil. Diss. Trier University, 1980.

Henke, Ernst Ludwig Theodor. *Georg Calixtus und seine Zeit.* 2 vols. Halle, 1853-1860.

Henke, Ernst. "Henke." *PRE* 7: 680-82. 3d ed. Leipzig, 1899.

Henkel, Dieter. *Staat und Evangelische Kirche im Königreich Hannover 1815-1833.* Studien zur Kirchengeschichte Niedersachsens, no. 8. Göttingen, 1938.

Hennecke, Edgar. "Zur Gestaltung der Ordination mit besonderer Rücksicht auf die Entwickelung innerhalb der lutherischen Kirche Hannovers." *Forschungen zur Geschichte Niedersachsens.* 1: no. 1, pp. 1-58. Hannover and Leipzig, 1906-07.

Herrlitz, Hans-Georg. *Studium als Standesprivileg: Die Entstehung des Maturitätsproblems im 18. Jahrhundert.* Fischer Taschenbücher, no. 3005. Frankfurt a.M., 1973.

Herrmann, Ulrich. "Modell der Schulreform: Das Braunschweigische Schuldirektorium 1786-1790." *Braunschweigisches Jahrbuch* 52 (1971): 163-81.

Herrmann, Ulrich. "Ernst Christian Trapp (1745-1818)." *Braunschweigisches Jahrbuch* 53 (1972): 183-95.

Heubach, Joachim. *Die Ordination zum Amt der Kirche.* Arbeiten zur Geschichte und Theologie des Luthertums, 2. Berlin, 1956.

Heussi, Karl. *Die Kirchengeschichtsschreibung Johann Lorenz von Mosheims.* Geschichtliche Untersuchungen, no. 1:4. Gotha, 1904.

Heussi, Karl. *Johann Lorenz von Mosheim: Ein Beitrag zur Kirchengeschichte des 18. Jahrhunderts.* Tübingen, 1906.

Heydorn, Heinz-Joachim, and Korneffke, Gernot, eds. *Studien zur Sozialgeschichte und Philosophie der Bildung: 1. Zur Pädagogik der Aufklarung.* List Taschenbücher der Wissenschaft, no. 1666. Munich, 1973.

Hinrichs, Carl. "Der Hallische Pietismus als politisch-soziale Reformbewegung des 18. Jahrhunderts." In his *Preussen als historisches Problem,* edited by Gerhard Oestreich, pp. 171-84. Berlin, 1964.

Hinrichs, Carl. *Preussentum und Pietismus.* Göttingen, 1971.

Hintze, Hedwig. *Staatseinheit und Föderalismus im alten Frankreich und in der Revolution.* Stuttgart, 1928.

Hintze, Otto. *Die Behördenorganisation und die allgemeine Staatsverwaltung Preussens im 18. Jahrhundert*. Acta Borussica, 6: no. 1. Berlin, 1901.

Hintze, Otto. *The Historical Essays of Otto Hintze*, edited by Felix Gilbert and Robert Berdahl. New York, 1975.

Hintze, Otto. "Die Hohenzollern und der Adel." In his *Regierung und Verwaltung*, edited Gerhard Oestreich, pp. 30-55. 2d ed. Göttingen, 1967.

Hintze, Otto. "Der preussische Militär- und Beamtenstaat im 18. Jahrhundert." *Regierung und Verwaltung*, edited by Gerhard Oestreich, pp. 419-28. Göttingen, 1967.

Hirsch, Emanuel. "Zum Verständnis Schwenckfelds." In *Festgabe für Karl Müller*, pp. 145-70. Tübingen, 1922.

Hirsch, Emanuel. *Die Unformung des christlichen Denkens in der Neuzeit: Ein Lesebuch*. Tübingen, 1938.

Hirsch, Emanuel. *Geschichte der neuern evangelischen Theologie im Zusammenhang mit den allgemeinen Bewegungen des europäischen Denkens*. 5 vols. Gütersloh, 1949-54.

Hirsch, Emanuel. *Hilfsbuch zum Studium der Dogmatik: Die Dogmatik der Reformatoren und der altevangelischen Lehrer quellenmaßig belegt und verdeutscht*. 4th ed. Berlin, 1964.

Hohlwein, H. "Thomasius." *RGG*, 6: cols. 866-67. 3d ed. Tübingen, 1962.

Holborn, Hajo. "Machtpolitik und lutherische Sozialethik." *Archiv für Reformationsgeschichte* 57 (1966): 23-32.

Holborn, Hajo. *Germany and Europe*. New York, 1970.

Holldack, Heinz. "Der Physiokratismus und die Absolute Monarchie." *Historische Zeitschrift* 145 (1931-32): 517-49.

Honecker, Martin. *Cura religionis Magistratus Christiani: Studien zum Kirchenrecht im Luthertum des 17. Jahrhunderts*. Jus Ecclesiasticum, no. 7. Munich, 1968.

Hubatsch, Walther, ed. *Absolutismus*. Wege der Forschung, no. 314. Darmstadt, 1973.

Hubrig, Hans. *Die patriotischen Gesellschaften des 18. Jahrhunderts*. Göttinger Studien zur Pädagogik, no. 36. Weinheim/Bergstrasse, 1957.

Inama. "Justi." *Allgemeine Deutsche Biographie*, 14: 747-53. Leipzig, 1881.

Jeismann, Karl-Ernst. *Das preußische Gymnasium in Staat und Gesellschaft. Die Entstehung des Gymnasiums als Schule des Staates und der Gebildeten, 1787-1817*. Industrielle Welt, no. 15. Stuttgart, 1974.

Johnson, Hubert C. *Frederick the Great and his Officials*. New Haven, Conn. 1975.

Junkin, Edward Dixon. *Religion versus Revolution: The Interpretation of the French Revolution by German Protestant Churchmen, 1789-1799*. Theol. dissertation. Basel University, 1968; Austin, Texas, 1974.

Kaiser, Gerhard. *Pietismus und Patriotismus im literarischen Deutschland: Ein Beitrag zum Problem der Säkularisation*, Veröffentlichungen des Instituts für Europäische Geschichte Mainz, 24. Wiesbaden, 1961.

Kantzenbach, Friedrich Wilhelm. "Das Phänomen der Entkirchlichung als Problem kirchengeschichtlicher Forschung und theologischer Interpretation." *Neue Zeitschrift für Systematische Theologie und Religionsphilosophie* 13 (1973): 82.

Kehr, Eckhart. "Zur Genesis der preussischen Bürokratie und des Rechtsstaates: Ein Beitrag zum Diktaturproblem." *Moderne deutsche Sozialgeschichte*, edited by Hans-Ulrich Wehler, Neue Wissenschaftliche Bibliothek, no. 10: 37-54. Cologne, 1966.

Kelle, Felix. *Martin Ehler's pädagogische Reformbestregungen*. Phil. dissertation. Leipzig University, 1907.

Kellenbenz, Hermann. "Probleme der Merkantilismusforschung." *Comité International des Sciences Historiques, XIIᵉ Congres. Rapports*, 4 (1965): 171-90.

Kiesel, Helmuth and Münch, Paul. *Gesellschaft und Literatur im 18. Jahrhundert*. Munich, 1977.

Klippel, Diethelm. *Politische Freiheit und Freiheitsrechte im deutschen Naturrecht des 18. Jahrhunderts*. Rechts- und Staatswissenschaftliche Veröffentlichungen der Görres-Gesellschaft, N.F., no. 23. Paderborn, 1976.

Knemeyer, Franz-Ludwig. *Regierungs- und Verwaltungsreformen in Deutschland zum Beginn des 19. Jahrhunderts*. Cologne and Berlin, 1970.

Knoke, K. "Der lutherische Bekenntnisstand der Prediger an der Universitätskirche zu Göttingen." *ZGNK* 23 (1918): 95-112.

Knoke, K. "Lectiones asceticae an der Göttinger Universität." *ZGNK* 25 (1920): 73-80.

Köhler, Manfred. "Über die soziale Bedeutung des protestantischen Pfarrhauses in Deutschland." Dissertation, Heidelberg University, 1952.

König, Helmut. *Zur Geschichte der Nationalerziehung in Deutschland im letzten Drittel des 18. Jahrhunderts.* Monumenta Paedagogica, no. 1. East Berlin, 1960.

König, Joseph. "Landesgeschichte." *Braunschweigische Landesgeschichte im Überblick*, edited by Richard Moderhack, pp. 61-110. 2d ed. Quellen und Forschungen zur braunschweigischen Geschichte, no. 23. Braunschweig, 1977.

Koldewey, Friedrich. *Geschichte der klassischen Philologie auf der Universität Helmstedt.* Braunschweig, 1895.

Koldewey, Friedrich. "Campe's Vorschläge zur Verbesserung des braunschweigischen Schulwesens." *Braunschweigisches Magazin* 2 (1896): 97-103.

Kopitzsch, Franklin, ed. *Aufklärung, Absolutismus und Bürgertum in Deutschland.* Nymphenburger Texte zur Wissenschaft Modelluniversität, no. 24. München, 1976.

Korff, H. A. *Geist der Goethezeit.* 5 vols. Leipzig, 1923-1957.

Koselleck, Reinhart. *Kritik und Krise. Eine Studie zur Pathogenese der bürgerlichen Welt.* Suhrkamp Taschenbuch Wissenschaft, no. 36. Frankfurt a.M., 1973.

Koselleck, Reinhart. "Begriffsgeschichte und Sozialgeschichte." *Historische Semantik und Begriffsgeschichte*, edited by Reinhart Koselleck, pp. 19-36. Sprache and Geschichte, no. 1. Stuttgart, 1979.

Krause, Reinhard. *Die Predigt der späten deutschen Aufklärung (1770-1805).* Arbeiten zur Theologie, no. 2 (Reihe 5). Stuttgart, 1965.

Kriedte, Peter; Medick, Hans; and Schlumbohn, Jürgen, eds. *Industrialisierung vor der Industrialisierung.* Veröffentlichungen des Max-Planck-Instituts für Geschichte, no. 53. Göttingen, 1977.

Kröger, Wolfgang. "Das Publikum als Richter: Lessing und die kleineren Respondenten im Fragmentenstreit." Theol. dissertation. Tübingen University, 1977.

Krumwiede, Hans-Walther. "Zur Entstehung des neuzeitlichen Staates und seiner Stellung zur Religion." *Evangelische Theologie* 36 (1976): 527-49.

Lampe, Joachim. *Aristokratie, Hofadel und Staatspatriziat in Kurhannover: Die Lebenskreise der hoheren Beamten and der kurhannoverschen Zentral- und Hofbehörden 1714-1760.* 2 vols. Untersuchungen zur Standesgeschichte Niedersachsens, no. 2/1. Göttingen, 1963.

Lampe, Walther. "Beitrag zur Personalgeschichte des hannoverschen Konsistoriums 1744-1844." *JGNK* 59 (1961): 105-9.

Lampe, Walther. "Grundsätzliches zur Frage der Prälatur in besonderer Verbindung zu den alten Provinziallandschaften." *JGNK* 63 (1965): 264-71.

Langen, August. *Der Wortschatz des deutschen Pietismus.* Tübingen, 1954.

Lau, F. "Orthodoxie, Altprotestantische." *RGG*, 4: col. 1724. 3d ed. Tübingen, 1960.

Leerhoff, Heiko. *Friedrich Ludwig von Berlepsch (1749-1818).* Veröffentlichungen der Historischen Kommission für Niedersachsen, no. 32, vol. 3. Hildesheim, 1970.

Leipoldt, Johannes, and Morenz, Siegfried. *Heilige Schriften: Betrachtungen zur Religionsgeschichte der antiken Mittelmeerwelt.* Leipzig, 1953.

Lenthe, Gebhard von. "Zur Geschichte des Beamtentums in Niedersachsen." *Beamtentum und Pfarrerstand 1400-1800*, edited by Günther Franz, pp. 239-47. Deutsche Führungsschichten in der Neuzeit, no. 5. Limburg/Lahn, 1972.

Leser. "Mauvillon." *Allgemeinen Deutsche Biographie*, 20: 715-16. Leipzig, 1884.

Leube, Hans. *Die Reformideen in der deutschen lutherischen Kirche zur Zeit der Orthodoxie.* Leipzig, 1924.

Levie, Dagobert de. "Patriotism and Clerical Office: Germany 1761-1773." *Journal of the History of Ideas* 14 (1953): 622-27.

Levie, Dagobert de. "The Patriotic Sermons of Christian Ludwig Hahnzog, Germany, 1785." *The Journal of Modern History* 26 (1954): 36.

Levie, Dagobert de. *Die Menschenliebe im Zeitalter der Aufklärung. Säkularisation und Moral im 18. Jahrhundert.* Bern, 1975.

Leyser, Jakob Anton. *Joachim Heirich Campe. Ein Lebensbild aus dem Zeitalter der Aufklärung.* 2 vols. 2d ed. Braunschweig, 1896.

Liebel, Helen P. *Enlightened Bureaucracy vs. Enlightened Despotism in Baden, 1750-1792.* Transactions of the American Philosophical Society, N.S. 55 (1965): 5.

Liebel, Helen P. "Der aufgeklärte Absolutismus und die Gesellschaftskrise in Deutschland im 18. Jahrhundert." *Absolutismus,* edited by Walther Hubatsch, pp. 488-544. Wege der Forschung, no. 314. Darmstadt, 1973.

Lieberg, Hellmut. *Amt und Ordination bei Luther und Melanchthon.* Forschungen zur Kirchen- und Dogmengeschichte, no. 11. Göttingen, 1962.

Lieberwirth, Rolf. *Christian Thomasius: Sein wissenschaftliches Lebenswerk. Eine Bibliographie.* Weimar, 1955.

Liermann, Hans. "Laizismus und Klerikalismus in der Geschichte des evangelischen Kirchenrechts." *Zeitschrift der Savigny-Stiftung für Rechtsgeschichte,* 70. *Kanonistische Abteilung,* 39 (1953): 1-27.

Lindemann, Klaus. *Geistlicher Stand und religiöses Mittlertum. Ein Beitrag zur Religionsauffassung der Frühromantik in Dichtung und Philosophie.* Gegenwart der Dichtung, 5. Frankfurt a.M., 1971.

Litzmann, Berthold. *Christian Ludwig Liscow in seiner litterarischen Laufbahn.* Hamburg and Leipzig, 1883.

Löwith, Karl. *From Hegel to Nietzsche.* Translated by David E. Green. London, 1964.

Lübbe, Hermann. *Säkularisierung: Geschichte eines ideenpolitischen Begriffs.* Munich, 1965.

Lütgert, Wilhelm. *Die Religion des deutschen Idealismus und ihr Ende.* 4 vols. Gütersloh, 1923-30. Reprint. 3 vols. Hildesheim, 1967.

Luthardt, Ernst. *Die Ethik Luthers in ihren Grundzügen.* Leipzig, 1867.

Lutheran Book of Worship. Edited by the Inter-Lutheran Commission on Worship. Minneapolis, Minn. and Philadelphia, Penn., 1978.

Maas, Ferdinand. "Josephinismus." *Lexikon für Theologie und Kirche* 5: cols. 1137-39. 2d ed. Freiburg i. Br., 1960.

McEachran, F. *The Life and Philosophy of Johann Gottfried Herder.* Oxford, 1939.

Mager, Inge. "Bibliographie zur Geschichte der Universität Helmstedt (mit besonderer Berücksichtigung der theologischen Fakultät)." *JGNK* 74 (1976): 237-42.

Mager, Inge. *Georg Calixts theologische Ethik und ihre Nachwirkungen.* Studien zur Kirchengeschichte Niedersachsens, no. 19. Göttingen, 1969.

Maier, Ernst von. *Hannoversche Verfassungs- und Verwaltungsgeschichte 1680-1866.* 2 vols. Leipzig, 1898-1899.

Malortie, C. E. von. *Der Hannoversche Hof unter dem Kurfürsten Ernst August und der Kurfürstin Sophie.* Hannover, 1847.

Manuel, Frank E. *The Eighteenth Century Confronts the Gods.* Cambridge, Mass., 1959.

Marahrens. "Instruktion für das Hospitium zu Loccum." *ZGNK* 29/30 (1924/25): 72-82.

Marino, Luigi. *I Maestri della Germania: Göttingen 1770-1820.* Turin, 1975.

Martiny, Fritz. *Die Adelsfrage in Preußen vor 1806.* Beiheft zur Vierteljahrschrift für Social- und Wirtschaftgeschichte, no. 35. Stuttgart, 1938.

Masur, Gerhard. "Naturrecht und Kirche. Studien zur evangelischen Kirchenverfassung Deutschlands im 18. Jahrhundert." *Historische Zeitschrift* 148 (1933): 29-70.

Maurer, Wilhelm. *Luthers Lehre von der drei Hierarchien und ihr mittelalterlicher Hintergrund.* Bayerische Akademie der Wissenschaften, Philosophisch-Historische Klasse, Sitzungsberichte, Jg. 1970, no. 4. Munich, 1970.

Meier, Ernst von. *Hannoversche Verfassungs- und Verwaltungsgeschichte, 1680-1866.* 2 vols. Leipzig, 1899.

Meijering, E. P. "Mosheim on the Philosophy of the Church Fathers." *Nederlands Archief voor Kerkgeschiedenis* 56 (1975): 367-83.

Meinecke, Friedrich. *"Die Entstehung des Historismus."* *Werke,* edited by Hans Herzfeld, Carl Hinrichs, and Walther Hofer, no. 3. Munich, 1959.

"Mercantilism." *Encyclopaedia Britannica,* 6:789. 15th ed.

Merker, Otto. "Karl August Freiherr von Hardenbergs Reformdenken in seiner hannoverschen Zeit 1771-1781." *Niedersächsisches Jahrbuch für Landesgeschichte* 43 (1976): 325-44.

Metz, J. B. and Rendtorff, Trutz, eds. *Die Theologie in der interdisziplinären Forschung*. Interdisziplinäre Studien, no. 2. Düsseldorf, 1971.

Meyen, Fritz. "Johann Friedrich Wilhelm Jerusalem, Abt von Riddagshausen." *Braunschweigische Jahrbuch* 53 (1972): 159-81.

Meyer, Johannes. "Literatur zur Einführung in die Kirchengeschichte Niedersachsens." *ZGNK* 41 (1936): 262-78.

Meyer, Johannes. "Geschichte der Göttinger theologischen Fakultät." *ZGNK* 42 (1937): 7-107.

Meyer, Johannes. *Kirchengeschichte Niedersachsens*. Göttingen, 1939.

Meyer, Philipp. "Der Quellenwert der Kirchen- und Schulberichte für eine Darstellung der Geschichte des kirchlichen Lebens unserer Heimat im Zeitalter der Aufklärung." *ZGNK* 19 (1914): 80-146.

Meyer, Philipp. "Die Entwicklung der Fürsorge für die Fortbildung der Geistlichen in den Braunschweig-Lüneburgischen Kurlanden während der Aufklärungszeit." *ZGNK* 34/35 (1929): 314-40.

Meyer Philipp. "Der obrigkeitliche Zwang in den deutschen evangelischen Landeskirchen des 16. bis 18. Jahrhunderts." *ZGNK* 34/35 (1929/39): 278-314.

Meyer, Philipp. *Die Pastoren der Landeskirchen Hannovers und Schaumburg-Lippes seit der Reformation*. 3 vols. Göttingen, 1941-53.

Meyer, Philipp. "Zur Verlesung landesherrlicher Verordnungen von den Kanzeln Niedersachsens im 16. bis 19. Jahrhundert." *JGNK* 48 (1950): 109-19.

Meyer, Philipp. "Die theologischen Prüfungen in den lutherischen Kirchen Calenberg-Göttingens und Lüneburgs bis zum Jahre 1868." *ZGNK* 52 (1954): 1-33; 53 (1955): 75-103.

Milske, Franz. "Joh. Peter Miller als Pädagog." Phil. dissertation. Würzburg University, 1921.

Moeller, Bernd. "Kleriker als Bürger." *Festschrift für Hermann Heimpel zum 70. Geburtstag am 19. September 1971. Zweiter Band*, pp. 195-224. Veröffentlichungen des Max-Planck Instituts für Geschichte, 36/II. Göttingen, 1972.

Moeller, Bernd. *Pfarrer als Bürger*. Göttinger Universitätsreden, no. 56. Göttingen, 1972.

Moeller, Bernd. "Mittelalter und Reformation." *Ökumenische Kirchengeschichte*, edited by R. Kottje and B. Moeller, vol. 2. 3 vols. Mainz and Munich, 1973.

Momigliano, Arnaldo. "Polybius' Reappearance in Western Europe." *Polybe*. Fondation Hardt, Entretiens, no. 20, pp. 345-72. Vandoeuvres and Geneva, 1973.

Mousnier, Roland. "Problèmes de méthode dans l'étude des structures sociales des seizième, dix-septième, dix-huitième siècles." *Spiegel der Geschichte: Festgabe für Max Braubach*, edited by Konrad Repgen and Stephan Skalweit, pp. 550-57. Münster/Westfalen, 1964.

Mühlpfordt, Günter. "Karl Friedrich Bahrdt und die radikale Aufklärung." *Jahrbuch des Institutes für Deutsche Geschichte*, Tel Aviv, edited by Walter Grab, 5 (1976): 49-99.

Müller, Max. "Basedow." *Allgemeine Deutsche Biographie*, 2: 113-124. Leipzig, 1875.

Müller, G. and Tholuck, F. "Carpzov." *PRE*, 3: 726-31. 3d ed. Leipzig, 1897.

Nissen, Walter. *Göttinger Gedenktafeln*. Göttingen, 1962.

Nürnberger, Richard. *Die Lehre von der Politik an der Universität Göttingen während der französischen Revolution*. Nachrichten der Akademie der Wissenschaften in Göttingen, 1. Philologisch-Historische Klasse, Jg. 1971, no. 2. Göttingen, 1971.

Obst, Helmut. *Der Berliner Beichtstuhlstreit: Die Kritik des Pietismus an der Beichtpraxis der lutherischen Orthodoxie*. Arbeiten zur Geschichte des Pietismus, no. 11. Witten, 1972.

Oestreich, Gerhard. "Eurooppalaisen Absolutismin Rakenneongelmia." *Historiallinen Aikakauskirja* 66 (1968): 234-49.

Oestreich, Gerhard. "Politischer Neustoizismus und Niederländische Bewegung in Europa und besonders in Brandenburg-Preußen." In his *Geist und Gestalt des frühmodernen Staates*, pp. 101-56. Berlin, 1969.

Overbeck, Franz. *Über die Christlichkeit unserer heutigen Theologie*. 2d ed. Leipzig, 1903. Reprint, Darmstedt, 1963.

Overbeck, Franz. *Christentum und Kultur*. Edited by Carl Albrecht Bernoulli. Basel, 1919. Reprint, Darmstadt, 1963.

Ozment, Steven. "Eckhart and Luther: German Mysticism and Protestantism." *The Thomist* 42 (1978): 259-80.

Palmer, R. R. *The Age of the Democratic Revolution: A Political History of Europe and America, 1760-1800.* 2 vols. Princeton, N.J., 1959, 1964.

Pariset, Georges. *L'État et les Églises en Prusse Sous Frédéric Guillaume Ier (1713-1740).* Thèse, Paris, 1896.

Parry, Geraint. "Enlightened Government and its Critics in Eighteenth-Century Germany." *The Historical Journal* 6 (1963): 178-192.

Paulsen, Friedrich. *Geschichte des gelehrten Unterrichts auf den deutschen Schulen und Universitäten.* 2 vols. 3d ed. Berlin and Leipzig, 1919-21.

Pelikan, Jaroslav. *"The Christian Tradition: A History of the Development of Doctrine." The Emergence of the Catholic Tradition (100-600),* 1. Chicago and London, 1971.

Pentzhorn, Edmund. *Thomas Abbt. Ein Beitrag zu seiner Biographie.* Phil. dissertation. Giessen University, 1884.

Peters, Martin. *Der Bahnbrecher der modernen Predigt Johann Lorenz Mosheim.* Leipzig, 1910.

Petri, Ludwig Adolph. *Die Bedürfnisse und Wünsche der protestantischen Kirche im Vaterlande.* Hannover, 1832.

Philipp, Wolfgang. "Rationalismus." *Evangelisches Kirchenlexikon,* edited by Heinz Brunotte and Otto Weber, 3: cols. 439-445. Göttingen, 1959.

Piepkorn, Arthur Carl. "The Sacred Ministry and Holy Ordination in the Symbolical Books of the Lutheran Church." *Concordia Theological Monthly* 40 (1969): 552-73.

Pinloche, Albert. *Geschichte des Philanthropismus.* 2d ed. Leipzig, 1914.

Plongeron, Bernard. "Bonheur et 'civilisation chrétienne': une nouvelle apologétique après 1760." Paper at the Fourth International Congress on the Enlightenment and the Sixth Annual Meeting of the American Society for Eighteenth-Century Studies, 13-20 July 1975, at Yale University.

Pocock, J. G. A. *Politics, Language and Time.* New York, 1973.

"Die Predigersynoden im Herzogthume Braunschweig. Geschichte derselben bis zum Anfange des gegenwärtigen Jahrhunderts." *Braunschweigisches Magazin,* Jg. 1866, pp. 209-224.

Preger, Wilhelm. *Die Geschichte der Lehre vom geistlichen Amte auf Grund der Geschichte der Rechtfertigungslehre.* Nördlingen, 1857.

Pressel, F. "Abbt: Thomas A." *Allgemeine Deutsche Biographie,* 1: 2-4, Leipzig, 1875.

Preus, Robert D. *The Theology of Post-Reformation Lutheranism: A Study of Theological Prolegomena.* Saint Louis, Mo., 1970.

Primer, Irwin, ed. *Mandeville Studies.* International Archives of the History of Ideas, no. 81. The Hague, 1975.

Raabe, Paul. "Die Zeitschrift als Medium der Aufklärung." *Wolfenbütteler Studien zur Aufklärung,* edited by Günter Schulz, 1: 99-136. Wolfenbüttel, 1974.

Raeff, Marc. "The Well-ordered Police State and the Development of Modernity in Seventeenth- and Eighteenth-Century Europe." *American Historical Review* 80 (1975): 1221-43.

Rahner, Hugo. "Die Vorstellung von der Gottesgeburt in der Seele bei den griechischen Kirchenvätern." *Zeitschrift für katholische Theologie* 59 (1935): 333-418.

Raumer, Kurt von. "Absoluter Staat, korporative Libertät, persönliche Freiheit." *Historische Zeitschrift,* 183: (1957): 55-96.

Reble, A. "Basedow." *RGG,* 1: col. 904. 3d ed. Tübingen, 1957.

Reble, A. "Philanthropinisten." *RGG,* 5: cols. 329-30. 3d ed. Tübingen, 1957.

Reble, A. "Neuhumanismus. II. Pädagogisch." *RGG,* 4: cols. 1418-1419. 3d ed. Tübingen, 1960.

Redwood, John. *Reason, Ridicule and Religion.* Cambridge, Mass., 1976.

Reik, Theodor. *Dogma and Compulsion.* Translated by Bernard Miall. 1951. Reprint. New York, 1973.

Reill, Peter Hanns. *The German Enlightenment and the Rise of Historicism.* Berkeley, Calif., 1975.

Reinhard, Johannes. *Die Prinzipienlehre der lutherischen Dogmatik von 1700 bis 1750.* Studien zur Geschichte der altprotestantischen Theologie, no. 1. Leipzig, 1906.

Reller, Horst. "Die Auswirkungen der Universität Helmstedt auf Pfarrer und Gemeinden in Niedersachsen." *JGNK* 74 (1976): 35-52.

Rendtorff, Trutz. "Christentum." *Geschichtliche Grundbegriffe. Historisches Lexikon zur politische-sozialen Sprache in Deutschland*, edited by Otto Brunner, Werner Conze, and Reinhart Koselleck, 1: 772-814. Stuttgart, 1972.

Rhamm, Albert. *Die Verfassungsgesetze des Herzogthums Braunschweig.* 2d ed. Braunschweig, 1907.

Riedel, Manfred. "Bürger, Staatsbürger, Bürgertum." *Geschichtliche Grundbegriffe. Historisches Lexikon zur politisch-sozialen Sprache in Deutschland*, edited by Otto Brunner, Werner Conze, Reinhart Koselleck, 1: 672-725. Stuttgart, 1972.

Ringer, Fritz K. *The Decline of the German Mandarins: The German Academic Community 1890-1933.* Cambridge, Mass., 1969.

Ritter, Gerhard. "Die Ausprägung deutscher und westeuropäischer Geistesart im konfessionellen Zeitalter." *Historische Zeitschrift* 144 (1934): 240-52.

Ritschl, Otto. *Dogmengeschichte des Protestantismus.* 4 vols. Göttingen, 1912-27.

Ritschl, Otto. "Das Theologumenon von der unio mystica in der späteren orthodox-lutherischen Theologie." *Harnack-Ehrung: Beiträge zur Kirchengeschichte ihrem Lehrer Adolf von Harnack dargebracht*, pp. 335-52. Leipzig, 1921.

Rössler, Emil F. *Die Gründung der Universität Göttingen.* Göttingen, 1855.

Roethe Gustav. "Göttingische Zeitungen von gelehrten Sachen." *Festschrift zur Feier des hundertfünfzigjährigen Bestehens der Königlichen Gesellschaft der Wissenschaften zu Göttingen*, pp. 567-675. Beiträge zur Gelehrtengeschichte Göttingens. Berlin, 1901.

Rosenberg, Hans. "Theologischer Rationalismus und vormärzlicher Vulgärliberalismus." *Historische Zeitschrift* 141 (1930): 497-541.

Rosenberg, Hans. *Bureaucracy, Aristocracy and Autocracy: The Prussian Experience 1660-1815.* Harvard Historical Monographs, no. 34. Cambridge, Mass., 1958.

Rotermund, Hans-Martin. *Orthodoxie und Pietismus: Valentin Ernst Löschers "Timotheus verinus."* Berlin, ca. 1954.

Ruprecht, Rudolf. *Der Pietismus des 18. Jahrhunderts in den Hannoverschen Stammländern.* Studien zur Kirchengeschichte Niedersachsens, no. 1. Göttingen, 1919.

Rupstein, Friedrich. *Dr. Heinrich Philipp Sextro, weiland Ober-Consistorial Rath, erster Hof und -Schloßprediger etc. zu Hannover. Eine Gedächtnißschrift seines Lebens und Wirkens wie seiner wohlthätigen Stiftungen.* Hannover, 1839.

Sabine, George H. *A History of Political Thought.* 3d ed. London, 1963.

"Salfeld, Abt zu Loccum." *Allgemeine hannoversche Biographie.* Hannover, 1916.

Salfeld, Eduard. "Der Landpfarrer und seine Gemeinde im Fürstentum Lüneburg zur Zeit der Orthodoxie." *ZGNK* 45 (1940): 203-24.

Saurer, E. "Kirchengeschichte als historische Disziplin?" *Denken über Geschichte*, ed. F. Engel-Janosi et al., pp. 157-69. Vienna, 1974.

Schian, Martin. *Die Sokratik im Zeitalter der Aufklärung.* Breslau, 1900.

Schian, Martin. *Orthodoxie und Pietismus im Kampf um die Predigt.* Studien zur Geschichte des neueren Protestantismus, no. 7. Gießen, 1912.

Schieder, Theodor. "Partikularismus und nationales Bewußtsein im Denken des Vormärz." *Staat und Gesellschaft im deutschen Vormärz 1815-1848*, pp. 9-38. 3d ed. Industrielle Welt, no. 1. Stuttgart, 1978.

Schlaich, Klaus. *Kollegialtheorie: Kirche, Recht und Staat in der Aufklärung.* Jus Ecclesiasticum, no. 8. Munich, 1969.

Schlaich, Klaus. "Der rationale Territorialismus. Die Kirche unter dem staatsrechtlichen Absolutismus um die Wende vom 17. zum 18. Jh." *Zeitschrift der Savigny-Stiftung für Rechtsgeschichte Kanonistische Abteilung* 54 (1968): 269-340.

Schleiff, Arnold. *Selbstkritik der lutherischen Kirchen im 17. Jahrhundert.* Neue Deutsche Forschungen Abt. Religions- und Kirchengeschichte, no. 6. Berlin, 1937.

Schlingensiepen-Pogge, Alexandra. *Das Sozialethos der lutherischen Aufklärungstheologie am Vorabend der Industriellen Revolution.* Göttinger Bausteine zur Geschichtswissenschaft, no. 39. Göttingen, 1967.

Schlumbohm, Jürgen. *Freiheit: Die Anfänge der bürgerlichen Emanzipationsbewegung in Deutsch-*

land im Spiegel ihres Leitwortes (ca. 1760-1800). Geschichte und Gesellschaft, no. 12. Düsseldorf, 1975.

Schmidt, Johann Dietrich. "Die theologischen Wandlungen des Christoph Friedrich von Ammon: Ein Beitrag zur Frage des legitimen Gebrauches philosophischer Begriffe in der Christologie." Theol. dissertation, Erlangen University, 1953.

Schmidt, Martin. "Bahrdt." *RGG*, 1: col. 845. 3d ed. Tübingen, 1957.

Schmidt, M. "Teilnahme an der göttlichen Natur. 2. Petrus 1,4 in der theologischen Exegese des Pietismus und der lutherischen Orthodoxie." *Dank an Paul Althaus: Eine Festgabe zum 70. Geburtstag*, pp. 171-201. Gütersloh, 1958.

Schmidt, M. *Wiedergeburt und neuer Mensch: Gesammelte Studien zur Geschichte des Pietismus.* Arbeiten zur Geschichte des Pietismus, no. 2. Witten, 1969.

Schmidt, Martin. "Der Pietismus in Nordwestdeutschland." *JGNK* 70 (1972): 147-77.

Schmidt, Martin. "Das pietistische Pfarrerideal und seine altkirchlichen Wurzeln." In *Bleibendes im Wandel der Kirchengeschichte,* edited by Bernd Moeller and Gerhard Ruhbach [apparently a *Festschrift* for Hans von Campenhausen], pp. 211-50. Tübingen, 1973.

Schmidt, Wilhelm. *Der braunschweigische Landtag von 1768-1770.* Dissertation. Göttingen University, 1912.

Schmitt, Hanno. "Leistungen, Widersprüche und Grenzen pädagogischer Reformarbeit am Ausgang des 18. Jahrhunderts Untersucht am Beispiel philanthropischer Erziehungstheorie und Reformpraxis im Herzogtum Braunschweig-Wolfenbüttel (1785-1790)." 2 vols. Dissertation Erziehungswissenschaften, Marburg University, 1977.

Schnath, Georg. *Geschichte Hannovers im Zeitalter der neunten Kur und der englischen Sukzession 1674-1714.* Veröffentlichungen der Historischen Kommission für Niedersachsen und Bremen, no. 18. 2 vols. Hildesheim, 1976.

Schneiders, Werner. *Die wahre Aufklarung. Zum Selbstverständnis der deutschen Aufklärung.* Munich, 1974.

Scholder, Klaus. "Herder und die Anfänge der historischen Theologie." *Evangelische Theologie* 22 (1962): 425-40.

Scholder, Klaus. "Grundzüge der theologischen Aufklärung in Deutschland." *Aufklärung Absolutismus und Bürgertum in Deutschland,* pp. 294-318. Nymphenburger Texte zur Wissenschaft Modelluniversität, edited by Franklin Kopitzsch, no. 24. München, 1976.

Schollmeier, Joseph. *Johann Joachim Spalding: Ein Beitrag zur Theologie der Aufklärung.* Gütersloh, 1967.

Schrenck, Gottlob. *Gottesreich und Bund im älteren Protestantismus vornehmlich bei Johannes Coccejus.* Beiträge zur Förderung christlicher Theologie. 2. Reihe, no. 5. Gütersloh, 1923.

Schüssler, Hermann. *Georg Calixt: Theologie und Kirchenpolitik.* Veröffentlichungen des Instituts für Europäische Geschichte Mainz, no. 25. Wiesbaden, 1961.

Schultz, Hermann. "Der Ordo salutis in der Dogmatik." *Theologische Studien und Kritiken* 72 (1889): 350-445.

Schultz, Robert C. *Gesetz und Evangelium.* Berlin, 1958.

Schultze, Johanna. *Die Auseinandersetzung zwischen Adel und Bürgertum in den deutschen Zeitschriften der letzten drei Jahrzehnte des 18. Jahrhunderts (1773-1806).* Historische Studien, no. 163. Berlin, 1925.

Schultzen, Friedrich and Müller, G. *Zum Jubiläum des Klosters Loccum.* Hannover, 1913.

Schumann, Reinhold. *Die Auffassung des Philanthropismus von Gesellschaft und Staat.* Phil. dissertation. Leipzig University, 1905.

Schwartz, Paul. *Der erste Kulturkampf in Preußen.* Berlin, 1925.

Seebaß, Georg and Freist, Friedrich-Wilhelm. *Die Pastoren der Braunschweigischen Evangelisch-Lutherischen Landeskirche.* 2 vols. Wolfenbüttel, 1974.

Seeberg, Erich. "Christian Thomasius und Gottfried Arnold." *Neue kirchliche Zeitschrift* 31 (1920): 337-58.

Seeberg, Erich. *Gottfried Arnold: Die Wissenschaft und die Mystik seiner Zeit.* Meerane i. Sa., 1923.

Seel, Hans. *Beiträge zur Geschichte des Begriffs einer deutschen Nationalerziehung am Ausgang des 18. Jahrhunderts*. Phil. dissertation. Münster University, 1925.

Seifert, Paul. *Die Theologie des jungen Schleiermacher*. Gütersloh, 1960.

Selle, Götz von. *Die Georg-August-Universität zu Göttingen 1737-1937*. Göttingen, 1937.

Sellin, Volker. "Friedrich der Große und der aufgeklärte Absolutismus." *Soziale Bewegung und politische Verfassung. Festschrift Werner Conze*, edited by Ulrich Engelhardt et al., pp. 83-112. Industrielle Welt, Sonderband. Stuttgart, 1976.

Sheehan, James F. "Begriffsgeschichte: Theory and Practice." *Journal of Modern History* 50 (1978): 312-19.

Sheldon, Henry C. *Sacerdotalism in the Nineteenth Century*. New York, 1900.

Sheldon, William Frederick. *The Intellectual Development of Justus Möser*. Osnabrücker Geschichtsquellen und Forschungen, no. 15. Osnabrück, 1970.

Skalweit, Stephen. "Edmund Burke, Ernst Brandes und Hannover." *Niedersächsisches Jahrbuch für Landesgeschichte* 28 (1956): 15-72.

Sommer, Louise. "Cameralism." *Encyclopedia of the Social Sciences* 3:158-61. New York, 1938.

Sperling, Eberhard. "Evangelische Klöster und Stifte in Niedersachsen." *JGNK* 72 (1974): 137-49.

Stech, Eugen. *Das Braunschweigische Schuldirektorium*. Langensalza, 1909.

Steinacker, Karl. *Abklang der Aufklärung und Widerhall der Romantik in Braunschweig*. Werkstücke aus Museum, Archiv und Bibliothek der Stadt Braunschweig, no. 10. Braunschweig, 1939.

Steinmetz, Rudolf. "Die Generalsuperintendenten in dem Herzogthum Bremen-Verden." *ZGNK* 11 (1906): 1-88.

Steinmetz, Rudolf. "Die Generalsuperintendenten von Calenberg." *ZGNK* 8 (1908): 25-267.

Stephen, Horst. *Herder in Bückeburg und seine Bedeutung für die Kirchengeschichte*. Tübingen, 1905.

Stephen, Horst and Leube, Hans. "*Die Neuzeit*." In *Handbuch der Kirchengeschichte*, vol. 4. 2d ed. Tübingen, 1931.

Stern, Selma. *Karl Wilhelm Ferdinand. Herzog zu Braunschweig und Lüneburg*. Veröffentlichungen der Historischen Kommission für Hannover, Oldenburg, Braunschweig, Schaumburg-Lippe und Bremen, no. 6. Hildesheim, 1921.

Stolzenburg, A. F. *Die Theologie des Jo. Franc. Buddeus und des Chr. Matth. Pfaff*. Neue Studien zur Geschichte der Theologie und der Kirche, no. 22. Berlin, 1926.

Stroup, John. "Protestant Churchmen in the German Enlightenment—Mere Tools of Temporal Government?" *Lessing Yearbook* 10 (1978): 149-89.

Swart, K. W. *The Sale of Offices in the Seventeenth Century*. The Hague, 1948.

Sybel, H. von. "Hardenberg," *Allgemeine Deutsche Biographie* 10:572-90. Leipzig, 1879.

Sykes, Norman. "Benjamin Hoadly, Bishop of Bangor." *The Social and Political Ideas of Some English Thinkers of the Augustan Age*, edited by J. F. C. Hearnshaw, pp. 112-55. London, 1928.

Tackett, Timothy. *Priest and Parish in Eighteenth-century France: A Social and Political Study of the Curés in a Diocese of Dauphiné 1750-1791*. Princeton, N.J., 1977.

Thadden, Rudolf von. *Restauration und Napoleonisches Erbe*. Veröffentlichungen des Instituts für Europäische Geschichte Mainz, no. 63. Wiesbaden, 1972.

Thielicke, Helmut. *The Ethics of Sex*. Translated by John W. Doberstein. New York, 1964.

Thimme, Friedrich. *Die Inneren Zustände des Kurfürstentums Hannovers unter der Französisch-Westfälischen Herrschaft 1806-1813*. 2 vols. Hannover and Leipzig, 1893.

Tholuck, Friedrich August Gottreu. *Vorgeschichte des Rationalismus. 2. Das kirchliche Leben des siebenzehnten Jahrhunderts, 2. Abtheilung*. Berlin, 1862.

Tholuck, Friedrich August Gottreu. *Geschichte des Rationalismus. 1. (einzige) Abteilung*. Berlin, 1865. Reprint. Aalen, 1970.

Tischhauser, Christian. *Geschichte der evangelischen Kirchen Deutschlands in der ersten Hälfte des 19. Jahrhunderts*. Basel, 1900.

Treue, Wilhelm. *Niedersachsens Wirtschaft seit 1760*. Schriftenreihe der Landeszentrale für politische Bildung in Niedersachsen Reihe B, no. 8. Hannover, 1964.

Trevor-Roper, H. R. *The European Witch-Craze of the Sixteenth and Seventeenth Centuries and Other Essays*. New York, 1969.

Trinterud, Leonard J., ed. *Elizabethan Puritanism*. New York, 1971.

Troeltsch, Ernst. *Protestantism and Progress*. Translated by W. Montgomery, 1912. Reprint. Boston, 1958.

Troeltsch, Ernst. *"Die Bedeutung des Protestantismus für die Entstehung der modernen Welt."* Beiheft 2 of *Historische Zeitschrift*. 2d ed. Munich, 1924.

Troeltsch, Ernst. "Das stoisch-christliche Naturrecht und das moderne profane Naturrecht." In his *Gesammelte Schriften*, edited by Hans Baron, vol. 4:166-90. Reprint. Aalen, n.d.

Troeltsch, Ernst. *The Social Teaching of the Christian Churches*. Translated by Olive Wyon. 2 vols. London, 1931, 1949.

Trost, Fritz. *Die Göttingische Industrieschule*. Arbeiten aus dem Forschungsinstitut für Fürsorgewesen in Frankfurt a.M., no. 4. Berlin, 1930.

Tschackert, Paul. "Bahrdt." *PRE*, 2:357-59. 3d ed. Leipzig, 1897.

Uhlhorn, Friedrich. "Die Bedeutung Georg Calixts für die lutherische Kirche der welfischen Lande." *ZGNK* 32/33 (1927/28): 201-17.

Valjavec, Fritz. *Die Entstehung der politischen Strömungen in Deutschland 1770-1815*. Munich, 1951.

Vehse, Eduard. *Geschichte der Höfe des Hauses Braunschweig in Deutschland und England. Die Hofhaltungen zu Hannover, London, und Braunschweig*. Geschichte der deutschen Höfe seit der Reformation, no. 22. Hamburg, 1853.

Vielhauer, Philipp. *Geschichte der urchristlichen Literatur*. Berlin, 1975.

Vierhaus, Rudolf. "Montesquieu in Deutschland: Zur Geschichte seiner Wirkung als politische Schriftsteller im 18. Jahrhundert." *Collegium Philosophicum. Studien Joachim Ritter zum 60. Geburtstag ...*, edited by Ernst-Wolfgang Böckenförde, pp. 403-37. Basel and Stuttgart, 1965.

Vierhaus, Rudolf. "Absolutismus." *Sowjetsystem und Demokratische Gesellschaft*, edited by C. D. Kernig et al., 1: col. 17-37. Freiburg i.B., 1966ff.

Vierhaus, Rudolf. "Politisches Bewusstsein in Deutschland vor 1789." *Der Staat* 6 (1967): 175-196.

Vierhaus, Rudolf. "Die Landstände in Nordwestdeutschland im späteren 18. Jahrhundert." *Ständische Vertretungen in Europa im 17. und 18. Jahrhundert*, edited by Dietrich Gerhard, pp. 73-93. Veröffentlichungen des Max-Planck-Instituts für Geschichte, no. 27. Göttingen, 1969.

Vierhaus, Rudolf. "Bildung." *Geschichtliche Grundbegriffe*, edited by Otto Brunner, Werner Conze, and Reinhart Koselleck, 1:508-51. Stuttgart, 1972.

Vierhaus, Rudolf, ed. *Eigentum und Verfassung*. Veröffentlichungen des Max-Planck-Instituts für Geschichte, no. 37. Göttingen, 1972.

Vierhaus, Rudolf. "Deutschland im 18. Jahrhundert: soziales Gefüge, politische Verfassung, geistige Bewegung." *Aufklarung, Absolutismus und Bürgertum in Deutschland*, edited by Franklin Kopitzsch, pp. 173-91. Nymphenburger Texte zur Wissenschaft Modelluniversität, no. 24. Munich, 1976.

Vierhaus, Rudolf. "Land, Staat und Reich in der politischen Vorstellungswelt deutscher Landstände im 18. Jahrhundert." *Historische Zeitschrift* 223 (1976): 40-60.

Vierhaus, Rudolf. "Zur historischen Deutung der Aufklärung: Probleme und Perspektiven." *Judentum im Zeitalter der Aufklärung*. Wolfenbütteler Studien zur Aufklärung, no. 4: 39-54. Wolfenbüttel, 1977.

Voltelini, Hans von. "Die naturrechtlichen Lehren und die Reformen des 18. Jahrhunderts." *Historische Zeitschrift* 105 (1910): 65-104.

Wagenmann. "Miller." *Allgemeine Deutsche Biographie*, 21: 749-50. 1885.

Wagenmann and Tschackert, Paul. "Less." *PRE*, 11: 404-6. 3d ed. Leipzig, 1902.

Walker, Mack. *German Home Towns: Community, State, and General Estate 1648-1871*. Ithaca, New York, 1971.

Wallmann, Johannes. *Der Theologiebegriff bei Johann Gerhard und Georg Calixt.* Beiträge zur historischen Theologie, no. 30. Tübingen, 1961.

Wallmann, Johannes. "Zwischen Reformation und Humanismus: Eigenart und Wirkungen Helmstedter Theologie unter besonderer Berücksichtigung Georg Calixts." *Zeitschrift für Theologie und Kirche* 74 (1977): 344-70.

Weidemann, Heinz. *Gerard Wolter Molanus, Abt zu Loccum.* Studien zur Kirchengeschichte Niedersachsens, nos. 3, 5. 2 vols. Göttingen, 1925, 1929.

Weill, Hermann. *Frederick the Great and Samuel von Cocceji.* Madison, Wisconsin, 1961.

"Welfen." *Der Grosse Brockhaus,* 12: 419. 12 vols. 17th ed. Wiesbaden, 1953-57.

Wendland, Walter. "Die praktische Wirksamkeit Berliner Geistlicher im Zeitalter der Aufklärung (1740-1806)." *Jahrbuch für Brandenburgische Kirchengeschichte* 11/12 (1914): 233-303.

Werner, Martin. *Die Entstehung des christlichen Dogmas problemgeschichtlich dargestellt.* 2d ed. Bern and Tübingen, 1941.

Werner, Martin. *Der protestantische Weg des Glaubens.* 2 vols. Bern 1955-62.

Williams, E. N. *The Ancien Régime in Europe.* Harmondsworth, Sussex, 1972.

Willson, A. Leslie. "Dichter-Priester, Bestandteil der Romantik." *Colloquia Germanica,* 1/2 (1968): 127-36.

Wilson, Bryan. "The Debate over Secularization." *Encounter* 45 (October, 1975): 77-83.

Wittram, Reinhard. *Das Nationale als europäisches Problem.* Göttingen, 1954.

Wittram, Reinhard. *Die Universität und ihre Fakultäten.* Göttinger Universitätsreden, no. 39. Göttingen, 1962.

Wotschke, Theodor. "Löschers Bemühungen um einen Theologenbund." *Zeitschrift für Kirchengeschichte* 47 (1928): 145-61.

Wotschke, Theodor. "Niedersächsische Mitarbeiter an den Unschuldigen Nachrichten." *ZGNK* 31 (1926): 73-112.

Zimmermann, Paul. "Ress, Johann Heinrich." *Allgemeine Deutsche Biographie,* 28:249-51. Leipzig, 1889.

Zimmermann, Paul. "Sextro." *Allgemeine Deutsche Biographie,* 34:77-79. Leipzig, 1892.

INDEX OF NAMES

INDEX OF SUBJECTS